Texas Government

POLICY & POLITICS

Eighth Edition

NEAL TANNAHILL
Houston Community College

PEARSON
Longman

New York San Francisco Boston
London Toronto Sydney Tokyo Singapore Madrid
Mexico City Munich Paris Cape Town Hong Kong Montreal

Vice President and Publisher: Priscilla McGeehon
Executive Editor: Eric Stano
Senior Marketing Manager: Elizabeth Fogarty
Media and Supplements Editor: Kristi Olson
Production Manager: Charles Annis
Project Coordination, Text Design, and Electronic Page Makeup: Shepherd, Inc.
Cover Design Manager: Wendy Fredericks
Cover Designer: Joseph DePinho
Cover Art: *Austin, Texas:* © Richard Cummins/Superstock, Inc.; *Map:* Map Resources Royalty Free/Fotosearch, LLC.
Photo Research: Photosearch, Inc.
Manufacturing Buyer: Lucy Hebard
Printer and Binder: Hamilton Printing Co.
Cover Printer: Phoenix Color Corp.

Library of Congress Cataloging-in-Publication Data

Tannahill, Neal R., 1949–
    Texas government : policy & politics / Neal Tannahill.
        p. cm.
    8th ed.
    Includes bibliographical references and index.
    ISBN 0-321-20282-1
        1. Texas—Politics and government—1951—Textbooks. 2. Local
    government—Texas—Textbooks. 3. Political planning—Texas—Textbooks. I. Title.

JK4816.T36 2003
320.4764—dc22   2004040135

Please visit our website at www.ablongman.com/tannahilltexas

ISBN 0-321-20282-1

1 2 3 4 5 6 7 8 9 10—HT—07 06 05 04

Contents

Preface

Textbooks should be designed with students in mind. I have written this textbook in a clear, straightforward fashion so students can easily understand concepts even if they have little background knowledge of Texas government and politics. I have also done my best to present the subject in an interesting fashion. Texas government is not boring and Texas government textbooks should not be boring either.

⭐ FEATURES

The text includes a number of features designed to help students learn and instructors teach.

- **Learning Objectives.** Each chapter contains a set of learning objectives. The objectives help students organize their study by identifying the most important points in each chapter.
- **Key Terms.** Words and phrases that have a specific meaning in the context of the subject matter appear in bold type, followed by a clear, straightforward definition. Students should not memorize the definition of the terms, but rather learn what they mean in the context of the chapter and be able to define and explain them in their own words. The list of terms at the end of each chapter helps students study by focusing their attention on important concepts.
- **Learning Activities.** I have included a learning activity in each chapter. Instructors may use the learning activities as homework assignments, group projects, or in-class exercises. The learning activities are designed to direct students to apply the information they learned in the chapter. They not only help students understand the materials in the text, but enable them to develop critical thinking skills as well.
- **Review Questions.** At the end of each chapter, I have included a set of review questions designed to help students focus their study. If students can answer the review questions, they will be well prepared to answer test questions.
- **National Perspective.** Each chapter includes a short essay about politics and government in another state. Students will better understand Texas government and politics in comparison with other state governments.
- **Getting Involved.** New to this edition, I have added a feature telling students how they can get involved in their communities, the college, and their

government by doing volunteer work, joining an interest group, or becoming a court appointed special advocate.

- **Glossary.** The textbook contains a glossary that includes the definitions of all the key terms listed in the text. If students forget what a term means, they can look it up quickly in the glossary without having to search for it in the text.

- **Texas Online.** Each chapter includes a feature with the addresses of Internet sites that deal with the subject matter of the chapter. Students can check out the sites that they find most interesting. In the process, they will learn more about the subject matter of the text.

- **What Is Your Opinion?** Each chapter includes a number of questions asking students their opinion about some of the political controversies discussed in the text. The questions are designed to be interesting and thought provoking.

- **Quotations.** I have sprinkled the text with quotations from political scientists and public figures commenting on the subject matter discussed in each chapter. Some of these quotations give insight into the text while others are just fun.

New to the Eighth Edition

The eighth edition of *Texas Government* includes an exciting new feature called "Getting Involved." It is designed to show students how they can get involved in their college, community, and government. Students discover, for example, how they can become volunteer deputy-voter registrars. They can learn not just how to register to vote themselves, but how to help their friends and neighbors register as well. Other examples of this feature encourage students to: form study groups, volunteer to teach children to read, contact their state legislators, and consider becoming a court appointed special advocate—representing the interests of children who appear before a state court.

Texas Government's eighth edition is completely up-to-date, containing thorough coverage of the latest developments in Texas politics. For instance, this edition includes an examination of the medical malpractice insurance reform, off-cycle congressional redistricting, homeowner insurance reform, the 2003 budget crisis, the school funding controversy, and the impact of No Child Left Behind in Texas. Students will learn why many Democratic House members fled to Ardmore, Oklahoma and why many Democratic state senators decamped to Albuquerque, New Mexico. They will read about the battles between doctors, lawyers, and insurance companies over the medical malpractice reform, and also discover why state colleges and universities have less money to spend, even though tuition and fees have gone up dramatically.

SUPPLEMENTS

- **Instructor's Manual/Test Bank.** The Instructor's Manual includes chapter outlines, chapter summaries, teaching suggestions, ideas for student projects, and discussion questions. The Test Bank contains hundreds of challenging multiple choice, short answer, and essay questions with an answer key.

- **TestGen-EQ Computerized Test Bank.** The printed Test Bank is also available electronically through our computerized testing system, TestGen-EQ. This fully networkable test generating software is now available on a cross-platform CD-ROM. TestGen-EQ's friendly graphical interface enables instructors to view, edit, add questions, transfer questions to tests, and print tests in a variety of fonts and forms. Search and sort features allow instructors to locate questions quickly and arrange them in preferred order. Six question formats are available, including short-answer, true-false, multiple-choice, essay, matching, and bimodal.

- **Study Guide.** The Study Guide helps students reinforce the themes and concepts they encounter in the text. It includes learning objectives, chapter outlines, chapter summaries, case studies, key terms, and practice tests for each chapter.

- **Companion Website.** A website is available to provide both students and instructors with additional resources. The site includes practice test questions, a syllabus builder, links to relevant sites on the Internet, and more. It can be accessed at **www.ablongman.com/tannahill**.

ACKNOWLEDGEMENTS

Many persons contributed significantly to the writing and production of this book. Eric Stano, Cristine Maisano, and the other professionals at Longman Publishing gave me sympathetic and professional help from the edition's beginning to its completion. I am also grateful to the scholars who reviewed the manuscript: Barbara Lenington, Texas A&M University; Mark A. Cichock, University of Texas at Arlington; Michael L. Dillard, St. Philip's College. Their comments proved invaluable in preparing the final text.

I am grateful to the government faculty at Houston Community College for their friendship and support. I have learned most of what I know about teaching from them. Thank you Ghassan Abdallah, Cecile (Cammy) Artiz, Evelyn Ballard, Harold "Hal" Comello, Dale Foster, Larry Gonzalez, Mark Hartray, Edmund "Butch" Herod, Brenda Jones, Aaron Knight, Gary LeBlanc, Raymond Lew, Joe C. Martin, Vinette Meikle Harris, David Ngene, Carlos Pierott, Donna Rhea, John Speer, Jaye

Ramsey Sutter, John Ben Sutter, R. Mark Tiller, and Linda Webb. I am also grateful for the hard work and dedication of the administration and staff of Houston Community College, including Charles Cook, Sue Cox, Mary Davis, and Susan Howard.

Finally, I wish to dedicate this book to my friends: Luis Arturo Nava, Anderson Brandao, Jason Orr, A. J. Hood, David Dupre, Robert Fisher, Ron Rueckert, Freda Coss, Kim Galle, and Hal Stockbridge.

Neal Tannahill
Houston Community College **neal.tannahill@hccs.edu**

INTRODUCTION

The Policymaking Process

LEARNING OBJECTIVES

After studying this Introduction, students should be able to do the following:

★ Describe the relationship between the policymaking environment and the policymaking process.

★ Distinguish among the five stages of the policy process using the issue of the death penalty as an example.

★ Discuss the dynamics of the policy cycle.

★ Identify the different types of political actors who may be involved in an issue network.

★ Explain the relationship between politics and the policymaking process.

★ Identify the reasons why it is important to study Texas government.

★ Define the key terms listed on page 14 and explain their significance.

Texas leads the nation in executions. Between 1977 and the end of 2003, the state of Texas put to death 313 convicted murderers, more than a third of the total executions nationwide.[1] Texas has carried out more than three times as many executions as Virginia, the state with the second greatest number of executions.[2] In January 2004, 445 men and 8 women awaited execution on death row at the Allan B. Polunsky Unit of the state prison system in Livingston.[3] Only the state of California had more people on death row than Texas.[4]

Capital punishment, the death penalty, is controversial. Death penalty advocates contend that criminals who take a life should pay for their crime with their own life. The death penalty protects law-abiding citizens by permanently removing violent criminals from society. The fear of the death penalty deters potential criminals from committing murder. Death penalty proponents also believe that an execution enables the family of a murder victim to reach closure and go on with their lives.

In contrast, death penalty opponents call capital punishment a barbaric relic of the nineteenth century, pointing out that the United States is the only industrialized democracy that still uses the death penalty against criminal defendants. Instead of deterring crime, they say, the death penalty may actually increase the violent crime rate by cheapening the value of human life. The opponents of capital punishment charge that it is biased because a large majority of persons who are sentenced to death and actually executed are poor, uneducated members of racial and ethnic minority groups.

★ THE STAGES OF THE POLICYMAKING PROCESS

The death penalty is an example of a **public policy,** which is the response, or lack of response, of government decision makers to an issue. Texas state and local government has policies addressing a wide range of issues, including education, water resource management, health care, and transportation. Capital punishment is part of the state's public policy response to the problem of violent crime.

The **public policy approach** is a comprehensive method for studying the process through which issues come to the attention of government decision makers, and through which policies are formulated, adopted, implemented, and evaluated. A study of capital punishment in Texas from a policy perspective would examine the legal, cultural, and socioeconomic factors shaping the policymaking environment. It would consider how and why violent crime became an issue of public concern and the process through which the state formulated and adopted a policy on capital punishment. It would examine the implementation of the death penalty, evaluate its effectiveness at reducing violent crime, and assess its impact on the state.

The Policymaking Environment

The set of factors outside of government that impacts the policymaking process either directly or indirectly is the **policymaking environment.** The policymaking process takes place within a cultural, socioeconomic, legal, and political context.

The policymaking environment is not one of the stages of the policymaking process; rather, it is the background in which the policymaking process takes place. The environment helps determine the problems that government attempts to solve, the set of policy alternatives that government decision makers will be willing to consider, the resources available to government to address the problem, and the relative strength of political forces involved in the policymaking process.

The most important environmental factors influencing capital punishment in Texas are the legal/constitutional setting and public attitudes toward violent crime. The state's death penalty statute must meet the constitutional standards set by federal and state courts. In 1972, for example, the U.S. Supreme Court ruled that death penalty laws throughout the nation were unconstitutional because they allowed judges and juries too much discretion, thereby opening the door to discriminatory practices.[5] Texas and other states subsequently rewrote their death penalty statutes to conform to the Court's objections.

The state's death penalty policy also reflects public opinion. According to public opinion polling data, Texans support the death penalty by a 76 percent to 17 percent margin, with the rest undecided.[6] Capital punishment is so popular in Texas that candidates for office often base their campaigns on support for the death penalty. When Texas Attorney General Mark White ran for governor in the early 1980s, for example, his campaign featured television advertisements showing pictures of the men who were executed during his tenure as attorney general.

> "You don't want to talk about instituting a state income tax or doing away with the death penalty. They're both considered—no pun intended—the kiss of death in Texas politics."
> —State Representative Elliott Naishtat, D., Austin

Agenda Building

The public policy process has five stages: agenda building, policy formulation, policy adoption, policy implementation, and policy evaluation. **Agenda building** is the process through which issues become matters of public concern and government action. Not all problems become the object of government action. Those problems that government officials actively consider how to resolve are part of the **official policy agenda.** In short, agenda building is the process through which issues become part of the official policy agenda.

Capital punishment has been part of the official policy agenda in Texas for decades. In the 1970s, state policymakers rewrote the state's capital punishment law to satisfy the objections of the U.S. Supreme Court. During the 1980s, appeals began to run out for some of the death-row inmates convicted under the new capital punishment law and prison officials developed a system for carrying out executions. In the early 1990s, the legislature and the state court system streamlined the capital appeals process to reduce the time between conviction and execution. In the early 2000s, the state has considered reforms designed to provide for postconviction DNA testing when DNA evidence is available that might prove an inmate's innocence and to improve the quality of legal representation available to persons charged with capital murder. The legislature has also considered whether juries should be allowed the option of assessing life in prison without possibility of parole as an alternative to the death penalty.

At any one time, the official policy agenda contains a relatively small number of major issues. In recent years, the official policy agenda for Texas state government has included the following issues:

- **Educational finance:** How can the state ensure that local school districts have adequate revenues to provide a quality education to the state's school children and that the money is collected fairly?
- **Educational accountability:** How can taxpayers be sure that they are getting their money's worth for the school taxes they pay?
- **Property tax reform:** How can the state protect property owners from rapidly rising property taxes without undermining the ability of local governments to fund the services they provide?
- **Medical malpractice reform:** What steps can the state take to prevent the cost of medical malpractice insurance from rising so high that doctors are forced to drop their practices?
- **Welfare reform:** What actions can the state government take to move people from welfare into the workforce?
- **Juvenile justice reform:** How can the state reduce the number of crimes committed by juveniles?
- **Insurance reform:** What steps can the state take to reduce insurance rates for Texas homeowners?
- **Security:** What steps should state and local governments do to protect against the danger of terrorist attack?

As students of Texas government using the policy approach, we would ask *how* each of these issues became part of the official policy agenda. Who raised each of these issues? What actions did individuals and groups take to get their issues addressed by government? Did other individuals and groups attempt to keep these issues off the official policy agenda? Why did the former succeed and the latter fail?

Agenda building not only identifies problems for government attention, but also defines the nature of those problems and therefore the eventual thrust of a policy solution.[7] Capital punishment, for example, can be defined in different terms. Death penalty advocates prefer to focus on the seriousness of violent crime and the length of delay between a death sentence and its imposition. In contrast, the opponents of capital punishment emphasize racial disparities in sentencing, the risk of executing an innocent person, and the relative cost of capital punishment compared to the expense of life in prison without parole. Whether state government attempts to streamline the appeals process to make it easier to carry out the death penalty, adopts reforms to protect against bias, or even eliminates capital punishment altogether depends on the way the issue is defined.

Policy Formulation

Policy formulation is the development of strategies for dealing with the problems on the official policy agenda. Once an issue becomes part of the official policy agenda, individuals and groups, both inside and outside of government, develop and propose approaches for addressing the problem. Defense attorneys, victims' rights organizations, legislators, prison officials, criminologists, prosecuting attorneys, civil rights activists, prison reformers, and the news media may all be involved in formulating policies affecting the death penalty.

Scholars who study public policymaking identify two models of policy formulation: the rational comprehensive model and the incremental model. The **rational comprehensive model of policy formulation** is an approach to policy formulation that assumes that policymakers establish goals, identify policy alternatives, estimate the costs and benefits of the alternatives, and then select the policy alternative that produces the greatest net benefit. In contrast, the **incremental model of policy formulation** is an approach to policy formulation that assumes that policymakers, working with imperfect information, continually adjust policies in pursuit of policy goals that are subject to periodic readjustment.[8]

Most political scientists believe that the rational comprehensive model is an unrealistic approach to policy formulation except when dealing with technical questions of limited scope. They believe that the incremental model of policy formulation more closely reflects the real world of public policymaking in which political actors disagree about policy goals, information about policy alternatives is imperfect, and resources to achieve goals are limited. At least for major issues, policy formulation involves policymakers developing strategies to achieve short-term goals, with both strategies and goals subject to modification. Furthermore, some scholars believe that the incremental approach is not only more realistic than the rational comprehensive model but also a more effective model for decision makers because it allows policymakers greater flexibility in modifying policy approaches to account for new information, changes in resource availability, and variation in political support.[9]

Consider the death penalty. Policymakers and other participants in the debate over the death penalty disagree about the goals of capital punishment and its effectiveness. Some participants in the policymaking process favor the death penalty in order to deter crime while others seek to punish offenders. Still another set of participants in the policymaking process hopes to minimize the application of the death penalty or eliminate it altogether. They argue that life in prison without possibility of parole achieves societal goals without the state taking life.

Scholars also disagree about the effect of capital punishment on the murder rate and its impact on society. The nature of the death penalty makes it difficult, if not impossible, to assess its impact with precision. How do we place a value on the life of a convicted murderer or the murderer's victim? In practice, current death penalty policy reflects a compromise developed by policymakers with different personal values, working with imperfect information, and facing conflicting political pressures on an emotional issue.

> "The death penalty is a necessary tool that reaffirms the sanctity of human life while assuring that convicted killers will never again prey upon others."
> —Michael D. Bradbury, California district attorney

Policy Adoption

Policy adoption is the official decision of a government body to accept a particular policy and put it into effect. The legislature passes and the governor signs a bill. The

L E A R N I N G   E X E R C I S E

Applying the Policymaking Model to a Current Policy Issue

Find and read a newspaper article dealing with a policy issue that is currently part of the official policy agenda for state and local government in Texas. Read the article and answer the following questions.

QUESTIONS TO CONSIDER

1. What issue does the article address?
2. Is this an issue for state government, local government, or both? What is the basis of your answer?
3. What stage or stages of the policymaking process does the article illustrate? Explain the basis for your answer.
4. What unit(s) of government does the article mention?
5. List all the participants mentioned in the article, including individuals and groups. Note whether each participant is part of government (such as a mayor, the governor, a state agency, or a member of Congress) or outside government (such as a newspaper reporter, a business executive, or an interest group).
6. According to the article, do the policy participants all share the same point of view about the issue? If not, compare and contrast the varying viewpoints and perspectives presented in the article.

Please identify the source of your article using the following format: Kathy Walt, "Despite Doubts, Most Texans in Poll Support Death Penalty," *Houston Chronicle*, June 22, 2000, p. 1A. Also, be prepared to give your instructor a photocopy of the article you read.

Texas Supreme Court issues a major ruling. A city council passes an ordinance. In practice, major government policies frequently reflect adoption decisions made at different points in time by different units of government. The legislature and the governor enacted the state's basic death penalty statute in 1973. They subsequently adopted amendments changing the method of execution from the electric chair to lethal injection, expanding the list of capital crimes, and modifying appeals procedures.

Policy Implementation

Policy implementation is the stage of the policy process in which policies are carried out. Implementation involves both government officials and individuals and groups outside of the government. A number of political actors participate in the implementation of the state's death penalty policy:

- District attorneys who determine whether to ask for the death penalty in a particular capital murder case.
- Juries and judges who decide whether to sentence a convicted defendant to death or life in prison.
- Officials in the Texas Department of Corrections who carry out death sentences.
- State and federal judges who hear appeals.
- Lawyers from the state attorney general's office who represent the state in court during the appeal process.

- Private defense attorneys who represent the defendant during the appeals process.
- The Board of Pardons and Paroles, which entertains requests for clemency.
- The governor who may grant a thirty-day reprieve on the execution of a death sentence and must concur with a decision of the Board of Pardons and Paroles to grant clemency.

Implementation is an essential part of the policy process. A policy in operation may evolve far differently from what its architects intended or expected. Sometimes policymakers misjudge the nature of a problem or underestimate the resources needed for its solution. Consider the implementation of capital punishment in Texas. Because of the length of the appeals process, the average stay on death row in Texas is 10.4 years.[10] In early 2004, the death row inmate with the longest tenure was Walter Bell, Jr. of Jefferson County, who was first sentenced to death in 1975.[11] Whereas death penalty opponents argue that appeals are necessary to ensure that innocent people are not put to death, critics charge that the current system is unfair to the relatives of murder victims and inhumane to people awaiting execution.

? WHAT IS YOUR OPINION?

Do convicted murderers spend too much time on death row before their sentences are carried out?

The implementation of the state's capital punishment statute varies from county to county. Many small counties rarely, if ever, send anyone to death row because they cannot afford the expense of conducting a capital murder trial, which can tie up a courtroom for weeks. In contrast, Harris County (which includes the city of Houston) has sentenced more people to death than any county in the United States. Figure I.1 depicts the number of Texas death row offenders sentenced from the state's six largest counties—Bexar County (San Antonio), Dallas County, El Paso County, Harris County, Tarrant County (Fort Worth), and Travis County (Austin). As the figure shows, Harris County has sent more convicted murderers to death row than the other five counties put together. Harris County's status as the death penalty capital of Texas reflects the philosophy of Harris County District Attorney Chuck Rosenthal and his predecessor, John B. Holmes, Jr. Under their direction, the district attorney's office in Harris County has asked juries to assess the death penalty more frequently than do the district attorneys' offices in other Texas counties.

Policy Evaluation

Policy evaluation is the assessment of policy. It involves questions of equity, efficiency, effectiveness, and political feasibility. Equity is the concept that similarly situated people be treated equally. Is the death penalty assessed in an even-handed fashion without regard to the gender, race, ethnicity, or financial status of the criminal and the victim? Death penalty opponents charge that capital punishment is usually assessed against persons with little status in society who cannot afford to hire an

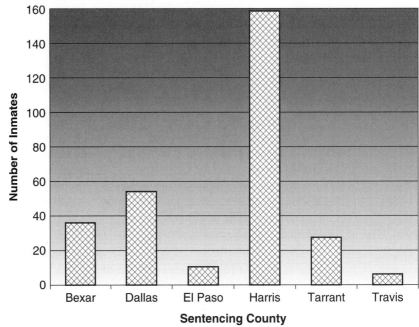

FIGURE I.1   Death Row Inmates, 2004

Source: Texas Department of Corrections

"One of the reasons
Harris County tries so
many capital murder
cases is simple
economics—we can
afford to."
—Harris County
District Judge
Michael McSpadden

effective legal defense. They also contend that the race of the crime victim affects the likelihood of a jury sentencing a convicted killer to die because persons convicted of murdering whites are more likely to be given the death penalty than people convicted of killing African Americans. In Texas, people charged with murder in urban counties, especially Harris County, are more likely to face a death sentence than people charged in other counties.

Efficiency is a comparison of a policy's costs with the benefits it provides. Because of the cost of trials and appeals in death penalty cases, capital punishment is actually several times more expensive than imprisoning a criminal for forty years or more. Nonetheless, the supporters of capital punishment believe that the costs of the legal process need to be balanced against the benefits of permanently eliminating a violent criminal from society.

Effectiveness is the extent to which a policy achieves its goals. Does the death penalty deter violent crime? The opponents of the death penalty point out that most studies find little, if any, relationship between the imposition of capital punishment and the incidence of murder. In contrast, advocates of capital punishment argue that deterrence would be enhanced if the time between conviction and execution were shorter.

Political feasibility refers to the ability of a policy to obtain public support. The Texas legislature will never repeal the death penalty as long as public opinion in the state supports capital punishment as strongly as it does today. Furthermore, the interest groups that defend the death penalty are more influential than the groups opposed to capital punishment.

Evaluation can be either normative or empirical. An **empirical analysis** is a method of study that relies on experience and scientific observation. An empirical analysis of capital punishment, for example, might explore the relationship between the death penalty and the murder rate. In contrast, a **normative analysis** is a method of study that is based on certain values. A normative analysis of the death penalty might consider the morality of the policy and the fairness of its implementation.

Policy evaluation sometimes highlights the distinction between policy outputs and policy outcomes. **Policy outputs** refer to actual government policies. **Policy outcomes** are the situations that arise as a result of the impact of policy in operation. Consider the distinction between policy outputs and outcomes as far as capital punishment is concerned. Thirty-eight states have capital punishment laws on the books, a policy output. In practice, however, many states seldom, if ever, carry out executions, a policy outcome. In 2002, only thirteen states conducted executions.[12] No state enforces the death penalty as aggressively as Texas.

The impact of policy evaluation on the policy process is known as **feedback.** If a policy is judged successful and the problem solved, officials may terminate the policy. Should the problem persist, the policy process may begin anew as groups and individuals once again push the issue to the forefront of the policy agenda.

"Things suck. We're all in trouble, serious trouble. It's on everybody's mind."
—Carl Buntion, Texas death row inmate

THE DYNAMICS OF THE POLICY PROCESS

Policymaking is more complex than the five-stage policy process would suggest at initial glance.

Policy Cycles

The term **policy cycle** refers to the passage of an issue through the policy process from agenda building through policy evaluation. Issues do not always travel smoothly through the policy cycle, moving from one stage to the next. No clear lines of demarcation can be drawn among the five stages of the policy process. The agenda setting and policy formulation stages sometimes overlap. For example, a number of religious leaders in Texas, including Joseph A. Fiorenza, the Roman Catholic Bishop of the Houston-Galveston diocese, have recently called for a moratorium on executions in Texas to allow time to review death penalty convictions because they believe that the capital punishment process is seriously flawed. The religious leaders are both attempting to raise an issue (the danger that the state may execute an innocent person) and propose a solution (a moratorium on the implementation of the death penalty to allow time to review questionable convictions). Similarly, policy implementation often has an aspect of policy adoption to it as agencies fill in the details of policies adopted by legislative bodies. Policy evaluations occur throughout the policy process, not just at its end.

Not every issue completes the policy cycle. Issues may be raised to the official policy agenda and policies formulated, but then forgotten as the attention of the general public and government officials turns to other, more pressing problems. Sometimes public officials, interest group spokespersons, or individual citizens will succeed in keeping an issue in the public eye until a policy solution is adopted and implemented. A triggering mechanism, such as a dramatic event, a news media report, or a scandal, is often necessary to force a public policy response to an issue. During the 2000 presidential campaign when Texas Governor George W. Bush ran for the White House, the national news media focused on many aspects of Texas politics and government, including the death penalty. The national attention helped set the agenda for a number of reform proposals in the 2001 legislative session, including proposals for postconviction DNA testing and life in prison without possibility of parole as an alternative punishment to the death penalty.

Finally, some issues, particularly major, controversial issues, such as the death penalty, travel through the policy process again and again over an extended period of time. Over the last thirty years, the issue of capital punishment has arisen repeatedly because of court rulings, controversies over the guilt or innocence of particular death row inmates, public concern over crime rates, media publicity about the length of time between sentencing and execution, and the 2000 presidential campaign. As long as the public remains deeply divided over capital punishment, the death penalty is likely to be a recurring item on the state's official policy agenda.

Issue Networks

The policymaking process involves a broad range of political actors, including government officials, the institutions of government, individual policy activists, political parties, the news media, and interest groups. Political scientists use the term **issue network** to describe a group of political actors that is concerned with some aspect of public policy. District attorneys, victims' rights organizations, defense attorneys, organizations opposed to capital punishment, legislators concerned about capital punishment, state and federal judges, the governor, and the members of the Board of Pardons and Paroles comprise the issue network for capital punishment in Texas. Issue networks vary from issue to issue. Although not all participants in an issue network are equally influential, no one individual or group is usually able to dominate policymaking on the issue. Instead, policy reflects the result of conflict (and occasionally compromise) among the participants.

Policymaking and Politics

Politics is the process that determines who shall occupy the roles of leadership in government and how the power of government shall be exercised. Politics exists because individuals and groups have different interests and different views about public policy. For example, the issue of whether county government should widen and extend a road might please land developers who hope to build a shopping center alongside the road, but displease area home owners who do not want additional traffic in their neighborhoods. The developers and the homeowners would oppose each other on this issue because their interests clash. Individuals and groups may also disagree

"I am confident that no Texan wants an innocent person to be condemned to death. A moratorium on capital punishment in order to fully examine our criminal justice system will give us assurance that, as far as humanly possible, the innocent will not be subjected to state-sponsored executions."
—Bishop Joseph A. Fiorenza

TEXAS ONLINE ★ Forces of Change

Texas Crime Victim Rights

State law grants crime victims certain rights, which can be found online at the following Internet address:

www.co.galveston.tx.us/distatty/texas_crime_victim_rights.htm

Study the website and answer the following questions.

QUESTIONS TO CONSIDER

1. Are close relatives of a murder victim considered victims under the law?
2. Do crime victims have the right to participate in the parole process for a defendant convicted of a crime against the victim?
3. Do crime victims have a right to be informed when a defendant is released on bond or on

> "Trying to take politics out of government is like trying to take math out of physics."
> —Paul Bergala, political consultant

on policy questions because their values differ. Whereas some people believe that the death penalty is morally wrong, other individuals think that it is morally just.

Political actors compete to shape public policy in ways that conform to their interests and values. Individuals and groups attempt to push issues to the forefront of the official policy agenda on which they want policy action while diverting attention from matters on which they prefer that the current policy remain unchanged. Once an issue is part of the official policy agenda, political actors seek to influence the policy formulation process in ways that further their interests. Individuals and groups who support the policy work for its adoption, while those who oppose the policy try to defeat it. Conflict continues during implementation, with competing interests attempting to shape implementation in ways beneficial to them. Finally, individuals and groups evaluate policies in accordance with their own perspectives, creating feedback designed to support the policy's continuance, encourage its revision, or urge its repeal.

WHY STUDY TEXAS GOVERNMENT?

Public opinion polls show that many Americans are cynical about government and uninterested in the way it works. Only 40 percent of the public trusts the government to do what is right most of the time.[13] Many people question the relevance of government to their daily lives and express little interest in public affairs. College students often tell their professors that they have registered for a course in Texas government only because it is required. They frankly admit that they have little interest in the subject and doubt that they will learn anything beneficial. International students in particular question the value of a class in Texas government.

Nonetheless, Texas government is profoundly important to the lives of Texas residents, regardless of their age, backgrounds, and careers. State and local government in Texas provides a broad range of essential government services, including law enforcement, fire protection, education, highways, mass transportation, welfare, job training, parks, airports, water and sewerage treatment, libraries, and public hospitals. Students attending public colleges and universities benefit directly from state-supported higher education. Everyone living in Texas, even temporary residents such as international students, benefits from understanding state and local laws and regulations concerning such matters as driver's licenses, automobile purchases, and renters' rights.

Laws and regulations adopted by state and local governments affect all Texans. Cities enact and enforce zoning ordinances, fire codes, and building codes to regulate land use and construction within city limits. Federal and state regulations affect air and water quality. The state criminal law governs many aspects of personal behavior. State agencies establish educational and technical requirements that must be fulfilled before individuals can engage in certain occupations and professions. Students take courses in Texas government because the Texas legislature requires that public college and university students must complete six semester-hours in American national, state, and local government, including study of the Texas Constitution.

? WHAT IS YOUR OPINION?

Do you agree with the legislative requirement that Texas college students must complete six semester hours in political science?

Texans pay for government through taxes and fees. State government and many local governments levy sales taxes on the retail purchase of a broad range of items. Property owners pay property taxes to municipalities, school districts, counties, and some other units of local government. Texans also pay fees to state and local governments in order to drive an automobile, operate a business, practice certain professions, sell liquor, obtain a marriage license, and go hunting or fishing.

State and local government affects not just individuals but society as a whole. In general, the actions of state and local governments affect the business climate in Texas, which in turn helps determine whether new companies relocate to the Lone Star State and whether firms already here expand their operations. Education, health care, welfare assistance, good roads, public transportation, sanitation, recreation facilities, law enforcement, environmental regulations, and fire protection make the state a better place to live and work. Tax rates and the impact of individual taxes on different income groups affect the distribution of wealth in society and influence the state's economy.

Students benefit from courses in Texas government because they can learn not just how state and local governments affect their lives, but also how they can influence public policy in the state. The essence of American democracy is that citizens govern themselves through their elected officials. Texans have the right (some would say *obligation*) not just to vote but also to communicate their policy preferences to their representatives. Government officials are responsive to the demands and requests of their constituents, especially officials at the state and local levels who work directly with individual citizens on a regular basis.

TEXTBOOK ORGANIZATION

The public policy approach provides the basis for the organization of this textbook. The book's first three chapters deal with the socioeconomic, cultural, and legal environments for policymaking in Texas. The types of issues that make the policy agenda, the policy approaches considered during policy formulation, and the basis of policy evaluation depend on the socioeconomic, cultural, and constitutional/legal context of policymaking. Chapter 1 focuses on the socioeconomic and cultural background of policymaking in the state. The Texas Constitution is the subject of Chapter 2. Chapter 3 deals with the national context of Texas policymaking, considering the impact of the federal system of government on state and local government in Texas.

Chapters 4, 5, 6, and 7 examine the political environment for policymaking. Chapter 4 focuses on individual participation whereas Chapter 5 looks at interest group participation. Chapter 6 considers political parties. Chapter 7 covers the topic of elections.

The next three chapters profile the policymaking institutions of state government. Chapter 8 examines the legislature; Chapter 9, the executive branch of state government; Chapter 10, the judicial branch. These chapters describe the structures of state government and discuss the role they play in the policymaking process.

Chapter 11 and Chapter 12 deal with local government in Texas. Chapter 11 considers city government while Chapter 12 looks at counties, school districts, and special districts. These chapters describe the structures of local government, identify their role in the policymaking process, and discuss some of the policies adopted and implemented by local governments.

The last chapter of the text focuses on a particular policy area, budgetary policy. It examines state taxes and spending priorities.

★ REVIEW QUESTIONS

1. How does the policymaking environment affect the policymaking process?

2. What are the five stages of the policymaking process?

3. How do the concepts of policy cycles and issue networks help explain how the policymaking process actually works?

4. What is the relationship between politics and the policymaking process?

5. Why is it important to study Texas government?

★ KEY TERMS

agenda building

capital punishment

empirical analysis

feedback

incremental model of policy
formulation

issue network

normative analysis

official policy agenda

policy adoption

policy cycle

policy evaluation

policy formulation

policy implementation

policy outcomes

policy outputs

policymaking environment

politics

public policy

public policy approach

rational comprehensive model
of policy formulation

★ NOTES

1. Texas Department of Criminal Justice, "Executives," available at **www.tdcj.state.tx.us**.
2. U.S. Bureau of Justice Statistics, *Capital Punishment*, annual reports, available at **www.tdcj.state.tx.us/stat/racial.htm**.
3. "Gender and Racial Breakdown of Death Row Offenders," Texas Department of Criminal Justice, available at **www.tdcj.state.tx.us/stat/annual.htm**.
4. California Department of Corrections, Populations Reports, available at **www.corr.ca.gov/OffenderInfoServices/Reports/PopulationReports.asp**.
5. *Furman v. Georgia*, 408 U.S. 238 (1972).
6. James Kimberly, "Texans Show Solid Support for Executions," *Houston Chronicle*, March 16, 2003, pp. 35, 43.
7. David A. Rochefort and Roger W. Cobb, "Problem Definition: An Emerging Perspective," in Rochefort and Cobb, eds., *The Politics of Problem Definition: Shaping the Policy Agenda* (Lawrence, KS: University of Kansas Press, 1994), pp. 1–31.
8. Christine H. Rossell, "Using Multiple Criteria to Evaluate Public Policies: The Case of School Desegregation," *American Politics Quarterly* 21 (April 1993): 155–184.
9. David Braybrooke and Charles E. Lindblom, *A Strategy of Decision* (New York: Free Press, 1970).
10. "Execution Statistics," Texas Department of Criminal Justice, available at **www.tdcj.state.tx.us/stat/annual.htm**.
11. "Offenders on Death Row," Texas Department of Criminal Justice, available at **www.tdcj.state.tx.us/**.
12. Curt Anderson, "Death Row Numbers in Decline," *Killeen Daily Herald*, December 16, 2002, available at **www.kdhnews.com**.
13. "Trust in the Federal Government, 1958–2000," *The NES Guide to Public Opinion and Electoral Behavior*, available at **www.umich.edu/~nes/nesguide/nesguide.htm**.

ONLINE PRACTICE TEST

Test your understanding of this chapter
with interactive review quizzes at

www.ablongman.com/tannahilltexas/introduction

CHAPTER ONE

The People, Economy, and Political Culture of Texas

The People of Texas
    Population Size and Growth
    Population Diversity
    Population Distribution

The Texas Economy
    An Economy in Transition
    Wealth, Poverty, and Economic Growth

Political Culture

Conclusion: The Socioeconomic Context
  of Policymaking
    Agenda Building
    Policy Formulation and Adoption
    Policy Implementation and Evaluation

LEARNING OBJECTIVES

After studying Chapter 1, students should be able to do the following:

★ Explain the relationship between education, economic growth, and demographic change in Texas.

★ Compare and contrast population growth in Texas with population growth nationwide.

★ Describe immigration patterns affecting the state of Texas.

★ Evaluate the advantages and disadvantages of rapid population growth.

★ Describe population growth in Texas during the 1990s, considering the growth rate and the affect of that growth on the racial/ethnic makeup of the state.

★ Trace the development of the state's economy, from the days of King Cotton to the present era of high technology economic development.

★ Identify the largest and most rapidly growing sectors of the state's economy today.

★ Compare household income and poverty rates in Texas with those of other states.

★ Describe the distribution of income in Texas.

★ Describe the political culture of Texas, considering the approaches of Elazar and the team of Rice and Sundberg.

★ Explain the relationship between changes in the state's demographic, economic, and cultural environment and policy change.

★ Define the key terms listed on page 33 and explain their significance.

Education is key to the future of Texas. Business managers decide to expand or relocate based on the availability of an educated workforce. Furthermore, individual income is directly related to educational attainment. In 2001, the median annual income of adults 25 years of age and older with a bachelor's degree or greater was $54,069. In contrast, the median annual income for adults with no more than a high school education was $28,343. High school dropouts made less than $20,000 a year.[1]

Unfortunately, Texas lags behind other states in educational attainment. In 2000, 79 percent of Texans 25 years of age and older had graduated from high school compared to a national high-school graduation rate of 84 percent. Texas also trailed the national average in the proportion of adults holding bachelor's degrees, 24 percent to 26 percent.[2] Today, only 4.9 percent of Texas residents are enrolled in higher education compared to 6.1 percent of the people in California, 6 percent in Illinois, and 5.6 percent in New York. To make matters worse, the rate of college enrollment in Texas is dropping. State officials estimate that the proportion of Texans attending college will fall to 4.6 percent or less by 2015.[3]

The problem for Texas is that the fastest growing segment of the population is also the least educated. Hispanic and African American Texans as a group are less educated and have lower incomes than non-Hispanic whites and Asian Americans. In 2001, Latinos comprised 32 percent of the state's population but only 23 percent of its college students. The comparable figures for African Americans were 12 percent and 11 percent.[4] Population experts project that the state's population will be 46 percent Latino and 10 percent African American by the year 2030. If the educational, occupational, and income status of Hispanic and African American Texans does not improve significantly, a majority of the state's working-age population will be poorly educated, low-income minority residents. Business and industry will be reluctant to relocate to a state without an educated workforce, tax collections will fall, and the state budget will be strapped trying to provide social services for a large population of low-income residents.[5]

"The future of Texas is tied to its minority populations. How well they do is how well Texas will do."
—Steve Murdock, demographer, Texas A&M University

The complex relationship between race and ethnicity, income and education, and public policy illustrates the importance of demographic, economic, and cultural factors on policymaking in Texas. This chapter examines some of the more significant factors shaping the environment for policymaking in Texas. The first section of the chapter profiles the people of Texas, considering the size of the state's population, population growth, population diversity, and the distribution of the state's people. The second section examines the state's economy, looking at economic trends, personal income, and poverty. The final section of the chapter deals with the subject of political culture.

The Texas legislature and the governor have attempted to increase diversity in the state's major universities by adopting the **top 10 percent rule,** which is a policy that guarantees the admission to state colleges and universities of students who graduate in the top 10 percent of their public high school classes without regard for their SAT or ACT scores. Because a majority of the state's public school students are either African American or Latino, state leaders hoped the rule would ensure the admission of a significant number of minority students to the University of Texas, Texas A&M University, and other state universities.

The top 10 percent rule is controversial. Critics charge that it has undermined the quality of incoming students at the state's best universities without enhancing diversity. Students admitted under the top 10 percent rule, which now make up about three-fourths of the freshman class at the University of Texas at Austin, have lower SAT and ACT scores on average than students otherwise admitted. Furthermore, the percentage of minority students has not gone up at the University of Texas or Texas A&M University. In contrast, the defenders of the policy point out that students admitted under the top 10 percent rule have earned better grades than students otherwise admitted. They also believe that the rule has made university admissions more diverse than they would have been otherwise.[6]

 WHAT IS YOUR OPINION?

If you were a member of the legislature, would you vote to repeal the top 10 percent rule?

THE PEOPLE OF TEXAS

The population of Texas is one of the largest and most diverse of any state in the nation.

Population Size and Growth

Texas is the nation's second most populous state. In July 2002, the U.S. Census Bureau estimated that the population of Texas was 21,779,893. Only California with 35.1 million people had a larger population.[7]

Figure 1.1 traces the growth of the state's population decade by decade from the 1970s through the 1990s and compares the population growth rate of Texas with the growth rate for the United States as a whole. As the figure shows, the state's population expanded the most rapidly between 1970 and 1980, which was a decade of significant economic growth. During the 1980s, the state's population grew at just less than 2 percent a year; the growth rate during the 1990s averaged 2.3 percent a year. In each of the three decades covered in the figure, the population of the **Lone Star State,** which is a nickname for Texas, increased at a more rapid pace than did the population of the nation as a whole. Furthermore, the U.S. Census Bureau estimates that the population of Texas has continued to grow at a relatively fast pace since the completion of the last census. Between July 2001 and July 2002, the state's population increased by 1.9 percent. Only Nevada, Florida, and Arizona grew more rapidly.[8]

Both natural population increase and immigration contribute to population growth in Texas. **Natural population increase** is the extent to which live births exceed deaths. The birth rate in Texas is the second highest in the nation.[9] Because the state's population is relatively young (a median age of 32.3 compared to a national average of 35.3),[10] the proportion of women of childbearing age is relatively high. The state's ethnic composition also contributes to rapid population growth. The birth rate for Mexican-American women, particularly recent immigrants, is

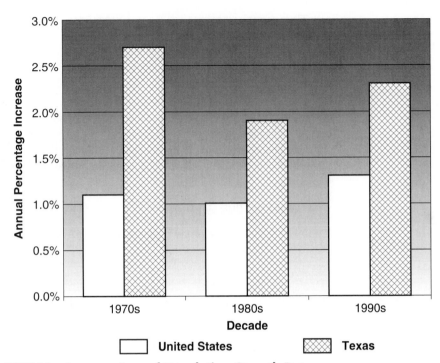

FIGURE 1.1   Average Annual Population Growth Rate
Source: U.S. Census Bureau

more than 50 percent higher than the birth rates for Latino women who are not of Mexican origin and for women who are African American or non-Hispanic white.[11]

The state's population also grows because of immigration. Between July 1, 2001 and July 1, 2002, Texas recorded a net gain of 202,499 residents from international and domestic immigration. The state experienced a net increase of 161,325 residents from international immigration and added another 41,174 people from domestic immigration.[12] Most migrants from within the United States are skilled workers who find jobs in the health care and **high technology industries,** which are industries that are based on the latest in modern technology, such as telecommunications and robotics. In contrast, immigrants from abroad tend to be poorly educated, low-skill workers who go to work in the tourism and construction industries.

Because of immigration, Texas has a large and diverse foreign-born population. The 2000 Census counted 2.4 million foreign-born residents of Texas, 11.5 percent of the state's population.[13] The foreign-born population of Texas is younger, poorer, and less well educated than are the state's native-born residents. More than three-fourths of the state's foreign-born residents are not American citizens.[14]

The state's relatively rapid population growth presents both opportunities and challenges for policymakers. Rapid population growth has led to greater representation for Texas in Congress, a bigger share of federal grant money, and an enlarged tax

"[Texas] gets a mix of the skilled migrants who make up the domestic migrant streams as well as . . . people who are unskilled (who) tend to be immigrants."
—William Frey, demographer

State law guarantees the admission to state colleges and universities of students who graduate in the top 10 percent of their public high school classes without regard for their SAT or ACT scores.

base. Because the number of seats in the U.S. House of Representatives each state receives is based on its population, relatively rapid population growth in the Lone Star State has translated into more representation in Congress. Texas gained three House seats after the 1990 Census and two more after the 2000 Census, giving the state 32 seats in the U.S. House. Population growth means an increase in federal financial aid because funding for many federal grant programs is based on population. Furthermore, population growth has generally meant a larger tax base for state and local governments. With more consumers to buy products, sales tax receipts have risen.

Population growth also presents policy challenges. Rapid population growth has placed a considerable strain on public services in Texas. More people mean more automobiles on city streets and freeways, more garbage to be collected and disposed of, more children to be educated, and more subdivisions for local law enforcement agencies to police. For example, school districts around the state will have to build additional classroom space to accommodate an expected 15 percent increase in elementary and secondary school students by the year 2007.[15]

TEXAS ONLINE ★ Forces of Change

Exploring Texas

Regardless of whether you are a newcomer to the Lone Star State or a native Texan, you will learn a good deal from the state's official government homepage:

www.texas.gov

Browse the website and answer the following questions.

QUESTIONS TO CONSIDER

1. What city in the state would you enjoy visiting? Why?
2. What is the state flower?
3. If you are new to Texas, how do you obtain a driver's license?

Population Diversity

The population of Texas is quite diverse. According to the 2000 Census, the population makeup in Texas is 52 percent non-Hispanic white, 32 percent Latino, 11 percent African American, and 3 percent Asian. American Indians comprise less than 1 percent of the state's population. About 1 percent of the state's population identify themselves as biracial or multiracial.[16] Although most Latino residents of Texas are Mexican American, the state's Hispanic population includes significant numbers of people who trace their ancestries to Cuba, El Salvador, or other Latin American countries. Similarly, the state's Asian population includes 27 different nationalities, the largest of which are Vietnamese, Chinese, Indian, Filipino, Korean, and Japanese.[17]

> "Anglos are very close to losing their majority status. Pick a year. In 2003, 2005, or sometime in the relatively near future, they'll drop below 50 percent."
> —Nestor Rodriquez, University of Houston

Texas's ethnic communities are distributed unevenly across the state. Most African American Texans live in the rural areas and small towns of east Texas, along the Gulf Coast, and in the state's metropolitan areas. Houston and Dallas are home to a third of the state's African American population.[18] Latinos are concentrated in south and west Texas, especially along the Mexican border. San Antonio, El Paso, Corpus Christi, Brownsville, McAllen, and Laredo all have Hispanic majorities.[19] Asians are clustered in the Gulf Coast region, whereas many Texans of German and Czech descent live in the Hill Country in central Texas. More than 90 percent of the state's foreign-born residents, regardless of racial/ethnic origin, live in metropolitan areas.[20]

Population Distribution

The population of Texas is not evenly distributed across the state. The most populous regions are central, south, north, and east Texas, and the Gulf Coast region. The most rapidly growing areas are the San Antonio-Austin region in central Texas, the Dallas-Fort Worth region in north Texas, the Houston area in southeast Texas, and the region near the border with Mexico. In contrast, the Panhandle region in northwest Texas and far west Texas (with the exception of the border area near El Paso) are sparsely populated and growing slowly if at all. In fact, many of the rural counties in west central Texas and the Panhandle lost population during the 1990s.[21]

Education is key to the future of Texas, especially the education of the state's growing Latino and African American populations.

Texas is an urban state, with 85 percent of its population living in metropolitan areas.[22] Table 1.1 identifies the largest cities in the state, showing both their population in 2000 and their rate of population growth during the 1990s. Three Texas cities—Houston, Dallas, and San Antonio—are among the ten largest cities in the United States. As Table 1.1 shows, most of the state's big cities increased their populations significantly during the decade. More than 90 percent of the state's population growth in the 1990s took place in metropolitan areas.[23]

Much of the growth in metropolitan areas occurred in the suburbs. Eight of the ten most rapidly growing counties in Texas were suburban counties. Collin County, which is north of Dallas, grew by 86 percent. Montgomery County and Fort Bend County, which are part of the Greater Houston metropolitan area, grew by 61 percent and 57 percent.[24]

The state's rural areas are growing slowly or, in some cases, losing population. Less than 10 percent of the 3.9 million residents added to the state's population during the 1990s lived in rural areas. The two most important industries for rural Texas, agriculture and oil, have changed to require fewer workers than before. Consequently, many rural areas have been losing population. During the 1990s, more than a third of Texas's rural counties lost population while every metropolitan county grew.[25]

TABLE 1.1   Population and Growth Rates for Texas Cities, 1990–2000

City	2000 Population	Percentage Change 1990–2000
Houston	1,953,631	19.8
Dallas	1,188,580	18.0
San Antonio	1,144,646	22.3
Austin	656,562	41.0
El Paso	563,662	9.3
Fort Worth	534,694	19.5
Arlington	332,969	27.2
Corpus Christi	277,454	4.3
Plano	222,030	72.0
Garland	215,768	19.4

Source: U.S. Census Bureau, available at **www.census.gov**.

 WHAT IS YOUR OPINION?

If you could afford to live anywhere, would you prefer to live in the city, the suburbs, or the countryside?

THE TEXAS ECONOMY

The economy is a key part of the policymaking environment in Texas.

An Economy in Transition

For most of Texas history, the state's economy was based on the sale of agricultural commodities and raw materials. In the nineteenth century, cotton and cattle formed the basis of economic activity. Unfortunately for the state, neither cotton nor cattle provided the necessary foundation for a manufacturing boom. Texas exported most of its ginned cotton for clothing production to other states or countries. Similarly, cattle ranchers drove their herds to railheads in Kansas for shipment to stockyards in the Midwest.

In 1901, oil was discovered at Spindletop near Beaumont. Subsequently, oil and gas deposits were found throughout the state and Texas became the nation's leading producer of oil and gas. In contrast to other commodities, oil spawned huge processing industries, including pipelines and refineries. The growth of petroleum-related businesses helped move the majority of Texans into urban areas by the 1950s.

Having an economy built on agriculture and oil has had a major impact on the state's development. In the nineteenth century, Texas's economic health depended on the prices of cotton and cattle. For much of the twentieth century, the state's economy rose and fell in line with oil prices. Because commodity

East Texas oil fields in 1903.

prices tend to fluctuate widely, Texas's economic history was one of booms and busts as prices for Texan products soared or collapsed. The state's economy boomed in the 1970s and early 1980s, for example, as oil prices rose to around $40 a barrel, but then sagged in the mid-1980s as the price of oil dipped to less than half its earlier level.

The nature of the state's economy has contributed to a relatively lopsided distribution of income. Texas has been a rich state, but most Texans have not been wealthy. To be sure, agriculture and oil were sources of significant wealth for the state's major landowners and oil producers. More Texans, however, were farm workers and oil-field roughnecks than large landowners or oil producers. Workers in these industries historically were poorly organized and poorly paid, at least in comparison with workers in the auto assembly plants or steel mills of northern states. Because people employed in industrial plants work together in close proximity, it is easier for them to organize and form unions to demand higher wages and better working conditions than farm workers and oil-field roughnecks who are dispersed, working outdoors.

The Texas economy is changing. As Figure 1.2 demonstrates, Texas oil production has been falling sharply and fairly steadily for years and continues to decline. Natural gas production has fallen as well. In 2003, the oil and gas business provided only 1.5 percent of the state's nonfarm payroll, down from 7.3 percent in the early 1980s.[26] As oil and gas production fell so did state severance tax revenues. (A **severance tax** is tax levied on natural resources at the time they are taken from the land or water.) Since the early 1970s, the proportion of state revenues generated by

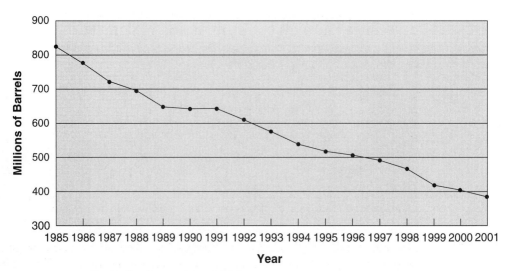

FIGURE 1.2 Texas Oil Production, 1985–2001
Source: Texas Railroad Commission

severance taxes on oil and gas production has declined from more than 20 percent of state revenues to less than 2 percent in 2002.[27]

Declining oil and gas production and stagnant farm prices have forced state leaders, both in government and private enterprise, to take steps to diversify the Texas economy. Although agriculture and petroleum are still important features of the state's economic picture, other industries are playing a greater role. Today, the state's economy is more diverse than ever before, resembling the national economy.

Table 1.2 shows the distribution of economic activity in the Lone Star State in 1990, 1995, and 2001. The largest sectors of the state's economy are 1) services, 2) trade, 3) finance, insurance, and real estate, and 4) manufacturing. The service sector of the economy includes health care, social services, and business services. The growing importance of trade to the state's economy reflects the emergence of the **global economy,** which is the integration of national economies into a world economic system in which companies compete worldwide for suppliers and markets. International trade has become increasingly important to the state's economy since the passage in 1994 of the **North American Free Trade Agreement (NAFTA),** which is an international accord among the United States, Mexico, and Canada to lower trade barriers among the three nations. In 2000, Texas companies exported nearly $112 billion of goods to 233 countries around the globe, placing Texas second only to California as an exporting state. The state's most important exports by value were computer and electronic products, chemicals, machinery, transportation equipment, and electrical equipment. Mexico is by far the state's primary international trading partner, followed by Canada, Japan, and Taiwan.[28]

The economic changes that are taking place in the state affect Texas's workforce. The most rapidly growing industries in the state, such as telecommunications and health care, employ workers with technical knowledge and a capacity to learn

TABLE 1.2 Texas Economic Sectors, 1990, 1995, and 2001

Sector	1990	1995	2001
Agriculture	1.5%	1.4%	1.2%
Mining (Oil and Gas)	8.4	6.6	6.3
Construction	3.7	4.3	4.8
Manufacturing	16.7	16.3	13.1
Transportation, communications, and utilities	9.7	10.8	11.1
Trade	15.3	16.3	16.7
Finance, insurance, and real estate	14.2	14.4	15.2
Services	17.9	18.0	20.6
Government	12.7	11.4	11.0

Source: Texas Comptroller of Public Accounts, available at **www.cpa.state.tx.us**.

> "We're going through a period in which trade and technology are like an economic natural disaster for the half of the working population that doesn't have a college degree."
> —Frank Levy, economist

new skills as technology changes. Texans who meet these criteria have a bright economic future. People who worked in high technology industries in Texas earned $64,100 on average in 1999 compared to $33,500 for the average worker in a private, nontechnology job.[29] In contrast, unskilled workers were lucky to find jobs that paid much more than minimum wage.

Wealth, Poverty, and Economic Growth

> "Texas is the big winner in free trade under NAFTA."
> —Charles Cervantes, U.S./Mexico Chamber of Commerce

Texas is a big state with a big economy. In 2002, the Texas **Gross State Product (GSP),** which is the total value of goods and services produced in a state in a year, was $750 billion.[30] Only California and New York had larger economies than Texas.[31] In fact, if Texas were an independent nation, it would have the seventh largest economy in the world, larger even than Canada, Mexico, and Spain.[32]

The Texas economy has been growing at a more rapid pace than the national economy. Figure 1.3 compares the annual growth rate of the Texas economy with the rate of economic growth for the entire nation from 1990 through 2002. As the figure indicates, Texas economic performance generally parallels that of the national economy. Both economies experienced periods of relatively slow economic growth in the early 1990s and then again in 2001–2002. In the meantime, both the national economy and the state economy enjoyed several years of brisk economic expansion in the mid- to late-1990s. The figure also shows that the Texas economy grew more rapidly than the national economy throughout the period. The economic slowdowns were not as slow in Texas, whereas the economic booms were more robust.

Nonetheless, Texas is a relatively poor state, at least in terms of individual and family income. The three-year median household annual income in Texas for 2000–2002 was $40,659 compared to a national figure of $43,052. Texas ranked 32nd among the 50 states.[33]

Household income varies depending on race and ethnicity. The average income for non-Hispanic white families in 2002 was $45,066 compared to $33,103 for Latino households and $29,026 for African American households.[34] Professor Stephen Klineberg, a Rice University sociologist, attributes the income disparity among ethnic and racial groups to an historic lack of access to quality education for

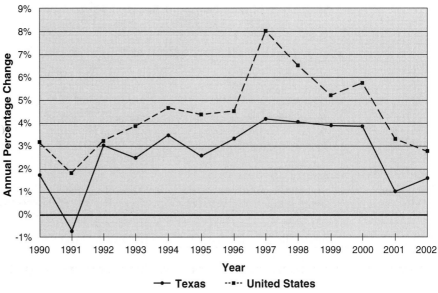

FIGURE 1.3   Changes In Economic Activity, 1990–2002
Source: Texas Comptroller of Public Accounts

African Americans and Latinos. Because the economy is changing, relatively few jobs are now available for people with weak job skills. "The good jobs that used to pay good money for unskilled or semi-skilled work are much harder to find these days," he explains.[35] As we discussed in the introduction to this chapter, the economic health of Texas hinges on the socioeconomic progress of the state's large and growing minority populations, especially its Latino and African American populations, and that progress depends on education.

The income differential between the wealthiest and the poorest families is greater in Texas than it is in other states and the income disparity is growing. Economists assess income inequality by ranking all families according to their income level, dividing them into five groups of equal size, and calculating the average income of each fifth. In the late 1990s, the average income for Texas families in the poorest fifth was $12,570 compared to an average income of $225,110 for families in the wealthiest fifth. The income disparity between the bottom and the top in Texas was greater than it was in all but two other states. Furthermore, the disparity is widening. During the 1990s, the average income of the poorest fifth of Texans grew by 14.5 percent compared to an increase of 31.5 percent for the wealthiest fifth.[36]

? WHAT IS YOUR OPINION?

Should the government adopt policies designed to narrow the wealth and income gaps between the poorest and wealthiest segments of the population?

LEARNING EXERCISE

The Texas Economy

How strong is the Texas economy today? You can find current state economic data online at the homepage of the Texas Comptroller of Public Accounts: **www.window.state.tx.us/**. Browse through the website to find data that assess the strength and performance of the state's economy. In particular, look for data that show changes in state economic performance over time or that compare the strength of the Texas economy with that of the United States as a whole.

Write a short essay in which you discuss Texas's economic performance today. The essay should describe the performance of the Texas economy across time and compare the strength of the economy in Texas today with the economy of the United States as a whole. Mention at least two economic indicators. Support your essay with charts, graphs, and tables depicting the data you find on the website. Make specific reference to those items in your essay. Finally, put in context the current performance of the state's economy with its historical performance as discussed in your textbook.

The poverty rate is relatively high in Texas. The government measures poverty on the basis of subsistence. By the official government definition, the **poverty line** is the amount of money an individual or family needs to purchase basic necessities, such as food, clothing, health care, shelter, and transportation. The actual dollar amount varies with family size and rises with inflation. In 2002, the poverty line stood at $18,390 for a family of four. During the three-year period of 2000–2002, the average poverty rate in Texas was 15.3 percent compared to 11.7 percent for the United States as a whole.[37]

Poverty is concentrated among racial minorities, single-parent families headed by women, and the very young. In 2002, the national poverty rate for non-Hispanic whites was 8.0 percent. It was 24.1 percent for African Americans, 21.8 percent for Latinos, and 10.1 percent for Asians and Pacific Islanders. More than 16 percent of the nation's children under age 18 live in families that are poor, while 26.5 percent of families headed by women with no husband present earn incomes below the poverty line.[38]

> "The biggest economic generator any community can have is a person with a college degree."
> —Leticia R. Van de Putte, Texas State Senator, D., San Antonio

POLITICAL CULTURE

Political culture refers to the widely held, deeply rooted political values of a society. Professor Daniel Elazar identifies three strains of political culture found in the United States: individualistic, moralistic, and traditionalistic.[39] The **individualistic political culture** is an approach to government and politics that emphasizes private initiative with a minimum of government interference. This political culture stresses the importance of the individual and private initiative. In this view of society, the role of government should be limited to protecting individual rights and ensuring

More than three million Texans, many of them children, live in poverty.

that social and political relationships are based on merit rather than tradition, family ties, or personal connections. Elazar says that individualistic political culture developed from the eighteenth- and nineteenth-century business centers in New York, Philadelphia, and Baltimore, and spread westward through the central part of the nation. Immigrants from areas dominated by the individualistic political culture settled in the northern and central parts of Texas in the mid-nineteenth century.

The **moralistic political culture** is an approach to government and politics in which people expect government to intervene in the social and economic affairs of the state, promoting the public welfare and advancing the public good. Participation in political affairs is regarded as one's civic duty. Elazar says the moralistic political culture developed from **Puritanism** (a religious reform movement) and New England town meetings, and spread westward through the northern part of the nation and down the West Coast. Texas has received relatively little immigration from areas where the moralistic political culture was important.

The **traditionalistic political culture** is an approach to government and politics that sees the role of government as the preservation of tradition and the existing social order. Government leadership is in the hands of an established social elite and the level of participation by ordinary citizens in the policymaking process is relatively low. The role of government is to protect and preserve the existing social order. Elazar says that the traditional form of political culture developed from the plantation society of the South and spread westward through the southern states. Many immigrants from areas where the traditionalistic political culture was strong settled in east Texas.

Elazar believes that the political culture of Texas is a hybrid, including both traditionalistic and individualistic elements, and he identifies some aspects of state politics that reflect these two strains of political culture. Texas's traditionalistic political culture, Elazar says, is represented in the state's long history as a one-party state, low levels of voter turnout, and social and economic conservatism. Elazar identifies the state's strong support for private business, opposition to big government, and faith in individual initiative as reflections of Texas's individualistic political culture.

Political scientists Tom W. Rice and Alexander F. Sundberg take a different approach to political culture. They focus on the concept of **civic culture,** which is a political culture that is conducive to the development of an efficient, effective government that meets the needs of its citizens in a timely and professional manner. States with a civic culture have innovative and effective government, they say, whereas states in which the culture is less civic have governments that are less responsive to citizen demands.

Rice and Sundberg identify four elements of a civic culture:

- **Civic engagement:** Citizens participate in the policymaking process in order to promote the public good.
- **Political equality:** Citizens view each other as political equals, with the same rights and obligations.
- **Solidarity, trust, and tolerance:** Citizens feel a strong sense of fellowship with one another, tolerating a wide range of ideas and lifestyles.
- **Social structure of cooperation:** Citizens are joiners, belonging to a rich array of groups, from recreational sports teams to religious organizations.

> "Texas isn't geography. It's history. It's a world in itself."
> —Edna Ferber, novelist

According to data gathered by Rice and Sundberg, Texas ranks 43rd among the 50 states in its level of civic culture. They found that most of the civic states are in the North, running from New England to the Northwest. In contrast, Rice and Sundberg found that most southern states are low in civic culture.[40]

Political culture is a useful concept for students of public policy because it leads us to focus on a state's history and development as important factors influencing politics and policy. Scholars who study the American states recognize variations in political behavior and beliefs among different regions of the country that can be explained on the basis of political culture. The concepts developed by Elazar and the team of Rice and Sundberg are useful tools for understanding policy differences among states that cannot be explained simply on the basis of socioeconomic factors.

NATIONAL PERSPECTIVE

Civil Unions in Vermont

The states of Texas and Vermont have contrasting political cultures that have produced dramatically different public policies. Texas has relatively low tax rates and low levels of government spending whereas Vermont is above average in both categories. In terms of budget priorities, Texas is a national leader in spending on prisons, but lags in welfare spending; Vermont is the opposite. Texas ranks 7th in the nation in spending **per capita** (per person) on prisons and 42nd in welfare spending per capita. In contrast, Vermont is 46th out of the 50 states in spending on prisons and 11th on welfare spending.*

Perhaps the greatest policy difference between Texas and Vermont is the way the two states relate to their gay and lesbian residents. Before the U.S. Supreme Court found the law unconstitutional in 2003, Texas was one of only a handful of states to outlaw same-gender sexual contact between consenting adults. "Deviate sexual intercourse" between two men or two women was a criminal offense in Texas, punishable by a maximum fine of $500. Although the Texas Homosexual Conduct Law was rarely enforced, it was used as a justification for discrimination against gay men and lesbians in employment, insurance benefits, child custody, and adoption.†

In contrast, Vermont is the most gay friendly state in the nation. Vermont not only prohibits discrimination on the basis of sexual orientation, but the state has become the first in the nation to offer civil unions as a legal alternative to marriage for gay men and lesbians. A **civil union** is a legal partnership between two men or two women that gives the couple all the benefits, protections, and responsibilities under law that are granted to spouses in a marriage. The Vermont Legislature passed and the governor of Vermont signed legislation granting gay men and lesbians the opportunity to form civil unions in the wake

of a decision by the Vermont Supreme Court. The court ruled that the Vermont Constitution required the state to provide eligible same-sex couples the opportunity to "obtain the same benefits and protections afforded by Vermont law to married opposite-sex couples." Under Vermont's civil union law, same-sex couples enjoy the same status as married couples when it comes to insurance, state tax laws, inheritance, probate, adoption, and hospital visitation.‡

Although states usually recognize marriages performed in other states, no state has yet recognized Vermont civil unions as binding outside the boundaries of Vermont. In fact, the U.S. Congress passed and President Bill Clinton signed the **Defense of Marriage Act (DOMA),** which is a federal law stipulating that each state may choose either to recognize or not recognize same-sex marriages performed in other states. Texas has adopted its own Defense of Marriage Act, declaring that a marriage between persons of the same sex or a civil union are "against public policy" and void in the state. Considering the political culture of Texas, it is unlikely that the Lone Star State will recognize Vermont civil unions as binding or adopt its own civil union law any time soon.

QUESTIONS TO CONSIDER

1. What are some possible explanations for the differences in public policies between Texas and Vermont?

2. What are some factors in the policymaking environment in Texas that would account for its policies dealing with gay men and lesbians?

3. What changes in the policymaking environment in Texas would have to occur before the state changed its policies toward gay men and lesbians?

State and Local Source Book 2000, published by *Governing: The Magazine of States and Localities,* 2000, pp. 12, 18, 33, and 42.
†*Lawrence v. Texas,* No. 02-102.

‡The Vermont Legislature, "Civil Unions," available at **www.leg.state.vt.us/baker/baker.cfm.**

CONCLUSION: THE SOCIOECONOMIC CONTEXT OF POLICYMAKING

The demographic, economic, and cultural environments affect every stage of the policymaking process.

Agenda Building

Because Texas is an urban state, issues such as mass transportation, air quality, crime, and inner city development more frequently appear on the official policy agenda than they would in a predominantly rural state. Population growth in the suburbs increases the influence of voices calling for lower property taxes, strong local schools, and highway construction to relieve traffic congestion. Similarly, the state's large racial and ethnic minority groups raise matters of particular concern to them, including issues of political representation and opportunity in employment and access to higher education. Texas's status as a border state ensures that immigration and trade issues frequently appear on the policy agenda.

Policy Formulation and Adoption

The demographic, economic, and cultural environments impact policy formulation. Political culture limits the range of alternatives to a policy problem. The political culture of Texas presupposes a minimal role for government. The state's economy impacts policy formulation as well. Economic growth generates tax revenues that can be used to expand government services or finance tax reductions. In contrast, an economic slump forces legislators and the governor to cut programs or increase taxes.

Environmental factors affect policy adoption. Although Latinos and African Americans comprise a substantial proportion of the state's residents, they lack economic power and, consequently, their political influence is less than their numerical representation in the state's population. As a result, state and local governments usually adopt policies that more closely reflect the desires of the non-Hispanic white majority than they do the state's racial and ethnic minority groups. Similarly, the weakness of organized labor and consumer interests in Texas ensures that the state adopts policies that more closely mirror the concerns of business owners and corporate managers than they do either labor or consumer interests.

Policy Implementation and Evaluation

Demographic, economic, and cultural factors influence policy implementation. Because of the state's geographical size and diversity, policy implementation sometimes varies from place to place. As we discussed in the introductory chapter, counties implement the state's capital punishment law differently because of disparities in

GETTING INVOLVED

Volunteering

Everyone should do volunteer work, especially college students. Volunteering is a way to give back to the community for the kindnesses of others. People who volunteer develop an attachment to their community by learning about the problems in their area and helping to solve them. Furthermore, volunteer work is a rewarding experience.

Your community has many fine organizations that welcome volunteers, including hospitals, schools, nursing homes, and animal shelters. Your college may have a service-learning program that matches volunteers with organizations needing help. Contact the organization of your choice and find out the procedures for volunteering. Even if you are only able to put in a few hours between semesters or on an occasional weekend, you will benefit from the experience.

It's your community—get involved!

resources. Large counties can aggressively pursue the death penalty whereas small counties lack the financial resources to prosecute more than a handful of capital punishment cases. Similarly, small rural school districts implement state educational policies differently than large urban districts.

Environmental factors also influence policy evaluation. Because Texas is a large and diverse state, it has a significant number of individuals and groups whose policy perspectives do not always coincide. Consequently, policy evaluation is more contentious than it would be in a more homogeneous state. Individuals and groups who lost out in the policy formulation and adoption stages evaluate a policy harshly, while those interests who initially supported the policy defend it.

Changes in the policymaking environment often lead to policy change. The number of political actors that are influential in the policy process has increased as the state's economic base has broadened. Oil and gas interests are still important but no longer dominant. Population change has also produced a change in the policy process. Newcomers to the state sometimes have different perspectives than those of native Texans. Historically, non-Hispanic White immigrants from other states have been more likely to identify with the Republican Party than have been native non-Hispanic White Texans.[41]

Studying Texas's social structure, economy, and political culture is important for students of Texas government because these factors provide the context for policymaking. They determine the types of political issues that make the official policy agenda, establish the boundaries of acceptable policy options available to public officials during the policy formulation and adoption stages, set the ground rules for policy implementation, and establish standards for evaluating policies. Finally, changes in the state's population, economy, and political culture will lead to changes in public policies. As we discussed in the introductory section of this chapter, education is critical to the state's economic future, especially the education of its large and growing minority populations.

★ REVIEW QUESTIONS

1. Why is the education of Latino and African American Texans important to the state's future?

2. Why has the population of Texas grown more rapidly than the national population growth rate?

3. How would you describe the diversity of the state's population?

4. Which areas and regions of the state grew the most rapidly during the 1990s? Which grew the most slowly?

5. How has the state's economy changed since the slump in the oil industry in the mid-1980s?

6. How does the Texas economy compare with the economy of the United States as a whole?

7. Is Texas a wealthy state?

8. How would you describe the political culture of Texas?

★ KEY TERMS

civic culture

civil union

Defense of Marriage Act (DOMA)

global economy

gross state product (GSP)

high technology industries

individualistic political culture

Lone Star State

moralistic political culture

natural population increase

North American Free Trade Agreement (NAFTA)

per capita

political culture

poverty line

Puritanism

severance tax

top ten percent rule

traditionalistic political culture

★ NOTES

1. U.S. Census Bureau, "Income 2001," available at **www.census.gov**.

2. U.S. Census Bureau, "Educational Attainment by States: 1990 and 2000," *Statistical Abstract of the United States, 2002*, available at **www.census.gov**.

3. Michael Arnone, "Texas Falls Behind in Plan to Enroll More Minority Students," *Chronicle of Higher Education*, January 17, 2003, p. A23.

4. *Chronicle of Higher Education Almanac Issue 2001–2002*, August 31, 2001, p. 89.

5. Martin Basaldua, "Closing the Gaps: Texas Higher Education Plan," Texas Higher Education Coordinating Board, 2000, available at **www.thecb.state.tx.us**.

6. Erik Rodriguez and Sharon Jayson, "10 Percent Law Not Doing Job at UT-Austin," *Austin American-Statesman*, May 25, 2003, available at **www.statesman.com**.

7. U.S. Census Bureau, "State Population Estimates, April 1, 2000 to July 1, 2002," available at **www.census.gov**.

8. U.S. Census Bureau, "Annual Population Change by State," available at **www.census.gov**.

9. U.S. Census Bureau, "Live Births by State: 2000," Statistical Abstract of the United States: 2002, available at **www.census.gov**.

10. U.S. Census Bureau, "Profile of General Demographic Characteristics for Texas: 2000," available at **www.census.gov**.

11. U.S. Census Bureau, "Fertility of American Women Current Population Survey—June 1998, Detailed Tables," available at **www.census.gov**.

12. U.S. Census Bureau, "Estimated Components of State Population Change: July 1, 2001 to July 1, 2002," available at **www.census.gov**.

13. U.S. Census Bureau, "Profile of the Foreign-Born Population in the United States: 2000," available at **www.census.gov**.

14. U.S. Census Bureau, "Profile of the Foreign-Born Population of the United States: 1997," available at **www.census.gov**.

15. *State Legislatures*, February 1998, p. 18.

16. U.S. Census Bureau, "Population by Race and Hispanic or Latino Origin," available at **www.census.gov**.

17. *Fiscal Notes*, November 1997, p. 3.

18. U.S. Census Bureau, "Population by Race and Hispanic or Latino Origin, for States, Puerto Rico, and Places of 100,000 or more Population: 2000," available at **www.census.gov**.

19. U.S. Census Bureau, "Percent of Population by Race and Hispanic or Latino Origin, for States, Puerto Rico, and Places of 100,000 or more Population: 2000," available at **www.census.gov**.

20. U.S. Census Bureau, "Profile of the Foreign-Born Population of the United States: 1997," available at **www.census.gov**.

21. Texas State Data Center and Office of the State Demographer, "Texas Population Growth in Texas Counties, 1850–2040," available at **txsdc.tamu.edu/maps/thematic/popgrowth.php**.

22. U.S. Census Bureau, "Metropolitan and Non-Metropolitan Population by State: 1980–2000," *Statistical Abstract of the United States: 2002*, available at **www.census.gov**.

23. U.S. Census Bureau, "Metropolitan and Non-Metropolitan Population by State: 1980–2000," available at **www.census.gov**.

24. "Texas Population Growth in Texas Counties, 1850–2040."

25. U.S. Census Bureau, *Census 2000 Geographic Definitions*, revised November 16, 2000, available at **www.census.gov**.

26. Texas Workforce Commission, "Texas Nonagricultural Wage and Salary Employment Seasonally Adjusted," available at **www.twc.state.tx.us**.

27. Texas Comptroller of Public Accounts, "Revenue by Source—Fiscal 2002," available at **www.window.state.tx.us/**.

28. Clint Shields, "From Texas to the World," *Fiscal Notes*, May 2003, pp. 8–9.

29. Tom Fowler, "Texas Ranks Among Best in Technology," *Houston Chronicle*, June 6, 2001, p. 4C.

30. Texas Comptroller of Public Accounts, "Spring 2002 Economic Forecast," available at **www.window.state.tx.us**.

31. U.S. Census Bureau, "Gross State Product in Current and Real (1996) Dollars: 1990–1999," *Statistical Abstract of the United States, 2002*, available at **www.census.gov**.

32. U.S. Census Bureau, "Gross State Product by Country: 1995–2000," *Statistical Abstract of the United States, 2002*, available at **www.census.gov**.

33. U.S. Census Bureau, "Income 2002," available at **www.census.gov**.

34. Ibid.

35. David Plesa, "Racial Income Gap Widens," *Houston Post*, April 16, 1993, p. A-1.

36. Economic Policy Institute, Center for Budget Priorities, "Pulling Apart: A State-by-State Analysis of Income Trends," available at **www.cbpp.org**.

37. U.S. Census Bureau, "Poverty in the United States 2002," available at **www.census.gov**.

38. Ibid.

39. Daniel Elazar, *American Federalism: A View from the States*, 2nd ed. (New York: Crowell, 1972), pp. 84–126.

40. Tom W. Rice and Alexander F. Sundberg, "Civic Culture and Government Performance in the American States," *Publius: The Journal of Federalism* 27 (Winter 1997):99–114.

41. Poll conducted by the University of Houston Center for Public Policy, quoted in *Houston Chronicle*, September 19, 1990, p. 1A.

ONLINE PRACTICE TEST

Test your understanding of this chapter
with interactive review quizzes at
www.ablongman.com/tannahilltexas/chapter1

Texas Constitution

LEARNING OBJECTIVES

After studying Chapter 2, students should be able to do the following:

★ Describe the role of the Texas Constitution in the controversy over education finance.

★ Compare and contrast state constitutions with the U.S. Constitution.

★ Trace the historical background of the Texas Constitution.

★ Identify the two main goals of the majority of delegates at the state constitutional convention of 1875 and describe the impact of those goals on the document they drafted.

★ Describe the principal features of the Texas Constitution.

★ Outline the process whereby the Texas Constitution can be amended and evaluate the significance of the changes that have been made through amendment.

★ Describe the means through which constitutions can change other than formal amendment and assess the relative importance of those means of change for the Texas Constitution.

★ Summarize the main criticisms of the Texas Constitution and trace the history of constitutional revision in the state.

★ Describe the role played by Texas courts and the Texas Constitution in the protection of civil liberties.

★ Assess the impact of the Texas Constitution on each stage of the policymaking process.

★ Define the key terms listed on page 58 and explain their significance.

The issue of education finance has been near the top of the official policy agenda in the Lone Star State longer than most Texans can remember. Public education is critically important not just to the state's 4 million public school students, but also to thousands of teachers and other school employees and to the communities in which they live. Moreover, education is expensive, the single largest expenditure for state and local government in Texas. In 2002, the average Texan paid nearly $1,200 in taxes to support public education.[1]

The state's education funding system is controversial because of its reliance on the **property tax,** which is a tax levied on the value of real property, such as land and buildings. Communities with substantial business property, industry, and wealthy neighborhoods can generate a significant amount of tax money for schools even with a relatively low tax rate. In contrast, less affluent communities can raise relatively little money even with a high tax rate. Consequently, wealthy districts can afford new school buildings, state-of-the-art science and computer labs, high teacher pay, and low student-teacher ratios, while poor districts cannot.

The controversy over school funding came to a head in 1989 with ***Edgewood v. Kirby,*** which was a lawsuit filed by a number of poor school districts, including the Edgewood ISD in San Antonio, against the state's system of education finance. The Texas Supreme Court held that the school finance system violated the Texas Constitution because it failed to treat all persons equally and because it was inefficient. The Court ordered the Texas legislature to change the system to ensure that school districts that levied the same tax rate would have roughly the same amount of tax revenue available for local use.[2] Eventually, the legislature settled on a plan capping local property tax rates at $1.50 per $100 of property valuation and forcing wealthy districts to transfer some of their revenue to poor districts. Some commentators referred to the system as the **Robin Hood Plan** because it took money from the rich and gave it to the poor.

Despite the passage of the Robin Hood Plan, legal challenges to the Texas school finance system continue. Several wealthy districts have filed suit against the system, charging that the state property tax cap that limits their ability to raise local money to support their schools amounts to an unconstitutional state property tax. They argue that the state spending and tax caps make it impossible for them to obtain the necessary funds to operate quality schools.[3] In the meantime, poor school districts are contemplating a new legal challenge of their own. This time their focus would be funding adequacy. They note that the Texas Constitution provides for an efficient state school system. The poor districts would argue that school funding is too low for the system to be efficient. They too believe that they do not have the money to provide a quality education for their students.

The governor and legislative leaders are committed to reforming the Texas school finance system to replace Robin Hood for both political and constitutional reasons. Robin Hood is quite unpopular in the suburbs and many Republican members of the legislature ran for office promising to replace the system. Because Robin Hood benefits more school districts than it hurts, however, a majority of legislators may be unwilling to dismantle the system unless they replace it with a new system that provides adequate funding to poor districts. Furthermore, any system that fails to address issues of funding equity among districts is probably unconstitutional. The dilemma for the legislature and the governor is that any new education funding system that repeals Robin Hood while protecting the interests of poor districts will require billions of additional state dollars. Most legislators and the governor have also promised not to raise taxes.

The controversy over education finance illustrates the relevance of the Texas Constitution to the policymaking process. Although school finance had been a perennial issue on the state's policy agenda, the legislature had taken only small steps toward addressing the controversy. By providing extra state money to poor districts, the legislature increased the minimum per-student funding available for districts with weak tax bases, while doing little to close the gap between poor districts and the wealthiest districts in the state. In *Edgewood* v. *Kirby*, the Texas Supreme Court ruled that the state constitution required that the funding gap between wealthy districts and poor districts be closed, and the only way the legislature could reduce the funding disparity among districts was to limit the amount of money available to wealthy districts. The continued legal wrangling over school finance ensures that the Texas Constitution will play an ongoing role in the school finance debate. Is the $1.50 property tax limit for school districts unconstitutional? Are public schools so poorly funded that the state's school system is inefficient? These are not just political questions but constitutional questions as well.

This chapter examines the Texas Constitution as an important element of the policymaking environment in the Lone Star State. The chapter begins with a discussion of the role of state constitutions in general. It explores the background of the Texas Constitution, describes the constitutional convention of 1875, and presents an overview of the document. The chapter discusses constitutional change and the role the Texas Constitution plays in protecting civil liberties. Finally, the chapter examines the impact of the Texas Constitution on the policymaking process.

> "A general diffusion of knowledge being essential to the preservation of the liberties and rights of the people, it is the duty of the legislature to establish and to make suitable provision for the support and maintenance of an efficient system of public free schools."
> —Texas Constitution, Article VII, Section 1

STATE CONSTITUTIONS

A **constitution** is the fundamental law by which a state or nation is organized and governed. The U.S. Constitution is the fundamental law of the United States. It establishes the framework of government, assigns the powers and duties of governmental bodies, and defines the relationship between the people and their government. Similarly, a state constitution is fundamental law for a state. The U.S. Constitution and the state constitutions together provide the total framework for government within the United States.

? WHAT IS YOUR OPINION?

Is the Robin Hood system of school funding fair?

Federal courts interpret the U.S. Constitution to allow substantial room for the development of state constitutional law in ways that do not conflict with the U.S. Constitution and in policy areas that are not preempted by federal legislation.[4] A

federal preemption of state authority is an act of Congress adopting regulatory policies that overrule state policies in a particular regulatory area. In other words, state constitutions and state laws are authoritative so long as they conflict with neither the U.S. Constitution nor federal law.

State constitutions differ from the U.S. Constitution in several respects. State constitutions may reflect different philosophies of government. The framers of the U.S. Constitution based the document on the principle of separation of powers, with a strong chief executive, a **bicameral legislature** (which is a legislative body with two chambers), and a judiciary appointed for life. Although every state constitution provides for **separation of powers** (which is the division of political authority among legislative, executive, and judicial branches of government), many state documents differ from the national constitution in important details. A number of state constitutions, including the Texas Constitution, give their governor fewer official powers than the U.S. Constitution grants the president. Indeed, the constitutions of Texas and several other states weaken their governors through means of the **plural executive,** which is the division of executive power among several elected officials. Most state constitutions, including the Texas Constitution, provide for the election of judges, and one state, Nebraska, has a **unicameral legislature,** which is a legislative body with one chamber.

Some state constitutions reflect a different approach to democracy than the U.S. Constitution embodies. The U.S. Constitution creates a **representative democracy** or a **republic,** which is a political system in which citizens elect representatives to make policy decisions on their behalf. The framers of the U.S. Constitution believed that elected representatives were needed to act as a buffer between the people and government policies. In contrast, some state constitutions include certain elements of **direct democracy,** which is a political system in which the citizens vote directly on matters of public concern. Almost half the states (but not Texas) provide for the **initiative process,** which is a procedure whereby citizens can propose the

GETTING INVOLVED

Joining a Student Club or Organization

If you join a student organization you will enjoy college more and probably make better grades as well. Joining a club will give you the chance to make new friends with similar interests and become acquainted with a faculty advisor outside the classroom setting. Because you will be better connected to the school you will be more likely to stay in school and finish your education.

Colleges and universities typically host a range of student clubs and organizations. Students at your school may participate in such organizations as an international student association, Campus Crusade for Christ, chess club, Young Democrats and Young Republicans, choir, gay/lesbian/bisexual students association, African-American student union, bridge club, Muslim students association, computer science club, Jewish life organization, Latino students association, karate club, premedical society, Catholic Student Union, math club, and Asian students association. The student life office at your college will have a list of student groups active on your campus.

It's your college—get involved!

adoption of a policy measure by gathering a prerequisite number of signatures. Voters must then approve the measure before it can take effect. State officials then place the measure on the ballot for approval by the voters. Initiative can be employed either to adopt measures or to repeal legislation enacted through the legislative process. Voters in California, Oregon, and other states with the initiative process have used it to make policy decisions concerning such issues as state tax rates, bilingual education, gay and lesbian rights, insurance rates, term limits for elected officials, and the provision of public services to illegal immigrants.[5]

In contrast to the U.S. Constitution, state constitutions have a quality of impermanence to them. Although the present state constitution of Massachusetts was written in 1780, only six state constitutions now in effect were drafted before 1850. The average state constitution lasts for 70 years.[6] About a fourth of the states have adopted new constitutions since World War II. Furthermore, most states have changed constitutions several times. Louisiana, for example, has had eleven constitutions; Georgia has had ten.[7]

Most state constitutions have more amendments than the U.S. Constitution, which has only 27. The average state constitution has been amended nearly a hundred times. The Constitution of South Carolina has been changed formally more than 450 times.[8] The Alabama Constitution has more than 700 amendments.[9]

Finally, state constitutions are on average four times longer than the U.S. Constitution. The Alabama Constitution at 315,000 words is the longest constitution in the nation, compared to only 7,400 words in the U.S. Constitution.[10] The Texas Constitution is 80,000 words. The length of state constitutions reflects the broader scope of state policy responsibilities compared with those of the national government. State constitutions deal with some matters not discussed at all in the U.S. Constitution, such as the structures, functions, and finances of local governments. State constitutions consider other issues, such as elections and land management, in greater detail than they are covered in the national document.

State constitutions also generally include numerous miscellaneous provisions that one observer calls "super legislation." These measures are the same quality and type as **statutory law** (law made by a legislature), but, for historical or political reasons, are upgraded to **constitutional law,** which is law that involves the interpretation and application of the constitution.[11] The South Dakota Constitution, for example, provides for state hail insurance; the Oklahoma Constitution requires that home economics be taught in public schools.[12]

BACKGROUND OF THE TEXAS CONSTITUTION

Texans adopted their first state constitution in 1845, when the Lone Star State joined the Union. As with most other state constitutions written in the first half of the nineteenth century, the Texas Constitution of 1845 was patterned after the U.S. Constitution. Following the national model, it created a government with legislative, executive, and judicial branches. Similar to the U.S. Constitution, the Texas Constitution of 1845 was a document of broad, general principles that allowed state government leeway to deal with policy problems as they arose. The voters would select the

Students crowded into a portable classroom at Frey School in the Edgewood Independent School District.

governor, lieutenant governor, and the members of the legislature. The governor would appoint other state executive officials and members of the state judiciary.

In 1850, Texas amended the state constitution to provide for election rather than appointment of state judges and most executive officeholders. This change reflected the principle of **Jacksonian democracy,** which was the view (associated with President Andrew Jackson) that the right to vote should be extended to all adult male citizens and that all government offices of any importance should be filled by election. The advocates of Jacksonian democracy believed that government is made responsive to the people through broad-based **suffrage,** which is the right to vote, and the **long ballot,** which is an election system that provides for the election of nearly every public official of any significance.

When Texas joined the Confederacy in 1861, the state changed its constitution. The new document declared the state's allegiance to the Confederacy and included a strong prohibition against the abolition of slavery. For the most part, however, this constitution closely resembled its predecessor.

In 1866, with the war lost, Texas rewrote its constitution once again in hopes of rejoining the Union under President Andrew Johnson's reconstruction plan. This new constitution repealed secession, repudiated the war debt, and recognized the supremacy of the U.S. Constitution. Although it abolished slavery, it fell short of granting equality to former slaves. African Americans could not testify in court cases in which other African Americans were not involved and were denied the right to vote. In most other respects, though, the constitution of 1866 simply reenacted provisions of the 1845 document.

The Texas Constitution of 1866 was short lived. By the time of its adoption, the Radical Republican majority in Congress had taken control of Reconstruction from President Johnson. The **Radical Republicans** were members of the Republican Party that wanted sweeping social change to take place in the South after the Civil War. Congress passed legislation over President Johnson's veto declaring that Texas and the other states of the Confederacy could not reenter the Union until they granted African Americans the right to vote, ratified the Thirteenth and Fourteenth Amendments to the U.S. Constitution, and drafted new state constitutions acceptable to Congress.

Because Union troops occupied Texas, the state had little choice but to accept the demands. Ninety Texans, representing a broad range of political factions, gathered in convention in June 1868 to draft another state constitution. The convention was a stormy one, with the delegates unable to agree on a document. In 1869, the military commander of Texas intervened to order the bits and pieces the convention had been working on gathered into a single document. The U.S. Congress accepted this new constitution and Texas was readmitted to the Union in 1870.

The Texas Constitution of 1869 created an active state government. Reverting to the procedure established in the original state constitution of 1845, it provided for the gubernatorial appointment rather than election of judges and most executive branch officials. It established annual sessions of the legislature and authorized increased salaries for state officials. The constitution also included a compulsory school attendance law and provided for state supervision of education.

For most white, ex-Confederate Texans, the constitution of 1869 represented defeat and humiliation. Many Texans regarded the document not as a Texas constitution at all but a document imposed on them by outside forces. Radical Republican Governor E. J. Davis held office under this constitution and the two were closely linked in the minds of the ex-Confederate Texans who considered Davis arrogant and corrupt. In particular, Democrats criticized the Davis administration for excessive spending, taxation, and borrowing.

Defenders of the Davis administration argued that the policies adopted by the governor and the Republican legislature were an appropriate effort to help the state recover from the Civil War. Under Davis, the state undertook programs to promote railroad construction, build an extensive network of roads, and construct a free public school system. Furthermore, Democratic Governor Richard Coke and the Democratic majority in the legislature who succeeded the Republicans in office were no more successful at dealing with the state's financial problems than their predecessors. In fact, the state budget deficit was higher in 1875 and 1876 under Coke than it had been in 1872 and 1873 under Davis.[13] A **budget deficit** is the amount of money by which annual budget expenditures exceed annual budget receipts.

Nonetheless, the association of the Texas Constitution of 1869 with Reconstruction guaranteed strong Democratic support for a new document. When Democrats regained control of state government in 1872 and 1873, their first priority was

The state capitol building in Austin.

to draft a new constitution for Texas. Governor Coke and Democratic legislative leaders initially proposed that a new constitution be written by the state legislature. When legislators deadlocked over a new document, however, the governor and the Democratic leaders had no choice but to call for the election of delegates to a state constitutional convention.

? WHAT IS YOUR OPINION?

Do you agree with the political philosophy underlying the concept of Jacksonian democracy?

CONSTITUTIONAL CONVENTION OF 1875

"The Constitution of 1876 was no lofty statement of principles and organic law, but a piece of detailed legislation born of reaction."

—Joe B. Frantz, historian

In the fall of 1875, 83 Texans gathered in Austin to draft a new constitution for the state. Although a number of Republicans, including several African Americans, served as convention delegates, a majority of delegates were white Democrats. Farmers, ex-Confederate officers, and lawyers were all well represented at the convention. The largest organized group of delegates was the Texas Patrons of Husbandry, better known as the **Grange,** an organization of farmers. Indeed, "retrenchment and reform," the Grangers' slogan, became the watchword of the convention.

The Grangers' slogan embodied two basic goals: to restrict the size and scope of state government and to control the excesses of big business. A majority of delegates at the convention wanted to restrain a state government that they believed was too large and expensive. To accomplish this task, the delegates abandoned one constitutional tradition while reinstating another. On one hand, the authors of the new constitution turned away from the pattern initially established in the Texas Constitution of 1845 of a general document phrased in broad terms, favoring instead a restrictive constitution of great length and detail. On the other hand, the delegates returned to the tradition of Jacksonian democracy, reinstating the long ballot and shortening the terms of office for elected officials.[14]

The convention restricted the authority of every branch and unit of Texas government. The new constitution weakened the office of governor by cutting the governor's salary and reducing the term of office from four to two years. It restricted the governor's power of appointment by creating a plural executive, which divided executive power among several elected officials, including a lieutenant governor, attorney general, comptroller, treasurer, and land commissioner. Executive officials elected independently from the governor would owe no allegiance to the governor. Indeed, they might be political rivals. The governor could appoint a number of lesser officials, but they would have little incentive to follow the governor's lead because the governor had no power to remove them before the end of their terms.

The constitution's framers limited the power of the legislature by cutting its meeting time and restricting the scope of its policymaking authority. They limited regular sessions of the legislature to 140 calendar days, every other year. They reduced legislative salaries and required that the legislature adopt a balanced budget unless four fifths of the membership agreed to deficit spending. Furthermore, by including long, detailed sections on education, finance, railroad regulation, and the like in the constitution, the framers forced legislators to propose constitutional amendments if they wanted to adopt policy changes in many areas.

The authors of Texas's new constitution employed several devices for reducing the power of the judicial branch of state government. They divided the state's court system into two segments, limiting the types of cases individual courts would be authorized to hear. In the best traditions of Jacksonian democracy, they provided for the election of judges to relatively brief terms. The framers also reduced judicial discretion by writing a long, detailed constitution that left relatively little room for judicial interpretation.

Nor did the framers of the Texas Constitution overlook local government. They specified the forms local governments must take and restricted local authority to levy taxes, provide services, adopt regulations, and go into debt. In many instances, local officials would have to ask the state legislature for permission to adopt even relatively minor policies. Changing local political structures would frequently necessitate a constitutional amendment.

Another major goal of the Granger-dominated convention was to control the excesses of big business. Consider the constitutional provisions dealing with banking. Many of the convention delegates were small farmers, used to living on the financial edge. They distrusted big, impersonal banks, which might be inclined to foreclose during hard times, preferring instead smaller, locally owned banks whose managers would be more understanding. Consequently, the convention prohibited **branch banking,** which is a business practice whereby a single, large bank conducts business from several locations. This provision ensured that banks would be locally owned rather than branches of large banks headquartered in Dallas or Houston.

The Constitution's deference to local values is reflected in its provisions dealing with liquor regulation as well. Although the Constitution empowered the legislature to regulate the manufacture, packaging, sale, possession and transportation of alcoholic beverages, it left the decision to legalize the sale of alcoholic beverages to local voters. **Local-option elections** (also known as wet-dry elections) are held to determine whether an area will legalize the sale of alcoholic beverages. The voters living in a city, county, or even in an area as small as a justice of the peace precinct may vote to keep their area dry, that is, to prohibit the sale of alcoholic beverages. Once an area goes dry, it cannot go wet unless the voters approve. Today, most of the state's counties north of Austin are dry whereas most of the counties south of Austin are wet.

The delegates at the constitutional convention believed in the old adage that a family's home is its castle and set about to protect it. They provided that a family **homestead** (that is, legal residence) could not be taken in payment of debt except for delinquent taxes and mortgage payments on a loan taken out to purchase the home itself. The framers added a measure to the constitution requiring that both spouses must give written consent before the homestead could be sold. The Constitution also prohibited garnishment of wages for payment of debt, except for the enforcement of court-ordered child support or spousal maintenance.

Although the Texas Constitution written in 1875 reflected the political concerns of rural-oriented Texans, the document was not far out of step with other state constitutions adopted in the late nineteenth century. The political currents of Jacksonian democracy flowed through much of the land, not just in Texas. Many states provided for the election of judges and a broad range of executive-branch officials. Short terms of office for governors and judges were fairly common. Furthermore, Texans were not the only Americans who distrusted public officials and worried about the corrupting influences of big banks, corporations, and railroads. It was not uncommon in the 1870s for states to adopt restrictive constitutions.[15]

"Humbly invoking the blessings of Almighty God, the people of the State of Texas do ordain and establish this Constitution."
—Preamble, Texas Constitution

Because the Texas Constitution prohibited branch banking, the legislature and the voters had to adopt a constitutional amendment to allow ATM machines.

The delegates finished their work in less than three months and in early 1876 the voters approved the new constitution by a margin of 2 to 1. With amendments, the constitution of 1876 remains today the fundamental law of the state of Texas.

OVERVIEW OF THE TEXAS CONSTITUTION

To students familiar with the U.S. Constitution, the most striking aspect of the Texas Constitution is its length. At 80,000 words, the Texas Constitution is one of the longest state constitutions in the nation. It can be found in most reference libraries, reprinted in the *Texas Almanac*, and online.

The Texas Constitution includes a number of features in common with the U.S. Constitution: a bill of rights, separation of powers with checks and balances, and the creation of a bicameral legislature. A **bill of rights** is a constitutional document

TEXAS ONLINE ★ Forces of Change

The Texas Constitution Online

You can find the Texas Constitution at the following Internet address:

www.capitol.state.tx.us/txconst/toc.html

Review the document and answer the following questions.

QUESTIONS TO CONSIDER

1. Does the Texas Constitution grant its residents the right to "keep and bear arms?" Based on your reading of the Constitution, would you say that Texans have an absolute right to carry guns in public?

2. Can the State of Texas impose an income tax?

3. In Texas, who or what has the power of impeachment?

guaranteeing individual rights and liberties. As with other provisions of the Texas Constitution, the Texas Bill of Rights is long, considerably longer than its counterpart in the national constitution. The Texas document contains 29 sections and includes most of the guarantees found in the national bill of rights, such as the protection of free speech and a free press, the guarantee of the right of trial by jury, and a safeguard against "unreasonable searches and seizures."

The Texas Bill of Rights does more than merely restate guarantees found in the American Constitution. The Texas document phrases the protection of rights positively rather than negatively. Consider the issue of freedom of expression. The First Amendment to the U.S. Constitution prohibits the abridgement of free expression: "Congress shall make no law . . . abridging the freedom of speech, or of the press." In contrast, the Texas Bill of Rights guarantees free expression: "Every person shall be at liberty to speak, write or publish his opinions on any subject . . . and no law shall ever be passed curtailing the liberty of speech or of the press." [Art. 1, Sect. 8.] One commentator believes that the provision in the Texas Constitution is potentially a stronger guarantee of free expression than the First Amendment to the U.S. Constitution. Whereas the U.S. Bill of Rights identifies rights the national government *may not infringe*, the Texas Bill of Rights lists rights state government *must protect*.[16]

The Texas Constitution protects the individual right of gun ownership. The Second Amendment to the U.S. Constitution declares that "the right of the people to keep and bear Arms shall not be infringed," but it couches that provision in the context of a state militia. Consequently, the federal courts have consistently held that the Second Amendment does not grant a federal constitutional right to own or carry weapons. In contrast, Article I, Section 23 of the Texas Constitution states that a citizen has the "right to keep and bear arms in the lawful defense of himself." Although the legislature can regulate "the wearing of arms, with a view to prevent crime," gun owners enjoy greater protection under the Texas Constitution than they do under the U.S. Constitution.

Furthermore, the Texas Bill of Rights includes a number of measures not found in the national bill of rights. Whereas the U.S. Constitution provides for the right to a jury trial only if defendants face more than six months in jail, the Texas Constitution guarantees the right to trial by jury for persons charged with any offense, even minor traffic violations. The Texas Constitution also contains two guarantees of equal rights more explicit and detailed than any comparable measure included in the U.S. Constitution. Both provisions are found in Article I, Section 3. The first measure is fairly broad: "All free men . . . have equal rights." The second guarantee, which was added in 1972, is known as the **Texas Equal Rights Amendments (ERA).** It is a provision in the Texas Constitution that states the following: "Equality under the law shall not be denied or abridged because of sex, race, color, creed, or national origin." [Art. I, Sect. 3a.]

The Texas Constitution establishes a separation of powers system with checks and balances. Similar to the national government, Texas state government has three branches: an executive branch headed by the governor, a bicameral legislature including the Texas House of Representatives and the Texas Senate, and a judicial branch. **Checks and balances** is the overlapping of the powers of the branches of government so that public officials limit the authority of one another. The governor's appointments, for example, must be confirmed by a two-thirds vote of the Texas Senate. Legislation must pass both the house and the senate before it has passed the Texas legislature. The governor can veto bills passed by the legislature, but the legislature can override the veto by a two-thirds vote of each house.

"If men were angels, no government would be necessary."
—James Madison, principle author of the U.S. Constitution

The Texas Constitution includes features not found in the U.S. Constitution. Some of these provisions involve policy matters of primary concern to state government. One section, for example, deals with voter qualifications and elections. Other sections outline the structures and responsibilities of local governments. Much of the length and detail of the Texas Constitution, though, can be attributed to the inclusion of long sections dealing with substantive policy areas. The framers of the constitution devoted thousands of words to such matters as railroad regulation, education, welfare, and taxation. Subsequent amendments have added thousands of words more.

CONSTITUTIONAL CHANGE

Constitutions that endure are living, growing documents. Constitutions change by means of formal amendment, practical experience, and judicial interpretation. The U.S. Constitution is a relatively brief document of general principles. Although it has been amended 27 times, scholars believe that practical experience and judicial interpretation have been more important means of constitutional change than written amendments. State constitutions are usually longer and more detailed than the national document, providing less opportunity for constitutional growth through practical experience and judicial interpretation. State constitutional change generally occurs most frequently through means of written amendments. This is certainly true for the Texas Constitution.

Change Through Amendment

A **constitutional amendment** is a formal, written change or addition to the state's governing document. The detailed style of the Texas Constitution has led to numerous amendments as each successive generation of Texans has attempted to adapt its features to changing times. Some amendments have been trivial, such as an amendment to allow city governments to donate surplus firefighting equipment to rural volunteer fire departments. Other amendments have dealt with weighty policy matters, such as an amendment authorizing the legislature to cap noneconomic damages such as pain and suffering awarded in lawsuits. The voters approved both amendments in 2003.

Through the years, amendments have produced several major changes in the Texas Constitution. The legislature and the voters have amended the constitution to strengthen the authority of state officials, especially the governor. Amendments have increased the term of office of the governor and the state's other elected executive officials from two years to four years and empowered the governor to remove his or her own appointees, pending senate approval. The constitution has also been amended to give the governor limited **budget execution authority,** which is the power to cut agency spending or transfer money between agencies during the period when the legislature is not in session.

The legislature and the voters have amended the Texas Constitution to enable state government to promote economic development. Amendments have eliminated the constitutional prohibition against branch banking, allowed local governments to give tax breaks to businesses relocating to Texas, and provided money for the development and conservation of the state's water resources. Other amendments have provided funds for highway construction, student loans, and college expansion.

The legislature and the voters have periodically approved amendments to enable the state to go into debt by issuing **general obligation bonds,** which are certificates of indebtedness that must be repaid from general revenues. Borrowing enables the state to spread the cost of major projects, such as prison construction and water development, over a period of time. Because the Texas Constitution prohibits the state from incurring debt that must be repaid from general revenues, the legislature has had to propose constitutional amendments to authorize borrowing. In 2003, the bonded indebtedness of the state of Texas was $6.7 billion, with the state paying $376 million a year in principal and interest out of general revenues.[17]

The process of amending the Texas Constitution is fairly straightforward. An amendment must first be proposed by a two-thirds vote of each house of the legislature. Then, it must be approved by a majority of the voters in an election. Through 2003, the voters had approved 432 amendments to the Texas Constitution of 609 proposed by the legislature.[18]

The amendment process is time-consuming and the electorate apathetic. Even in the most favorable circumstances, the interval between the formulation of a proposed amendment and its ultimate approval or rejection by the voters is measured in years. Furthermore, elections to ratify constitutional amendments generate relatively little voter interest. As Figure 2.1 indicates, the number of Texas voters who decided the fate of the nineteen proposed constitutional amendments on the ballot

"It's a good thing it has been amended many times. If it had not been, ministers of the gospel would not be able to be legislators. If you had ever participated in a duel, you would not be allowed to hold public office. And indeed, if you had ever received any kind of public financial assistance, you wouldn't even be allowed to vote."

—Elton Bomer, former Texas secretary of state

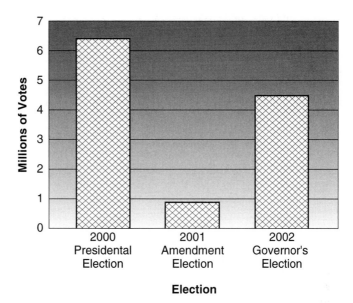

FIGURE 2.1   Votor Turnout
Source: Texas Secretary of State

in 2001 was considerably less than the number of Texans who participated in the 2000 presidential election or the 2002 governor's election.

Political science research indicates that citizen participation in the amendment process may have some policy consequences. Studies show that voters who take part in amendment elections tend to be older, better educated, and wealthier than the electorate for candidate elections. They are also more likely to be white. Voters around the nation have been generally inclined to favor amendments that restrict the rights of people accused of crimes, while supporting constitutional changes to expand other types of individual rights.[19]

Nearly every state allows its citizens to vote on constitutional amendments, and defenders of the process say that the people should have a voice in the adoption of changes in their state's fundamental law. They define the issue in terms of democracy. Although the legislature can propose constitutional change, the voters should have the final word on whether changes are adopted.

In contrast, critics argue that most citizens are not well enough informed to make reasonable judgments about the details of state constitutional law. For example, Texas voters have twice rejected efforts to repeal a provision in the Texas Constitution requiring companies who seek investment from the Texas Growth Fund to disclose whether they do business with the white-minority governments of South Africa and Namibia. With the introduction of democratic, majority-rule governments in those countries, the original rationale for the sanctions no longer applies. Even though there is no organized opposition to repeal the measure, the voters, apparently confused by the issue, have failed twice to ratify amendments repealing the provision.

"I guess people don't understand what they're voting on. Neither the League nor anybody else has come up with any arguments against [the amendment requiring companies to disclose ties to the governments of South Africa and Namibia]."
—Julie Lowenberg, Texas League of Women Voters

The Texas legislature sometimes words amendments with an eye toward deceiving voters. The Texas Constitution requires that the state publish a summary and a brief explanation of proposed constitutional amendments in newspapers at least twice before the day of the election. In 1989, the summary for one proposed amendment clearly explained that the amendment would increase the pay for members of the Texas legislature from $7,200 to $23,358 a year. It would raise the salaries of the Speaker of the house and the lieutenant governor even more. On the ballot, however, the description of the measure began as follows: "The constitutional amendment to *limit* the salary. . . ." Poorly informed voters might well have voted to raise legislative salaries while believing they were doing the opposite. In this instance, at least, the legislature's effort at deception failed because the amendment was defeated.

The legislature also manipulates the timing of amendment ratification elections to influence their outcome. In 2003, the legislature passed a constitutional amendment to clarify that the legislature has the constitutional authority to limit the amount of noneconomic damages that a jury could award in a personal injury lawsuit. The legislature adopted the amendment to head off legal challenges against laws limiting the right of individuals to sue over faulty products, personal injuries, or medical malpractice. Instead of scheduling the ratification election for November, when amendment ratification elections are typically held, the legislature set the vote for a Saturday in September. Critics charged that legislative leaders reasoned that the amendment would be more likely to pass if it were held in a low-turnout special election in September than it would in November when a Houston city election would bring large numbers of minority voters to the polls that might vote against it.

> "Deception has become an accepted practice in the legislature's dealings with voters."
> —Douglas Harlan.
> Journalist

> "[Legislative leaders are] afraid of the people of color in Harris County. They're afraid of maximum participation. That's offensive."
> —State Senator Leticia Van de Putte, D., San Antonio

Change Through Practice and Experience

Not all constitutional changes result from formal constitutional amendment. Many of the fundamental features of American national government have developed through practice and experience. Consider the military powers of the president. The U.S. Constitution declares that the president is the commander in chief of the armed forces. To determine what this important constitutional power really entails, however, one must look to its practical application by actual presidents, such as Lincoln during the Civil War or Franklin Roosevelt during World War II. When President George W. Bush commanded the American armed forces to attack Iraq to overthrow the regime of Saddam Hussein, for example, no one seriously questioned the president's constitutional authority to order the military into combat despite the lack of a congressional declaration of power because previous presidents had taken similar action.

Because of its detail and specificity, the Texas Constitution has not grown as much through practice and experience as the U.S. Constitution, but some changes have occurred through that means. For example, the office of lieutenant governor of Texas as outlined in the state constitution resembles that of the vice president of the United States, which, historically, has been a relatively weak office. In practice, however, the lieutenant governor has become one of the most important policy leaders in the state, far more important in state government than the vice president has been on the national scene. This is an important development in the fundamen-

LEARNING EXERCISE

Predicting Amendment Success

Does the electoral success of state constitutional amendments depend on the way they are described on the ballot? Many proposed amendments deal with issues about which the average voter has little knowledge or interest because most amendments receive minimal press attention. Indeed, the only information that many voters have about proposed amendments is the caption that actually appears on the ballot. Consequently, amendments that have attractively worded captions may have a better chance at passage than amendments with less appealing captions.

The ten statements printed below are the captions of amendments that actually appeared on the ballot within the last few years. Based only on caption wording, which of these amendments do you think passed? Be prepared to explain the reasoning behind your answer.

QUESTIONS TO CONSIDER

1. The amendment to provide for the surety of a grain warehouse fund to be established by the grain industry for the protection of farmers.
2. The amendment to raise the maximum property tax rate that may be adopted by certain rural fire prevention districts, but only if approved by the districts' residents.
3. The constitutional amendment providing that the trustees of a local public pension system must administer the system for the benefit of the system's participants and beneficiaries.

4. The constitutional amendment to promote the reduction of pollution and to encourage the preservation of jobs by authorizing the exemption from *ad valorem* taxation of real and personal property used for the control of air, water, or land pollution.
5. The amendment to limit school tax increases on the residence homestead of the surviving spouse of an elderly person if the surviving spouse is at least 55 years of age.
6. The amendment allowing state employees to receive compensation for serving as a member of a governing body of a school district, city, town or other local governmental district.
7. The amendment to provide that a member of the legislature is eligible to be elected or appointed and to serve in a different state office but may not receive an increase in compensation granted to that office during the legislative term to which he was a member.
8. The constitutional amendment prohibiting a personal income tax without voter approval and, if an income tax is enacted, dedicating the revenue to education and limiting the rate of local school taxes.
9. The constitutional amendment to allow a person who holds the office of municipal court judge to hold at the same time more than one civil office for which the person receives compensation.
10. The amendment authorizing the legislature to provide assistance to encourage economic development in the state.

*Amendments 1, 3, 4, 5, 8, and 10 passed; amendments 2, 6, 7, and 9 failed.

tal structures of Texas government that resulted not from formal amendment but through the informal processes of practice and experience.

Change Through Judicial Interpretation

Many scholars believe that the most important mechanism through which the U.S. Constitution has changed has been judicial interpretation. Federal court rulings have defined constitutional principles in such key policy areas as school integration, voting rights, freedom of expression, freedom of religion, and the rights of persons accused of crimes. Because of the more detailed nature of state constitutions, judicial interpretation has historically been a less significant means for constitutional change at the state level than it has been at the national level. Today, however, this situation may be changing. State courts have begun to play an increasingly important policymaking role through the interpretation of state constitutions, especially in the area of state funding for public education.

? WHAT IS YOUR OPINION?

Are state constitutional amendment elections so complicated that ordinary citizens cannot make intelligent choices?

Constitutional Revision

Many critics of the Texas Constitution believe that Texas should have a new state constitution. The League of Women Voters, the Texas Bar Association, a number of public officials, and many political scientists (including most textbook authors) charge that the document is so long and detailed, and so often amended, that many citizens (and even many public officials) do not understand it. A simpler, more straightforward document, they say, would increase respect for and understanding of state government.

The most telling criticism of the Texas Constitution is that it hinders the formulation, adoption, and implementation of sound public policy. During the 1980s and early 1990s, and then again in 2003, the legislature was forced to deal with a serious budget shortfall, necessitating spending cuts, tax increases, or both. The legislature's ability to set spending priorities, however, was limited by constitutionally **dedicated funds,** which are constitutional or statutory provisions that set aside revenue for particular purposes. For example, the **Dedicated Highway Fund** is a constitutionally earmarked account containing money set aside for building, maintaining, and policing state highways. The **Permanent University Fund (PUF)** is money constitutionally set aside as an endowment to finance construction, maintenance, and some other activities at the University of Texas, Texas A&M University, and other institutions in those two university systems. In preparing the budget, legislators did not have the option of cutting highway funds to avoid a tax increase or diverting construction money from the University of Texas and Texas A&M University systems to other colleges and universities. The state constitution would not allow it. Instead, the legislature had to raise taxes and fees and/or look for budget cuts in areas not protected by constitutionally dedicated funds.

Critics of the Texas Constitution charge that it is loaded with provisions that hinder the operation of efficient government. The governor has insufficient power, they say, to manage the state bureaucracy, the legislature meets too briefly and infrequently to resolve the state's policy problems, and the election of judges makes for a judiciary excessively dependent on interest group campaign contributions. The critics believe that many of the problems facing the state will not be resolved until the Texas Constitution is significantly revised or rewritten entirely.

"I'm afraid we're running an eight-track stereo government in a CD-ROM society."
—Kevin Brady, former legislator

The Dedicated Highway Fund is a constitutionally earmarked account containing money set aside for building, maintaining, and policing state highways.

The most recent efforts at **constitutional revision,** which is the process of drafting a new constitution, have failed. In 1972, Texas voters approved a constitutional amendment to call a state constitutional convention with members of the legislature serving as convention delegates. The ground rules for the convention required a two-thirds vote of approval for a new constitution, but two thirds of the legislator-delegates could not agree on a new document. Three years later, the legislature tried to make the best of the situation by dropping most of the controversial items that had deadlocked the constitutional convention and dividing the document into a series of amendments to submit to the voters. If the voters approved all of the amendments, the state would effectively have a new constitution.

The campaign for the new constitution was hard fought, with state officials, interest groups, local officeholders, and a host of others getting involved. The proponents, including many state officials, newspaper editorial writers, and scholars, argued that the revision would produce a more efficient and effective state government. In response, the opponents, including many local officials and a number of interest groups, warned that the new constitution would increase the power of state government too much and might well lead to the adoption of a state income tax. In the end, the opponents of the new constitution won big as voters rejected all of the amendments by an overwhelming margin.

In the late 1990s, two respected members of the legislature once again raised the issue of constitutional revision. They proposed a new constitution of only 19,000 words that would be a more general statement of fundamental law than the document it would replace. Their proposed constitution would strengthen the powers of the governor, reorganize the executive branch to reduce the number of elected

"It's time for Texas to have a constitution that's appropriate for the twenty-first century."
—Bill Ratliff, lieutenant governor

NATIONAL PERSPECTIVE

Constitutional Revision in Alabama

Constitutional revision has become part of the official policy agenda for the state government of Alabama. Although the League of Women Voters, major state newspapers, and university professors have been calling for constitutional change for decades, the issue did not gain serious momentum until the creation in 2000 of Alabama Citizens for Constitutional Reform (ACCR), a public interest group dedicated to the adoption of a new state constitution.* ACCR leaders, including business people, local officials, and college professors gave speeches, issued press releases, and wrote articles making the case for a new state constitution. The ACCR generated enough public interest in constitutional reform to catch the attention of the state's politicians. During the 2002 election, both major party candidates for governor and many candidates for the Alabama legislature declared their support for constitutional change. In 2003, the new governor, Bob Riley, appointed a citizen's commission to draft a series of constitutional proposals that the legislature and voters could adopt in the form of constitutional amendments.†

The critics of the Alabama Constitution, which was ratified in 1901, argue that it is not just outmoded but an embarrassment to the state as well. At 315,000 words, the Alabama Constitution is the longest in the nation, four times longer than the Texas Constitution. It has been amended more than 700 times. The document also includes a number of offensive provisions left over from the days of racial segregation, including a prohibition against interracial marriage and a requirement for racially segregated schools. Although these measures are no longer legally binding, their presence in the constitution is inconsistent with the image that state leaders want to convey.

The proponents of constitutional revision in Alabama contend that the current document concentrates too much power in Montgomery, the state capital. Cities and counties have so little authority that they cannot tax to build a new school or sewer system unless the legislature proposes a constitutional amendment and statewide voters approve it. Consequently, local officials have little power to address local issues while state legislators must spend an inordinate amount of time on local matters rather than major state problems.

Not everyone in Alabama supports constitutional revision. Some conservatives warn that a new constitution would lead to higher taxes. If a new constitution makes it easier for local governments to adopt taxes without navigating the amendment process, they will be more likely to raise taxes. The **Christian Coalition,** a conservative Christian organization, also opposes constitutional revision, fearing that a new constitution would ease restrictions on gambling.

QUESTIONS TO CONSIDER

1. Which state is in more need of a new constitution—Alabama or Texas? What is the basis for your judgment?
2. What lessons can constitutional revisionists in Texas learn from the Alabama experience?
3. Why is constitutional revision difficult to achieve?

*Albama Citizens for Constitutional Reform, available at **www.constitutionalreform.org**.
†Mike Sherman, "Work Begins on Constitution," *Montgomery Advertiser,* February 1, 2001, available at **www.montomeryadvertiser.com**.

officials, replace the election of judges with a merit selection process, and reorganize the judicial branch of government. Their proposal never came to a vote in the legislature, however, because most legislators wanted to avoid having to address controversial issues. Lieutenant Governor Bill Ratliff explained the situation as follows: "The members of the legislature did not see a strong enough necessity for a new constitution to cast a vote that might have beat them."[20]

CIVIL LIBERTIES AND THE TEXAS CONSTITUTION

Civil liberties concern the protection of the individual from the unrestricted power of the government. Throughout most of this century, individuals and groups who have believed that their rights were infringed by the actions of state and local government have turned not to state courts for protection under state bills of rights, but to the federal courts and the national bill of rights. During the 1950s and 1960s in particular, the U.S. Supreme Court acted to protect individuals from racial discrimination, guarantee freedom of expression, and expand the rights of people who were accused of crimes. In Texas, federal court rulings have dealt with such issues as racial segregation in the public schools, overcrowding in the state's prison system, the rights of children of illegal aliens to receive a free public education, and abortion rights.

Today, civil liberties lawyers, criminal defense attorneys, and minority rights advocates believe they can no longer count on the U.S. Supreme Court to rule on their behalf. Under the influence of conservative justices appointed by Presidents Nixon, Reagan, and George H. W. Bush, the Court has either cut back on rights granted citizens in the 1950s and 1960s or refused to expand those rights. Out of necessity, those seeking the protection of civil liberties have turned their attention to state courts and state constitutions.

As the U.S. Supreme Court has interpreted the individual rights guarantees of the U.S. Constitution more restrictively, state constitutions, as interpreted by state courts, have begun to play a more prominent role as defenders of individual rights. Since 1970, state courts around the nation have issued more than 700 rulings providing broader rights than those recognized by the U.S. Supreme Court or new rights not found in the U.S. Bill of Rights. The areas in which state courts have been most active are abortion rights, criminal procedure, church/state relations, and gender discrimination.[21]

In Texas, state courts have relied on the Texas Constitution to expand civil liberties in several policy areas involving the **equal protection of the law,** which is the legal principle that state laws may not arbitrarily discriminate against persons. The Texas Supreme Court has held that "similarly situated individuals must be treated equally under [state law] . . . unless there is a rational basis for not doing so."[22] In *Edgewood* v. *Kirby*, for example, the Texas Supreme Court ruled that the state's system of financing public education violated the Texas Constitution because it resulted in unequal treatment for school children residing in different school districts.[23]

The emergence of the Texas Constitution as an instrument for the protection of civil liberties is a relatively recent development. Whether it is a lasting development will depend on the state's judges and the voters who elect them. Will the justices serving on the state's two highest courts, the Texas Supreme Court and the Texas Court of Criminal Appeals, dare to make controversial decisions considering that they must stand periodically for reelection? Election-minded justices may be eager to rule in favor of school children, but will they be just as willing to uphold the rights of gay men and lesbians, atheists, persons accused of crimes, or other individuals and groups who may not be popular with the average Texas voter?

Consider the legal challenge to the state's homosexual conduct law. In 1998, Harris County sheriff's deputies, responding to a false tip about an armed intruder, entered a home and discovered John G. Lawrence and Tyron Garner having sex. The deputies arrested the men on charges of "deviant homosexual conduct." Lawrence and Garner pled "no contest" to the charges so they could challenge the constitutionality of the law on appeal. Subsequently, a three-judge appeals panel ruled on a 2-to-1 vote that the state's sodomy law violated the Texas ERA because it singled out gay men and lesbians. The judges ruled that the state had no rational basis for punishing gay male and lesbian couples for behavior that is legal for heterosexual couples.

Conservative opponents of the court's decision to overturn the sodomy law focused their criticism on the two judges who issued the ruling. The chairman of the Harris County Republican Party circulated a letter demanding that the two judges who voted to strike down the law either reverse their ruling or resign from office. The Texas Republican Party even included a provision in its **party platform,** a statement of party principles and issue positions, that the voters should defeat the two judges at the polls. Although the two judges who issued the initial ruling held their ground, the other members of the appellate court apparently caved in to the pressure. In an unusual move, all nine members of the appeals court agreed to reconsider the decision of the three-judge panel. They voted 7-to-2 to reverse the decision of the three-judge panel and reinstate the law.

In 2003, the U.S. Supreme Court ruled that the Texas homosexual conduct law violated the U.S. Constitution. After Lawrence and Garner lost in state court, they turned to the federal court system. "[Lawrence and Garner] are entitled to respect for their private lives," declared the Court. "The State cannot demean their existence or control their destiny by making their private sexual conduct a crime."[24]

> "The burden of preserving our precious civil rights and liberties falls heavily on the shoulders of judges who must stand for election and raise large sums of money to defend what their conscience and learning tell them is fair and just."
> —James C. Harrington, Texas Civil Liberties Union

★ CONCLUSION: THE CONSTITUTIONAL CONTEXT OF POLICYMAKING IN TEXAS

The Texas Constitution is an important part of the policymaking environment for state and local government in Texas.

Agenda Building

Some issues appear on the state's official policy agenda because of the constitution or because of its interpretation by state courts. Although the controversy over public school finance was long simmering, it was not until the Texas Supreme Court ruled that the current finance system violated the Texas Constitution that the legislature and governor were forced to address the issue.

Policy Formulation and Adoption

The state constitution affects policy formulation by limiting the options available to policymakers. It sets a framework within which policymakers must work. *Edgewood v. Kirby* not only forced the legislature to address school funding issues but also to consider and eventually adopt a solution that the legislature would have been unlikely to seriously consider otherwise. The legislature and the governor adopted the Robin Hood Plan because they believed that the Texas Supreme Court was unlikely to accept a lesser solution as constitutional.

The governor and the legislature will also have to work within the framework of the Texas Constitution as they formulate an alternative to Robin Hood. The constitution prohibits a state property tax and defines the circumstances under which the state can adopt an income tax. The legislature and the governor cannot adopt an income tax unless the voters approve and the revenues generated by the tax must be used to reduce local school property taxes and fund public education.

The Texas Constitution establishes the ground rules for policy adoption. Measures cannot become law unless they are passed in identical form by both houses of the legislature and signed by the governor. If the governor vetoes a measure, the constitution provides that it dies unless it is passed again by a two-thirds margin in both chambers of the legislature.

Policy Implementation and Evaluation

The Texas Constitution fragments policy implementation by dividing administrative responsibilities among dozens of elected or appointed executive officials, boards, commissions, and agencies. Neither the governor nor any other state executive official has the authority to oversee or coordinate policy implementation. Elected officials answerable only to the voters administer tax collection, oil and gas regulation, land management, and agriculture policy. In the meantime, appointed boards that answer directly to no one administer the state's health programs, operate the prison system, regulate utility companies, and license professionals ranging from medical doctors to hair stylists.

The Texas Constitution ensures that policy evaluation is haphazard and uncoordinated. With relatively little administrative authority, the governor has few incentives and no real power to conduct systematic evaluation studies or put their recommendations into practice. Although the legislature has the authority to evaluate policy and the power to use feedback from the evaluation to make policy changes, short, biennial sessions make evaluation difficult. In practice, the legislature and other state offices have created evaluation mechanisms, but their effectiveness is reduced because of structural limitations imposed by the constitution.

★ REVIEW QUESTIONS

1. How does *Edgewood* v. *Kirby* illustrate the role of the Texas Constitution in the policymaking process?

2. How do state constitutions compare and contrast with the U.S. Constitution?

3. What important historical factors shaped the development of the Texas Constitution of 1876?

4. In what ways did the Texas Constitution of 1876 restrict the power of state government?

5. How has the Texas Constitution changed since its adoption in 1876?

6. What is the process for amending the Texas Constitution?

7. Why do some people believe that Texas needs a new constitution?

8. What role does the Texas Constitution play in protecting civil liberties?

9. How does the Texas Constitution affect policymaking in Texas?

★ KEY TERMS

bicameral legislature

bill of rights

branch banking

budget deficit

budget execution authority

checks and balances

Christian Coalition

civil liberties

constitution

constitutional amendment

constitutional law

constitutional revision

dedicated funds

Dedicated Highway Fund

direct democracy

Edgewood v. *Kirby*

equal protection of the law

federal preemption of state authority

general obligation bonds

Grange

homestead

initiative process

Jacksonian democracy

local-option elections

long ballot

party platform

Permanent University Fund (PUF)

plural executive

property tax

Radical Republicans

representative democracy *or* republic

Robin Hood Plan

separation of powers

statutory law

suffrage

Texas Equal Rights Amendment (ERA)

unicameral legislature

★ NOTES

1. Texas Education Agency, "State Funding," available at **www.tea.state.tx.us**.

2. *Edgewood* v. *Kirby*, 777 S.W.2d 391 (1989).

3. John Kirsch, "Rich Districts Will Get Their Day in Court," *Fort Worth Star-Telegram*, May 30, 2003, available at **www.dfw.com**.

4. *State Constitutions in the Federal System* (Washington, DC: Advisory Commission on Intergovernmental Relations, 1989), ch. 2.

5. David M. Hedge, *Governance and the Changing American States* (Boulder, CO: Westview, 1998), pp. 32–33.

6. Christopher W. Hammons, "Was James Madison Wrong? Rethinking the American Preference for Short, Framework-Oriented Constitutions," *American Political Science Review* 93 (December 1999): 837.

7. Lawrence W. Friedman, "An Historical Perspective on State Constitutions," *Intergovernmental Perspective* Spring 1987, pp. 9–13.

8. Robert S. Lorch, *State and Local Politics: The Great Entanglement*, 5th ed. (Englewood Cliffs, NJ: Prentice-Hall, 1995), p. 12.

9. Alabama Citizens for Constitutional Reform, available at **www.constitutionalreform.org**.

10. Hammons, "Was James Madison Wrong?" p. 840.

11. Friedman, "An Historical Perspective on State Constitutions," pp. 9–13.

12. Hammons, "Was James Madison Wrong?" p. 840.

13. John Walker Mauer, *Southern State Constitutions in the 1870s: A Case Study of Texas*, Ph.D. Thesis, Rice University, Houston, Texas, 1983, p. 152.

14. Mauer, *Southern State Constitutions in the 1870s*, p. 152.

15. Friedman, "An Historical Perspective on State Constitutions," pp. 9–13.

16. James C. Harrington, "The Texas Bill of Rights and Civil Liberties," *Texas Tech Law Review* 17 (1986): 1487.

17. Comptroller of Public Accounts, "General Obligation Bonds and Revenue Bonds Payable from General Revenue," available at **www.cpa.state.tx.us/treasops/bondapp.html**.

18. Legislative Reference Library of Texas, "Constitutional Amendments," available at **www.lrl.state.tx.us/legis/constAmends/lrlhome.cfm**.

19. Janice C. May, "Constitutional Amendment and Revision Revisited," *Publius: The Journal of Federalism* 17 (Winter 1987): 153–79.

20. Quoted in Clay Robison, "Weak State Government Paved Way for Lobbyists," *Houston Chronicle*, December 29, 2002, p. 25A.

21. Jim Kincaid and Robert F. Williams, "The New Judicial Federalism: The States' Lead in Rights Protection," in Thad L. Beyle, ed., *State Government: CQ's Guide to Current Issues and Activities 1993–94* (Chapel Hill: University of North Carolina Press, 1993), p. 183.

22. *Whitworth v. Bynum*, 699 S.W.2d 194 (1985).

23. *Edgewood v. Kirby*, 777 S.W.2d 391 (1989).

24. *Lawrence v. Texas*, No. 02-102.

ONLINE PRACTICE TEST

Test your understanding of this chapter
with interactive review quizzes at

www.ablongman.com/tannahilltexas/chapter2

CHAPTER THREE

The Federal Context
of Texas Policymaking

LEARNING OBJECTIVES

After studying Chapter 3, students should be able to do the following:

★ Compare and contrast the roles played by the federal government and state government in the formulation, adoption, and implementation of air pollution abatement policy in the state of Texas.

★ Describe the federal system, discussing the relative positions of the federal government and the states.

★ Assess the impact of the U.S. Constitution and federal courts on policymaking in Texas, discussing *Brown* v. *Board of Education of Topeka, Ruiz* v. *Estelle,* and *Roe* v. *Wade.*

★ Evaluate the effect of federal law on policymaking in Texas, considering in particular the role of federal preemption and federal mandates.

★ Describe the process through which federal grant programs are adopted and implemented.

★ Distinguish between categorical and block grants, evaluating the arguments in favor of each type of grant.

★ Evaluate the arguments for and against entitlement programs.

★ Distinguish between project and formula grant programs.

★ Identify and discuss the various types of conditions that the federal government places on the receipt of federal funds.

★ Evaluate the importance of federal programs to state and local governments in Texas.

★ Assess the impact of the federal system on each stage of the policymaking process in Texas.

★ Define the key terms listed on page 80 and explain their significance.

Texas has an air pollution problem. More than half the state's residents live in areas that do not meet the minimum standard for ground-level ozone. Ozone, which is caused by automobile and industrial plant emissions, can be harmful to people, animals, crops, and other materials. It can inflame the cells that line the lungs, aggravate asthma, and cause permanent lung damage. The affects can be particularly serious in children and in people with chronic lung diseases.[1] The **Environmental Protection Agency (EPA),** which is the federal agency responsible for enforcing the nation's environmental laws, identifies four major areas of the state that do not meet federal air-quality standards for ozone pollution: Dallas-Fort Worth, Houston-Galveston, Beaumont-Port Arthur, and El Paso. Meanwhile, air quality in Austin, San Antonio, Longview-Marshall, Corpus Christi-Victoria, and Tyler barely meets the standard.[2]

Poor air quality in Texas threatens not just the public health, but the state's economic health as well. The federal Clean Air Act sets air-quality goals and requires that states achieve the goals by 2007. Texas and other states that do not currently meet the standard must adopt and implement a plan to reduce harmful air emissions. If the EPA determines that a state has failed to adopt and implement a plan adequate to reduce harmful emissions, the state must satisfy the EPA's objections within 18 months or face sanctions. The sanctions could include restrictions on the construction or expansion of industrial plants and the loss of federal funding for transportation projects in the affected area.[3]

The **Texas Commission on Environmental Quality (TCEQ)** is the state agency responsible for enforcing pollution control regulations in Texas. The TCEQ has developed a State Implementation Plan (SIP), addressing air-quality issues in each area of the state that is not in compliance with the law. The state's SIP includes more effective automobile emissions testing, the use of cleaner diesel fuel, a reduction in the emission of nitrous oxide by industrial plants, and an early morning ban on heavy-duty construction equipment in the summer in affected areas.[4]

The implementation of the federal Clean Air Act in Texas begins this chapter on the federal context of policymaking for Texas government. The chapter identifies the role of state and local governments in the federal system of American government. It explores the impact of the U.S. Constitution and federal courts on state and local governments by examining three important cases in constitutional law. The chapter also studies the influence of federal law on state and local policymaking, considering federal preemption of state authority and federal mandates. The next section of the chapter describes federal grant programs and examines their influence on the state and local policymaking process. The chapter concludes with a discussion of the impact of the federal government and the federal system on policymaking in Texas.

?   WHAT IS YOUR OPINION?

Would you be willing to drive less in order to reduce air pollution?

ROLE OF THE STATES IN THE FEDERAL SYSTEM

Policymaking in Texas takes place within the context of America's federal system of government. A **federal system** *or* **federation** is a political system that divides power between a central government, with authority over the whole nation, and a series of state governments. In a federal system, both the national government and the states enjoy **sovereignty,** which is the authority of a state to exercise legitimate powers within its boundaries, free from external interference. The national government and the states derive their authority not from one another but from the U.S. Constitution. Both levels of government act directly on the people through their officials and laws, both are supreme within their proper sphere of authority, and both must consent to constitutional change.

"It's about people's health and cleaning up the air."
—Hazel Barbour, TCEQ

The national government is constitutionally the dominant partner in America's federal system. Article VI of the U.S. Constitution includes a passage known as the **National Supremacy Clause,** which is a constitutional provision that declares that the Constitution, the laws made under it, and the treaties of the United States are the supreme law of the land. In short, the National Supremacy Clause states that the legitimate exercise of national power supersedes state action when the two conflict.

Nonetheless, state and **local governments,** which are subunits of states, enjoy considerable policymaking authority. States and localities provide their residents with a wide range of services. The major budget items for state and local governments in Texas and around the nation are education, health care, public safety, and transportation. State and local governments build and repair roads, put out fires, educate youngsters, spray mosquitoes, vaccinate children, provide parks and recreation facilities, police neighborhoods, operate hospitals, provide water and sewer service, pick up garbage, and administer welfare programs for the poor.

State and local governments regulate a wide range of industries, including insurance, finance, oil and gas, and utilities. State governments require business owners to obtain licenses and follow state guidelines in operating their establishments. They license a wide range of professions, including doctors, lawyers, realtors, accountants, nurses, and hair stylists. Cities regulate land use, establish construction codes, and inspect food vendors.

States and localities levy taxes. The most important tax sources for state and local governments nationwide are sales, property, excise, and income taxes. All of these taxes are important in Texas except the income tax. Texas is one of only a handful of states that does not levy a personal income tax.

In many policy areas, state governments rather than the federal government have taken the policymaking lead. Partisan wrangling and budget deficits have hamstrung Congress and the president, preventing them from addressing many of the nation's pressing domestic policy problems. Both chambers of Congress have been closely divided between the two political parties. Control of the U.S. Senate and House has sometimes been divided between the two parties; Congress and the presidency have often been under the control of different parties as well. **Blame avoidance,** which is the effort on the part of government officials to assign responsibility

N A T I O N A L   P E R S P E C T I V E

Drilling for Oil in Alaska

The petroleum industry is more important to Alaska than it is to Texas. In 2003, taxes and royalties on oil and gas production accounted for more than two-thirds of state tax revenue in Alaska. Because of petroleum revenue, individual Alaskans enjoy the lowest state taxes in the nation, with no personal income tax and a relatively low sales tax.*

The state of Alaska and the federal government are locked in a controversy over extending oil development in the state. The most promising area for future oil development in the United States is located on Alaska's North Shore in the Arctic National Wildlife Refuge (ANWR). Oil industry executives and most elected officials in Alaska argue that the ANWR oil fields can be developed without causing serious harm to the Arctic environment. A majority of Alaska residents, including native Alaskans who live in the effected area, support drilling as well. In contrast, environmentalists believe that oil exploration in the ANWR would threaten the fragile ecology of the region.

The future of oil development in the ANWR depends on the federal government. When Congress created the ANWR in 1980, it designated the coastal plain for eventual development. In 1995, Congress included a provision in a budget measure to open the coastal plain for oil drilling, but it died when President Bill Clinton vetoed the bill. The prospects for future oil development in the ANWR improved substantially in 2000 with the election of George W. Bush, a Texas oilman, to the presidency. Bush supports opening the ANWR for oil drilling and has made that position the centerpiece of his administration's energy policy. Although the U.S. House of Representatives has voted in favor of drilling, the Senate has so far blocked the proposal.

QUESTIONS TO CONSIDER

1. Do you favor or oppose oil exploration in the ANWR? Why?
2. Why do you think most elected officials in Alaska favor oil development in the ANWR?
3. Should the decision whether to drill in the ANWR be made by the state government of Alaska or by the federal government?

*Alaska State Budget, available at **www.gov.state .ak.us/**.

---

for policy failures to someone else, has taken precedence over problem solving. In the meantime, Congress and the president have lacked resources to address domestic policy problems because of record-high budget deficits. (A **budget deficit** is the amount of money by which annual budget expenditures exceed annual budget receipts.)

While Congress and the president have been unable to agree on a national health system, for example, many state governments have pieced together a health insurance system for low-income families using the Medicaid program and the Children's Health Insurance Program (CHIP). The **Medicaid program** is a federal program designed to provide health insurance coverage to poor people, the disabled, and elderly Americans who are impoverished. The **Children's Health Insurance Program (CHIP)** is a federal program designed to provide health insurance to children from low-income families whose parents are not poor enough to qualify for Medicaid. States have extended Medicaid to cover working families above the poverty line who cannot afford health insurance, adults with disabilities who cannot get insurance, women with breast cancer or cervical cancer, and people with HIV.[5]

Health care is not the only policy area where states rather than the federal government have taken the policymaking lead. Many states have deregulated electric utilities. Although electricity deregulation proved disastrous in California, other states, including Texas, have deregulated the industry without major problems. State governments won a multibillion dollar settlement from the tobacco industry for a lawsuit filed to recover the cost of smoking-related illnesses covered by Medicaid. Furthermore, some of the most important recent domestic policy initiatives adopted by the federal government, including welfare reform and education reform, were modeled on programs developed at the state level.

STATES, THE COURTS, AND THE CONSTITUTION

The U.S. Constitution is the supreme law of the land. It takes legal precedence over state constitutions, state laws, state administrative procedures, and the actions of local government. State and local officials pledge to uphold the U.S. Constitution and most of them take that responsibility quite seriously. When the legislature considers changes in the state's capital punishment law, for example, much of the debate centers on the likelihood that any proposed revision will survive a constitutional challenge. Individuals and groups who believe that the policies of state and local government violate the U.S. Constitution may file suit in federal court, asking the court to intervene. We can illustrate the importance of federal court rulings on policymaking in Texas by examining three historic cases: *Brown v. Board of Education of Topeka*, *Ruiz v. Estelle*, and *Roe v. Wade*.

School Desegregation

Brown v. Board of Education of Topeka (1954) dealt with the constitutionality of state laws requiring racially segregated schools. The Brown family, residents of Topeka, Kansas, wanted their daughter Linda to attend the public school nearest their home. The law of the state of Kansas required separate schools for white and African American youngsters. Because the school nearest the Brown home was for whites only, Linda, who was African American, would have to travel across town to another school. With the legal support of the **National Association for the Advancement of Colored People (NAACP),** which is an interest group organized to represent the interests of African Americans, the Browns filed suit against the state. They charged that the law requiring a racially segregated public school system violated the **Equal Protection Clause,** which is the constitutional provision found in the Fourteenth Amendment of the U.S. Constitution that declares that "No State shall . . . deny to any person within its jurisdiction the equal protection of the laws."

The U.S. Supreme Court ruled that the state law was unconstitutional because it denied equal educational opportunities to African American students. "Segregation of white and colored children in public schools has a detrimental effect upon the colored children," wrote Chief Justice Earl Warren in the Court's opinion. "A sense of inferiority affects the motivation of the child to learn."[6]

Brown v. *Board of Education of Topeka* ultimately had a profound impact on policymaking in Texas. Even though the case involved a state law in Kansas, the precedent set by the Supreme Court in its ruling applied to all similar statutes throughout the United States. As was true for most southern states, Texas had a **dual school system,** that is, separate sets of schools for white and African American youngsters. The state was eventually forced to dismantle its dual school system and adopt policies aimed at achieving racial integration of public schools.

Prison Overcrowding

Ruiz v. *Estelle* (1972) addressed the issue of living conditions in the Texas Department of Corrections (TDC). In 1972, a group of prison inmates filed suit in federal court, claiming that living and working conditions in Texas prisons constituted "cruel and unusual punishment," forbidden by the Eighth Amendment to the U.S. Constitution. They charged that the state's prison system was severely overcrowded, the prison staff was too small to maintain security, working conditions were unsafe, disciplinary procedures were severe and arbitrary, and medical care was inadequate.

In 1980, federal District Judge William Wayne Justice ruled against the state of Texas, ordering sweeping changes in the Texas prison system. Although an appeals court later overturned part of Judge Justice's ruling, it upheld the key points of his decision. Eventually, the state settled the suit by agreeing to limit inmate population to 95 percent of prison capacity, separate hard-core offenders from inmates convicted of nonviolent crimes, improve the guard-to-inmate ratio, and upgrade inmate medical treatment.[7]

The *Ruiz* case forced Texas to limit its prison population. Initially, the state responded with early release, turning offenders out on **parole,** which is the conditional release of convicted offenders from prison to serve the remainder of their sentences in the community under supervision. In the long run, the state complied with the court's decision to reduce overcrowding by dramatically increasing the capacity of its prison system.

Abortion

Roe v. *Wade* (1973) dealt with the issue of abortion. "Jane Roe," an anonymous woman living in Dallas, challenged the constitutionality of a Texas law prohibiting abortion except to save the life of a woman. The U.S. Supreme Court found the Texas statute unconstitutional, saying that a woman's right to personal privacy under the U.S. Constitution included her decision to terminate a pregnancy within six months of inception.

The Supreme Court explained the ruling by dividing a pregnancy into three trimesters. During the first trimester (a three-month period), state governments could not interfere with a physician's decision, reached in consultation with a pregnant patient, to terminate a pregnancy. In the second trimester, a state could regulate abortion only to protect the health of the woman. In the third trimester, after the fetus has achieved viability (the ability to survive outside the womb), the Court ruled that states could choose to prohibit abortion, except when necessary to preserve the life or health of the woman.[8]

Linda Brown and her family were the plaintiffs in the _Brown_ v. _Board of Education of Topeka_ case, in which state laws requiring racial segregation in public schools were ruled to be unconstitutional.

"Under house Bill 15, a woman who gets an abortion must view 20 colored pictures showing every gestational development. If our Constitution gives a woman a choice to get an abortion, why make such a traumatic time even more difficult?"
—State Senator Eliot Shapleigh, D., El Paso

In subsequent cases, the Supreme Court modified its ruling in _Roe_ v. _Wade_ to allow states greater leeway to limit abortion rights. Although the Court reaffirmed a woman's right to choose to abort a fetus before viability, it ruled that a state could regulate access to abortion as long as the regulations did not place an "undue burden" on a woman's right to choose. The Court's majority defined an undue burden as one that presented an "absolute obstacle or severe limitation" on the right to decide to have an abortion. State regulations that simply "inhibited" that right were permissible.[9]

The Texas legislature and the governor have taken advantage of the Supreme Court's flexibility on state abortion regulation by adopting a parental notification law and mandating a 24-hour waiting period for all women seeking an abortion. A 1999 measure prohibits Texas physicians from performing an abortion on a pregnant minor unless they provide the minor's parent or guardian with a 48-hour notice. The law does not require parental consent. If the minor does not wish to have her parent or guardian notified of her intent to have an abortion, she may ask a judge to waive the requirement. The judge may grant the waiver based on one of the following circumstances:

GETTING INVOLVED

Contacting Your Representative in Washington, D.C.

In America's federal system of government, individuals are citizens of the United States and citizens of the state in which they live. If you live in the Lone Star State, you are both an American citizen and a citizen of Texas. You receive services, pay taxes, and are subject to the laws and regulations of both the national government and the state of Texas.

American citizens have the constitutional right to participate in the policymaking process for both the national government and their state government. They may vote in both national and state elections and contact their elected representatives at both levels of government to make their policy preferences known.

The names, postal addresses, and e-mail addresses of the people who represent you in Congress are available online. The website for the U.S. Senate is available at **www.senate.gov**. The website for the U.S. House is at **www.house.gov**. Each site has an interactive window that enables you to identify the names of your representatives. You can also find contact information. Write or e-mail your U.S. senators and U.S. representative, expressing your point of view on the Clean Air Act, No Child Left Behind, Medicaid, or any other federal or national issue about which you have an opinion.

It's your country—get involved!

- The minor is sufficiently mature and well enough informed to make a decision to have an abortion without notice to parent or guardian.
- The notification would not be in the best interests of the minor.
- The notification may lead to the minor's physical, sexual, or emotional abuse.[10]

In 2003, the legislature and governor adopted additional restrictions on abortion. Before performing an abortion, a physician must provide a pregnant patient with a state-created packet that includes information about the health risks associated with abortion, alternatives to terminating a pregnancy, and color images of fetal development. The woman must then wait 24 hours before having the abortion.

Roe v. *Wade* and other court cases dealing with abortion rights affected Texas law by restricting the state's ability to adopt policies controlling access to abortion. Before *Roe*, the state was free to adopt any policy ranging from legalization of abortion in most circumstances to the prohibition of abortion in almost all circumstances. Because of *Roe*, abortion is now legal in every state, including Texas, whether legislators and governors like it or not. In 1999, Texas physicians performed 80,739 abortions in the state.[11]

> "Abortion at any stage is more risky than taking a mole off. . . . This bill will make abortions safer for those who choose to get them."
> —State Senator Robert Deuell, R., Greenville

? WHAT IS YOUR OPINION?

Do you agree with the Texas law that forces women to wait 24 hours before they can have an abortion? Why or why not?

STATES AND FEDERAL LAW

Federal laws apply to state and local governments as long as Congress acts within the scope of its powers under the U.S. Constitution. Article I, Section 8 of the Constitution grants Congress authority to legislate in a range of policy areas, including trade, immigration, patent and copyright law, and national defense. In practice, Congress has made frequent use of the Interstate Commerce Clause as a basis for legislation affecting the states. The **Interstate Commerce Clause** is the constitutional provision giving Congress authority to "regulate commerce . . . among the several states." Congress has used this constitutional provision as a basis for legislation dealing with such diverse subjects as cable television regulation, agricultural price supports, and racial discrimination.

The federal laws and regulations that have the greatest impact on state and local policymaking take the form of federal preemption and federal mandates. Federal preemption *prevents* states from adopting their own policies in selected policy areas whereas federal mandates *require* certain state policy actions.

Federal Preemption

The federal government prevents state and local governments from making policy in some policy areas. An act of Congress adopting regulatory policies that overrule state policies in a particular regulatory area is known as **federal preemption of state authority.** Congress has passed more than a hundred laws preempting state regulation, including preemption of state policies dealing with cellular phone rates, nuclear power safety, private pension plans, and trucking rates.[12]

Preemption is controversial. The proponents of preemption believe that uniform national regulatory standards are preferable to state-by-state regulation. In contrast, critics of preemption contend that congressional efforts to override state authority violate state's rights principles that hold that state legislators know best what policies are most appropriate for their states.

Ironically, business interests, who often oppose regulation in general, typically support federal preemption of state regulations. Firms doing business nationwide would rather adapt to a uniform national policy than conform to 50 different state regulations. As one state official put it, "A lot of . . . companies feel it is easier to work with Congress than fifty state legislatures."[13] Business interests would also prefer that Congress adopt a relatively mild nationwide regulatory standard than deal with tough regulations at the state level.

> "I would rather deal with one federal gorilla than fifty state monkeys."
> —Industry official

Federal Mandates

A **federal mandate** is a legal requirement placed on a state or local government by the national government requiring certain policy actions. The **Americans with Disabilities Act (ADA),** which is a federal law intended to end discrimination against disabled persons and eliminate barriers preventing their full participation in American society, imposes a broad range of federal mandates. The ADA has been interpreted to require that new buses purchased by mass transit systems must have wheelchair lifts, rest rooms in public buildings must be accessible to disabled people, and city streets that are resurfaced have curb cuts.[14] The ADA mandates that when a new building goes up or an old building undergoes a major renovation, it must be made accessible to people with disabilities, and accommodations must be made for employees with disabilities. Because of the ADA, colleges and universities typically provide special assistance to students with disabilities, such as sign-language interpreters for students who have hearing impairments and additional time to take exams for students with learning disabilities.

State and local government officials often resent federal mandates because they are sometimes so detailed that they force states to abandon their own policy innovations in favor of a one-size-fits-all federal prescription. Consider the **No Child Left Behind Act,** which is a federal law that requires state governments and local school districts to institute basic skills testing as a condition for receiving federal aid. The

The ADA requires that public buildings be accessible to persons with disabilities.

measure, which was named for a slogan used by the George W. Bush presidential campaign, forces states to administer tests in mathematics and language arts for students in grades three through eight by the 2005–2006 school year. Schools must conduct science tests once in grades three through five, six through nine, and ten through twelve by 2007–2008. The results of the tests must be used to assess school performance and track the progress of individual students. Poor performing schools that fail to improve will eventually face the loss of federal aid money.[15] State officials argue that No Child Left Behind is so complex that school officials will be forced to spend all of their time and money testing and tracking students rather than implementing the educational reforms they think will work best.

> "You get the feeling sometimes that the feds are just not on the same map as state and local governments."
> —Lynn Cutler, former presidential adviser

State officials also complain about cost shifting from the federal government to the states. The War on Terror, for example, has become a major drain on the finances of state and local government. Because the nation's cities, power plants, bridges, refineries, and monuments are potential targets for terrorists, state and local authorities have been forced to increase security. They have also had to invest millions of dollars in training and equipment for police officers, fire fighters, and other emergency responders so they will be ready in case of an attack. State officials believe that the cost of homeland security should be borne by the national government because national security has historically been a federal function. Nonetheless, the federal government has shifted most of the cost of homeland security to the states. Although President Bush proposed providing $3.5 billion to the states for the First Responders Initiative grant program in his 2002 budget, Congress appropriated less than a billion dollars in additional money.[16]

> "The big frustration is that we're fighting a war in the Middle East and a war in our cities, trying to defend ourselves against terrorism, and the cities are not getting financial support to do their share of it."
> —Mayor Kenneth Barr, Fort Worth

FEDERAL GRANT PROGRAMS

Federal grant-in-aid programs, which are programs through which the national government gives money to state and local governments for expenditure in accordance with set standards and conditions, play a significant role in state policymaking. In 2002, the federal government gave $352 billion to state and local governments, 17.5 percent of the federal budget.[17] Nearly 90 percent of the funds went directly to state governments rather than localities, although much of that money was passed on by the state to local agencies for health and human services, housing and urban development, transportation, and education.[18]

Program Adoption

Congress and the president adopt federal grant programs through the legislative process. Both houses of Congress must agree to establish a program and the president must either sign the legislation or allow it to become law without signature. If the president vetoes the measure, it can become law only if Congress votes to override the veto by a two-thirds margin in each house.

Federal programs must be authorized and funds appropriated for their operation. The **authorization process** is the procedure through which Congress legislatively establishes a program, defines its general purpose, devises procedures for its operation,

TEXAS ONLINE ★ Forces of Change

The Texas Office of State-Federal Relations

The Texas Office of State-Federal Relations is a state agency established to lobby Congress on behalf of state government and to ensure that state officials are kept up-to-date on federal policy developments that might affect Texas. Browse the agency homepage and answer the questions that follow:

www.osfr.state.tx.us/

QUESTIONS TO CONSIDER

1. What is the mission statement of the agency?
2. What sort of information does the homepage contain?
3. Does the summer internship program interest you?

specifies an agency to implement the program, and indicates an approximate level of funding for the program. The authorization process does not actually allocate money for the program. Congress sometimes specifies that programs must periodically be reauthorized. The **appropriation process** is the procedure through which Congress legislatively provides money for a particular purpose. The appropriation process takes place annually.

The adoption of the Help America Vote Act of 2002 illustrates the distinction between authorization and appropriation. Congress passed and President George W. Bush signed the measure to reform state election systems after the debacle of the Florida presidential election controversy in 2000. The law requires states to maintain a database of registered voters, provide voting systems with minimum error rates, set voter identification requirements, provide access for people with disabilities, and draft procedures for resolving voter complaints.[19] Although the measure authorized $4 billion to cover the cost for new voting machines and other improvements, Congress failed to include the money in the annual appropriation bill, leaving the states to bear the cost of the measure on their own.[20]

> "The federal government is passing the buck, but not the bucks to the states."
> —Alan Rosenthal, Eagleton Institute of Politics

Types of Federal Programs

Federal programs come in a variety of forms.

Categorical and Block Grants   A **categorical grant program** is a federal grant-in-aid program that provides funds to state and local governments for a fairly narrow, specific purpose, such as removing asbestos from school buildings or acquiring land for outdoor recreation. In this type of program, Congress allows state and local officials little discretion as to how money is spent. Categorical grants comprise 97 percent of all federal grants, accounting for 79 percent of federal grant money to state and local governments.[21]

A **block grant program** is a federal grant-in-aid program that provides money for a program in a broad, general policy area, such as elementary and secondary edu-

Federal grant money supports highway construction in Texas.

cation, or transportation. State and local governments have more discretion in spending block grant funds than they have for categorical grant money. Nonetheless, over time Congress tends to attach conditions to the receipt of block grant funds, thus reducing the flexibility of state and local officials. When Congress and the president created the Surface Transportation Program in 1991, for example, they gave states a lump sum of money to spend on highways and other transportation projects in accordance with statewide objectives. Subsequently, Congress and the president have added restrictions, requiring that 10 percent of the funds must be used to improve the safety of state highways and that 10 percent must be spent on "transportation enhancement" activities, such as hike and bike trails.[22]

Policymakers disagree about the relative merits of categorical and block grants. The proponents of categorical grants argue that they enable Congress to identify particular policy problems and ensure that the money that Congress provides targets those problems. Categorical grants, they say, allow Congress to set national goals and apply national standards to achieve those goals. If local officials are given too much discretion, they may use grant money to reward campaign supporters or pay back political debts. In contrast, the supporters of block grants contend that state and local officeholders know better what their residents want and need than do officials in Washington, D.C. Block grants enable the officials closest to the people to direct the federal dollars to where they will do the most good.

? WHAT IS YOUR OPINION?

If you were a member of Congress, would you prefer block grants or categorical grants?

Entitlement Programs   Some federal programs, including Medicaid, the School Lunch Program, and Unemployment Compensation, are **entitlement programs,** which are government programs providing benefits to all persons qualified to receive them under law. Congress sets eligibility standards based on such factors as age, income, and disability. Individuals who meet the criteria are entitled to receive the benefits.

Spending for entitlement programs does not go through the appropriation process. The amount of money the federal government spends each year on Medicaid and other entitlement programs depends on the number of eligible recipients who apply for benefits and the cost of providing those benefits. If Congress and the president want to reduce (or increase) spending for an entitlement program, they must pass legislation to change the program.

Entitlement programs are controversial. The proponents of entitlement programs say that they represent a national commitment to address certain important policy issues, including health care for the poor and the disabled (Medicaid), nutritious lunches for low-income school children (the School Lunch Program), and income security for unemployed workers (Unemployment Compensation). Program recipients do not have to depend on Congress and the president to appropriate money each year for their benefits because they are entitled to them by law. In contrast, the critics of entitlement programs charge that they are budget busters. Spending for entitlement programs goes up each year automatically as the number of beneficiaries rises and the cost of providing services increases, regardless of the budgetary situation.

"You measure a government by how few people need help."
—Patricia R. Schroeder, former member of Congress

Project and Formula Grants   Federal grants differ in the criteria by which funding is awarded. A **project grant program** is a grant program that requires state and local governments to compete for available federal money. State and local governments present detailed grant applications which federal agencies evaluate in order to make funding decisions. The Department of Education, for example, administers project grants dealing with a range of educational initiatives, such as teacher training, math and science education, and preparing students for the demands of today's workforce. Public schools, colleges, and universities make applications to the agency which then decides which grant proposals merit funding.

A **formula grant program** is a grant program that awards funding on the basis of a formula established by Congress. In contrast to project grants, formula grants provide money for every state and/or locality that qualifies under the formula. The Clean Fuels Formula Grant Program is a formula grant administered by the Department of Transportation that allocates money to transit authorities to assist in the purchase and use of low-emissions buses and related equipment. The program awards funds based on a formula that includes area population, the size of the bus fleet, the number of bus passenger miles, and the severity of the area's air pollution problem.[23]

Grant Conditions

Federal grants usually come with conditions. A **matching funds requirement** is the legislative provision that the national government will provide grant money for a particular activity only on condition that the state or local government involved supply a certain percentage of the total money required for the project or program. For example, if the total cost of a sewage treatment plant in Laredo is $20 million, the national government may supply $16 million (80 percent) while requiring the city to match the federal money with $4 million of local funds (20 percent). Even federal programs that do not require financial participation by state and local governments often require contributions in-kind. The national government covers the entire cost of the **Food Stamp Program,** which is a federal program that provides vouchers to low-income families and individuals that can be used to purchase food, but state governments must administer its operation.

Matching funds requirements sometimes force states and localities to devote growing sums of money to particular programs. Consider the impact of the Medicaid program on state budgets. The national government and the states split the cost of Medicaid, with the federal government picking up 50 percent to 80 percent of the expense, depending on a state's wealth. The cost division in the Lone Star State is 60 percent for the federal government and 40 percent for the state of Texas. Medicaid expenditures have increased rapidly because Congress and the states have expanded eligibility to include more people and because of the rising cost of medical services for recipients, especially for prescription drugs. Medicaid expenditures grew by 11 percent in 2001, 13 percent in 2002, and an estimated 15 percent in 2003, with no relief in sight.[24] Even though the federal government picks up at least half of the additional costs, states must cover the rest of the expense from their own funds.[25] As a result, Medicaid spending is the fastest growing item in most state budgets, representing, on average, 13 percent of state general fund expenditures.[26]

Congress imposes legislative mandates on recipients of federal funds. Some mandates apply to grant recipients in general. These include provisions in the area of equal rights, equal access for the disabled, environmental protection, historic preservation, and union wage rates for construction workers on federally funded projects. Furthermore, individual programs often have particular strings attached. In order to receive money from the 1994 Crime Act to construct, expand, and operate correctional facilities, states had to adopt "truth in sentencing" laws that accurately showed the amount of time persons convicted of crimes would spend behind bars. States had to ensure that violent criminals served at least 85 percent of their prison sentences. The federal government also required states to impose stiff penalties for criminal offenders and adopt programs to protect the rights of crime victims.[27]

Congress sometimes uses federal grant money to compel states to adopt policies favored in Washington, D.C. although not necessarily in state capitals. In the 1970s and 1980s, Congress threatened states with the loss of federal highway grant money

The School Lunch Program is a federal program that provides free or inexpensive lunches to children from poor families.

unless they adopted the 55 miles per hour speed limit and raised their minimum legal drinking age to 21. Although Congress has dropped the speed limit requirement, it now requires that states ban open containers and revoke the driver's licenses of repeat DUI offenders. If states fail to comply with the open container ban and driver's license revocation rule, the federal government transfers a portion of their highway construction money into a fund that can only be used for highway safety.

Congress initially took an incentive approach to setting a national standard of 0.08 blood-alcohol content to determine if a driver is legally intoxicated. Although some states already followed the 0.08 standard, most states, including Texas, had set the drunk-driving level at a blood-alcohol content of 0.10. Instead of penalizing states that failed to adopt the 0.08 standard with loss of federal funds, Congress established a fund to pay a cash bonus to states that voluntarily adopted the tougher blood-alcohol standard. Two years later, however, Congress decided that the incentive plan was not working well enough, so it adopted legislation mandating the loss of highway funds for states that failed to adopt the 0.08 standard by October 1, 2003.

LEARNING EXERCISE

Texas in the Federal System

The federal government has a substantial impact on the policymaking process in Texas, affecting a wide range of state and local policies. Your assignment is to find a newspaper article illustrating the impact of a unit of the federal government on one or more units of government in Texas. The unit of national government could be Congress, a federal court, or a federal agency, such as the EPA or the Department of Defense. The unit of Texas government could be a state agency, such as the University of Texas at Austin or TCEQ, or a unit of local government, such as a city, school district, or county government. An appropriate article might discuss a federal grant program, a federal regulation that affects state/local government, or a federal court ruling that impacts the state of Texas, a city in Texas, a school district, or a Texas county.

Be sure the article you select includes at least one unit of government at the national level and one at the state or local level. Do not choose an article that deals with two branches of the national government such as Congress and the president. Articles that address the relationship between the national government and a private organization, such as a business or an interest group, do not match the assignment either.

You can look for suitable articles in newspapers online or thumb through actual newspapers. Some of the state's more prominent newspapers can be found online at the following Internet addresses:

Austin American-Statesman: **www.statesman.com**

Dallas Morning News: **www.dallasnews.com**

El Paso Times: **www.elpasotimes.com**

Fort Worth Star Telegram: **www.dfw.com**

Houston Chronicle: **www.houstonchronicle.com**

Once you have found a suitable article, write a short essay about the article in which you do the following:

- Summarize the article.
- Identify the unit of national government and the unit of Texas state/local government mentioned in the article.
- Explain why the article illustrates the impact of the national government on state and/or local government in Texas.
- Identify the source of the article.

"Blackmailing by the feds has taken away representative government."
—Rep. Todd Taylor, Iowa legislature

Although most states (including Texas) complied with the federal requirement rather than risk the loss of highway funding, state officials complained about Congress forcing its policy preferences on the states. "If states want 0.08, that's fine," said an Iowa legislator. [But] "if Congress says you have to have it, they've [sic] overstepped their bounds."[28]

Federal Money and Texas

State and local governments in Texas receive billions of dollars in federal funds annually. Federal aid accounts for 15 percent of combined state and local revenue, with federal grants providing money to the state for health care and nutrition for low-income families, highway construction, and homeland security and emergency preparedness.[29] The state's school districts receive federal grant funds for special education, bilingual education, and the School Lunch Program. Federal money flows to Texas cities for such activities as sewage treatment plant construction, parkland acquisition, neighborhood revitalization, and airport construction.

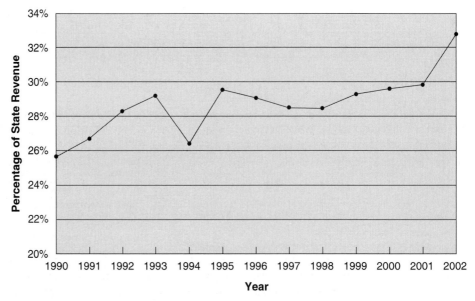

FIGURE 3.1   Federal Funds as Percent of State Revenue
Source: Texas Comptroller of Public Accounts

Figure 3.1 documents the growth in federal aid to state government in Texas. Between 1990 and 2002, the relative importance of federal funding to state government in Texas increased irregularly from less than 26 percent in 1990 to more than 32 percent in 2002. Although Medicaid funding alone accounted for more than 40 percent of the increase in federal grant funds during the 1990s, it was not the only federal program to grow. Funding for three-fourths of federal programs increased during the 1990s, including money for programs dealing with natural resources and the environment, transportation, community and regional development, income security, and education and training.[30]

CONCLUSION: THE FEDERAL CONTEXT OF POLICYMAKING IN TEXAS

The federal system affects every stage of the policymaking process in Texas.

Agenda Building

The federal government frequently raises issues that must be addressed by state and local governments in Texas. The federal Clean Air Act requires Texas to address air pollution problems. *Brown* v. *Board of Education of Topeka* and subsequent federal court cases dealing with school desegregation forced the state and its school districts to desegregate the public schools. Prison reform became a major item on the state's official policy agenda only after *Ruiz* v. *Estelle*. It is unlikely that any of these issues would have become part of the official policy agenda in Texas when they did and in the form they did were it not for federal action.

Policy Formulation and Adoption

The federal system affects policy formulation. The consideration of policy options by state and local officials often depends on the availability of federal funds and the limitations imposed by federal guidelines. Nearly half the total state budget is written to conform to federal mandates, provide matching funds for federal programs, or comply with federal court orders.[31] Furthermore, state and local policymakers typically design policies dealing with health, welfare, law enforcement, education, job training, prison management, and other areas with the goal of increasing federal funding. For example, college and university officials often develop programs based on their likelihood of winning federal grant funding.

The federal government influences state policy adoption. Most states, including Texas, raised their drinking ages to 21 and lowered their speed limits to 55 miles per hour because Congress threatened them with the loss of federal highway grant money should they do otherwise. Texas adopted a testing program for automobile emissions in order to comply with federal clean air requirements. State officials revised welfare policies to comply with the provisions of welfare reform.

Policy Implementation and Evaluation

The federal system affects policy implementation. When a state or local government accepts federal funds, it must agree to follow federal guidelines in program implementation, such as filing an environmental impact statement for construction projects, paying union wage scale to contract workers, and ensuring accessibility for disabled persons. Because most major policy areas in Texas (including education, transportation, and health care) involve at least some federal money, federal regulations have a major impact on policy implementation.

State and local governments implement many federal programs. Congress sets program goals, establishes guidelines, and then charges the states with implementation. State governments enjoy the leeway to implement the programs as they see fit within the guidelines set by the federal government. Consider the federal Clean Air Act. The law requires Texas to reduce pollution to meet federal air-quality standards, but the EPA does not specify the steps Texas must take to achieve the goal. Texas has leeway to develop a plan to meet local needs as long as the plan reduces pollution enough to meet the standard.

Finally, the federal system influences policy evaluation. Federal officials act as policy evaluators, determining whether grant proposals merit continued funding or if state policies are constitutional. Furthermore, state policymakers often judge policies on the number of federal dollars they are able to bring to the state or whether the policies can pass muster when challenged in federal court.

★ REVIEW QUESTIONS

1. Why have state governments begun to take the policymaking lead in many issue areas rather than the federal courts?

2. How do the federal courts and the U.S. Constitution impact state policymaking in such areas as school integration, prison management, and access to abortion?

3. How do federal preemption and federal mandates affect state policymaking?

4. How are federal grant programs adopted and implemented?

5. What are the different types of grant programs?

6. What sorts of conditions does the federal government place on the receipt of federal funds?

7. How important are federal grants to state and local governments in Texas?

8. How does the federal government affect each stage of the policymaking process in Texas?

★ KEY TERMS

Americans with Disabilities Act (ADA)

appropriation process

authorization process

blame avoidance

block grant program

budget deficit

categorical grant program

Children's Health Insurance Program (CHIP)

dual school system

entitlement programs

Environmental Protection Agency (EPA)

Equal Protection Clause

federal grant-in-aid programs

federal mandate

federal preemption of state authority

federal system or federation

Food Stamp Program

formula grant program

Interstate Commerce Clause

local governments

matching funds requirement

Medicaid program

National Association for the Advancement of Colored People (NAACP)

National Supremacy Clause

No Child Left Behind Act

parole

project grant program

sovereignty

Texas Commission on Environmental Quality (TCEQ)

★ NOTES

1. Environmental Protection Agency, "The Ozone Problem," available at **www.epa.gov**.

2. Texas Commission on Environmental Quality, "The Quest for Clean Air," available at **www.tceq.state.tx.us**.

3. Texas Commission on Environmental Quality, "Avoiding the Penalty Box," available at **www.tceq.state.tx.us**.

4. Texas Commission on Environmental Quality, "State Implementation Plan," available at **www.tceq.state.tx.us**.

5. Trinity D. Tomsic, "Managing Medicaid in Tough Times," *State Legislatures* (June 2002): 13–17.

6. *Brown v. Board of Education of Topeka*, 347 U.S. 483 (1954).

7. *Ruiz v. Estelle*, 503 F. Supp 1265 (S.D. Tex 1980); 679 F 2d 115 (5th Cir. 1982).

8. *Roe v. Wade*, 410 U.S. 113 (1973).

9. *Planned Parenthood of Southeastern Pennsylvania v. Casey*, 505 U.S. 833 (1992).

10. Texas Family Code 33.002-33.004.

11. Texas Department of Health, "Bureau of Vital Statistics 1999 Annual Report," available at **www.tdh.state.tx.us**.

12. Ellen Perlman, "The Gorilla that Swallows State Laws, " *Governing* (August 1994): 9.

13. Idaho Attorney General Jim Jones, quoted in Martha M. Hamilton, "On Second Thought, We'd Prefer the Feds on Our Backs," *Washington Post National Weekly Edition*, December 14, 1987, p. 32.

14. John M. Goshko, "The Big-Ticket Costs of the Disabilities Act," *Washington Post National Weekly Edition*, March 20–26, 1995, p. 31.

15. Public Law 107-110.

16. Deanna Boyd, "Anti-Terrorism Efforts Are Costing Cities Dearly," *Fort Worth Star-Telegram*, March 20, 2003, available at **www.dfw.com**.

17. Office of Management and Budget, "Summary Comparison of Total Outlays for Grants to State and Local Gov-

ernments: 1940–2008," *The Budget for Fiscal Year 2004, Historical Tables,* available at **www.whitehouse.gov/omb/budget**.

18. "Federal Aid to States and Localities," *Governing State and Local Source Book 2003*, p. 30.

19. Public Law 107-252.

20. Alan Greenblatt, "Squeezing the Federal Turnip," *Governing* (March 2003): 29.

21. Robert J. Dilger, "The Study of American Federalism at the Turn of the Century," *State and Local Government Review* 32 (Spring 2000): 103.

22. Texas Comptroller of Public Accounts, "Theory of Devolution," *Fiscal Notes* (July 1996): 4.

23. Department of Transportation, "Fact Sheet: Clean Fuels Formula Grant Program," available at **www.fhwa.dot.gov/tea21/factsheets/clnfuel.htm**.

24. Martha P. King, "Hurdles of Health Care Reform," *State Legislatures* (January 2003): 22.

25. Texas Department of Health and Human Services, "Texas Medicaid in Perspective," April 2002, available at **www.hhsc.state.tx.us**.

26. Tomsic, "Managing Medicaid in Tough Times," p. 14.

27. "The New Crime Bill," *State Legislatures* (November 1994): 27.

28. Anya Sostek, "Slow to Toe the DUI Line," *Governing* (May 2003): 42.

29. "State and Local Sourcebook, 2003," p. 32.

30. Dilger, "The Study of American Federalism at the Turn of the Century," p. 100.

31. *Texas Weekly*, December 5, 1994, p. 6.

ONLINE PRACTICE TEST

Test your understanding of this chapter
with interactive review quizzes at

www.ablongman.com/tannahilltexas/chapter3

Political Participation

LEARNING OBJECTIVES

After studying Chapter 4, students should be able to do the following:

★ Evaluate the arguments for and against the initiative process.

★ Trace the history of voting rights in Texas, explaining the significance of the poll tax, white primary, and *Smith* v. *Allwright* in the struggle for minority voting rights in Texas.

★ Identify the various means by which individuals can participate in the policymaking process.

★ Describe the rules and procedures for registering and voting in Texas.

★ Compare voter participation rates in Texas with the rates in other states.

★ Explain why participation rates in Texas are relatively low compared to other states.

★ Describe variations in participation rates based on income, age, race/ethnicity, and gender.

★ Compare and contrast the Texas electorate with the state's population in terms of income, education, and age.

★ Describe the role of participation in the policymaking process.

★ Define the key terms listed on page 103 and explain their significance.

Should citizens be able to bypass their elected representatives to adopt policies by popular vote? Nearly half the states (but not Texas) have the **initiative process,** which is a procedure whereby citizens can propose the adoption of a policy measure by gathering signatures on a petition. The number of signatures ranges from 2 percent to 15 percent of the total vote in the most recent statewide election, depending on the state. Some states also require that petition signatures be gathered throughout the state rather than in one geographical area. If enough valid signatures are collected, state officials place the measure on the ballot for approval by the voters. In recent years, the initiative process has been used to address a number of important policy issues, including bilingual education, property tax rates, gay and lesbian rights, the death penalty, insurance rates, term limits for elected officials, casino gambling, and the rights of crime victims.[1]

The advocates of the initiative process believe that it enhances participation by more closely linking citizens to their government. Initiative allows voters to overcome the opposition of their elected representatives to adopt policy proposals they favor. Consider the issue of **term limitation,** which is the movement to restrict the number of terms public officials may serve. Even though public opinion polls indicate that term limitation is popular with voters, state legislatures almost invariably reject the idea because legislators do not want to vote themselves out of office. In most states with the initiative process, the voters have used it to bypass the legislature and adopt term limits themselves.

Initiative proponents believe that allowing citizens to vote on policy questions enhances public interest in and knowledge about political issues. Given the power to make policy decisions themselves, voters will take seriously the responsibility to be informed. Indeed, research finds that citizens in initiative states are more knowledgeable about politics than citizens in noninitiative states.[2] Referendum campaigns will focus on the merits of policy issues rather than the character of candidates. Furthermore, initiative advocates believe that the process will increase voter turnout because citizens will see a direct link between their participation and public policy.

The supporters of initiative also argue that it will reduce the role of special interests. Elected officials are too closely tied to special interest money to make policy decisions that reflect the public interest instead of the policy preferences of lobbyists. Initiative allows citizens to express their policy preferences directly without being compromised by interest group influence.

In contrast, the critics of the initiative process contend that it diminishes the quality of democracy. Referendum campaigns often feature simplistic slogans and shallow discussions of complex issues. Voter turnout for referendum elections is generally less than it is for candidate elections. Also, many voters ignore referenda placed at the end of a long ballot.[3]

Critics believe that the initiative process often works to the detriment of minority groups. Ballot measures in a number of states have dealt with the establishment of English as a state's official language, bilingual education, the provision of social services to illegal immigrants, affirmative action, and gay and lesbian rights. In most cases, the proposed measure was designed to diminish the rights of minority groups

"I support initiative and referendum. I strongly believe that Texans want and deserve a greater say in their government."
—Bob Bullock, lieutenant governor of Texas, 1991–1999

rather than expand or protect them. Colorado voters, for example, approved an amendment to their state constitution that not only repealed all local ordinances and statewide policies protecting gay men and lesbians from discrimination but also prohibited the future enactment of similar measures. The U.S. Supreme Court subsequently overturned the amendment as a violation of the **Equal Protection Clause,** which is the constitutional provision found in the Fourteenth Amendment of the U.S. Constitution that declares: "No State shall . . . deny to any person within its jurisdiction the equal protection of the laws."[4]

Although the advocates of initiative argue that it is citizen democracy in action, opponents point out that interest groups often drive the process. Groups that fail to achieve their policy goals through the legislative process contract with a company to collect signatures on a petition. Instead of citizens asking their neighbors to sign a petition to support a cause they embrace, professional collectors gather signatures door-to-door and at shopping malls on a commission basis. Once a proposition earns a place on the ballot, groups for and against its adoption mount expensive media campaigns, which, critics charge, are often filled with misinformation. Furthermore, the voters who participate in a referendum election are typically wealthier than are the people who vote in candidate elections.[5]

> "Far from replacing group lobbying efforts, initiative and referenda campaigns provide an alternative channel for the very group activities the reformers denounce."
>
> —Betty Zisk,
> political scientist

Finally, the opponents of initiative argue that it produces bad public policy. The advantage of the legislative process, they say, is that it allows for deliberation, discussion, and eventual compromise. In contrast, initiative presents voters with an all-or-nothing proposition.

The controversy over the initiative process introduces the general topic of participation in the policymaking process in Texas. Political participation is important because it is the mechanism that links citizens to their government. The advocates of the initiative process offer it as a reform to make government more responsive to citizen concerns. In contrast, critics charge that initiative fails to achieve that goal.

This is the first of four chapters dealing with participation in the policymaking process in Texas. Each chapter considers who participates in the policymaking process, how participation takes place, and what effect participation has on policy. This chapter examines individual participation, focusing primarily on voting and voting rights. Chapter 5 looks at interest groups, Chapter 6 considers political parties, and Chapter 7 deals with elections.

? WHAT IS YOUR OPINION?

Should the state of Texas adopt the initiative process?

VOTING RIGHTS AND MINORITY PARTICIPATION

Only white males enjoyed the right to vote when Texas joined the Union in 1845. Much of the subsequent history of the state is the story of the efforts of women and the members of racial and ethnic minority groups to gain the right to vote and participate meaningfully in Texas politics.

Women's Suffrage

In the nineteenth century, politics was a man's world, not just in Texas but in the entire United States. The women's rights movement began in the North in the 1840s as an offshoot of the **abolition movement,** which was a political reform effort in early nineteenth-century America whose goal was the elimination of slavery. In Texas, the weakness of the abolition movement hindered the cause of women's rights. The drive for women's **suffrage,** that is, the right to vote, did not begin to pick up steam in the state until 1903 with the founding of the Texas Woman Suffrage Association. In 1915, the state legislature narrowly rejected an amendment to the Texas Constitution calling for women's suffrage. Three years later the legislature approved a law allowing women to vote in primary elections. Finally, in 1919, the U.S. Congress proposed a constitutional amendment granting women the right to vote nationwide. Texas was the first state in the South to ratify the Nineteenth Amendment, which became law in 1920, giving women in Texas and all across America the right to vote.[6]

> "The right of citizens of the United States to vote shall not be denied or abridged by the United States or by any State on account of sex."
> —Nineteenth Amendment to the U.S. Constitution

Minority Voting Rights

Winning the right to vote and having that vote counted was a more elusive goal for Texans of African and Hispanic descent than it was for women.

African American Enfranchisement after the Civil War   Before the Civil War, nearly all African Americans who lived in Texas were slaves; none could vote or hold public office. The war ended slavery, but the state's white political establishment refused to enfranchise former slaves. (**Franchise** is the right to vote; to **enfranchise,** means to grant the right to vote.) The Texas Constitution of 1866, written under President Andrew Johnson's Reconstruction plan, denied African Americans the right to vote and hold public office. The U.S. Congress, however, refused to accept the Johnson plan for Reconstruction. In 1867, Congress passed legislation over Johnson's veto that placed the South under military rule and forced southern states to grant African Americans the right to vote.

African Americans registered to vote for the first time in Texas in 1867. The following year they cast ballots in an election to select delegates to a state constitutional convention. Of the 90 delegates chosen, nine were African American men, and all were Republicans. In 1869, African American voters helped elect E. J. Davis governor. In the same election, eleven African Americans won seats in the state legislature.

After the early 1870s, Texas politics began to return to the pattern in place before the Civil War. The Democratic Party regained control of the legislature in the 1872 election and recaptured the governor's mansion a year later. Meanwhile, some white Texans organized chapters of the Ku Klux Klan to threaten and intimidate African American leaders. At times, the Klan resorted to violence to assert white control.

Nonetheless, African Americans continued to participate in Texas politics. Six African Americans were among the delegates elected to the constitutional convention of 1875. Furthermore, with the exception of the legislature elected in 1887, all legislatures chosen from 1868 through 1894 included African American members. All told, 41 African Americans served in the Texas legislature between 1868 and 1900.[7]

Minority Disfranchisement   In the early twentieth century, the white establishment in Texas restricted the voting rights of minorities in order to maintain political power. After Reconstruction, Texas was a one-party state. The Democratic Party, which was controlled by wealthy economic interests, held virtually every elective office in the state. **Disfranchisement,** the denial of voting rights, was the response of the political establishment to the attempt of the Populist Party to win power by uniting lower-income voters of all races against the wealthy economic interests who controlled state politics. Conservative political leaders in Texas (and throughout the South) used racial issues to divide the working class. They hoped to ensure their long-term control of state government by disfranchising African Americans (and many poor whites and Latinos as well).[8]

The poll tax and the white primary were the main instruments of disfranchisement. The **poll tax,** which was a tax that prospective voters had to pay in order to register to vote, kept low-income people of all races from voting. In 1902, the Texas legislature proposed and the voters passed a state constitutional amendment requiring a poll tax. The tax was $1.50 or $1.75 a year (depending on the county), not an insignificant sum in early twentieth-century Texas. (In today's value, the poll tax would be $30 or $35.) Before the implementation of the poll tax, more than 60 percent of voting-age Texans typically participated in presidential elections. In contrast, election turnout dipped to 30 percent of voting-age adults in 1904 after the poll tax went into effect.[9]

The **white primary,** which was an election system that prohibited African Americans from voting in Democratic primary elections, ensured that white voters would control the Democratic Party. In 1903, the state Democratic Party executive committee suggested that all county party committees exclude African Americans from party primary elections. A **primary election** is an intraparty election during which a party's candidates for the general election are chosen. By the 1920s, most counties with significant African American populations used the white primary and in 1924 the Texas legislature adopted the procedure statewide. Because the Democratic Party dominated Texas politics in those days, the Democratic primary was the most important election in the state. Whoever won the primary election invariably won the general election. Consequently, the exclusion of African Americans from participation in the Democratic primary not only barred them from influence in Democratic Party politics but also from meaningful participation in Texas politics in general.

Boss Control in South Texas   Although the white primary did not keep Latinos from the ballot box, political bosses often controlled their votes. In heavily Hispanic south Texas in particular, ranch-owners (some of whom were Latino) controlled both local economies and local politics. The boss would pay the poll tax

Texans once had to pay a poll tax in order to register to vote.

for his workers (most of whom were Hispanic) and then instruct them how to vote. With their jobs depending on it, workers had little choice but to do as they were told.

Many Texans know the story of Archer Parr, the so-called Duke of Duval County, which is located in south Texas just west of Corpus Christi. For years, Parr ran Duval County as his own political kingdom. The most famous example of Parr's influence came in 1948 when a young member of Congress named Lyndon B. Johnson ran for the U.S. Senate against the former governor Coke Stevenson. Parr supported Johnson, but the day after the election it appeared that Stevenson had won the statewide vote by a razor-thin margin. One ballot box remained uncounted, however, Box 13 in neighboring Jim Wells County, where Parr's influence extended. Johnson won Box 13 almost unanimously and "Landslide Lyndon" became an 87-vote winner. Remarkably, 200 voters at Box 13 arrived to cast their ballots in alphabetical order. The affair still inspires death-bed confessions.[10]

> "More men have been elected between sundown and sunup than ever were elected between sunup and sundown."
> —Will Rogers, political humorist

The Struggle for Minority Voting Rights   African Americans in Texas turned to the federal courts for help in regaining the right to vote. Lawrence A. Nixon, an El Paso physician, challenged the constitutionality of the Texas White Primary Law in federal court. In 1927, the U.S. Supreme Court unanimously struck down the law as a "direct and obvious infringement" of the Equal Protection Clause of the Fourteenth Amendment to the U.S. Constitution.[11]

The Texas legislature responded to the ruling by repealing the White Primary Law and replacing it with a statute allowing the state executive committee of each political party to "prescribe the qualifications of its own members." The executive committee of the state Democratic Party then declared that only whites could vote in Democratic primary elections. Dr. Nixon again carried the fight to the U.S. Supreme Court and once again the Court invalidated the Texas law. The vote on the Court was close, however, five to four.[12]

Next, the legislature repealed all laws dealing with primary elections and the Texas Democratic Party declared itself a private organization whose membership was exclusively white. Only party members could vote in Democratic primary elections. African Americans again turned to the federal courts with Richard R. Grovey, a Houston barbershop owner, filing suit. This time, however, the courts refused to help. In 1935, the U.S. Supreme Court unanimously upheld the white primary on grounds that the state of Texas was not involved. The Court ruled that the Fourteenth Amendment did not apply to the Democratic Party because the party was a private organization.[13]

The white primary survived until 1944 when the U.S. Supreme Court decided *Smith* v. *Allwright*, reversing its earlier ruling. This case involved a suit brought by Lonnie Smith, a Houston dentist who was an African American community leader and political activist. The Court ruled eight to one that the Democratic Party acted as an agent of the state when it conducted primary elections. Consequently, the Court declared, the exclusion of African Americans from the Democratic primary was an unconstitutional violation of the Fifteenth Amendment to the U.S. Constitution, which grants African Americans the right to vote.[14]

The white primary was history, but other forms of voting discrimination persisted. In Fort Bend County, for example, white officials arranged a whites-only preprimary called the Jaybird primary. White voters would cast their ballots for the winner of the Jaybird primary in the regular Democratic primary, thus minimizing the impact of the African American vote. The U.S. Supreme Court overturned this procedure in 1953.[15]

The poll tax was the next to fall. In 1962, the U.S. Congress proposed a constitutional amendment to prohibit poll taxes in elections for the presidency or Congress. When it was ratified as the Twenty-fourth Amendment in 1964, the Texas poll tax could be collected only for state and local elections. Two years later, the U.S. Supreme Court struck that down as well as a violation of the Equal Protection Clause of the Fourteenth Amendment.[16] The poll tax was now just as dead as the white primary.

The Texas legislature and the governor responded to the loss of the poll tax by establishing the most difficult and restrictive system of voter registration in the nation. Prospective voters had to register between October 1 and January 31 each year. Anyone who lacked the foresight to sign up three months before the spring primaries and nine months before the November general election was out of luck. In practice, this system worked against poor persons of all races. It survived until 1971 when, as with so many other Texas election procedures, it was struck down by the federal courts.[17]

"[T]he opportunity for choice [of elected officials] is not to be nullified by a state through casting its electoral process in a form which permits a private organization to practice racial discrimination in the election."
—Smith v. Allwright

"A government is free in proportion to the rights it guarantees to the minority."
—Alf Landon, Republican presidential candidate in 1936

PARTICIPATION IN TEXAS POLITICS

A **democracy** is a system of government in which the people hold ultimate political power. Most political scientists believe that a successful democracy depends on citizen participation in the policymaking process.

Forms of Participation

Individual Texans can participate in the policy process in a number of ways: voting, campaigning, joining political groups, contacting public officials, and participating in protest demonstrations and unconventional political acts.

In 2002, the number of voters aged 65 or older outnumbered younger voters below the age of 30 by a two-to-one margin.

Voting   To vote in Texas, individuals must be 18 years of age as of the next election, American citizens (either native-born or naturalized), and residents of Texas. Newcomers need not wait to establish residency; anyone who has a Texas home address is eligible to vote. Persons who have been declared mentally incapacitated by the final judgment of a court of law are disqualified from voting. Individuals who have been convicted of serious crimes (felonies) lose the right to vote as well, at least temporarily. Convicted criminals in Texas are eligible to vote again after they have fully completed their sentences, including time served on probation or parole. (**Probation** is the suspension of a sentence, permitting the defendant to remain free under court supervision, whereas **parole** is the conditional release of convicted offenders from prison to serve the remainder of their sentences in the community under supervision.)

Individuals must register before they can vote. Registration becomes effective 30 days after an application is received, so prospective voters must apply at least a month before the election in which they want to cast a ballot. Either the county tax assessor-collector's office or, in smaller counties, the county clerk or an election administrator handles voter registration. Voter registration applications are readily available in driver's license offices, libraries, and other government offices and public places. They are printed in both English and Spanish, are easy to complete, and require only a person's name, gender, birth date, address, court of naturalization (if applicable), and signature.

Voter registration is permanent as long as voters keep their addresses current with county election officials. People who change addresses within the same county may return to their old polling place to vote for 90 days after their move. Every two years, however, county election officials mail out new voter registration certificates and purge from the voter rolls the names of people who are no longer at their listed addresses. Consequently, people who move must take the initiative to report changes of address in order to remain registered. Texans who relocate from one county to another must register again in their new county of residence. People who lose their voter certificates can request replacements from county election officials.

Voters cast their ballots in election precincts near their homes. An **election precinct** is a voting district. Rural counties may have only a handful of precincts, but

TEXAS ONLINE ★ Forces of Change

Online Voter Registration

Anyone with Internet access can obtain a voter registration application at the following Internet address: **www.sos.state.tx.us/elections/voter/reqvr.shtml**

Read the online voter information and answer the following questions.

QUESTIONS TO CONSIDER

1. Why do you think the application asks for your date of birth?
2. Why does it ask for your address?
3. Do you think that ordinary citizens are able to complete the voter registration application without assistance?

urban counties have hundreds. Harris County, the state's most populous county, has more than 900 election precincts. Precinct polling places are generally located in public buildings, such as schools or fire stations. Newspapers usually print a list of polling locations a day or so before an election. Prospective voters can also learn the polling place for their election precinct by telephoning the county clerk's office or checking a county website.

Texans can vote early if they wish. State law once limited early voting (formerly called absentee voting) to individuals who planned to be out of town on the day of the election or at least *said* they planned to be out of town—some people voted absentee in order to avoid Election-Day lines. In 1987, the legislature revised the election code to allow people to vote early without having to give an explanation and many Texans now take advantage of no-excuse early voting. The period for early voting begins 17 days before an election and ends four days before. Locations for early voting may be limited to the county clerk's office at the courthouse or a handful of branch offices located throughout the county.

It is also possible to vote early by mail. Individuals who expect to be out of the county on the day of the election and during the early voting period may write the county clerk's office and request a mail ballot. People age 65 and older and those who are disabled or ill may vote by mail as well. Students away at school have the option of voting by mail or registering and voting in the county where they attend classes.

Early voting affects both the composition of the electorate and the strategy of election campaigns. Research shows that early voting increases election turnout by less physically active older adults who might have difficulty getting to the polls on Election Day.[18] Candidates take advantage of early voting by organizing early get-out-the-vote drives. Because state law requires election officials to keep a running list of who has voted early and who has not, campaigns can concentrate on getting people to the polls who are most likely to be their supporters.

> "Voting is the first duty of democracy."
> —Lyndon B. Johnson, President of the United States, 1963–1969

Campaigning   People can participate in politics by working on election campaigns. Although this is the age of television campaigns and the Internet, volunteers still have a place in election campaigns because electronic wizardry is too expensive for many campaigns. Underfinanced campaigns can often compensate for a lack of money with well-organized volunteer efforts. Many local election contests rely almost exclusively on volunteers.

Campaigns ask volunteers to do work that demands energy and attention to detail. Volunteers often help with mass mailings. Although campaign professionals believe that direct mail is an effective means for getting a candidate's message across, sending letters and campaign literature to thousands of potential voters is a huge job. Computers can do the work, but that approach is expensive. Consequently, many campaigns use volunteers to flare envelopes, fold literature, stuff the literature into envelopes, seal the envelopes, affix address labels, and bundle the envelopes for mailing.

Some of the most important volunteer work involves staffing telephone banks. Campaigns spend thousands of dollars having dozens of phones installed a few weeks before the election. They either hire workers or recruit volunteers to call registered voters from lists that can be obtained from the county tax office. When volunteers call potential voters, they identify themselves as workers on the campaign of Candidate A and then ask: "Can Candidate A count on your support in the upcoming election?" The goal is to identify supporters and undecided voters. On Election Day, campaign volunteers call supporters and remind them to vote. Meanwhile, other volunteers mail literature to people who claimed to be undecided.

There is almost no end to the work volunteers perform in an election campaign. They assemble yard signs and distribute them to the candidate's supporters. They answer office telephones and deliver soft drinks and snacks to other volunteers. (One of the cardinal rules of a successful campaign is to feed the volunteers.) On Election Day, volunteers drive people who lack transportation to the polls and pass out campaign literature outside polling places.

? WHAT IS YOUR OPINION?

Can someone who does not vote still be a good citizen?

Other Forms of Participation   Voting and campaigning are not the only ways people participate in politics. People participate by working through a group. One person casting a single ballot or working alone for a candidate is not as effective as a group of people working together. Many Texans make their voices heard by taking part in such political organizations as the National Rifle Association (NRA), Mothers Against Drunk Driving (MADD), and the League of United Latin American Citizens (LULAC). The **National Rifle Association (NRA)** is an interest group organized to defend the rights of gun owners and defeat efforts at gun control. **Mothers Against Drunk Driving (MADD)** is an interest group that supports the reform of laws dealing with drunk driving. The **League of United Latin American Citizens (LULAC)** is a Latino interest group.

People participate in the policy process by contacting government officials. Citizens may send e-mail messages to their state legislators or telephone city council members. Individuals may speak before the board of trustees of the local school district or community college.

Some Americans participate in politics by engaging in protest demonstrations, rallies, and marches. In recent years, Texans have engaged in demonstrations to influence government policy on issues such as abortion, the war against Iraq, and state budget cuts for health care and children's services. Americans have a constitutional right to express their political views and that includes the right to protest publicly. As long as protestors do not break the law (by blocking traffic, for example), they are acting legally within the spirit and the letter of the U.S. Constitution.

Finally, some people go beyond peaceful protest to engage in acts of political violence, including the bombing of abortion clinics and destruction of property. Although political violence will draw attention to a cause, it is often counterproductive because it provokes a backlash. Most mainstream antiabortion groups, for example, disassociate themselves from individuals who advocate violence against abortion providers because they believe that violence undermines their cause with mainstream voters.

NATIONAL PERSPECTIVE

Mail Voting in Oregon

The state of Oregon conducted the 2000 presidential election entirely by mail. Election officials mailed out ballots to all registered voters between 18 and 14 days before Election Day. Voters could mail back the completed ballots up until the date of the election or drop them off at designated sites. Oregon now conducts all primary and general elections by mail.

Oregon election officials believe that mail balloting increased voter participation. In 1996, approximately 1.4 million Oregon voters cast ballots for president the old-fashioned way, in person and by traditional absentee ballot. The figure represented 71 percent of the state's registered voters. In contrast, the 2000 presidential election turnout was 1.6 million, 80 percent of registered voters.*

Mail balloting is popular with Oregon voters. Nearly three-fourths of the state's voters tell survey researchers that they prefer voting by mail to traditional in-person voting. Younger adults and voters over the age of 50 are the biggest supporters of the new system. They like mail balloting not only because it is convenient, but also because it gives them time to discuss races with their friends and family before deciding how to vote.[†]

QUESTIONS TO CONSIDER

1. Do you see any disadvantages to voting by mail?
2. Would you like to vote by mail rather than in person?
3. Do you think Texas and other states will adopt a mail voting system such as the Oregon procedure?

*Bill Bradbury, Oregon Secretary of State, "Report of the Oregon Elections Task Force," 2001, available at www.sos.state.or.us/

[†]Dave Scott, "Ways to Turn Out Voters," *State Government News* (February 2000): 18–19.

Participation Rates in Texas

Most adult Texans do not vote, even in high profile presidential elections. Figure 4.1 summarizes participation in the 2000 presidential election in Texas. As the figure indicates, nearly 14.5 million Texans were old enough to vote in 2000. Of that number, 12.4 million, 85 percent of the voting-age population, were registered to vote. Voter turnout, meanwhile, was 6.4 million, 44 percent of voting-age adults.

Turnout in elections that are not as high profile as a presidential contest is usually less than it is in a presidential race. Only 30 percent of the state's voting-age population participated in selecting a governor in 2002. Rick Perry, who was elected governor with 2.6 million votes, won the electoral support of just 17 percent of the state's potential electorate. Voter participation in the 2001 constitutional amendment election was even smaller, with less than 6 percent of the voting-age adult population.[19]

Compared with other states, the level of political participation in Texas is relatively low, at least in terms of voter turnout. Although voting is not the *only* form of participation, it is the most common form and the most easily measured. Figure 4.2 shows that less than 50 percent of the state's voting-age adult population has turned out to vote in every presidential election since 1980. Furthermore, each year voter turnout in Texas was well below the national average.

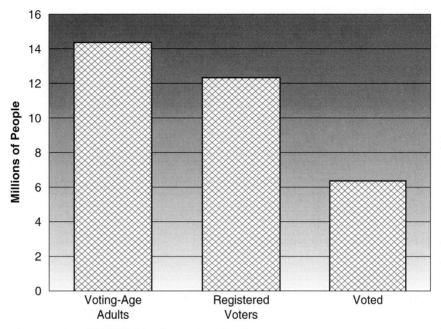

FIGURE 4.1 Participation in the 2000 Election
Source: Texas Secretary of State

Political scientists identify several factors that may account for the relatively low rate of political participation in the state. High levels of participation are associated with older, better-educated populations with relatively high incomes. Compared with other states, income levels in Texas are lower, the age distribution is younger, and levels of educational achievement are below average. All of these factors are related to lower levels of political participation.

The weakness of political parties and labor unions in Texas may be associated with relatively low levels of voter turnout. Strong parties and unions are able to educate citizens about politics and motivate them to participate politically.[20] They recruit voters. Political parties in Texas are generally less organized than parties in many other states. Furthermore, labor unions in Texas are weaker than unions in the Northeast and Midwest.

The relatively high percentage of recent immigrants to Texas may help account for the state's low participation rates. In general, newcomers to an area need a few years to settle into their new communities before becoming active in state and local political affairs. People vote because they are concerned about their communities, and new residents take time to identify with their new communities.[21] Newcomers to an area must also take the time to register to vote.[22] Furthermore, many of the state's immigrants are not yet American citizens and therefore they are ineligible to vote.

Finally, some political scientists believe that election frequency and ballot complexity reduce election turnout.[23] Considering the frequency of elections in Texas

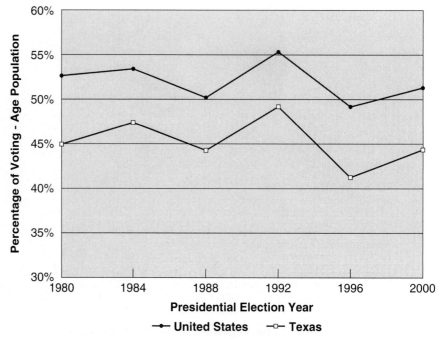

FIGURE 4.2 Voter Turnout, United States and Texas
Source: U.S. Census Bureau, Texas Secretary of State

and the length and complexity of the ballot (19 constitutional amendments in 2001!), it would be understandable if many of the state's voters suffer burnout.

Patterns of Participation

Participation rates vary among individuals based on income, age, and race/ethnicity. Middle- and upper-income groups participate at a higher rate than lower-income groups. According to **exit polls,** which are surveys based on random samples of voters leaving the polling place, 52 percent of Texas voters in 2000 had annual household incomes in excess of $50,000. In contrast, only 22 percent of the state's voters earned incomes of $30,000 or less.[24] The household income of the average voter was substantially higher than household income of the average Texan, which was less than $38,000 a year in 2000.[25]

The relationship between income and participation also holds true for forms of participation other than voting. A survey of local party activists in Texas and other southern states found that a majority of the activists of both political parties had family incomes of $40,000 a year or more.[26] Lower-income people are also considerably less likely to make campaign contributions than are the wealthy.[27]

Political participation increases with age until advanced age and ill health force the elderly to slow down.[28] National surveys show that voter participation by people under the age of 30 is typically 20 to 30 percentage points lower than it is among

More than 25 percent of Texas voters in 2000 were Latino, African American, or Asian American.

people over 30.[29] Younger adults have fewer resources and are less interested in the policy process than older adults. Young people today are also more cynical about politics and less engaged than earlier generations.[30] As adults mature, their incomes increase and their skills develop. Older adults establish roots in their communities that increase their interest and awareness of the political process.

The overall participation rates for African Americans and non-Hispanic whites are similar, while participation rates for Hispanics are substantially lower than they are for other racial and ethnic groups. According to the 2000 Census, the population of Texas was 52 percent non-Hispanic white, 32 percent Latino, 11 percent African American, 3 percent Asian, and 2 percent "other."[31] In contrast, the 2000 electorate in Texas was 73 percent non-Hispanic white, 10 percent Latino, 15 percent African American, 2 percent Asian, and 1 percent "other."[32] Both non-Hispanic whites and African Americans were overrepresented among voters, whereas Latinos and Asians were underrepresented.

Racial/ethnic patterns of participation reflect the importance of recruitment to political participation.[33] Political scientists would anticipate that participation rates for African American and Latino citizens would be lower than those for non-Hispanic whites because of income and age differences. As a group, minority citizens are less affluent and younger than non-Hispanic whites. Nonetheless, participation rates for African Americans exceed expectations because of the effectiveness of

"Young people today are not viewing politics as being relevant to their lives."
—Linda Sax, survey researcher

LEARNING EXERCISE

Participation Interview

Political scientists employ various research techniques to study political participation. Survey research is a method that scholars can use to study the behavior and attitudes of large groups of people. By using scientific sampling methods, survey researchers can study such topics as the relationship between age and voter turnout. Survey research has shown, for example, that voting participation increases with age until advanced age and ill health force the elderly to slow down.* In contrast, individual interviews enable researchers to examine the behavior and attitudes of individuals in more depth than survey research generally allows. Although it would not be valid for a scientist to generalize about an entire population from one interview or a small number of interviews, the insights gained from interviews are valuable for designing survey research studies and interpreting their results.

Your assignment is to interview someone you know about political participation and prepare a report documenting and discussing your research. You should begin by developing a set of questions designed to gather the following information about the individual that you interview:

• Age, race, gender, occupation, educational level, and income level.

• History of voting participation in elections for various offices, including president, governor, and local office.
• Attitude about voting.
• Reasons for voting (or not voting) in particular elections.

Keep in mind that some information can be obtained without asking. You will not need to ask your Aunt Millie, for example, if she is male or female or if she is white, African American, or Latino. You may also want to estimate her general age and general level of income rather than ask her those questions because she might be offended by the questions or unwilling to give you personal information.

Prepare your questions before the interview takes place and rehearse them so you can conduct a smooth interview. Be sure to get all the information you need, but do not waste the interviewee's time. Be prepared to take notes or tape record the interview.

Interview someone who is eligible to vote in Texas. The person can be a friend, acquaintance, or relative, but not someone who is taking a course in political science this semester. After you have completed the interview, prepare a written report in which you describe the person you interviewed and discuss that person's participation history and attitude toward political participation. When possible, relate the information you learned in your interview to political science research on political participation.

---

*M. Kent Jennings and Gregory B. Markus, "Political Involvement in the Later Years: A Longitudinal Survey," *American Journal of Political Science* 32 (May 1988): 302–16.

organizations in the African American community such as churches and political groups at stimulating participation. In contrast, participation rates for Latino Texans reflects the relative weakness of Latino political organizations at turning out the vote. Also, many of the state's Latino residents are not citizens or are younger than 18 years of age.

Men and women are equally likely to vote, but men are more likely than women to engage in other forms of political participation. Women comprised 51 percent of the Texas electorate in 2000, reflecting the gender distribution of the state's adult population.[34] Women and men are also equally likely to participate in election cam-

TABLE 4.1   Representation Based on Income, Education, and Age, 1986 Data

Population Characteristic	Texas	Mean of Fifty States
Income	50	67
Education	46	58
Age	43	47

Source: Robert A. Jackson, Robert D. Brown, and Gerald C. Wright, "Representation, Turnout, and the Electoral Representativeness of U.S. State Electorates," *American Politics Quarterly* 26 (July 1998): 259–87.

paigns. In contrast, women are less likely than men to contribute money to political campaigns, contact public officials, and join political organizations.[35]

Is the Texas Electorate Representative of the State's Population?

Political scientists Robert A. Jackson, Robert D. Brown, and Gerald C. Wright have published research comparing the population of each state with those people who vote.[36] To what degree, they ask, does the electorate resemble the state's adult population in terms of income, education, and age? Jackson, Brown, and Wright use a 100-point scale to show the results of their research. If the state's electorate has the same proportion of poor people as the state's population, the income score for that state would be 100. A score of 75 indicates that the state's electorate includes only 75 percent as many low-income people as the state's population.

Table 4.1 compares the scale scores for Texas with the national mean for the 50 states. Voters as a group are wealthier, better educated, and older than the state's adult population. This is true not only in the Lone Star State but also in other states. The Texas electorate, however, is less representative of the state population than the average state electorate, especially in terms of income and education. The proportion of poor people in the electorate in Texas is only 50 percent as large as it is in the state's adult population. The comparable figure for the average state is 67 percent. In sum, the poor are underrepresented among voters in all states, but they are more underrepresented in Texas than the average state.

The underrepresentation of Texans who are poor is the legacy of the state's long history of public policies designed to limit the right to vote to middle-class and upper-income white people. The white primary, poll tax, and restrictive voter registration requirements all discouraged or prevented poor Texans from registering to vote. Although federal intervention has forced the state to expand its electoral system to broad-based participation, the legacy of exclusion still affects voter turnout today. Parents who could not vote were unable to serve as participation role models for their children. Adult Texans who grew up in households with adults who could not vote are less likely to participate politically than are citizens who were raised in families that participated in the political process.

Ed Garza was elected mayor of San Antonio in 2001. As the state's electorate has grown more diverse, the number of Latino and African American officeholders has increased.

★ CONCLUSION: PARTICIPATION AND POLICYMAKING

Abraham Lincoln, the great American president of the Civil War era, described democracy as government of the people, by the people, and for the people. Political scientists would probably qualify Lincoln's characterization to add that democracy is government of, by, and for those people who participate. People who cannot participate in the policymaking process or who choose not to participate have no influence.

For decades, political participation in Texas was restricted to a narrow segment of society. The white primary coupled with boss control in south Texas limited meaningful participation to non-Hispanic whites. The poll tax ensured that middle- and upper-income voters would dominate elections. Minority citizens and low-income residents of all races had relatively little input into the state's policymaking process.

Federal intervention and demographic change have transformed the face of political participation in Texas. Court rulings, a constitutional amendment, and federal laws have knocked out the white primary, the poll tax, and other devices designed to restrict participation. Meanwhile, the potential electorate has expanded dramatically as the state's population has grown more diverse. African American, Latino, and Asian voters combined represented more than a fourth of the Texas electorate in 2000 and their numbers are certain to grow as the Latino and Asian populations age and obtain citizenship status and as older non-Hispanic white citi-

"Every election we see a higher percentage of Hispanics voting. It's a very young population and has had less education than other groups, but those differences are starting to go away."
—Jerry Polinard, political scientist

zens die. The Texas electorate in 2020 will be dramatically different in terms of race and ethnicity from the Texas electorate of the late twentieth century.

Agenda Building

For most of the twentieth century, the policy agenda in Texas reflected the values of the middle- and upper-income non-Hispanic whites who participated in the policymaking process. State and local government addressed issues of economic development, transportation, crime, and the defense of traditional values. Many Latino, African American, and low-income white Texans wanted government to address other issues, such as racial and ethnic discrimination, job training for low-skill workers, educational opportunities for their children, and health care for low-income families. Their voices were not heard because they were unable to participate meaningfully in the policymaking process.

As the Texas electorate has grown more diverse, the policy agenda has changed to include some of the concerns of the African American, Latino, and low-income residents of the state. In recent years, the state government has considered policies designed to address such issues as health care for children in low-income families, access to higher education for minority students, bias-motivated crimes, and racial profiling by state and local police officers. **Racial profiling** is the practice of a police officer targeting individuals as suspected criminals on the basis of their race or ethnicity.

Policy Formulation and Adoption

For decades, state government in Texas formulated and adopted conservative public policies favored by the state's non-Hispanic middle- and upper-income white electorate. **Conservatism** is the political view that seeks to preserve the political, economic, or social institutions of society against abrupt change. Conservatives generally oppose most government economic regulation and heavy government spending while favoring low taxes and traditional values. State government kept taxes low, relying on consumer taxes such as the sales tax instead of taxes on income. Government regulations were designed to promote business expansion rather than protect workers, consumers, or the environment. State services focused on promoting economic growth instead of providing services to help low-income families. Public policies reflected traditional social values by requiring racial segregation, prohibiting abortion, and outlawing same-gender sexual relations.

Many of the state's minority and low-income residents favored liberal policies, but they had no influence because they were unable to participate meaningfully in the policy process. **Liberalism** is the political view that seeks to change the political, economic, or social institutions of society to advance the development and well-being of the individual. Liberals believe that government should foster social progress by promoting social justice, political equality, and economic prosperity. Liberals usually favor government regulation and high levels of spending for social programs. On social issues, such as abortion and pornography regulation, liberals tend to support the right of adult free choice against government interference.

As the electorate has expanded, state officials have formulated and adopted public policies that reflect the interests of the state's more diverse electorate. In recent years, the Texas legislature has adopted legislation to increase the state's minimum wage to match the federal minimum, expand Medicaid coverage to include more low-income people, and enact hate-crimes legislation. The **minimum wage** is the lowest hourly wage that an employer can pay covered workers. **Medicaid** is a federal program designed to provide health insurance coverage to poor people, disabled persons, and elderly Americans who are impoverished. **Hate-crimes legislation** refers to a legislative measure that increases penalties for persons convicted of criminal offenses motivated by prejudice based on race, religion, national origin, gender, or sexual orientation.

Policy Implementation and Evaluation

Individual Texans play relatively little direct role in policy implementation. People support the efforts of police to enforce the law by reporting offenses to law officers and assisting in criminal investigations. Individuals may also file lawsuits to challenge the way state agencies implement policy.

Individuals play a larger role in policy evaluation than they do in policy implementation. Political scientists believe that citizens often base their voting choice on their evaluation of the effectiveness of public policies. The concept that voters choose candidates based on their perception of an incumbent candidate's past performance in office or the performance of the incumbent party is known as **retrospective voting.** If citizens are pleased with the performance of the government, they vote to reelect incumbent officeholders. (An **incumbent** is a current officeholder.) If they are unhappy with governmental performance, they vote against incumbent officials.

The changing face of the Texas electorate has changed the tone of policy evaluation. For decades, the only voices that counted in Texas politics were the voices of middle- and upper-income non-Hispanic whites. As the electorate has expanded, evaluation has changed. Consider the issue of racial profiling. The issue became part of the policy agenda in response to criticism from African American and Latino Texans who perceived that police officers frequently identified minority residents as criminal suspects based solely on their race or ethnicity. African American and Latino Texans have long been concerned about law enforcement practices in Texas, but only within the last few decades have they gained political influence necessary to have their concerns heard and acted on by state officials.

Conservative voices still dominate Texas politics, but they are no longer the only voices heard. The collapse of legal barriers to participation has enabled African American and Latino Texans to participate meaningfully in the state's policy debate. Furthermore, the rapid growth of the state's minority population ensures that African American, Latino, and Asian interests will have more policymaking influence in the twenty-first century than they did in the twentieth century.

★ REVIEW QUESTIONS

1. What are the arguments for and against the initiative process?

2. What measures were used in Texas to restrict the voting rights of minorities and how were those measures overcome?

3. What ways do individuals participate in Texas politics?

4. How do participation rates in Texas compare with those in other states?

5. Why are voter participation rates in Texas lower than those in other states?

6. Is the Texas electorate unrepresentative of the state's population?

7. How are changes in the state's electorate affecting the policymaking process?

★ KEY TERMS

abolition movement

conservatism

democracy

disfranchisement

election precinct

enfranchise

Equal Protection Clause

exit polls

franchise

hate-crimes legislation

incumbent

initiative process

League of United Latin American Citizens (LULAC)

liberalism

Medicaid

minimum wage

Mothers Against Drunk Driving (MADD)

National Rifle Association (NRA)

parole

poll tax

primary election

probation

racial profiling

retrospective voting

suffrage

term limitation

white primary

★ NOTES

1. David M. Hedge, *Governance and the Changing American States* (Boulder, CO: Westview, 1998), pp. 32–33.

2. Mark A. Smith, "Ballot Initiatives and the Democratic Citizen," *Journal of Politics* 64 (August 2002): 892–903.

3. Stephen M. Nichols, "State Referendum Voting, Ballot Roll-off, and the Effect of New Electoral Technology," *State and Local Government Review* 30 (Spring 1998): 107.

4. *Romer v. Evans*, 517 U.S. 620 (1996).

5. Nichols, p. 107.

6. Elizabeth A. Taylor, "The Woman Suffrage Movement in Texas," *Journal of Southern History* 17 (May 1951): 194–215.

7. Merline Pitre, *Through Many Dangers, Toils and Snares: Black Leadership in Texas, 1868–1900* (Austin: Eakin Press, 1985).

8. V. O. Key, Jr., *Southern Politics in State and Nation* (New York: Alfred A. Knopf, 1949).

9. *Historical Statistics of the United States* (Washington, DC: U.S. Government Printing Office, 1975), pp. 1071–72.

10. Dudley Lynch, *Duke of Duval* (Waco: Texian Press, 1978).

11. *Nixon v. Herndon*, 273 U.S. 536 (1927).

12. *Nixon v. Condon*, 286 U.S. 73 (1932).

13. *Grovey v. Townsend*, 295 U.S. 45 (1935).

14. *Smith v. Allwright*, 321 U.S. 649 (1944).

15. *Terry v. Adams*, 345 U.S. 461 (1953).

16. *United States v. Texas*, 384 U.S. 155 (1966).

17. *Beare v. Smith*, 321 F. Supp. 1100 (1971).

18. William Lyons and John M. Scheb II, "Early Voting and the Timing of the Vote: Unanticipated Consequences of Electoral Reform," *State and Local Government Review* 31 (Spring 1999): 148.

19. Texas Secretary of State, "Turnout and Voter Registration Figures (1970–current)," available at **www.sos.state.tx.us/**.

20. G. Bingham Powell, Jr., "American Voter Turnout in Comparative Perspective," *American Political Science Review* 80 (March 1986): 17–43.

21. André Blais, *To Vote or Not to Vote?* (Pittsburgh: University of Pittsburgh Press, 2000), p. 13.

22. Peverill Squire, Raymond E. Wolfinger, and David P. Glass, "Residential Mobility and Voter Turnout," *American Political Science Review* 81 (March 1987): 45–65.

23. Richard W. Boyd, "Election Calendars and Voter Turnout," *American Politics Quarterly* 14 (January–April 1986): 89–104.

24. "Exit Polls for Texas," available at **www.cnn.com/election/2000/results/index.epolls.html**.

25. U.S. Census Bureau, "Income 1999," available at **www.census.gov**.

26. Charles D. Hadley and Lewis Bowman, eds., *Party Activists in Southern Politics* (Knoxville, TN: University of Tennessee Press, 1998), p. 6.

27. Sidney Verba, Kay Lehman Schlozman, and Henry E. Brady, *Voice and Equality: Civic Volunteerism in American Politics* (Cambridge, MA: Harvard University Press, 1995), p. 190.

28. M. Kent Jennings and Gregory B. Markus, "Political Involvement in the Later Years: A Longitudinal Survey," *American Journal of Political Science* 32 (May 1988): 302–16.

29. Lynn M. Casper and Loretta E. Bass, "Voting and Registration in the Election of November 1996," (Washington, DC: Bureau of the Census, 1998), **www.census.gov/population/www/socdemo/voting.html**.

30. Sheilah Mann, "What the Survey of American College Freshmen Tells Us about Their Interest in Politics and Political Science," *PS: Political Science and Politics* (June 1999): 263–68.

31. U.S. Census Bureau, "Population by Race and Hispanic or Latino Origin," available at **www.census.gov**.

32. "Exit Polls for Texas," available at **www.cnn.com/election/2000/results/index.epolls.html**.

33. Henry E. Brady, Sidney Verba, and Kay Lehman Schlozman, "Beyond SES: A Resource Model of Political Participation," *American Political Science Review* 89 (June 1995): 271–94.

34. "Exit Polls for Texas," available at **www.cnn.com/election/2000/results/index.epolls.html**.

35. Verba, Schlozman, and Brady, *Voice and Equality: Civic Volunteerism in American Politics*, p. 255.

36. Robert A. Jackson, Robert D. Brown, and Gerald C. Wright, "Representation, Turnout, and the Electoral Representativeness of U.S. State Electorates," *American Politics Quarterly* 26 (July 1998): 259–87.

Interest Groups

LEARNING OBJECTIVES

After studying Chapter 5, students should be able to do the following:

★ Describe the key issues underlying the debate over medical malpractice insurance reform and identify the groups active on either side of the controversy.

★ Identify the various types of interest groups active in Texas politics and evaluate their relative influence on the policymaking process.

★ Identify the basic political goals for each of the following types of interest groups: business groups and trade associations; professional associations; organized labor; agricultural groups; racial and ethnic minority groups; religious groups; and citizen, advocacy, and cause groups.

★ Describe the tactics that interest groups employ to achieve their goals.

★ Describe the techniques used by successful lobbyists to influence the policymaking process.

★ Evaluate the scheme devised by Thomas and Hrebenar for classifying the influence of interest groups in the state policymaking process.

★ Describe the role that interest groups play in the state's policymaking process.

★ Define the key terms listed on page 126 and explain their significance.

Many Texas doctors complain that the high cost of medical malpractice insurance is driving them out of business. Between 1987 and 2002, malpractice insurance premiums rose by 400 percent in Texas.[1] Some physicians, especially doctors with high-risk specializations, declare that they can no longer afford to remain in practice. According to the American Medical Association (AMA), the annual cost of malpractice insurance for a Texas physician ranges from $10,000 to $117,000 a year, depending on the specialization.[2]

The **Texas Medical Association (TMA),** a professional organization of physicians, believes that the solution to the problem is a cap on the amount of money a jury can award in noneconomic damages. Economic damages awarded in a medical malpractice lawsuit include lost wages and the cost of medical care. Noneconomic damages include money to compensate for disfigurement, loss of companionship, pain, suffering, and **punitive damages,** which are monetary awards given in a lawsuit to punish a defendant for a particularly evil, malicious, or fraudulent act. The TMA notes that the California legislature capped noneconomic damages in medical malpractice cases at $250,000 in 1975. Since then, medical malpractice premiums in California have risen by only 167 percent compared to an increase of 500 percent in the rest of the country.[3]

The **Texas Trial Lawyers Association (TTLA),** which is an organization of attorneys who represent plaintiffs in personal injury lawsuits, blames bad doctors and a weak stock market for rising medical malpractice premiums rather than excessive jury awards. The TTLA notes that data provided by the insurance companies show that noneconomic damages awarded by juries in medical malpractice cases have actually been falling. In 1988, Texas juries awarded $60 million in noneconomic damages and $88 million in economic damages. In 2000, jury awards for noneconomic damages stood at $40 million while economic awards had risen to $298 million.[4] The TTLA contends that malpractice awards have been climbing because the Texas State Board of Medical Examiners has failed to purge the profession of the small number of bad doctors who are guilty of malpractice. Between 1997 and 2002, the Board of Medical Examiners failed to revoke the license of a single physician for committing medical errors.[5] Furthermore, the TTLA believes that insurance companies are increasing premiums to make up for poor investments. When the stock market is doing well, insurance companies make enough money on investments to keep their premiums low. When the market is weak, as it was in the early years of this decade, insurance companies increase premiums to make up for their investment losses.[6]

The battle over medical malpractice insurance reform features some of the most powerful interest groups in Texas politics. An **interest group** is an organization of people who join together voluntarily on the basis of some interest they share for the purpose of influencing policy. Although the TMA and the TTLA are the main combatants, other groups are involved as well. Business groups and trade associations support the efforts of the TMA because they want the legislature to limit lawsuits in general, not just medical malpractice lawsuits. The revision of state laws to limit the ability of plaintiffs in personal injury lawsuits to recover damages in court is known as **tort reform.** Meanwhile, consumer groups, such as Public Citizen and Texas Watch, join forces with the TTLA to oppose medical malpractice reform in particu-

"[Medical malpractice insurance premiums] are driving physicians across the country out of business."
—Dr. Donald Palmisano, American Medical Association

lar and tort reform in general because they want to defeat legislation that would make it more difficult for injured consumers to file suit and recover damages.

> "Limits on medical malpractice insurance penalize patients most severely injured by medical malpractice."
> —Carlton Carl, Association of American Trial Lawyers

Interest groups are important participants in the policymaking process. Groups on both sides of the controversy over medical malpractice insurance attempt to influence the policymaking process by contributing to the election campaigns of candidates for governor, the legislature, and judicial offices. Groups for and against medical malpractice reform conduct public relations campaigns to sway public opinion. They lobby lawmakers and other officials to formulate, adopt, and implement the policies they prefer. Finally, groups attempt to influence policy evaluation by interpreting the impact of policies in a light favorable to their interests.

This chapter is the second in a series of four chapters examining the political environment for policymaking. Chapter 4 discussed political participation in Texas. Chapters 6 and 7 will focus on political parties and elections. This chapter studies the role of interest groups in the policymaking process. It identifies the major interest groups active in the state, discusses the strategies and tactics interest groups employ to achieve their goals, and evaluates the impact of groups on the policymaking process.

? WHAT IS YOUR OPINION?

Do you favor capping the amount of money that juries can award for noneconomic damages in medical malpractice cases?

★ INTEREST GROUPS IN TEXAS POLITICS

> "People think they are not in power, and the special interests are—and I think they are right."
> —Don McAdams, former Texas legislator who is now a lobbyist

Most Texans have an interest in the policies of state and local government in Texas, but not all Texans have organized to promote and defend their interests. Compare and contrast the position of college students with that of the people who manage large energy companies, such as Reliant Energy and Texas Utilities. Both groups have an interest in state and local government. Public policies dealing with college funding, university admissions, course transfers, tuition, and the availability of scholarships and financial aid affect college students. In the meantime, energy company executives have an interest in electricity deregulation, property taxes, and government regulations dealing with environmental pollution, electric power transmission, and workplace safety. College students and energy company executives are not equally organized. College students have little if any interest group representation. Although student organizations exist at many of the state's colleges and universities, their primary focus is not political. In contrast, energy company executives are organized both by firm and by industry groups. They are widely regarded as being among the most influential voices in state and local government.

We begin our study of interest groups by identifying the most important organized interests in Texas politics. Who are the interests, how well are they organized, what do they want from state and local government, and how effective are they at achieving their goals?

Business Groups and Trade Associations

Business groups and trade associations are the most powerful interest groups in Texas politics. Other groups may be influential at particular levels of government, on certain issues, and at certain points in the policy process, but business interests are important everywhere, from the county courthouse to the governor's mansion. Whereas other interests focus on one issue or a narrow range of issues, business voices are heard on virtually every major policy issue, whether education finance, insurance regulation, medical malpractice insurance reform, water development, or transportation.

Business interests pursue their political goals both as individual firms and through trade associations. Bank of America, Reliant Energy, SBC Communications, State Farm Insurance, and other large business enterprises are major players in state politics. Business groups also work through **trade associations,** which are organizations representing the interests of firms and professionals in the same general field. The Texas Association of Builders, for example, is a trade association representing the interests of building contractors. The Mid-Continent Oil and Gas Association is a trade association that speaks for the interests of the major oil producers, whereas the Texas Independent Producers and Royalty Owners Association is a trade association for relatively small, independent oil and gas companies. The **Texas Association of Business (TAB)** is a trade association for business firms ranging from giant corporations to small neighborhood business establishments. The TAB, which includes local chambers of commerce in its organizational structure, is perhaps the single most powerful interest group organization in the state.

Business groups and trade associations are effective because they are organized, well-financed, and skilled in advocating their positions. Business people usually know what they want from government and have the financial and organizational resources to pursue their goals aggressively. Furthermore, business groups as a whole enjoy a relatively favorable public image. Although the alcohol, gambling, and tobacco industries have public relations problems, most Texans have a favorable image of business in general, especially small business.

"We're going to have to get about the business of creating jobs and driving the economy, and the only way to do that is with a healthy business climate."
—Chuck McDonald, political consultant

Business groups and trade associations generally agree on the need to maintain a **good business climate,** which is a political environment in which business would prosper. Business people believe that tort reform is an important element of a good business climate because it reduces the premium costs to business of insurance against lawsuit judgments. In general, a good business environment includes low tax rates on business, laws that restrict union influence, and regulation favorable to business growth. More and more, business interests also support education to train the skilled, well-educated workforce needed for high-tech development.

When business groups and trade associations are united, they usually get what they want in Texas. The battle over tort reform illustrates the power of business interests united behind a particular policy objective. During the 1990s, the Texas legislature passed and the governor signed legislation enacting the following tort reform measures:

- **Frivolous lawsuits:** The legislature and the governor adopted legislation allowing judges to punish plaintiffs for filing lawsuits that the court

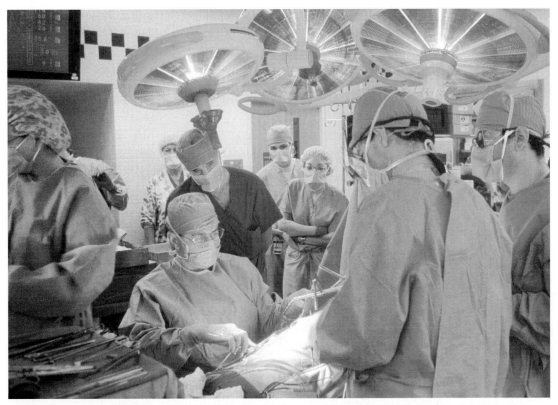

Many Texas physicians complain that the high cost of medical malpractice insurance is driving them out of business.

determined were without merit. The judge could fine the plaintiff or order the plaintiff to pay the attorney's fees for the defendant.

- **Punitive damages:** The legislature and the governor made it more difficult for plaintiffs to recover punitive damages. They also capped the amount of punitive damages that could be awarded to twice the economic damages suffered by the plaintiff, such as medical bills and lost wages, plus no more than $750,000 for pain and suffering.

- **Forum shopping:** The legislature and the governor limited the locations in which a plaintiff could file a personal injury lawsuit to the county of the principal office of the defendant, the site where the injury occurred, and the residence of the defendant.

- **Joint and several liability reform:** The legislature and the governor limited the applicability of **joint and several liability,** which is the legal requirement that a defendant with "deep pockets" held partially liable for a plaintiff's injury must pay the full damage award for those defendants unable to pay. In most personal injury lawsuits, a defendant cannot be held 100 percent responsible for a judgment unless the defendant is deemed at least 50 percent responsible for the injury.[7]

- **Lawsuit immunity:** The legislature and the governor have passed legislation sheltering some potential defendants from liability suits, including medical providers who volunteer their help to charitable organizations. The state also prevents city governments from filing product liability lawsuits against firearms manufacturers.

In 2003, the legislature and governor reacted to the crisis over medical malpractice insurance by adopting a new set of tort reform measures:

- **Caps on noneconomic damages:** Patients injured by medical malpractice can recover no more than $250,000 in noneconomic damages from a physician or other health care provider. If a hospital, clinic, or nursing home is also found liable, the patient can recover a maximum $250,000 each from two other parties for a total cap of $750,000.

- **Protection against product liability suits:** The manufacturers of defective products are shielded from liability if they followed federal standards or regulatory requirements.

- **Joint and several liability reform:** Juries may allocate fault among all responsible parties, including parties with no financial assets. In cases involving automobile accidents, juries may also be informed whether the injured party was wearing a seat belt or in a car seat when apportioning liability.

Business groups also enjoy considerable influence with the judicial branch of Texas government, which is responsible for implementing tort reform legislation. Business interests who lose personal injury lawsuits or consumer fraud cases are more than twice as likely to win on appeal in the courts of appeal as are individual consumers who appeal.[8] Business groups are even more successful before the Texas Supreme Court. According to a study conducted by Texas Watch Foundation, a consumer research and education organization, insurance and corporate defendants won 79 percent of the cases during the 2002–2003 session of the Texas Supreme Court. Consumer interests won just 19 percent of the time. No clear winner could be determined in the other 2 percent of cases.[9]

Business interests are more influential in Texas politics than they are in national politics because they have fewer competitors in Texas than they do at the national level or in many other states. Organized labor, consumer groups, environmental organizations, and other groups that often oppose business interests on various policy issues are relatively weak in the Lone Star State. The best that the organizations opposed to tort reform have been able to accomplish, for example, has been to limit the extent of their defeat. The TTLA, the major organization against tort reform, enjoys considerable financial resources, but it has been outspent and out-organized by business interests. In 2002, 46 of the top 50 contributors to candidates for statewide executive positions and legislative office in Texas were business executives; only two were attorneys.[10]

Nonetheless, business interests do not get everything they want in Texas because they are not always united. Big business and small business sometimes have different

"The only folks hurt in the pocketbook by this lawsuit-reform measure are the plaintiffs' lawyers."
—Governor Rick Perry commenting on the 2003 tort reform measure

perspectives. During a recent legislative session, for example, some of the state's largest landfill operators—Browning Ferris Industries, Waste Management, Inc., and USA Waste—joined forces to fight a bill that would have reduced environmental standards on landfills. The big firms opposed the measure because they had already invested millions of dollars to comply with state requirements and did not want smaller competitors to be able to compete with them without paying the price.[11]

Business interests in different fields sometimes clash as well. Downtown business interests and suburban retailers fight over the location of civic centers and sports facilities, Sunday-closing laws, and urban mass transit. Downtown interests prefer economic development policies aimed at attracting office-space occupants and retail customers to the central business district, such as the construction of new downtown sports and theater complexes. In contrast, suburban interests favor policies that promote suburban development, such as highway construction and flood control.

Professional Associations

Professional associations are politically influential because of the relatively high socioeconomic status of their members. Doctors, dentists, lawyers, realtors, and other professionals generally have the financial resources to make their voices heard. Furthermore, they enjoy an added advantage in that many elected officials come from the ranks of professionals, especially lawyers. Public officials who happen to be lawyers, for example, are more likely to understand and sympathize with the policy perspectives of attorneys than are officials who lack legal training.

Professional associations concern themselves with public policies that affect their members. Doctors and lawyers battle one another over medical damage award caps in malpractice lawsuits. Real estate professionals are primarily concerned with public policies affecting real estate transactions, such as home equity lending and professional licensure.

Organized Labor

Organized labor is relatively weak in Texas. State laws make it difficult for unions to organize workers and easy for business to use nonunion labor. Texas is a "right to work" state. A **right to work law** is a statute prohibiting a union shop. A **union or closed shop** is a workplace in which every employee must be a member of a union. In states without right to work laws, the employees in a particular workplace may vote whether to create a union shop. If a majority of the workers agree, everyone employed in the plant must join the union and pay union dues. Union membership becomes mandatory. In a right to work state, union organizers are forced to recruit members individually.

Nationally, labor unions are strongest in the large, industrialized states of the Northeast and Midwest, the region known as the **Frostbelt.** In 2002, a fourth of the workforce in New York belonged to unions while the unionization rate in Michigan was 21.1 percent. In contrast, organized labor is not nearly as well established in the states of the South and Southwest, the **Sunbelt.** Only 5.1 percent of Texas workers belonged to unions in 2002 compared to a national unionization rate of 13.2 percent. Texas ranked 48th among the 50 states in the level of unionization.[12]

TEXAS ONLINE ★ Forces of Change

Texas Interest Groups

Many of the state's interest groups have websites publicizing issue positions, mission statements, news, and contact information.

- Lone Star Chapter of the Sierra Club (environmental group): **www.texas.sierraclub.org/**
- Texas Right to Life Committee (antiabortion group): **www.texasrighttolife.com/**
- Public Citizen (consumer rights and environmental group): **www.citizen.org/texas/**
- Texas Public Interest Research Group (public interest advocacy group founded by students): **www.volunteersolutions.org/ut/org/215394.html**
- Children's Defense Fund of Texas (advocacy group for children): **www.cdftexas.org/issues/**
- Texas AIDS Network (AIDS advocacy group): **www.texasaids.net/contributions_main.htm**
- Texas Eagle Forum (interest group focusing on traditional values): **www.texaseagle.org/**
- Texas Abortion and Reproductive Rights Action League (pro-choice group): **www.taral.org/html/**
- Texas Freedom Network (interest group focusing on opposition to religious conservatives): **www.tfn.org/**
- American Civil Liberties Union of Texas (interest group focusing on civil liberties issues): **www.aclutx.org/**
- Texas League of United Latin American Citizens (Latino rights organization): **www.texaslulac.org/**
- League of Women Voters of Texas (nonpartisan group focusing on voter education): **www.lwvtexas.org/**
- Texas State Conference of NAACP Branches (African American rights organization): **www.texasnaacp.org/**

- Texas Common Cause (nonpartisan group focusing on campaign finance reform and ethics in government): **www.ccsi.com/~comcause/**
- Texas Watch (consumer group): **www.texaswatch.org/**
- Texas State Rifle Association (group opposed to gun control): **www.tsra.com/**
- The Metropolitan Organization (Houston-area faith-based nonpartisan organization focusing on civic education): **www.tmohouston.net/**
- Texas Christian Coalition (conservative Christian group): **www.texascc.org/**
- Gay and lesbian political groups (gay and lesbian rights organizations):
  Houston—**www.hglpc.org/pages/1/index.htm**
  Dallas—**www.divanet.com/dgla/**
  Austin—**www.outaustin.org/**
  San Antonio—**saerpc.unitysa.org**
  El Paso—**www.members.aol.com/EquityEP/**
- National Organization for Women chapters in Texas (women's rights organizations): **www.now.org/chapters/tx.html**

Check out the websites of one of the groups and answer the following questions.

QUESTIONS TO CONSIDER

1. What issues does the group stress in its website?
2. Does it appear that the group is more interested in raising money, recruiting volunteers, or both?
3. Would you describe the group's website as organized and informative? Why or why not?

In Texas, labor unions are strongest in the state's more heavily industrialized areas, such as the Texas Gulf Coast and the Dallas-Fort Worth area. Organized labor has political influence in Houston, Dallas, and Fort Worth, and labor unions may be the single most important political force in Pasadena, Deer Park, and the Golden Triangle area of Beaumont, Port Arthur, and Orange. Unions also have influence within the organization of the state Democratic Party.

Most Texas unions belong to the **American Federation of Labor-Congress of Industrial Organizations (AFL-CIO),** which is a national association of unions.

The Texas AFL-CIO includes Texas affiliates of the Communications Workers of America, International Brotherhood of Electrical Workers, Fire Fighters, American Federation of Government Employees, National Association of Letter Carriers, International Association of Machinists, Oil, Chemical, and Atomic Workers, American Federation of State, County, and Municipal Employees (AFSCME), and Texas Federation of Teachers. The fastest growing unions are those representing service sector workers and government employees.

Private-sector unions are concerned with employee compensation, working conditions, job availability, job training, and state laws affecting the ability of unions to organize. The AFL-CIO favors increasing the state minimum wage, which covers farm workers and other employees not covered by the federal minimum wage. The **minimum wage** is the lowest hourly wage that an employer can pay covered workers. Unions also favor education, job training, and other social programs that benefit working class families.

Public employee organizations are similar to private sector unions in that they want higher wages, secure jobs, salaries based on seniority rather than merit, attractive fringe benefits, and good working conditions. Teachers' organizations, for example, worry about state reductions in their health insurance and retirement benefits. Fire and police unions are concerned with the state civil services' rules for municipal fire and police employees. Public employee organizations also address issues related to the professional concerns of their members. Teachers groups, for example, participate in policy debates over school funding and the ratio of students to teachers. Police organizations take positions on proposals to revise the state's criminal laws.

Agricultural Groups

Agricultural interests have long been powerful in Texas politics. In the nineteenth century, the most influential political voices in the state were those of major landowners and the rural population was large enough to overwhelm the city vote in statewide elections. Even after Texas became an urban, industrial state, rural interests continued to exercise disproportionate power. Rural areas were overrepresented in the legislature and farm groups were politically skillful.

Urbanization has weakened agricultural interests in Texas, but farm groups retain influence. As a group, farmers and ranchers are politically astute, organized, and knowledgeable about how to exert influence in state politics. In fact, a great deal of agriculture in Texas has become agribusiness, run by corporations that possess all the political skills and advantages of big business in general. Also, many of the policy goals of agricultural interests have long since been achieved and entrenched in law or the state constitution. As a result, agricultural interest groups have the advantage of defending ground already won rather than pushing for new policies.

Agriculture is a tenuous business and farmers are well aware that government actions can frequently determine whether they make a profit or go broke. Taxes are an area of concern. Farmers on the outskirts of metropolitan areas, for example, can be hurt by rising property taxes. As the big city sprawls in their direction, the value of their land goes up, but so do their property taxes. Their crops, though, are worth no more. Farm groups have lobbied successfully to have farmland taxed on its value as farmland, not on its value as the site of a future subdivision. Agricultural interests have also won tax breaks on the purchase of farm machinery, seed grain, and fertilizer.

Agricultural groups have other interests as well. They are concerned with state laws and regulations affecting agriculture, such as livestock quarantine requirements and restrictions on the use of pesticides. They support generous state funding for agricultural research conducted at Texas A&M University. Water development and conservation are increasingly becoming important for agricultural interests concerned about irrigation farming.

As with business interests, agricultural groups in Texas are not always united. The concerns of the family farm and agribusiness do not always coincide. Many government programs that benefit the corporate farm have hurt the small farmer. Regional disputes also flare. For example, west Texas agricultural interests once advocated a plan for pumping water from east Texas to their part of the state. Farm and ranch interests in east Texas fought the plan, fearing it would hurt agriculture in their region.

Racial and Ethnic Minority Groups

Racial and ethnic minority groups enjoy some political influence in Texas. The two best-known minority rights organizations in the state are affiliates of well-known national organizations. The Texas **League of United Latin American Citizens (LULAC)** is a Latino interest group and the Texas chapter of the **National Association for the Advancement of Colored People (NAACP)** is an interest group organized to represent the interests of African Americans.

Minority groups are interested in the enforcement of laws protecting the voting rights of minority citizens, the election and appointment of minority Texans to state and local offices, college and university admission policies, and inner-city development. In recent sessions of the legislature, Latino and African American members have pushed for passage of legislation concerning hate crimes and racial profiling. **Hate-crimes legislation** refers to legislative measures that increase penalties for persons convicted of criminal offenses motivated by prejudice based on race, religion, national origin, gender, or sexual orientation. **Racial profiling** is the practice of a police officer targeting individuals as suspected criminals on the basis of their race or ethnicity. Latino and African American legislators have also pushed

GETTING INVOLVED

Joining a Group

People who want to influence policy in a particular issue area should join a group. The Texas Online feature found on p.112 includes the websites of a number of interest groups active in Texas politics. Each of these groups is a membership organization in that it invites the participation of ordinary citizens.

Contact the group whose values and viewpoints most nearly conform to your own and find out how you can join the group and contribute to its work. Get on the group's mailing list, give money to the organization, attend meetings, and volunteer.

It's your government—get involved!

for changes in the state's **capital punishment** (death penalty) law to provide jurors with the option of sentencing persons convicted of capital murder to life without parole rather than death by lethal injection. Many minority-rights advocates believe that the death penalty is often implemented in a fashion that discriminates against minority defendants.

Racial and ethnic minority groups are considerably more influential in Texas politics today than they were in the early 1960s. More African American and Latino Texans are registered to vote than ever before. In 2000, Latino, African American, and Asian Texans comprised more than 25 percent of the statewide vote.[13] No serious candidate for statewide or municipal office in the state's big cities can afford to ignore African American and Hispanic concerns. Latino and African American legislators have also become an important voting bloc in the state legislature.

Nonetheless, racial and ethnic minority groups are not as powerful as the more established interest groups in the state. Racial and ethnic minority groups are sometimes divided among themselves and almost always short of funds. Many minority residents are not registered to vote; others stay home on Election Day. Furthermore, African American and Hispanic voters do not necessarily follow the political lead of groups such as LULAC and the NAACP.

The League of United Latin American Citizens (LULAC) is an interest group representing the political concerns of Americans of Hispanic descent.

Religious Groups

Churches and other religious institutions provide the foundation for a number of political organizations. Roman Catholic and Protestant churches in poor and minority areas have helped organize political groups to support health care, education, and neighborhood improvement for the state's poor people. These organizations include Communities Organized for Public Service (COPS) in San Antonio, Interfaith Alliance in the Rio Grande Valley, The Metropolitan Organization (TMO) in Houston, and the El Paso Inter-religious Sponsoring Organization (EPISO).

The most active and probably most influential religiously oriented political groups statewide are associated with the **religious right,** who are individuals who hold conservative social views because of their religious beliefs. Perhaps the most important conservative religious organization in Texas is the **Christian Coalition.** It opposes abortion, pornography, sex and violence on television, gay and lesbian rights, sex education, and evolution. The Christian Coalition favors sexual abstinence before marriage, prayer in schools, home schooling, and family values in general.

Conservative Christian groups are influential within the state Republican Party and in low-turnout elections. In recent years, Conservative Christians have comprised a majority of the delegates to the state convention of the Texas Republican Party. Furthermore, the Christian Coalition and other groups allied to the conservative Christian movement have elected candidates to a number of local school boards and the state board of education.

> "There's not anything wrong in trying to get God's people to vote."
>
> —The late W. A. Criswell, pastor, First Baptist Church, Dallas

Citizen, Advocacy, and Cause Groups

Citizen groups are organizations created to support government policies that they believe will benefit the public at large. **Common Cause** is a group organized to work for campaign finance reform and other good government causes. Common Cause supports campaign finance reform and ethics regulations for public officials. Texas Public Interest Research Group (Tex-PIRG) is a consumer rights organization.

Advocacy groups are organizations created to seek benefits on behalf of persons who are unable to represent their own interests. The Children's Defense Fund, for example, is an organization that attempts to promote the welfare of children. The Texas AIDS Network represents the interests of people with HIV/AIDS.

Cause groups are organizations whose members care intensely about a single issue or a group of related issues. The **Texas Right to Life Committee,** for example, opposes abortion whereas the **Texas Abortion and Reproductive Rights Action League (TARAL)** favors abortion rights. The **Sierra Club** is an environmental organization. Other cause groups include the **National Rifle Association (NRA), National Organization for Women (NOW),** and the **American Association of Retired Persons (AARP).** The NRA is an interest group organized to defend the rights of gun owners and defeat efforts at gun control. NOW is a group that promotes women's rights. The AARP is an interest group representing the concerns of older Americans.

> "A group contributes to a legislator that they [sic] know is philosophically aligned with them [sic], so that legislator is going to go and vote in their [sic] way because they share common philosophies."
>
> —Mike Martin, former member of the Texas legislature

Citizen groups, advocacy groups, and cause groups vary in political influence. The Texas NRA is the dominant force in the state on the issue of gun control. Texas has some of the most gun-friendly firearms regulations in the country. In contrast, the Lone Star Chapter of the Sierra Club struggles to have a significant political impact.

INTEREST GROUP TACTICS

Interest groups employ a variety of tactics in an effort to achieve their goals.

Electioneering

Interest groups attempt to influence public policy by participating in the electoral process. Groups with a large membership and/or influence beyond their ranks try to affect election outcomes by endorsing favored candidates and delivering a bloc vote on their behalf. Unions, racial and ethnic minority groups, and some citizen groups regularly use this strategy. In 2002, for example, the Texas Right to Life Committee endorsed Republican Governor Rick Perry for governor while the Texas AFL-CIO threw its support behind Tony Sanchez, the Democratic Party nominee for governor.

"We openly support tort reform candidates from both parties. We play for big stakes, and we play fair, and we play to win."

—Dick Trabulsi, Jr., chair, TLR PAC

The most effective tool interest groups have for affecting election outcomes is money. Interest groups contribute to candidates they support through their **political action committees (PACs),** which are organizations created to raise and distribute money in political campaigns. People associated with the interest group such as union members and business executives contribute money to the group's PAC, which, in turn, gives money to candidates for office. Executives with Reliant Energy, for example, contribute to Reliant Energy PAC. Texas physicians give money to the TMA PAC, while trial lawyers contribute to the TTLA PAC.

Texas does not limit the amount of money individuals, businesses, or PACs can contribute in election campaigns and some interest groups take advantage of the opportunity to give large amounts of money to the candidates of their choice. Groups involved in the tort reform debate were particularly generous during the 2001–2002 election cycle. Figure 5.1 graphs the amount of campaign contributions given by three of the major financial players in the battle over medical malpractice reform— TMA PAC, TTLA PAC, and Texans for Lawsuit Reform (TLR) PAC, which is a PAC organized by business interests who support tort reform. As the figure shows, the two PACs supporting tort reform significantly outspent the trial lawyers' PAC.

Interest groups consider several factors in determining which candidates to support. When all other considerations are equal, groups back candidates who are sympathetic with their policy preferences. In the 2002 election campaign, the TMA PAC and TLR PAC supported candidates favoring tort reform, mostly Republicans, whereas the TTLA PAC gave its money to tort reform opponents, mostly Democrats. Interest groups also consider the likelihood of a candidate's winning the election because groups want to back winners. Interest group leaders would rather give to a strong candidate who is only somewhat supportive of their group than throw their money away on an almost certain loser who is completely behind the group's

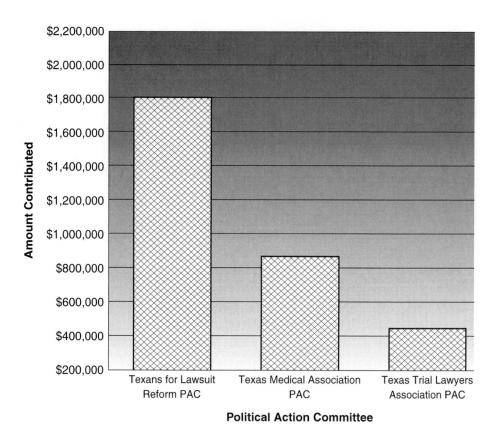

FIGURE 5.1 **Campaign Contributions, 2001–2002**
Source: National Institute of Money in State Politics

"I don't give my people's money to those I think are going to lose."
—George Gould, PAC Manager

goals. Interest groups typically contribute more generously to incumbents than challengers because they know that an **incumbent,** that is, a current officeholder, is more likely to win than a challenger. Finally, interest groups prefer giving to incumbent officeholders who hold important policymaking positions, such as the members of the key policymaking committees in the legislature. Elected officials who hold important posts, such as the chairs of key committees in the legislature, are in better position to return favors than officeholders who have little power.

The political money game can be hazardous to the health of an interest group that winds up on the losing side of an election contest. Consider the experience of the Texas Automobile Dealers Association (TADA). Automobile dealers are business people who are traditionally allied with the Republican Party. In 1998, for example, the TADA PAC contributed nearly $600,000 to various Texas candidates, mostly to Republicans, including $98,500 to George W. Bush, the Republican candidate for governor.[14] In 2001, however, Republican Governor Rick Perry angered the automobile dealers by vetoing both of their top legislative priorities. One measure would have allowed dealers to increase the documentary fee they charge on new car sales from $50 to $75; the other would have allowed dealers to sell "gap insurance" to cover the shortfall when an outstanding loan exceeds the value of a new car that is totaled.[15] The car dealers retaliated against the governor by throwing their support to his Democratic opponent in the 2002 election. TADA contributed $50,000 to Sanchez while individual car dealers gave thousands more. When Perry won the race anyway, the automobile dealers moved quickly to try to repair relations with the governor. Shortly after the election, TADA gave $50,000 to the Perry campaign matching the amount it had earlier given Sanchez.[16] Giving money to a candidate after an election is over is known as **catching the late train.** The group also hired a former top aide to Governor Perry as a lobbyist. Gene Fondren, the longtime head of the auto dealers PAC, explained the situation facing TADA as follows: "We did not support the governor, and when you take that kind of a risk, particularly with an incumbent, it's always painful. And we have worked hard to make amends."

Lobbying

Lobbying is the communication of information by a representative of an interest group to a government official for the purpose of influencing a policy decision. Interest group lobbyists are at work on all levels of Texas government and at every stage of the policy process. In 2001, more than 1,600 registered lobbyists spent from $104 million to $230 million attempting to influence the Texas legislature and state agencies. (Because state reporting requirements allow interest groups to report their expenditures by checking a bracketed range, it is impossible to calculate lobby expenditures with more precision.) SBC Communications, Electronic Data Systems Corp., Reliant Energy, TXU Corp., and Exxon Mobil Corp. ran the best-funded lobby operations, each spending more than $1.5 million.[17] In sheer numbers of lobbyists, the most active industry lobbyists in Texas are insurance, health services, and oil and gas.[18]

The traditional approach of lobbyists in Texas was **social lobbying,** which is the attempt of lobbyists to influence public policy by cultivating personal, social relationships with policymakers. Cynics referred to the practice as "booze, bribes, and babes." Lobbyists would ply their trade by meeting legislators and executive branch officials at a local barbecue restaurant for an evening of ribs, beer, and storytelling.[19]

Lobbyists are now more professional probably because government officials are more sophisticated. Professional lobbyists are skilled technicians, knowledgeable both in how to approach public officials and in the subject matter vital to their groups. The basic stock in trade of the skilled lobbyist is information. In fact, interest groups are sometimes the main source of information on a piece of legislation. "We have 140 days to deal with thousands of bills," said one state senator. "The lobbyists are providers of information about those issues. I don't know how we could operate without them."[20]

Research shows that the most successful lobbying efforts are those that are supported by campaign contributions during election season and reinforced by contacts from constituents.[21] Interest groups lay the groundwork for effective lobbying by giving money for political campaigns. Although campaign contributions do not necessarily buy votes, they do generally guarantee access to decision makers by lobbyists.

"The question you really need to ask members [of the legislature] is not whether they remember you gave to them, but whether they can remember who gave to their opponents. They can all recite that; they know that list by heart. That one, they carry to the grave."
—Bruce Gibson, former member of the Texas legislature and now an executive with Reliant Energy

"The average taxpayer doesn't have a seat at the table."
—Craig McDonald, Texans for Public Justice

"The lobby dollars are not to buy votes; it's [sic] to educate members."
—Mike Krusee, State Representative, R., Round Rock

NATIONAL PERSPECTIVE

Campaign Contribution Limits in Minnesota

Minnesota law limits the amount of money interest groups can contribute to candidates for legislative or executive office. During an election year, PACs and individuals can give no more than $500 to a candidate for governor or the state legislature, $200 to a candidate for attorney general, and $100 to a candidate for other statewide offices. In other years, contribution limits are even lower—$100 per candidate.*

Minnesota's strict campaign finance law limits the amount of money available to candidates. In 2002, total campaign spending in Minnesota was $9.8 million, $1.95 for every resident in the state. In contrast, candidates in Texas spent $216 million, $9.92 per resident. The disparity in political spending per voter is more dramatic. In 2002, Minnesota candidates spent $4.35 for every vote cast compared with $47.47 per vote in Texas.[†]

Minnesota's contribution limit influences the dynamics of election contests. Jesse Ventura, the former professional wrestler, won election as governor of Minnesota in 1998 as the candidate of the **Reform Party,** which is the political party founded by Dallas billionaire Ross Perot. Ventura defeated two well-known opponents, Republican Norm Coleman and Democrat Hubert Humphrey III, despite raising barely $1 million. The contribution limit helped Ventura because it prevented either of his opponents from rais-

ing more than $2.5 million.[‡] In mid-October when polls showed Humphrey and Coleman neck and neck with Ventura running third, the two major party candidates decided to focus their campaigns on defeating each other while ignoring Ventura. As Election Day approached, the polls showed Ventura moving up, but neither Humphrey nor Coleman had enough money to buy television time for attack ads to stem Ventura's momentum. Were it not for the contribution limits, Coleman and Humphrey could have raised millions of dollars more in campaign contributions from interest groups that could have been used to cut Ventura down to size. Without significant interest group support, Ventura would have lacked the money to respond to the attacks and would almost certainly have lost the election.[§]

QUESTIONS TO CONSIDER

1. Would you favor campaign contribution limits in Texas similar to the limits in Minnesota?

2. Do you think it is likely that the Texas Legislature will adopt campaign finance limits? Why or why not?

3. Who would benefit from campaign contribution limits in Texas? Who would be harmed by contribution limits?

---

*Minnesota Secretary of State, available online at **www.sos.state.mn.us**.
[†]National Institute on Money in State Politics, available at **www.followthemoney.org**.

[‡]National Institute on Money in State Politics, available at **www.followthemoney.org**.
[§]Stephen I. Frank and Steven C. Wagner, *We Shocked the World: A Case Study of Jesse Ventura's Election as Governor of Minnesota* (Orlando, FL: Harcourt College Publishers, 1999).

Interest groups back their legislative lobbyists by mobilizing group members in the home districts of legislators to contact their representatives. For example, the TMA asks its physician members to personally contact public officials who happen to be their patients. Even though the doctors who make the contacts with policymakers are not professional lobbyists, they are particularly effective because they already have a personal relationship with the public official.

CALVIN AND HOBBES

Public Relations Campaigns

"There are only so many hours in a day, and when you're trying to figure out who to fit into your day, you obviously pay attention to the people who helped put you in."
—John Bryant, former member of Congress from Texas

Interest groups attempt to influence policy by building public support for their points of view. They recognize that public officials, especially elected officials, are unlikely to jeopardize their political future by publicly supporting an unpopular cause, regardless of PAC money and lobbying. Interest groups understand that their lobbying efforts will be more effective if policymakers know that group goals enjoy public support.

The groups supporting tort reform have conducted a sophisticated public relations campaign to win support for their point of view. They have purchased billboards and run television and radio advertisements against what they called "lawsuit abuse." They have also used radio talk shows and other media to publicize examples of what they considered unreasonable jury judgments, such as the story of a woman who sued McDonald's restaurant chain after hot coffee spilled in her lap. According to a survey conducted in 2003 by the Scripps Howard Texas Poll, the public relations campaign of the tort reform supporters has been effective. By a 57 percent to 33 percent margin, Texans favored a $250,000 cap on noneconomic damages in medical malpractice lawsuits.[22]

Litigation

"Anybody who accepts $100,000 from a PAC belongs, body and soul, to that PAC."
—Babe Schwartz, former member of the Texas legislature who is now a lobbyist

Sometimes interest groups use litigation (i.e., lawsuits) to achieve their goals. The NAACP and the Mexican American Legal Defense and Education Fund (MALDEF) have gone to court many times to argue cases involving school desegregation, education finance, and voting rights. For example, MALDEF provided legal support to the poor school districts that sued the state over its education funding system in the case known as *Edgewood v. Kirby.*[23]

Litigation has been an important political tool for interest groups, but it has its limitations. Court action is both time-consuming and expensive. Not all groups can afford it. Also, litigation is reactive. Lawsuits are inevitably filed in response to policy actions with which a group disagrees. Court actions can sometimes succeed in

> "Anytime someone, whether a person or a PAC, gives you a large sum of money, you can't help but feel the need to give them extra attention, whether it is access to your time or, subconsciously, the obligation to vote with them."
>
> —John Bryant, former member of Congress from Texas

overturning policies already in place, but they are usually an ineffective means for initiating policies.

Protest Demonstrations

Groups that cannot afford public relations experts and advertising campaigns attempt to influence public opinion by means of protest demonstrations. Civil rights groups used this technique in the 1960s. Today, it is occasionally employed by a variety of groups pursuing many different goals, ranging from antinuclear groups opposing construction of a nuclear power plant to antipornography crusaders picketing convenience stores that sell *Playboy* magazine. In general, protest demonstrations are a tactic employed by groups unable to achieve their goals through other means. Sometimes the protest catches the attention of the general public and pressure is brought to bear on behalf of the protesting group. In most cases, though, protests have only a marginal impact on public policy.

> "I don't think money buys anything [concrete]. But it does [buy] access; it puts you in position [when you want] appointments. But I don't think you can buy votes."
>
> —former Speaker of the House Billy Clayton who is now a lobbyist

Political Violence

Occasionally, frustrated groups go beyond peaceful protest to violent, illegal activities. During the 1960s, some groups opposed to the war in Vietnam took over college administration buildings or burned Reserve Officer Training Corps (ROTC) offices on campus. The Ku Klux Klan has also been linked to violence in the state. Although political violence usually begets a negative response from the political establishment, violence can occasionally succeed in calling the public's attention to an issue that might otherwise be ignored.

 WHAT IS YOUR OPINION?

Is violence on behalf of a political cause ever justified?

Alliances

Interest groups find power in alliances with other interest groups and political parties. The battle over medical malpractice reform in particular and tort reform in general pitted two powerful interest group-political party alliances against one another. The TMA, business groups as a whole (especially insurance companies and construction companies), and the Republican Party lined up in favor of tort reform while the trial lawyers, consumer groups, and the Democratic Party were opposed. The tort reformers got most of what they wanted out of the legislature because their interest group alliance was better funded and better organized than their opponents. Furthermore, the Republican Party had won electoral control of all three branches of state government, including both chambers of the Texas legislature.

L E A R N I N G   E X E R C I S E

Group Political Action

The tactics interest groups employ depend on the resources at their disposal, their goals, and the political circumstances in which they find themselves. This exercise is designed to allow students to use their creativity to solve a community problem by creating a group and using one or more of the tactics discussed in this chapter. Your instructor will divide the class into six groups. The students in each group should assume that they have formed an organization, an interest group, to attempt to solve one of the problems below. Each group must develop a plausible solution to its assigned problem, making a realistic assessment of the resources the group will have at its disposal. The solution does not necessarily have to include government action. In completing this exercise, students should consider the range of tactics interest groups use to attempt to achieve their goals. Be prepared to present your proposed solution to the entire class and explain why it is likely to work.

The groups and their problems are as follows:

GROUP A: A sexually oriented business is scheduled to open two blocks from your home, just around the corner from an elementary school. Your neighbors want to prevent its opening because they are concerned about property values and the possible negative effect of the business on neighborhood youngsters going back and forth to school.

GROUP B: The state Department of Mental Health and Mental Retardation has purchased property in your neighborhood with the intent of opening a halfway house where mentally retarded persons would live while holding down jobs in the community. You and some of your friends support the concept, but you are aware that other people in the neighborhood are organizing to prevent the house from opening. You and your friends would like to take steps to defuse opposition to the home and make its residents feel welcome.

GROUP C: Because of budget constraints, the mayor and city council are considering budget cuts that would lead to the closure of the branch library in your neighborhood. You and several other students use the library regularly and want it to remain open.

GROUP D: You discover that your child's high school is dispensing birth control pills to students. You strongly oppose the idea and want to stop it.

GROUP E: You learn that your child's elementary school teacher leads his class in prayer every morning at the beginning of the school day. Although you and your family faithfully practice your religion, you believe that school officials should not be leading students in prayers that may not be consistent with the beliefs of all students. You have spoken to the school principal, but she has not been receptive to your complaints.

GROUP F: A fire at an apartment complex in your part of town has left several low-income families homeless. They have lost most of their belongings and have neither the funds nor insurance to get back on their feet. You and some of your neighbors want to help them, but you cannot afford to meet all of their needs.

CONCLUSION: INTEREST GROUPS AND POLICYMAKING

Interest groups are important participants in the state's policymaking process. Political scientists Clive S. Thomas and Ronald J. Hrebenar classify states as to the relative influence of groups in state politics. They identify the following types of states:

- **Dominant states:** In these states, the policymaking influence of interest groups is overwhelming and consistent. Thomas and Hrebenar put seven states in this category: Alabama, Florida, Louisiana, New Mexico, Nevada, South Carolina, and West Virginia.

- **Complementary states:** In these states, groups either must work with or, alternatively, are constrained by other elements of the state's political system, such as its political culture or a strong executive branch. Seventeen states fall into this category: Colorado, Connecticut, Indiana, Maine, Maryland, Massachusetts, Michigan, Missouri, New Hampshire, New Jersey, New York, North Carolina, North Dakota, Pennsylvania, Utah, Washington, and Wisconsin.
- **Subordinate states:** Interest groups are subordinate to other elements of the state's political climate. No states fall into this category.
- **Dominant/Complementary states:** These states alternate between the dominant and complementary categories. This category includes 21 states: Alaska, Arizona, Arkansas, California, Georgia, Hawaii, Idaho, Illinois, Iowa, Kansas, Kentucky, Mississippi, Montana, Nebraska, Ohio, Oklahoma, Oregon, Tennessee, Texas, Virginia, and Wyoming.
- **Complementary/subordinate states:** The states in this category alternate between the complementary and subordinate classifications. This group includes five states: Delaware, Minnesota, Rhode Island, South Dakota, and Vermont.

Thomas and Hrebenar classify Texas as a dominant/complementary state. The Lone Star State alternates between periods when the influence of interest groups is overwhelming and times when groups are constrained by other elements of the state's political system. In Texas, the governor and legislative leaders are powerful enough to limit the influence of interest groups if they wish. Nonetheless, the governor and legislative leaders do not always choose to restrain the power of groups because they may support the goals the groups are trying to achieve. Furthermore, the state's executive and legislative officials are not involved in every policy issue and in every detail of the issues in which they do participate.[24]

? WHAT IS YOUR OPINION?

Do interest groups have too much influence in Texas?

Agenda Building

Interest groups participate in every stage of the policymaking process. Groups attempt to set the policy agenda and define the way issues on the agenda are perceived. Medical malpractice reform became part of the official agenda in Texas because of the efforts of the TML, TLR, and other groups advocating changes in the state's tort laws. The proponents of tort reform campaigned to define the issue in terms of lawsuit abuse by publicizing instances of frivolous lawsuits and excessive jury awards. In contrast, the TTLA and consumer groups defended the civil justice system by arguing that most jury awards are reasonable and that excessive awards are almost always overturned or reduced on appeal. The TTLA attempted to define the issue in terms of consumer rights.

Policy Formulation and Adoption

Interest groups play a prominent role in policy formulation. Groups formulate policy proposals by drafting measures that can then be introduced as legislation by sympathetic members of the legislature or local governing bodies. Groups also attempt to influence the details of policy proposals being considered by legislative bodies and government agencies. The medical malpractice reform proposals considered by the 2003 session of the legislature were written in close consultation with the TMA and other tort reform proponents. In the meantime, tort reform opponents, recognizing that they lacked the votes to defeat the measures outright, attempted to modify the details of the legislation to minimize its impact.

Interest groups affect policy adoption both by influencing the identity of elected officials and by lobbying policymakers. The proponents of tort reform were in good position to accomplish many of their goals in 2003 because their candidate for governor and most of the legislative candidates that they backed had won. The lobbying battle was not over whether tort reform would pass because the votes were already in place. Instead, the fight was over the exact shape of the legislation.

Policy Implementation and Evaluation

Interest groups influence policy implementation through electioneering and lobbying. In Texas, many of the executive and judicial branch officials who carry out policies are elected. For example, a majority of the members of the Texas Supreme Court, the state's highest court for civil disputes, has won election with the support of tort reform advocates. Furthermore, groups interested in policy implementation frequently lobby state agencies and local officials in charge of carrying out policies just as they lobby legislators.

Interest groups participate in policy evaluation as well, hoping to shape policy feedback in accordance with their particular points of view. Tort reform proponents produced data supposedly showing that the average Texas household benefited by more than $1,000 a year in reduced prices and increased personal income because of the tort reforms adopted in the 1990s. In contrast, the opponents of tort reform charged that tort reform proponents used questionable methods to generate data to prove their case.[25] Instead, they argue that tort reform had failed to produce lower insurance rates and consumer prices.

By and large, interest group participation in Texas politics has a conservative impact on public policy because the most powerful interest groups in the state typically promote conservative policy preferences. Business groups and trade associations favor low overall tax rates with a tax structure dependent on consumer taxes, limited government services, and government regulations designed to foster business development. In contrast, the interest groups that counterbalance business forces in other states and at the national level, especially organized labor, consumer organizations, and environmental groups, are relatively weak in Texas.

★ REVIEW QUESTIONS

1. What role did interest groups play in the controversy over medical malpractice reform?
2. Which groups are the most influential in Texas politics and what factors account for their influence?
3. What are the policy goals of the various interest groups active in Texas politics?
4. Why are business interests more influential than organized labor?
5. What tactics do interest groups use to influence the policymaking process?
6. What factors do interest groups consider in determining which candidates to support?
7. What approaches do lobbyists use to influence public policy?
8. Compared with other states, how important are interest groups in Texas politics?
9. What role do interest groups play in each stage of the policymaking process in Texas?

★ KEY TERMS

advocacy groups

American Association of Retired Persons (AARP)

American Federation of Labor-Congress of Industrial Organization (AFL-CIO)

capital punishment

catching the late train

cause groups

Christian Coalition

citizen groups

Common Cause

Frostbelt

good business climate

hate-crimes legislation

incumbent

interest group

joint and several liability

League of United Latin American Citizens (LULAC)

lobbying

minimum wage

National Association for the Advancement of Colored People (NAACP)

National Organization for Women (NOW)

National Rifle Association (NRA)

political action committees (PACs)

punitive damages

racial profiling

Reform Party

religious right

right to work law

Sierra Club

social lobbying

Sunbelt

Texas Abortion and Reproductive Rights Action League (TARAL)

Texas Association of Business (TAB)

Texas Independent Producers and Royalty Owners Association

Texas Medical Association (TMA)

Texas Right to Life Committee

Texas Trial Lawyers Association (TTLA)

tort reform

trade associations

union or closed shop

★ NOTES

1. Guillermo X. Garcia, "Group Says Tort Reform Won't Fix Medical Crisis," *San Antonio Express News*, April 17, 2003, available at **www.mysanantonio.com**.
2. "States Said to be in Trouble," *USA Today*, April 27, 2003, available at **www.usatoday.com**.
3. Gary Boulard, "The Doctors' Big Squeeze," *State Legislatures* (December 2002): 26.
4. David Pasztor, "Malpractice Pain Awards Haven't Risen, Study Finds," *Austin American-Statesman*, March 18, 2003, available at **www.austin360.com**.
5. Doug J. Swanson, "Patients' Deaths Haven't Moved State Board to Act," *Dallas Morning News*, July 28, 2002, available at **www.dallasnews.com**.
6. Alan Greenblatt, "Medical Mayhem," *Governing* (April 2003): 36.
7. Texas Department of Insurance, "Tort Reform Statutes," available at **www.tdi.state.tx.us**.
8. Janet Elliott, "Defendants Fare Better on Appeal, Study Finds," *Houston Chronicle*, Nov. 6, 2003, p. 27A.
9. Court Watch, "Shifting Sands for Consumers: Court Watch 2002–2003 Annual Report," available at **www.texaswatch.org**.
10. Texans for Public Justice, "Money in PoliTexas: A Guide to Money in the 2002 Texas Elections," available at **www.tpj.org**.
11. *Texas Weekly*, March 31, 1997, p. 3.
12. Bureau of Labor Statistics, "Union Affiliation of Employed Wage and Salary Workers by State," available at **www.bls.gov**.
13. "Exit Polls for Texas," available at **www.cnn.com/election/2000/results/index.epolls.html**.
14. National Institute on Money in Politics, available at **www.followthemoney.com**.
15. Terry Box and Pete Slover, "Car Dealers Make U-Turn to Sanchez," *Dallas Morning News*, July 18, 2002, available at **www.dallasnews.com**.
16. National Institute on Money in Politics, available at **www.followthemoney.com**.
17. Laylan Copelin, "More Money Flowing from State Lobbyists," July 3, 2002, *Austin American-Stateman*, available at **www.statesman.com**.
18. Center for Public Interest, "The Fourth Branch of State Government," available at **www.publicintegrity.org**.
19. Keith E. Hamm and Charles W. Wiggins, "Texas: The Transformation from Personal to Informational Lobbying," in Ronald J. Hrebenar and Clive S. Thomas, eds., *Interest Group Politics in the Southern States* (Tuscaloosa, AL: University of Alabama Press, 1992), p. 163.
20. Brent Manley, "Texas Lobbyists' Big Bucks Get Bigger," *Houston Post*, March 18, 1984, pp. 1A, 18A.
21. John R. Wright, "Contributions, Lobbying, and Committee Voting in the U.S. House of Representatives," *American Political Science Review* 84 (June 1990): 417–38.
22. Janet Elliott, "Most Texans Favor Cap in Medical Malpractice," *Houston Chronicle*, May 17, 2003, p. 36A.
23. *Edgewood v. Kirby*, 777 S.W.2d 391 (1989).
24. Clive S. Thomas and Ronald J. Hrebenar, "Interest Groups in the States," in Virginia Gray and Herbert Jacob, eds., *Politics in the American States*, 6th ed. (Washington, DC: CQ Press, 1996), p. 152.
25. Suzanne Staton, "Billion Dollar Boom?" *Fiscal Notes* (January 2001): 10–11.

ONLINE PRACTICE TEST

Test your understanding of this chapter with interactive review quizzes at

www.ablongman.com/tannahilltexas/chapter5

Political Parties

LEARNING OBJECTIVES

After studying Chapter 6, students should be able to do the following:

★ Describe the party system in the United States and Texas.

★ Describe the party organization of the two major parties at the national and state level.

★ Trace the history of political parties in Texas from the late nineteenth century through the present.

★ Compare and contrast the Texas Democratic and Republican Parties today in terms of voter support and offices held.

★ Identify the groups of voters who generally support each of the major political parties in terms of income, race and ethnicity, region, and place of residence.

★ Identify the interest groups associated with each of the state's major political parties.

★ Compare and contrast the state's two major parties in terms of issue orientation.

★ Evaluate the policy impact of the emergence of the GOP as the state's dominant political party.

★ Identify the factors affecting the future of party politics in Texas.

★ Describe the role of political parties in the state's policymaking process.

★ Define the key terms listed on page 153 and explain their significance.

Texas Democratic Party leaders described the three candidates at the top of the Democratic ticket in the 2002 state election as a "Dream Team" that would return Democrats to power in the Lone Star State for the first time in nearly a decade. Tony Sanchez, the party's candidate for governor, was a wealthy south Texas oilman who promised to spend as much of his own money as necessary to win. Because Sanchez was the first Latino ever to win a major party nomination for governor, Democratic leaders hoped that Hispanic voters would turn out in record numbers to back Sanchez and help the entire slate of Democratic candidates. Ron Kirk, the African American mayor of Dallas, was the party's candidate for the U.S. Senate. With Kirk at the top of the ballot, the Democrats counted on a big turnout of African American voters. The third member of the Dream Team was John Sharp, the former state comptroller. Party leaders anticipated that Sharp, the non-Hispanic white member of the group, would appeal to white voters living in rural areas, small towns, and the suburbs.

Unfortunately for the Democrats, the Dream Team fizzled. Sanchez, Kirk, and Sharp all lost. Sharp ran the closest race, losing to Republican David Dewhurst by 52 percent to 46 percent. (Candidates for the Libertarian Party and the Green Party split the other 2 percent of the vote.) In the meantime, Republican Governor Rick Perry trounced Sanchez, 58 percent to 40 percent, and John Cornyn, the Republican nominee for the U.S. Senate, defeated Kirk by 55 percent to 43 percent.[1]

The 2002 election left the Republican Party in firm control of Texas government. Republicans held the three highest profile elective offices in the state: Perry was governor while Cornyn and Kay Bailey Hutchison represented Texas in the U.S. Senate. Every member of the Texas Railroad Commission, Texas Supreme Court, and Texas Court of Criminal Appeals was Republican. A majority of the members of both houses of the Texas legislature and the Texas Board of Education were Republican as well. The Republican Party also held a majority of county offices and district judgeships in most large urban and suburban counties. Texas Democrats could console themselves only with a shrinking majority in the state's U.S. congressional delegation. Democrats continued to hold most elected county offices and judicial positions in rural counties. Although the mayors of Dallas, Fort Worth, Houston, San Antonio, and Austin were Democrats, all were chosen in **nonpartisan elections,** which are election contests in which the names of the candidates appear on the ballot but not their party affiliations.[2]

This chapter on political parties is the third in a series of four chapters examining the political environment for policymaking. Chapter 4 discussed political participation in Texas, while Chapter 5 dealt with interest groups. Chapter 7 will focus on elections. This chapter begins by describing the party system in Texas and the United States. It traces the state's party history and examines party organization at the national and state levels. The chapter compares the state's major parties in terms of strength, base of support, interest group alliances, and issue positions. It concludes by discussing the role of political parties in the policymaking process.

"If God were nominated as a Democrat, He couldn't win in Texas."

—Jerry Polinard, political scientist

THE PARTY SYSTEM

A **political party** is a group of individuals who join together to seek public office in order to influence public policy. Parties are similar to interest groups in that both types of political organizations attempt to influence the policymaking process and both are interested in election outcomes. The difference is that political parties attempt to win control of the machinery of government by nominating candidates for elected office, who then run under the party label and, if successful, identify with the party while in office. The Republican Party, the Democratic Party, the Texas Association of Business (TAB), and the Texas Trial Lawyers Association (TTLA) all participate in the election process and all attempt to influence public policy, but only the Republicans and the Democrats actually put forward candidates for office under their organizational name. They are political parties whereas the other two organizations are interest groups.

Throughout most of its history, the United States has had a **two-party system,** which is the division of voter loyalties between two major political parties, resulting in the near exclusion of minor parties from seriously competing for a share of political power. Since the Civil War era, the Democrats and the Republicans have been the two dominant parties in American national politics. The Libertarian, Green, and Reform parties are minor parties that have tried to have an impact in Texas politics. Except for the election of a small number of Libertarian candidates at the local level, minor party candidates have had little success in the Lone Star State. After the 2002 election, every member of the Texas legislature and every member of the congressional delegation from Texas were Republicans or Democrats.

Despite a national two-party system, many states have experienced periods of one-party dominance. The most significant example of one-party control took place in the South after the end of the Civil War era. For about a century, every southern state, including Texas, was under the firm and usually unchallenged political control of the Democratic Party. Political conflicts still occurred in the South, but they took place within the Democratic Party between factions divided over issues or personalities. A **party faction** is an identifiable subgroup within a political party.

PARTY ORGANIZATION

The Democratic and Republican Parties have both national and state party structures.

The National Party Organizations

A national committee and chair head the national party organization. The national committee consists of a committeeman and committeewoman from each state and the District of Columbia, chosen by their state or the district party organization. The national committee elects the national chair. When the party controls the White House, the national chair is usually the handpicked choice of the president.

NATIONAL PERSPECTIVE

Minor Parties in New York

Voters in New York choose among candidates for the two major parties and several minor parties. State law allows a political party to receive a place on the official ballot if its supporters can collect 20,000 petition signatures. The party holds its ballot slot as long as its candidate for governor receives at least 50,000 votes. Since 1970, the New York ballot has consistently included candidates for the Conservative, Liberal, and Right to Life Parties in addition to the Democrats and Republicans. In recent years, the ballot in New York has also included the Independence, Green, and Working Families Parties.

Minor parties in New York have been successful at holding their places on the ballot because of the state's cross-endorsement rule. An individual can run for office as the candidate of more than one party. In 2000, for example, Hillary Rodham Clinton ran for the U.S. Senate as the candidate of both the Democratic Party and the Liberal Party while her chief opponent, Rick Lazio, was the candidate of both the Republican Party and the Conservative Party. People who want to vote for a minor party candidate who is cross-endorsed by a major party do not have to worry about throwing their votes away because the candidate receives the sum total of votes cast for that candidate, whether they came from minor party or major party voters.

New York's minor parties are more interested in influencing policy than electing candidates. The Liberal Party's primary goal is to make the state's Democratic Party more liberal. Most of the Liberal Party's endorsed candidates are Democrats, but if party leaders believe that the Democratic candidate is not sufficiently liberal, the party can run its own candidate or make no endorsement in the race, thereby taking votes away from the Democratic candidate. Sometimes the Liberal Party will even endorse a moderate Republican. Similarly, the Conservative Party works to push the Republican Party in a conservative direction by withholding support from GOP nominees who are not conservative enough for Conservative Party tastes.

The New York Right to Life Party focuses on a single issue, opposition to abortion. It selects its candidates based solely on their position on the issue of abortion. The Right to Life Party occasionally cross-endorses one of the major party candidates, usually the Republican candidate. Most of the time, however, the Right to Life Party nominates its own candidate and uses the campaign as an opportunity to discuss opposition to abortion.

QUESTIONS TO CONSIDER

1. Would you like for Texas to have election laws similar to those in New York that allow minor parties to cross-endorse major party candidates?

2. If you lived in New York, would you consider minor party endorsements in deciding which candidate to support?

3. Would you ever consider voting for a minor party candidate who was not also endorsed by a major party, knowing full well that the candidate had no realistic chance of winning? Why or why not?

The national party organizations have become important sources of financial support and technical expertise to state party candidates. Although the national political party organizations can give no more than $5,000 to candidates for Congress in direct contributions, they can spend considerably more money on a candidate's behalf. **Coordinated expenditures** are funds spent by a national party organization to support the party's candidates, including expenditures for polls, advertising, issue research, and fundraising. Coordinated expenditures by political parties are spent, as

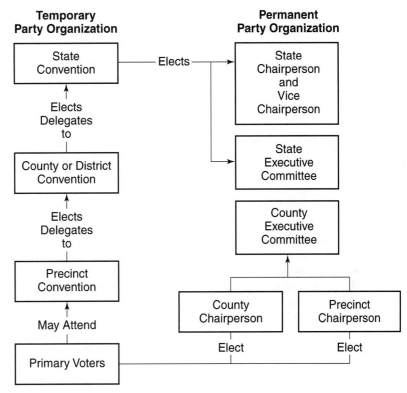

FIGURE 6.1   Texas Party Structures

their name implies, in coordination with the candidate's campaign. Furthermore, individuals interested in running for state or national office can attend candidate training sessions sponsored by the national party organizations at which they learn how to build a campaign organization, raise money, deal with the media, identify issues, and present themselves to voters.

Although both of the major national political parties have become adept at raising money, the national Republican Party typically has more money to support the efforts of its candidates and its state parties than does the national Democratic Party. In the 2001–2002 election cycle, the national Republican Party raised $472 million nationwide compared with $272 million by the Democrats.[3] Furthermore, the Republican Party is more effective than the Democratic Party at targeting competitive races where the money will do the most good.[4]

"Party committees now primarily provide services to candidates."
—Robert Biersack, political scientist

Texas Party Organizations

Political parties in Texas have both temporary and permanent party organizations. Figure 6.1 depicts the various structures.

Temporary Party Organization   The temporary party organization of each party assembles for a few hours or days in general election years (even-numbered years—2002,

2004, etc.) to allow rank-and-file party supporters a chance to participate in the party's decision making process. In the evening of the March primary after the polls have closed, Texans have the opportunity to attend precinct conventions, usually in the same location as the polling place, with Republicans gathering in one area and Democrats in another. Citizens who voted in the primary election are eligible to participate in the precinct convention of the party in whose primary they voted. The turnout at precinct conventions is usually light, especially in nonpresidential years. The main business of precinct conventions is to elect delegates to the county or state senatorial district conventions, which are held on the second Saturday after the primary. In large urban counties with more than one state senatorial district (Harris, Dallas, Bexar, and Tarrant Counties), delegates elected at precinct conventions attend state senatorial district conventions. In other counties, they attend a county convention. The number of delegates an election precinct may send to the county or district convention depends on the size of the vote in that precinct for the party's candidate in the last governor's election.

The county and district conventions are larger and more formally organized than precinct conventions, and they generally last longer, sometimes a full day. The convention usually includes speeches by party leaders and officeholders, and the delegates will likely debate and vote on a number of resolutions. Once again, the main business of the meeting is to select delegates to the next highest level—in this case, the state convention. The number of delegates each county or district convention sends to the state convention depends on the size of the vote for the party's candidate in the last governor's election in the county or district.

The Republican and Democratic Parties hold their state conventions in June. This meeting is the largest, most formal, and longest of all, generally lasting most of a weekend. As at a district/county convention, delegates must sign in and present their credentials, and party leaders give their best political speeches. The state convention certifies party nominees for the fall general election, adopts a state **party platform** (which is a statement of party principles and issue positions), elects the state party chairperson and vice chairperson, chooses members of the state executive committee, and selects individuals to serve on the national party executive committee. The state convention also gives the party the opportunity to showcase itself and its candidates for the upcoming general election.

In presidential election years, the state party convention selects delegates to the national party convention. State law provides that delegates to the national party conventions be pledged to support presidential candidates in rough proportion to the candidates' strength in the spring presidential preference primary. In addition to selecting delegates to the national party convention, each state party convention also names a slate of potential presidential electors to cast Texas's Electoral College votes should the party's presidential candidate carry the state in the November general election. The **Electoral College** is the system established in the U.S. Constitution for the selection of the president and vice president of the United States.

Permanent Party Organization   Each party has a permanent party organization that operates year-round. At the base of the permanent party organization are the precinct

The Texas delegation at the 2000 Democratic National Convention cheers the Gore nomination.

chairpersons, elected by party voters in each of the state's precincts, except in those areas where one party is so weak that no one can be found to accept the job. Precinct chairpersons conduct primary elections by staffing the polling place on Election Day. They may also work to organize the precinct for their party.

The county executive committee is the next highest level of permanent party organization. It includes all the precinct chairpersons in the county and the county chairperson, who is elected by party voters countywide. The county executive committee receives filing petitions and fees from primary election candidates for countywide offices and is responsible for placing candidates' names on the ballot. The county executive committee also arranges for county and district conventions.

The state executive committee is the highest level of party organization in the state. It includes the party chair and vice chair and a committeeman and committeewoman representing each of Texas's 31 state senatorial districts. The State Democratic Executive Committee (SDEC) includes a party treasurer as well. The main duties of the SDEC and the State Republican Executive Committee (SREC) are to certify statewide candidates for the spring primary, arrange state party conventions, raise money for party candidates, and, in general, promote the party. In particular, state party chairs serve as media spokespersons for their party.

TEXAS ONLINE ★ Forces of Change

Political Parties in Texas

The Texas Democratic, Green, Libertarian, Reform, and Republican Parties all have homepages. Learn more about the state's political parties by checking out their websites.

Democratic Party: **www.txdemocrats.org**
Texas Green Party: **www.txgreens.org**
Texas Libertarian Party: **www.lp.org/organization/TX**
Texas Reform Party: **www.texasreformparty.org**
Texas Republican Party: **www.texasgop.org**

Review each of the websites and answer the following questions.

QUESTIONS TO CONSIDER

1. Which website is the most visually attractive? Why?
2. Which website is the least visually attractive? Why?
3. Pick out one website and write a short review, discussing its main features, strong points, and weaknesses.

HISTORY OF THE TEXAS PARTY SYSTEM

"The Civil War made the Democratic Party the party of the South and the Republican Party the party of the North."

—V. O. Key, Jr., political scientist

The recent success of the Texas Republican Party is remarkable considering the history of party competition in the state. For nearly a century, Texas was a one-party state and that party was the Democrats. Older Texans remember a time when nearly every elected official was a Democrat and the Republican Party was so weak that it failed even to field candidates for many state and local offices.

The Civil War and Reconstruction produced the one-party Democratic South. Because of its association with the Union during the Civil War era, most native white southerners hated the Republican Party. In Texas, the **Grand Old Party (GOP),** as the Republican Party was known, could count on the loyalty of African Americans, German Americans living in the Hill Country who had opposed secession before the Civil War, and few others. With the Republican Party in disrepute, the Democrats were the dominant party not only in Texas but also throughout the South, so much so in fact that political commentators coined the phrase **Solid South** to refer to the usual Democratic sweep of southern state electoral votes in presidential election years. In Texas, Democrats won nearly every statewide race, most seats in Congress and the state legislature, and the overwhelming majority of local and judicial contests, frequently without Republican opposition.

Large landowners and industrialists controlled the Democratic Party of the late nineteenth and early twentieth centuries. The public policies they favored reflected a political philosophy of **conservatism,** which is the political view that seeks to preserve the political, economic, and social institutions of society against abrupt change. Conservatives generally oppose most government economic regulation and heavy government spending while favoring low taxes and traditional values.

By the 1930s, an identifiable liberal faction emerged to challenge conservative dominance of the Democratic Party. **Liberalism** is the political view that seeks to change the political, economic, or social institutions of society to foster the development of the individual. Liberal Democrats in the Lone Star State supported Democratic President Franklin Roosevelt and his **New Deal program,** which was the name given to Roosevelt's legislative program for countering the Great Depression. Liberal Democrats called for a more active role for state government in the fields of education, job training, health care, and public assistance to the poor. To pay for these programs, liberal Democrats proposed higher taxes on business and industry, and on people earning substantial incomes. Liberal Democrats in Texas called for the elimination of the white primary and the poll tax. They supported an end to discrimination against African Americans and Latinos.

The liberal wing of the Texas Democratic Party achieved some political success during the 1930s as the Great Depression caused many Texans to question the wisdom of the state's conservative public policies. The high point for the liberals was the election of liberal Democrat James Allred as governor in 1935 and 1937. During the Allred administration, the legislature and the governor enacted several liberal programs designed to combat the Great Depression. Support for the liberal Democrats came primarily from a loose coalition of unemployed persons, working-class whites, labor union members, Jews, university people, some professionals, Latinos, and African Americans. The latter were now beginning a wholesale change of allegiance from the GOP to the party of Franklin Roosevelt.

The conservative Democrats reestablished themselves as the dominant wing of the Democratic Party during the 1940s. With the Depression over, the economic issues raised by liberal Democrats were less effective. Conservative Democrats claimed that the return of economic prosperity proved the correctness of their philosophy. Another advantage for conservatives was that they enjoyed easier access to the financial resources needed to wage a modern political campaign in a large and rapidly growing state than did the liberal Democrats. Furthermore, working-class and minority voters who made up the core of support for the liberal Democrats were less likely to vote than the middle- and upper-income non-Hispanic white supporters of the conservative Democrats.

The period running from the early 1950s through the late 1970s was a time of transition for party politics in the Lone Star State. By the 1950s, the liberal wing of the Texas Democratic Party had become a formidable political force. Although conservative Democrats still held the upper hand, liberal challengers had to be taken seriously. Liberal Democrats scored a major breakthrough in 1957, when Ralph Yarborough, a liberal Democrat, won a special election to the U.S. Senate. He held the seat through 1970. Liberal Democrats also captured a few seats in Congress, won a number of positions in the state legislature, and ran credible races for the party's gubernatorial nomination.

Liberal Democrats gained strength because the Democratic electorate was changing. The legal barriers that had kept many African Americans, Latinos, and poor whites from the polls were coming down, primarily because of the intervention of the federal courts and the U.S. Congress. The liberal wing of the party also benefited from the defection of some conservative voters to the GOP. A poll taken in the mid-1960s found that 37 percent of Texans who said they were once conservative Democrats had left the party, either to become Republicans (23 percent) or independents (14 percent).[5] The exodus of conservative voters from the Democratic Party made it easier for liberal candidates to win Democratic primary elections.

In the meantime, the Texas Republican Party was coming to life. The emergence of the GOP as a political force in Texas can be traced to the 1950s and the presidential candidacy of General Dwight D. Eisenhower. The personal popularity of Eisenhower as a war hero brought a flood of new faces into the Republican camp, many of which were former Democrats. Furthermore, many conservative Democrats, including Governor Allan Shivers, deserted their party's presidential nominee, Governor Adlai Stevenson of Illinois, to openly support the Republican presidential candidate. Eisenhower carried the state in both 1952 and 1956.

Texas Republicans built their party throughout the 1960s and 1970s. They elected candidates to the U.S. Congress and the Texas legislature and won a number of local races, particularly in urban areas. Perhaps their most important victory came in 1961 when Republican John Tower, a young college professor at Midwestern State University in Wichita Falls, won a special election to serve the remainder of Lyndon Johnson's U.S. Senate term after Johnson resigned to become vice president. Tower won reelection in 1966, 1972, and 1978.

Surveys of party identification among voters traced the Republican surge. For decades, the most common political animal in the Lone Star State was the Yellow Dog Democrat. This was a Texan, it was said, who would vote for a yellow dog were it the Democratic candidate. In other words, a **Yellow Dog Democrat** was a loyal Democratic Party voter. In 1952, 66 percent of Texans called themselves Democrats, while only 6 percent declared allegiance to the Republican Party. Twenty years later, the margin was a bit closer, 57 percent to 14 percent.[6] By 1984, however, Democrats outnumbered Republicans by only 33 percent to 28 percent.[7]

> "I have seen the conservative Democrats getting smaller and smaller each year, and I think a lot of conservative Democrats are going to be faced with making the same decision that I made."
> —Kent Hance, former Democrat turned Republican

What accounts for the rise of the GOP as a significant electoral force in Texas? First, the legacy of the Civil War finally began to diminish in importance, especially for younger Texans. Surveys showed that younger voters were more likely to identify with the GOP than older people.[8] Second, many conservative white Democrats became disenchanted with what they saw as an increasingly liberal national Democratic Party. While some conservative southern Democrats openly defected to GOP ranks, other conservatives remained nominal Democrats but supported Republicans in statewide and national races whenever the Democratic nominee seemed too liberal for their taste. Finally, the Texas Republican Party benefited from the migration of white-collar workers from outside the South. Many of these Republican newcomers had supported the GOP in their old states and simply brought their party loyalties with them to their new homes in Texas.

The 1978 election marked the emergence of a competitive two-party system in Texas. For the Democrats, the most significant development came in the spring primary election, when Attorney General John Hill, a liberal Democrat, defeated incumbent Governor Dolph Briscoe, a conservative Democrat. Hill's victory demonstrated that liberal Democrats could compete with conservative Democrats on an equal footing. The determining political event in 1978 for the GOP came in the fall general election when Bill Clements defeated Hill to become the first Republican elected governor in more than a century. The election of Clements demonstrated that well-funded Republican candidates could win

The suburbs have become Republican strongholds.

statewide elections in Texas, especially against Democrats from the liberal wing of the party.

From 1978 to 1994, Texas party politics were more competitive than ever before. The GOP enjoyed an advantage at the top of the ballot, winning most races for governor and U.S. senator. The Republican presidential nominee carried the state every time during this period. In contrast, Democrats were considerably more successful in contests below the top of the ballot. Throughout the period, Democrats won most statewide executive offices below the level of governor, held majorities in the Texas House and Texas Senate, elected most of the state's judges, and held most county offices.

"Politically, Texas is now an indisputably Republican state." —Michael Barone and Grant Ujifusa, journalists

Texas is still a two-party state, but the Republican Party has become the dominant party. Since 1994 when Republican gubernatorial nominee George W. Bush defeated incumbent Democratic Governor Ann Richards, the GOP has established itself as the majority party in contests for statewide office and the legislature. The Republican Party has made dramatic gains in races for judicial office and won numerous local offices as well.

Figure 6.2 documents the rise the rise of the Texas GOP by charting the growth of Republican strength in the Texas House of Representatives. Between 1981 and 2001, the Republican delegation in the Texas House more than doubled, increasing from 35 to 72 members. The Republican Party fell short of a ma-

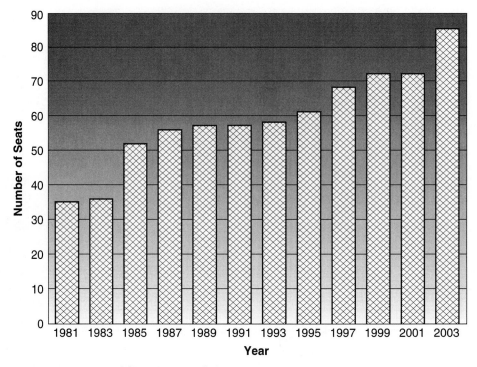

FIGURE 6.2   **Republican Strength in Texas House**

jority in the 150-member chamber until the 2002 election, which was a break-through election for House Republicans.

THE PARTY BALANCE

Democratic leaders had high hopes for the 2002 election. Although the GOP had held the governorship and most statewide offices since 1994, many Democrats believed that the Republicans owed their success more to the personal appeal of George W. Bush than to the strength of the Republican Party. Texas was a Bush state for sure, but it was not necessarily a Republican state.

The Democrats put forth a maximum effort to win the 2002 election. In addition to the Dream Team of Sanchez, Kirk, and Sharp, the Democratic Party boasted a full slate of strong candidates for statewide offices. Democrats vigorously contested many legislative and county races as well. With Sanchez and his family giving nearly $60 million to his own campaign, the Democrats even raised more money than the GOP, $107 million compared to $106 million for the Republicans.[9]

Table 6.1 documents the extent of the Republican victory in 2002. After the election, Republicans occupied both of the state's U.S. Senate seats and the six state exec-

TABLE 6.1   Party Affiliation of Elected Officials in Texas, 2003

Office	Total Number of Officials	Democrats	Republicans
U.S. Senate	2	0	2
U.S. House	32	17	15
State Executives*	6	0	6
Texas Senate	31	12	19
Texas House	150	62	88
Texas Supreme Court	9	0	9
Texas Court of Criminal Appeals	9	0	9
Texas Railroad Commission	3	0	3
Texas State Board of Education	15	5	10

*Governor, lieutenant governor, attorney general, comptroller, agriculture commissioner, and land commissioner.

> "The striking thing about the Democratic Party is that it's essentially nonexistent. What happens when you run as a Democrat for any statewide office is that you do your own fundraising, you get together your own staff, you put together your own campaign—there is nothing in place for you."
>
> —Molly Ivins, journalist

utive offices, including the offices of governor, lieutenant governor, attorney general, comptroller, land commissioner, and agriculture commissioner. The GOP held a majority in both chambers of the Texas legislature and on the Texas State Board of Education. Every member of the Texas Supreme Court, Texas Court of Criminal Appeals, and Texas Railroad Commission was a Republican. Most district judges and county officials in Harris, Dallas, Bexar, and Tarrant Counties were Republicans as well.

An analysis of the 2002 election returns suggests that the baseline Republican vote was nearly 58 percent of the electorate. Most Democratic candidates struggled to reach the 42 percent mark. The contests for the Texas Court of Criminal Appeals are a good measure of party strength because the individual candidates are not well known and seldom raise enough money to mount the media-based campaign necessary to build name recognition. Without information about the individual candidates, voters typically base their choices on party affiliation. When the Democratic Party dominated Texas politics, Democrats routinely swept races for the Court of Criminal Appeals. For the last decade, however, the GOP has won every race for the Texas Court of Criminal Appeals. In 2002, the Republican candidates for the three Court of Criminal Appeals races won 57–58 percent of the vote.[10]

VOTING PATTERNS

Voting patterns in Texas reflect differences in income, race and ethnicity, region, and place of residence.

Income

Voting patterns reflect income, with higher-income citizens supporting Republican candidates and lower-income voters backing Democrats. Exit polls taken during the 2000 presidential election showed a clear relationship between income and voter

"Politics generally comes down, over the long run, to a conflict between those who have and those who have less."
—V. O. Key, Jr., political scientist

choice. Democrat Al Gore led Republican George W. Bush by a comfortable 59 percent to 37 percent margin among voters with incomes between $15,000 and $30,000 a year. With each succeeding income bracket, however, Gore lost support and Bush gained. Among Texas voters making over $100,000 a year, Bush trounced Gore by a margin of 71 percent to 25 percent.[11]

Race and Ethnicity

Voting patterns vary based on race and ethnicity. Minority voters, especially African Americans, support the Democrats. In 2000, African American Texans backed Gore over Bush by a lopsided margin, 91 percent for Gore to 5 percent for Bush. Gore also carried the Latino vote in Texas but by a closer margin, 54 percent to 43 percent. In contrast, Bush led among non-Hispanic white voters, 73 percent to 24 percent for Gore.[12]

Region

Historically, Texas voting patterns have had a regional flavor. East Texas and south Texas, especially the counties along the Mexican border, have been Democratic strongholds. West Texas, the Panhandle region, and central Texas, excluding the city of Austin, have been areas of Republican strength. The party balance in other regions of the state has been relatively close.

As the Republican Party has gained strength in Texas, regional voting patterns have shifted. The border region along the Rio Grande River remains firmly in the Democratic camp, but east Texas is changing. Democrats still hold most local offices in east Texas, but Republican candidates for statewide and national office often run strong in the region.

"Particular businesses such as insurance and home builders have interest in reduced regulations, and Republicans think that's good public policy. It's a shared vision that low taxes and reduced regulations are positive for Texas over the long term."
—Cal Jillson, political scientist

Place of Residence

The GOP is strongest in the suburbs whereas Democrats run best in the inner city. In the meantime, the rural areas of the state, which were once solidly Democratic, are now trending Republican, at least for national and statewide office. Democrats hold inner-city congressional districts in Houston, Dallas, San Antonio, Austin, and El Paso whereas Republicans have won most of the state's predominantly suburban congressional districts. The state's most rapidly growing suburban counties (Collin and Denton Counties in the Dallas-Fort Worth area and Fort Bend and Montgomery Counties in the Houston area) are Republican strongholds.

INTEREST GROUP-POLITICAL PARTY ALLIANCES

Political parties and interest groups form informal alliances. Interest groups assist political parties by providing campaign funds and organizational support to party candidates. Groups contribute money directly to the party and its candidates or provide indirect support through **independent expenditures,** which are funds spent on behalf of a candidate that are not coordinated with the candidate's campaign. Groups en-

TABLE 6.2   Political Party and Interest Group Alliances

Groups Allied with the Democratic Party	Groups Allied with the Republican Party
• Organized labor	• Business groups and trade associations
• Environmental organizations	• Professional organizations
• Consumer groups	• Farm groups
• African American rights organizations	• Religious conservatives
• Hispanic rights groups	• National Rifle Association
• Gay and lesbian rights organizations	• Right to Life Advocates
• Teachers' groups	• Tort reform organizations
• Texas Abortion and Reproductive Rights Action League	
• Trial lawyers	
• Women's rights groups	

dorse candidates and distribute campaign literature to group members and people who would likely sympathize with the group's goals. Interest groups may also provide lobbying support for policies the party favors.

Table 6.2 lists the interest groups generally associated with the Texas Democratic and Republican Parties. Although the list of groups allied with the Democratic Party is longer than that associated with the GOP, the groups in the Democratic column are not necessarily more effective politically. With the exception of trial lawyers, who support the Democrats, the groups allied with the Republican Party have more money to devote to political action than do the groups who support the Democratic Party. Many of the groups allied with the Democrats, such as teacher's organizations and labor unions, have a large membership base that can be tapped for volunteer campaign support. Their numbers are somewhat offset, however, by the dedication of activists associated with the Right to Life Committee and various conservative religious groups supporting the Republican Party.

Although political parties and interest groups form alliances, groups are not wholly owned subsidiaries of parties. Not all African Americans, Latinos, and gay men and lesbians support the Democratic Party by any means; some are Republican. For example, the Log Cabin Republicans is an organization of gay and lesbian Republicans. Furthermore, groups and group members may not agree with a political party on every issue or endorse all of its candidates.

ISSUE ORIENTATION

The two major political parties in Texas agree on the fundamental principles of America's political and economic systems. Neither party wants to secede from the Union, rejoin Mexico, or establish a monarchy. Both Democrats and Republicans favor good schools, safe streets, clean air, and a strong economy. The two parties disagree on some of the details of policy, particularly on the role of government in society.

Table 6.3 compares the 2002 platforms of the state's two major political parties on selected issues. As the table shows, the two parties agreed on some matters. Both

LEARNING EXERCISE

Party Platforms and Support Groups

Political parties take issue positions designed to appeal to those groups of voters who compose their electoral coalition. Match the issue positions listed below with one or more of the party's support groups identified in Table 6.2. You may wish to review the policy goals of various interest groups discussed in Chapter 5 before completing this assignment.

Match the following Democratic platform positions with one or more of the groups allied with the Democratic Party:

- Opposes private school vouchers.
- Supports bilingual education.
- Endorses the "top 10 percent" university admissions policy.
- Opposes English-only laws.

- Favors increasing the minimum wage.
- Supports abortion rights.
- Endorses a federal law to prohibit employment discrimination on the basis of sexual orientation.

Match the following Republican platform positions with one or more of the groups allied with the Republican Party:

- Favors repealing the corporation franchise tax.
- Supports elimination of joint and several liability.
- Calls for repeal of minimum wage laws.
- Supports a constitutional amendment to ban abortion.
- Calls for repeal of no-fault divorce laws.
- Opposes laws granting civil rights protection to gay men and lesbians.

the Democrats and the Republicans opposed the adoption a state income tax and favored the election of state judges. Both parties expressed reservations about the **Texas Assessment of Knowledge and Skills (TAKS)** program, although neither party platform identified TAKS by name. The TAKS, which replaced the Texas Assessment of Academic Skills (TAAS), is a state mandated basic-skills test designed to measure student progress and school performance. High school students must pass the test before they can graduate. The Democratic platform advocated the use of a more complete evaluation system of students rather than just one test and the GOP platform deplored the amount of time devoted to test preparation rather than teaching basic skills.

On other issues, the Democrats and Republicans adopted positions that were clearly different. Whereas the Democrats supported abortion rights, the GOP platform called for the adoption of a constitutional amendment to outlaw abortion. The Democrats endorsed bilingual education; the Republicans rejected it. The Democrats advocated campaign finance reform to limit campaign contributions and candidate spending; the Republicans rejected all campaign finance reform proposals except for full disclosure of the sources of campaign contributions. Whereas the Democratic platform endorsed the state law that guarantees the top 10 percent of every public high school class admission to the public college or university of their choice, the GOP document declared that college admissions should be based only on merit and ability without regard for class standing or the school students attended.

The party platforms show that the two parties have different perspectives on the role of government. The Democrats believe that government should play a role in

"Government exists to help us achieve as a community what we cannot achieve as individuals."
—2002 Texas Democratic Party platform

Many of the delegates at recent state Republican Party conventions have been associated with the Christian Coalition or other conservative religious organizations.

"The family is respon-
sible for its own wel-
fare, education,
moral training, con-
duct, and property."
—2002 Texas
Republican Party
platform

solving social problems. The Democratic platform supports adequate funding for public education, Medicaid, and the Children's Health Insurance Program (CHIP). The Democrats favor government regulation designed to protect the environment, guarantee a choice of physicians to patients enrolled in health maintenance organizations (HMOs), and help low-income wage earners. On social issues, Democrats support abortion rights and favor the adoption of a federal law to protect gay men and lesbians from job discrimination. In contrast, the Republicans believe that government's primary role is to support traditional family values rather than solving social problems. The GOP platform proposes the repeal of the property tax, which is the major source of tax revenue for local governments in Texas, and the reduction of the sales tax, which is the major source of tax revenue for state government. The Republicans propose reducing or eliminating a broad range of state spending programs and oppose creating new programs. The Republicans believe that government should strengthen traditional marriage by making divorce more difficult, outlawing same-sex marriage, and prohibiting homosexuals from adopting children or from having custody of children.

Both of the major political parties in Texas are divided over policy issues. The historic division of the Democratic Party between liberals and conservatives persists,

TABLE 6.3   Texas Democratic and Republican Party Platforms, 2002, Selected Issues

Issue	Democratic Platform Position	Republican Platform Position
State taxes	Opposes the adoption of a state income tax. Calls for a constitutional amendment to ban taxes on food and prescription medicine.	Opposes the adoption of a state income tax. Favors reducing the state sales tax rate, repealing the corporation franchise tax, and abolishing the property tax.
School finance	Supports "sufficient and fair" state funding for public education so that the cost is not passed on to local property taxpayers.	Proposes a state constitutional amendment that would require that all money raised within a school district be used within that school district.
HMO regulation	Declares that HMO members should have the right to choose any physician who will accept the HMO fee structure.	No position.
Vouchers and school choice	Favors giving parents state funding vouchers and then letting them choose the public school that best meets the needs of their children. Opposes private school vouchers.	Favors giving parents state funding vouchers and then letting them choose among public schools, private schools, parochial schools, or home schooling contingent on the passage of a state constitutional amendment shielding private and parochial schools from state oversight.
Medicaid	Texas should provide sufficient funds to maximize the amount of federal Medicaid money coming to Texas.	No position.
Children's Health Insurance Program (CHIP)	Favors expansion of the program to cover all uninsured children in the state.	No position.
Basic skills testing	Improve the accountability system by relying on a more complete evaluation than just one standardized test score.	Deplores the amount of time devoted to test preparation rather than teaching basic skills.
Bilingual education	Supports bilingual education and multi-language instruction that allows English-speaking children to learn a second language.	Calls for the termination of bilingual education programs.
Higher education	Endorses state law that guarantees the top 10 percent of every public high school class admission to the public college or university of their choice.	Advocates a single standard of college and university admission based on merit and ability without regard for class standing or the school students attended.

although without the intensity of earlier days. Most real conservatives have long since left the party to join the GOP. Nonetheless, a survey of local Democratic Party activists in Texas finds a 43 percent to 26 percent split between liberals and conservatives, with another 31 percent declaring they are "middle of the road."[13] Furthermore, the Democratic members of Congress from Texas range from quite conservative to very liberal. Democratic Representative Charles Stenholm (west Texas) has a

Issue	Democratic Platform Position	Republican Platform Position
Tort reform, which is the revision of state laws to limit the ability of plaintiffs in personal injury lawsuits to recover damages in court.	Supports access to justice through the ability to join together to seek redress for personal injury and property damages.	Favors elimination of **joint and several liability,** which is the legal requirement that a defendant with "deep pockets" held partially liable for a plaintiff's injury must pay the full damage award for those defendants unable to pay. Demands that parties who file frivolous lawsuits be forced to pay the attorney fees for the successful defendant.
Judicial selection	Supports the election of state judges as well as meaningful judicial campaign finance reform.	Supports the election of state judges. Favors the establishment of consistent guidelines for contributions to campaigns of state judges.
Minimum wage	Calls for enforcement of minimum wage laws.	Calls for the repeal of the minimum wage.
Environmental protection	Supports the enforcement of the federal Clean Air Act, but opposes lowering the speed limit to 55 mph.	Opposes Environmental Protection Agency (EPA) management of Texas air-quality issues such as regulation of speed limits on Texas highways.
Abortion	Women should have access to the full range of reproductive choices, including bearing healthy children and preventing unintended pregnancy.	Declares that the unborn child has an individual fundamental right to life that cannot be infringed. Supports a constitutional amendment to ban abortion.
Divorce	No position.	Calls for repeal of no-fault divorce laws.
Campaign finance reform	Favors limiting both campaign contributions and expenditures.	Opposes campaign finance reforms other than full disclosure of contributions.
Election reform	No one should be denied the right to vote because of language barriers or confusing voting systems.	Supports requiring the reregistration of voters every four years. Opposes Internet voting.
Gay and lesbian rights	Endorses a federal law to prohibit employment discrimination based on sexual orientation.	Opposes repeal of the state's homosexual conduct law. Opposes laws granting civil rights protection to gay men and lesbians. Declares that homosexuals should not be allowed to adopt or have custody of children.

decidedly conservative voting record in Congress, while Representatives Eddie Bernice Johnson (Dallas) and Sheila Jackson Lee (Houston) are unabashed liberals.[14]

The state Republican Party is also divided, but not along conservative/liberal lines. The Texas Republican Party is firmly conservative. Eighty-six percent of Republican Party activists in Texas call themselves conservative compared with 12 percent who say they are middle of the road and a mere 2 percent who declare themselves liberal.[15] Meanwhile, the Republican congressional delegation is decidedly conservative. In 2002, no GOP House member from Texas scored less than 76 percent on a scale created by the American Conservative Union (ACU) to gauge the conservatism of members of Congress based on their voting records on selected foreign policy, social, and budget issues. Most Republican House members had scores of 90 percent or more.[16]

The Republican Party of Texas is divided between social conservatives and business-oriented conservatives. The social conservatives are primarily concerned with moral and cultural issues. They oppose abortion, gambling, and gay and lesbian rights while supporting parental choice, school prayer, and teaching **creation science,** which is an approach to the origin of the universe that is consistent with the biblical story of creation. In contrast, business conservatives focus on such issues as state taxes, tort reform, government regulation, and economic development.

Social conservatives dominate the state party organization whereas candidates supported by business-oriented conservatives are more successful at the ballot box. Social conservative activists have taken control of the state Republican Party organization through participation in precinct conventions. A majority of the delegates at recent state Republican Party conventions have been associated with the social conservative wing of the party. They have chosen their leaders to serve as state party chair and written platforms that reflect their values.[17] The 2002 Republican Party platform is sprinkled with references to God and includes long sections condemning abortion and homosexuality.

The social conservatives have not been successful at winning elections, at least not for high-profile offices. None of the state's more prominent Republican elected officials is closely associated with the social conservative wing of the party. On occasion, Republican Governors George W. Bush and Rick Perry clashed openly with social conservatives. In 2001, for example, Governor Perry signed hate-crimes legislation over the strong opposition of social conservatives who objected because the measure included coverage of crimes committed on the basis of sexual orientation. **Hate-crimes legislation** is a legislative measure that increases penalties for persons convicted of criminal offenses motivated by prejudice based on race, religion, national origin, gender, or sexual orientation.

?   WHAT IS YOUR OPINION?

Which party's platform more closely matches your political views— the Democratic or the Republican?

THE IMPACT OF PARTISAN CHANGE

Texas has undergone a political transformation. In less than 30 years, Texas has gone from a state in which Democrats captured almost every elective office to one in which the Republican Party controls all three branches of state government and many local governments as well. Has the dramatic change in the state's partisan balance been accompanied by a similarly remarkable change in policy?

The simple answer is no. Public policies in Texas have always reflected the state's individualistic-traditionalist political culture regardless of the political party in control of state government. The **individualistic political culture** is an approach to government and politics that emphasizes private initiative with a minimum of government interference. The **traditionalistic political culture** is an approach to government and politics that sees the role of government as the preservation of tradition and the existing social order. Historically, Texas has boasted low tax rates, poorly funded public services, minimal regulation of private business activity, and social policies designed to embrace and promote traditional Christian values. By and large, the new Republican leaders of state government have adopted policy initiatives consistent with the basic approach to state government taken by generations of Democratic officeholders in years past.

Consider the policy decisions of the Seventy-eighth session of the Texas legislature, which met in 2003. Facing a $10 billion budget shortfall, the governor and the legislature balanced the budget without raising taxes, primarily by cutting state spending. As for social issues, the legislature passed and the governor signed a bill outlawing same-sex marriage; they made abortion more difficult by imposing a 24-hour waiting period for women seeking to end a pregnancy. The legislature and the governor also adopted a package of tort reform measures.

Each of the legislature's actions reflected the conservative philosophy of the majority Republican Party, but none of them was a dramatic departure from policies enacted by previous Democratic legislatures and Democratic governors. The legislature and governor reduced state spending in 2003 in order to avoid a tax increase, but the programs were already poorly funded. The Democrats who once controlled the state presided over a government that was the least generous in the nation in terms of funding public services. In 2000, Texas ranked 50th in state government spending per capita.[18] Texas government has never been especially friendly to gay and lesbian rights or supportive of abortion rights. The enactment of a ban on same-sex marriage in 2003 was more symbolic than substantive because Texas law already defined marriage as a union between a man and a woman. Before the U.S. Supreme Court ruled

GETTING INVOLVED

Volunteer to Support Your Political Party

Political parties are a means for individuals to influence the policymaking process. The Texas Online feature found on page 136 includes the websites of the five most important political parties in Texas politics. Each party website includes information on how Texans can contact the party and get involved in its work. Contact the party of your choice and offer to help. Volunteers support their party by registering vot-ers, helping out in the local office, raising money, and researching issues. People who get involved with their party may eventually win the opportunity to attend the county, state, or national convention. Some may even decide to run for office and may be elected.

It's your country—get involved!

Michael Williams is a Republican member of the Texas Railroad Commission. If the Republican Party hopes to continue to be the dominant political party in Texas, it must broaden its appeal to minority voters.

the law unconstitutional, Texas was one of a handful of states that criminalized private, consensual sexual conduct among adults of the same gender. The Texas legislature has never passed pro-choice legislation, regardless of the party in control. Furthermore, the tort reforms adopted in 2003 only added to an extensive list of lawsuit restrictions enacted when Democrats still ran the legislature.

THE FUTURE OF PARTY POLITICS IN TEXAS

The Republican Party is likely to maintain its hold on state government at least through for the rest of the decade. The defeat of the Dream Team and the entire Democratic ticket was so overwhelming that it is unlikely that potentially strong Democratic candidates will venture a race for statewide office because they will doubt their chances to win.[19] The Democratic Party will also have trouble raising

"It's not a flawed strategy—it was a strategy ahead of its time. In ten or twelve years, if they [the Democrats] are getting 60 percent of the Mexican-American vote in the state, they'll start winning every statewide election."
—Jerry Polinard, political scientist

money to mount serious statewide races. Consequently, the Democrats may be forced to concede high-profile races for the U.S. Senate and governor to the Republicans.

The problem for the Democratic Party is weak minority turnout and relatively little support among non-Hispanic white voters. Democratic party leaders hoped that the presence of Sanchez and Kirk at the top of the ticket would motivate Latino and African American voters to cast ballots in record numbers in 2002. Minority turnout surged in some areas, but the overall voter participation rate for Latinos and African Americans was disappointing. Balloting in heavily Hispanic Brownsville, Corpus Christi, and El Paso was up only 5 percent from the 1998 election, which had set a modern-day record for low turnout. In the meantime, non-Hispanic white voters have flocked to the GOP. Although Sanchez took 80 percent or more of the Latino and African American vote, election analysts estimated that he received less than 30 percent of the non-Hispanic white vote.[20] No one can win a statewide election today with less than 30 percent of the non-Hispanic white vote.

In the long run, demographic change may restore the Democratic Party to power in Texas. The Dream Team may have been ahead of its time. Racial and ethnic minority groups will soon comprise a majority of the state's population and Latino Texans will likely become the state's largest ethnic group, outnumbering non-Hispanic whites sometime between the years 2020 and 2030.[21] Every year, the Latino share of the state's electorate grows as more and more Latino Texans obtain American citizenship or reach voting age. Unless Republican candidates capture a larger percentage of Hispanic votes than they usually do today, they will have trouble winning statewide elections.

"Hispanics must have an important role in the future of the Texas Republican Party. If they don't, when people discuss minorities in the years ahead, they won't be talking about Hispanics. They'll be referring to Texas Republicans."
—Bill Clements, former Republican governor of Texas

Republican leaders recognize the need to extend their party's appeal to minority voters. Republican Governors Clements, Bush, and Perry appointed Latinos and African Americans to high profile positions as secretary of state or to fill vacancies on the Texas Railroad Commission and the Texas Supreme Court. Bush campaigned hard to win Latino votes, speaking Spanish in campaign appearances and in radio campaign ads. Nonetheless, the efforts of party leaders to attract Latino voters to the GOP have been undermined by a party platform opposing bilingual education and calling for the adoption of American English as the official language of Texas and the United States.

CONCLUSION: POLITICAL PARTIES AND POLICYMAKING

Political scientists use the concept of responsible parties to discuss the relationship between political parties and public policy. A **responsible party** is a political party that clearly spells out issue positions in its platform and, when in office, faithfully carries them out. Cohesive, well-organized political parties raise issues to the official policy agenda in their platforms and other party pronouncements. Once in power, party members in the legislature and executive branch can formulate and adopt policies to address the issues the party raised. Party members in the executive and judicial branches of government implement policy. Party leaders then defend policies of their making and criticize policies associated with the opposing party.

Political parties in the United States and Texas fail to fully live up to the responsible party model. Although both parties adopt platforms, party candidates and officeholders do not always embrace every item in the platform. Governor Bush disagreed with some elements of the 1998 Texas Republican platform, such as its advocacy of English as the official state language. He simply ignored some of the document's other provisions, including its advocacy of a biblically based school curriculum. Consequently, party activists included a provision in the 2002 Texas Republican Party platform directing the party campaign committee "to strongly consider candidates' support of the party platform when granting financial or other support."[22] For years, political parties hardly mattered in Texas politics because Texas was a one-party state. Now that Texas has become a two-party state, parties do matter, but they do not dominate the policymaking process. In the legislature and the executive branch, party affiliation probably has less impact on policy than other factors, such as the ideology of individual officeholders and the wishes of the legislators' constituents.

Political scientists use the concept of issue networks to describe policymaking in America. An **issue network** is a group of political actors that is concerned with some aspect of public policy. They may include technical specialists, journalists, legislators, the governor, other state executive officials, interest groups, bureaucrats, academic experts, individual political activists, and political parties. In Texas, political parties play a role in the policymaking process, but their influence is tempered by the participation of other political actors.

Agenda Building

Political parties participate in agenda building. Parties identify issues in their platforms and party candidates discuss issues during election campaigns. Party officeholders promote issues from their positions in government. During the 2002 election campaigns, both major party candidates pledged to reform insurance regulation and address school finance. Governor Perry and most Republican candidates promised to repeal the **Robin Hood Plan,** which was the reform of the state's school finance system designed to increase funding for poor school districts by redistributing money from wealthy districts. Both candidates for governor declared that they would increase spending for education and hold the line on taxes.

Policy Formulation and Adoption

Parties participate in policy formulation and adoption. Parties and party candidates suggest solutions to policy problems. Once in office, party leaders may work together to adopt policies reflecting their party's position. Governor Perry and the Republican legislative leadership worked together to pass tort reform in 2003. The governor declared that tort reform was a major goal during his 2002 election campaign and he asked the legislature to act. Republican leaders in both chambers helped push through a tort reform legislation and then Perry signed it into law.

Policy Implementation and Evaluation

Political parties play a role in policy implementation. Most of the officials who head the units of government responsible for policy implementation are either elected under the party label or appointed by elected officials who ran for office under the party name. They may use their position to further their party's policy objectives. Some of the Republican members of the State Board of Education, for example, have worked to shape the school curriculum and to adopt textbooks that reflect the socially conservative views of the GOP platform.

Party leaders evaluate public policies. The party out of power typically attacks the work of the governing party while the incumbent party defends its position. In 2003, for example, Texas Democrats blasted the work of the Republican controlled legislature, declaring that the budget cuts adopted by the legislature and the governor would hurt teachers, elderly people, school children, and the poor. In contrast, GOP leaders defended the budget, declaring that the legislature and the governor kept their promise not to raise taxes.

★ REVIEW QUESTIONS

1. What was the strategy behind the Dream Team and how successful was it?

2. What is the relationship between the national political party organization and party candidates at the state level?

3. Why was the Democratic Party the dominant political party in Texas for nearly a century after the end of the Civil War era?

4. Why has the Republican Party now become stronger than the Democratic Party in Texas?

5. Which groups of voters typically support the Democrats? Which groups usually support Republican candidates?

6. How do the Texas Democratic and Republican Parties differ in terms of issue positions?

7. How has the emergence of the GOP as the dominant party in Texas affected public policy?

8. What is the future of party politics in Texas?

9. What role do political parties play in the policymaking process in Texas?

★ KEY TERMS

conservatism
coordinated expenditures
creation science
Electoral College
Grand Old Party (GOP)
hate-crimes legislation
independent expenditures
individualistic political culture
issue network

joint and several liability
liberalism
New Deal program
nonpartisan election
party faction
party platform
political party
responsible party

Robin Hood Plan
Solid South
Texas Assessment of Knowledge and Skills (TAKS)
tort reform
traditionalistic political culture
two-party system
Yellow Dog Democrat

★ NOTES

1. "2002 General Election, Race Summary Report, Texas Secretary of State," available at **www.sos.state.tx.us**.

2. Colleen McCain Nelson, "Democrats Hang on to Mayors' Jobs," *Dallas Morning News*, June 8, 2003, available at **www.dallasnews.com**.

3. Federal Election Commission, available at **www.fec.gov**.

4. Malcolm E. Jewell and Sarah M. Morehouse, *Political Parties and Elections in American States*, 4th ed. (Washington, DC: Congressional Quarterly Press, 2001), p. 49.

5. James A. Dyer, Arnold Vedlitz, and David B. Hill, "New Voters, Switchers, and Political Party Realignment in Texas," *Western Political Quarterly* 41 (March 1988): 156.

6. Clay Robison, "Texas GOP Beats Dems in Key Areas," *Houston Chronicle*, November 28, 1989, p. 16A.

7. *Texas Weekly*, July 15, 1991, p. 5.

8. "The Two Souths," *National Journal*, September 20, 1986, pp. 2218–20.

9. National Institute on Money in State Politics, available at **www.followthemoney.org**.

10. "2002 General Election, Race Summary Report, Texas Secretary of State," available at **www.sos.state.tx.us**.

11. Exit poll data, available from **www.cnn.com/election/2000/results/index.epolls.html**.

12. Exit poll data, available from **www.cnn.com/election/2000/results/index.epolls.html**.

13. Robert P. Steed, "Parties, Ideology, and Issues: The Strategy of Political Conflict," in Steed, John A. Clark, Lewis Bowman, and Charles D. Hadley, eds., *Party Organization and Activism in the American South* (Tuscaloosa, AL: University of Alabama Press, 1998), p. 87.

14. Michael Barone with Richard E. Cohen and Grant Ujifusa, *The Almanac of American Politics 2002* (Washington, DC: National Journal, 2001), pp. 1450–1520.

15. Steed, "Parties, Ideology, and Issues," p. 87.

16. American Conservative Union, available at **www.conservative.org**.

17. Nate Blakeslee, "Have Republicans Lost the Fire?" *Texas Observer*, March 2, 2001, pp. 4–5.

18. "State Governments—Expenditures and Debt by State: 2000," *Statistical Abstract of the United States 2002*, available at **www.census.gov**.

19. Wayne Slater and Pete Slover, "Energized GOP: Let's Go," *Dallas Morning News*, November 7, 2002, available at **www.dallasnews.com**.

20. Jay Root and John Moritz, " 'Dream Team' No Match for GOP in Texas," *Fort Worth Star-Telegram*, November 7, 2002, available at **www.dfw.com**.

21. Rad Sallee, "Texas' Population is Changing," *Houston Chronicle*, April 22, 1994, p. 36A.

22. *2002 State Republican Party Platform*, available at **www.texasgop.org**.

ONLINE PRACTICE TEST

Test your understanding of this chapter
with interactive review quizzes at

www.ablongman.com/tannahilltexas/chapter6

Elections

LEARNING OBJECTIVES

After studying Chapter 7, students should be able to do the following:

★ Describe the long ballot in Texas and evaluate its advantages and disadvantages.

★ Identify and describe the various types of elections held in Texas.

★ Describe the process through which Texans participate in the presidential nomination process for the two major political parties.

★ Identify the officials in Texas that are elected at large and those that are elected by districts.

★ Discuss the impact of one person, one vote on legislative redistricting.

★ Describe the impact of the Voting Rights Act on legislative redistricting.

★ Assess the role of politics on redistricting, focusing on the battle over redistricting following the 2000 census and the off-cycle redistricting struggle in 2003.

★ Evaluate the role of money in Texas elections— where it originates, how it is spent, and what difference it makes.

★ Describe campaigns for major office in Texas.

★ Describe the role that each of the following plays in voter choice: political party identification, issues, incumbency, campaigns, candidate image, retrospective and prospective voting, and national factors.

★ Evaluate the role of elections in the policymaking process.

★ Define the key terms listed on page 183 and explain their significance.

In 2003, Democratic legislators made history by leaving the state. When Republican legislative leaders attempted to pass a congressional redistricting plan that could reduce the number of Democrats serving in the U.S. Congress from 17 to as few as 10, more than 50 Democratic members of the Texas House of Representatives secretly traveled to Ardmore, Oklahoma where they would be outside the jurisdiction of Texas law enforcement officials who had been sent to find them and bring them back to Austin. The strategy for the Democrats was to prevent the house from having a quorum, which is the number of members that must be present for the chamber to conduct official business. Because the rules of the house set a quorum at two-thirds of the 150-member body, the absence of more than 50 Democratic legislators blocked the redistricting bill, at least for the time being. Once the deadline for passing legislation expired in the house, the Democrats returned to the state and the legislature resumed its business.

Although the trip to Ardmore prevented the legislature from passing a redistricting plan in its regular legislature session, the success of the house Democrats was short lived. Soon after the regular session ended, Republican Governor Rick Perry called the legislature into special session to consider redistricting. This time it was the turn of the senate Democrats to leave the state. Eleven of the 12 Democratic members of the Texas senate held out in Albuquerque, New Mexico for weeks, preventing the 31-member senate from having a quorum. With the governor threatening to call one special session after another, the Democrats eventually broke ranks. Democratic Senator John Whitmire of Houston returned to Texas, the senate established a quorum, and the legislature eventually passed a redistricting plan.

"I'm the majority leader and we want more seats."
—House Majority Leader Tom DeLay

The drama over congressional redistricting illustrates the importance of election rules and procedures. Battles over redistricting are intense because the shape of legislative districts determines the outcome of elections. In turn, election outcomes affect public policy by selecting the individuals and the party that hold government office.

This chapter on elections is the last in a set of four chapters examining the political environment for policymaking. Chapter 4 dealt with participation. Chapter 5 addressed the topic of interest groups in Texas. Chapter 6 focused on political parties.

★ THE LONG BALLOT

Texas has the **long ballot,** which is an election system that provides for the election of nearly every public official of any significance. A conscientious Texas voter who never misses an election has the opportunity to cast a ballot for each of the following public officials:

- The president and vice president
- Two U.S. senators
- One member of the U.S. House of Representatives
- The governor of Texas and five other state executive officials
- Three railroad commissioners
- One member of the state board of education
- One state senator

- One state representative
- Nine members of the Texas Supreme Court
- Nine members of the Texas Court of Criminal Appeals
- At least 2 and perhaps as many as 60 or more state appellate and district court judges
- Numerous local officials, including county executives, county judges, city officials, and members of school district boards of trustees.

The ballot is especially long in the state's urban counties where a large number of state district court judges must stand for election. In 2002, Harris County voters faced a ballot with 130 offices listed.

The long ballot is not unusual in America, but few states vote on as many officials as Texas. Only four states elect more statewide executive officeholders than Texas; three states select only a governor statewide.[1] Considering the number of candidates and constitutional amendments Texas voters must decide, the Lone Star State may well have the longest, most complicated election ballot in the nation.

The long ballot is controversial. Its defenders believe that election is the best way to ensure that public officials remain accountable to the people. If citizens grow unhappy with some aspect of state government, they can simply vote the responsible officials out of office. In contrast, critics of the long ballot argue that most Texans lack information to make intelligent voting choices on many down-ballot races. Not knowing the qualifications of the candidates, voters may cast ballots for persons with familiar or catchy names who may be unqualified for the offices they seek.

? WHAT IS YOUR OPINION?

Is the ballot too long for Texas voters to be able to make informed choices?

TYPES OF ELECTIONS

Texans have the opportunity to cast ballots in different types of elections held at various times throughout the year.

General Elections

The **general election** is a statewide election to fill national, state, and some local offices, held on the first Tuesday after the first Monday in November of even-numbered years. Voters may choose among candidates put forward by the Democratic and Republican Parties and, sometimes, by minor parties, such as the Libertarian Party and the Green Party. The ballot may also include the names of independent candidates not affiliated with any political party. The state's two major parties are guaranteed space on the ballot, but minor parties and independent candidates must collect signatures equivalent to 1 percent of all the votes cast for governor in the last general election to qualify for the ballot. In 2002, minor party and independent candidates needed the signatures of 37,380 registered voters who had not participated in the March primary. A party can hold its ballot slot as long as one of its candidates receives at least 5 percent of the statewide vote.

State law allows either split-ticket or straight-ticket voting. **Split-ticket voting** refers to citizens casting their ballots for candidates of two or more parties for different offices during the same election. **Straight-ticket voting** involves citizens casting their ballots only for the candidates of one party. The general-election ballot includes a straight-ticket box to allow voters to cast straight-ticket ballots by marking a single box rather than having to vote individually on all of a party's candidates. In 2002, 54 percent of Harris County voters cast a straight-ticket ballot.[2]

The candidate with the most votes wins the general election, regardless of whether that candidate has a majority (more than 50 percent) of the ballots cast. There are no runoffs. Suppose that Democrat Mary Jones, Republican Joe Nava, and Raymond Smith, a Libertarian, run for the office of county sheriff. The outcome of the election is as follows:

Jones	18,344
Nava	18,501
Smith	3,189

Under the state's election laws, Nava wins the election despite having taken less than a majority of the total votes cast in the election because the candidate with the most votes wins the general election.

Primary Elections

Although minor parties may select their general-election candidates at a state convention, Texas law requires that major parties must choose their candidates in a **primary election,** which is an intraparty election at which a party's candidates for the general election are chosen. Democrats compete against other Democrats, Republicans against Republicans. In Texas, primary elections take place on the first Tuesday in March of even-numbered years.

The two basic kinds of primary election methods are the closed primary and the open primary. The **closed primary** is an election system that limits primary election participation to registered party members. Many party leaders favor the closed primary because they believe that it prevents the supporters of the opposition party from influencing the selection of candidates for their party. Why should Democrats be allowed to help select Republican nominees and vice versa? In contrast, the **open primary** is an election system that allows voters to pick the party primary of their choice without disclosing their party affiliation. Some party leaders favor the open primary because they believe that it will produce nominees who can appeal to independent voters and supporters of the other party more than the closed primary can. Candidates with broad appeal are more likely to win the general election than are candidates who can only attract the votes of other Democrats or Republicans.

The Texas primary system is a cross between an open primary and a closed primary. In contrast to the practice in many states, Texas does not require that citizens disclose their party affiliation when they register to vote. On primary Election Day, however, voters must publicly choose the party in whose primary they wish to par-

Texas voters choose among candidates for dozens of offices.

ticipate. They cannot vote in both primaries. Once a voter declares a choice, the election judge stamps the voter registration card "Voted in the Republican (or Democratic) primary."

Primary election participation has changed as the fortunes of the state's two major political parties have changed. From the 1870s until the middle of the twentieth century, most of the state's voters participated in the Democratic primary. A majority of Texans identified with the Democratic Party and the Democratic primary had the more hotly contested races. In recent years, participation in the Republican primary has risen as the Grand Old Party (GOP) has gained strength and the Republican primary has featured interesting and important races for president, governor, and senator.

Figure 7.1 compares Democratic and Republican primary election turnout in statewide (nonpresidential) election years from 1978 to 2002. In 1978, Democratic primary voters outnumbered GOP primary participants by a better than ten to one margin. Subsequently, the Democratic primary electorate shrank while the number of people voting in the Republican primary increased. In 1998, nearly as many Texans voted in the GOP primary as took part in the Democratic primary. In 2002, Democratic primary turnout rebounded because of competitive races for governor and senator while Republican turnout was little changed from 1998.

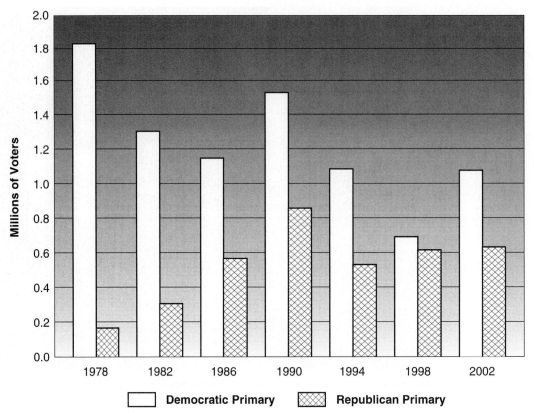

FIGURE 7.1   Primary Turnout, 1978–2002
Source: Texas Secretary of State

Each party's set of primary voters reflects its socioeconomic profile. The overwhelming majority of Republican primary participants are middle- and upper-income non-Hispanic whites living in the suburban areas of the state's major urban centers. In contrast, a majority of Democratic primary voters are minority. Political scientist Dan Weiser estimates that the 2002 Democratic primary turnout was 39 percent non-Hispanic white, 35 percent Latino, and 26 percent African American.[3]

To win a primary election, a candidate must receive a majority of the votes cast (50 percent plus one vote). If no one receives a majority in a multicandidate race, the two highest finishers meet in a runoff. Suppose that Joe Nava, Elizabeth Long, and Lee Chen are running for the Republican nomination for the office of county sheriff and the vote totals are as follows:

Nava   4,102
Long   2,888
Chen   2,009

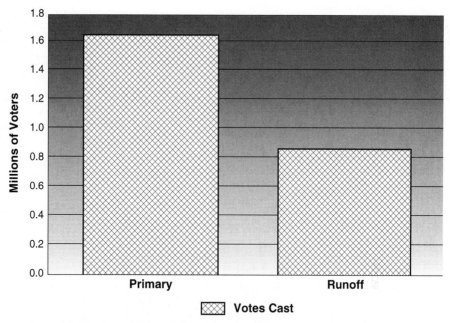

FIGURE 7.2   Primary and Runoff Turnout, 2002
Source: Texas Secretary of State

Nava and Long would face one another in the primary runoff because neither received a majority of the votes cast. Chen is eliminated because he finished third.

A **runoff primary election** is an election between the two top finishers in a primary election when no candidate received a majority of the vote in the initial primary. In Texas, the primary runoff takes place on the first Tuesday in April, a month after the initial primary. People who voted in the March primary may only vote in the same party's runoff election. They cannot switch parties for the runoff. Citizens who failed to vote in March can vote in either party's runoff primary. The winner of the runoff is the party's official nominee for the fall general election.

On average, voter turnout in a runoff primary election is only about two-thirds as high as turnout in the initial primary.[4] The drop-off in numbers in a runoff is particularly dramatic when no major statewide contests are on the runoff ballot for governor or senator to spur voter interest. Figure 7.2 compares voter turnout in the primary election and the runoff primary in 2002. Although more than 1.6 million Texans voted in the Republican and Democratic primaries, fewer than 850,000 voters returned for the runoff a month later.

The Presidential Delegate Selection Process

Every four years, Texans have the opportunity to participate in the process through which the Democratic and Republican Parties choose their presidential candidates by selecting delegates to attend the national conventions of the two major parties.

The procedure for selecting delegates to national party conventions varies from state to state. About two-thirds of the states select delegates by means of a **presidential preference primary election,** which is an election in which party voters cast ballots for the presidential candidate they favor and in so doing help determine the number of convention delegates that candidate will receive. Other states choose national convention delegates by the **caucus method of delegate selection,** which is a procedure for choosing national party convention delegates that involves party voters participating in a series of precinct and district or county political meetings. The process begins with party members attending precinct conventions where they elect delegates to district meetings. The district meetings in turn select delegates to the state convention. Finally, the state party convention chooses national convention delegates.

In Texas, the state Republican Party chooses delegates to the national party convention through a presidential preference primary. To receive any delegates, a presidential candidate has to win at least 20 percent of the vote in one or more U.S. congressional districts. Any candidate who gets a majority of the vote in a congressional district claims all of that district's delegates. A candidate who gets more than 20 percent but less than a majority receives a share of the delegates allotted to that district. In 2000, George W. Bush captured the entire Texas delegation to the Republican National Convention by winning more than 85 percent of the primary vote.

The Texas Democratic Party selects national convention delegates through a system that combines the primary and caucus methods. More than half the state's Democratic delegates are awarded to presidential candidates in rough proportion to the percentage of votes they receive in a presidential preference primary as long as a candidate qualifies by winning at least 15 percent of the statewide vote. Candidates also win delegates based on the results of a caucus process. Finally, the party reserves a number of delegate positions for **super delegates,** Democratic officeholders and party officials who attend the national party convention as delegates who are not officially pledged to support any candidate. Vice President Al Gore won most of the Texas delegates chosen to attend the 2000 Democratic National Convention.

The Texas legislature has periodically tinkered with the timing of the spring primary in hopes of increasing the state's influence in the presidential selection process. In 1987, the legislature moved the spring primary date from May to March in hopes of enhancing the state's impact on the presidential nomination process. Despite its size, Texas had had relatively little influence in presidential nomination contests because each party's presidential nomination was long since decided by the time Texas got around to selecting its convention delegates. The legislature hoped that by moving the state's presidential delegate selection process up a couple of months that presidential candidates would be forced to campaign in the Lone Star State and appeal to Texas voters. The scheme failed, however, because other state's moved their primaries and caucuses up as well. In 2000, both Bush and Gore had their party's nomination wrapped up even before Texans went to the polls. Consequently, in 2003, the Texas legislature tried once again to increase the state's role in the presidential selection process by moving the primary up another week, from the second Tuesday in March to the first Tuesday in March.

NATIONAL PERSPECTIVE

The Open Primary in Louisiana

Louisiana has a unique primary system. Every candidate competes for votes in an open primary, regardless of party affiliation. If one candidate wins a majority of the vote, that candidate is elected. Otherwise, the two top finishers face each other in a runoff election, regardless of party affiliation. In theory, the runoff could involve two Democrats, two Republicans, or one candidate from each party. In 2002, for example, nine candidates competed in the open primary for the U.S. senate, including four Republicans, two Democrats, a Libertarian, and two independents. The two top candidates, incumbent Democrat Mary Landrieu and Republican Suzanne Haik Terrell, met in a runoff, which Landrieu won.

Democratic Governor Edwin Edwards invented the open primary and got the state's Democratic controlled legislature to adopt it as a device to slow the rise of the state's Republican Party. To win office, Democrats had to survive a bruising Democratic primary election and then defeat a Republican opponent in the general election who usually had not had to face a Republican primary opponent. Edwards figured that the open primary would erase the Republican advantage by forcing all the candidates into the same set of elections.

Although the open primary has not prevented Republicans from making substantial inroads in Loui-

siana politics, it probably was responsible for Edwards winning a fourth nonconsecutive term as governor in 1991. The three main contenders, Edwards, Republican state legislator David Duke, and incumbent Republican Governor Buddy Roemer, carried considerable political baggage into the race. Many Louisiana voters thought that Edwards was a crook because he had spent most of his career fighting off corruption charges. Duke was notorious as a former Nazi sympathizer and leader of the Ku Klux Klan. Finally, Roemer had angered many voters because he broke his promise not to raise taxes. Most experts on Louisiana politics believed that Roemer would have been able to defeat either Edwards or Duke in a runoff, but he finished third. Edwards easily defeated Duke in the runoff and became governor of Louisiana once again.

QUESTIONS TO CONSIDER

1. What are the advantages of an open primary system such as the one in Louisiana?
2. What are the disadvantages of an open primary?
3. Would you like to see Texas adopt an open primary system? Why or why not?

Local Elections

Under state law, local elections for city, school district, and special district officials must be held on one of four dates: the third Saturday in January, the first Saturday in May, the second Saturday in August, or the first Tuesday after the first Monday in November. Local governments usually conduct their elections in odd-numbered years so they will not coincide with general elections for president, senator, and governor. Most city governments choose officials by majority vote, with a runoff election if no one candidate receives a majority in a multicandidate field. Most school districts choose the members of their boards of trustees by plurality vote—the candidate who receives the most votes wins regardless of whether it is a majority. The state constitution *requires* majority election for terms of office greater than two years. State law allows cities and school districts to cancel elections if all candidates are running unopposed and no other issues are on the ballot.

Most local contests in Texas are **nonpartisan elections,** which are election contests in which the names of the candidates appear on the ballot but not their party affiliations. The supporters of nonpartisan elections argue that the elimination of political parties from local elections reduces corruption. Furthermore, they say that nonpartisan elections free local politics from state and national political controversies. In contrast, critics of nonpartisan elections believe they work to the advantage of upper-income groups because they reduce the amount of information available to voters about candidates. In partisan elections, the single most important piece of information voters have about candidates is the party label. In nonpartisan elections, voters do not know the party attachments of the candidates. They must do some research on candidates if they are going to vote in their own best interest. Upper-income persons are in a better position to determine which candidates best represent their interests because they are better able to learn about candidates than low-income people are.

Scholarly research largely supports the critics of nonpartisan elections. Turnout for nonpartisan elections is generally lower than turnout for partisan elections. Without party labels on the ballot to guide their choice, some potential voters stay home because they are unable to distinguish among the candidates. Furthermore, some people who do cast ballots base their voting decisions on such factors as incumbency, gender, and the perceived ethnicity of the candidates based on their names.[5]

> "Politics is the gentle art of getting votes from the poor and campaign contributions from the rich by promising to protect each from the other."
> —Edward Bennett Williams, attorney

Special Elections

A **special election** is an election called at a time outside the normal election calendar. Special elections may be used to approve local bond issues, which we discuss below, or to fill unexpected vacancies in the state legislature or the state's congressional delegation. Vacancies in executive and judicial offices are generally filled by gubernatorial appointment. When a vacancy occurs—say because a legislator resigns—the governor calls a special election. Special elections are nonpartisan, although party organizations often get involved. A candidate must receive a majority of the votes cast (50 percent plus one) to win a special election. Otherwise, the two leading candidates meet in a runoff.

Noncandidate Elections

Texas voters have the opportunity to participate in a number of noncandidate elections, including bond elections, recall elections, and referenda. A **bond** is a certificate of indebtedness issued to investors who loan money for interest income; in lay terms, a bond is an IOU. A **bond election** is an election for the purpose of obtaining voter approval for a local government going into debt. Approval for state government indebtedness is obtained through the adoption of a constitutional amendment.

Recall is a procedure allowing voters to remove elected officials from office before the expiration of their terms. If enough signatures can be gathered on petitions, disgruntled citizens can force a recall election to remove the targeted official and voters decide whether to keep the officeholder or declare the office vacant. The vacancy will then be filled in a special election. In 2003, California voters recalled Governor Gray Davis and replaced him with Hollywood actor Arnold Schwarzenegger, but that could not happen in the Lone Star State because state officials are not subject to the recall. In Texas, the power of recall is limited to the citizens of some city governments.

Many cities (but not the state government) provide for the **initiative process,** which is a procedure whereby citizens can propose legislation by gathering a certain number of signatures on a petition. Election officials then place the measure on the ballot for approval by the voters. Some cities also allow citizens to repeal ordinances passed by city council through a similar process. In some municipalities, city officials may place nonbinding referenda on the ballot. Furthermore, the executive committees of the state Republican and Democratic Parties sometimes include nonbinding referenda proposals on their spring primary ballots.

Texans vote on other measures as well. Voters must approve amendments to the state constitution. The legislature usually places amendments on the November ballot, in both even- and odd-numbered years. Voters must also approve the establishment and dissolution of special districts, such as hospital districts or municipal utility districts. Finally, **local-option elections** are elections held to determine whether an area will legalize the sale of alcoholic beverages.

? WHAT IS YOUR OPINION?

Does Texas have too many elections?

★ ELECTION DISTRICTS

Texas voters select public officials in a combination of at-large and district elections. An **at-large election** is a method for choosing public officials in which every citizen of a political subdivision, such as a state or county, votes to select a public official. The president and vice president, two U.S. senators, governor, lieutenant governor, comptroller of public accounts, land commissioner, attorney general, agricultural commissioner, three railroad commissioners, nine justices of the Texas Supreme Court, and nine justices of the Texas Court of Criminal Appeals are all elected in at-large, statewide elections. Furthermore, a number of local officials, including county and district judges, sheriffs, city mayors, city council members, and school district trustees are elected at large.

A **district election** is a method for choosing public officials in which a political subdivision, such as a state or county, is divided into districts and each district elects one official. Members of the Texas legislature, U.S. Congress, and State Board of Education (SBOE) are elected from districts. For example, the 150 members of the Texas House of Representatives are elected one each from 150 state representative districts. The state's 31 state senators are chosen from 31 state senatorial districts. A number of local officials, including county commissioners, city council members in some cities, and the members of boards of trustees in some school districts, are also elected from single-member districts.

REDISTRICTING

Election districts must be redrawn every ten years to adjust for changes in population. The process of redrawing the boundaries of legislative districts is known as **redistricting.** The Texas legislature is responsible for redrawing Texas house districts, Texas senate districts, U.S. congressional districts, and the districts for the state board of education. Local governing bodies, such as city councils and commissioners courts, redraw the districts of local officials. The national census, which is taken every ten years, provides the population data for redistricting.

One Person, One Vote

State legislatures have not always been conscientious about redistricting. During the first half of the twentieth century, the legislatures of a number of states including Texas failed to redistrict despite dramatic population movement from rural to urban areas because rural legislators did not want to relinquish control. As a result, the population size of some legislative districts varied dramatically. In 1961, the ratio between the most populous and the least populous U.S. congressional district in Texas was 4.4 to 1. The ratio was 8 to 1 for state senate districts and 2 to 1 for state house districts.[6]

The U.S. Supreme Court addressed this issue in a series of cases that established the doctrine of **one person, one vote,** which was the judicial ruling that the Equal Protection Clause of the Fourteenth Amendment to the U.S. Constitution requires that legislative districts be apportioned on the basis of population.[7] If one legislative district has substantially more people than another district, then the people living in the smaller district have more political influence than do the residents of the larger district. Suppose an urban district has ten times more people than a rural district. The people in the rural district would have ten times the influence in the election of a legislator or a member of Congress. Compared with the citizens living in the large urban district, the voters in the smaller rural district would effectively have ten votes. The Supreme Court ruled the Constitution requires that citizens have equal political influence regardless of where they live. "One person, one vote," ruled the Court, not "one person, ten votes." District boundaries would have to be drawn to ensure nearly equal population size. Although the Court allowed some leeway in state legislative and local district size, it required that U.S. congressional districts have almost exactly the same number of people. In 2002, for example, a federal court overturned Pennsylvania's redistricting plan because two U.S. house districts varied in size by 19 people—646,361 compared to 646,380![8]

The Supreme Court's one-person, one-vote decisions had a significant impact on policymaking in Texas. Because of the Court's rulings, urban areas gained representation while rural interests lost ground. The legislative delegation for Harris County, the state's most populous county, increased from 1 state senator and 12 members of the house to 4 senators and 19 house members.[9] African Americans, Latinos, and Republicans, all groups that are more numerous in urban areas than rural, increased their representation in legislative bodies. Urban problems such as education, transportation, race relations, crime, and health care won a more prominent place on the state's policy agenda.[10]

The Voting Rights Act (VRA)

The **Voting Rights Act (VRA)** is a federal law designed to protect the voting rights of racial and ethnic minorities. The VRA makes it illegal for state and local governments to enact and enforce election rules and procedures that diminish African American and Latino voting power. Furthermore, the **preclearance provision of the VRA** requires that state and local governments in areas with a history of voting discrimination submit redistricting plans to the U.S. Department of Justice for approval *before* they can go into effect. Congress and the president included the preclearance provision in the VRA in order to stay one step ahead of local officials who would adopt new discriminatory electoral procedures as soon as the federal courts threw out an old procedure. The preclearance provision of the VRA only applies to states and parts of states that have substantial racial and language minority populations with relatively low rates of voter participation. Texas is covered along with all or part of 15 other states: Alabama, Alaska, Arizona, California, Florida, Georgia, Louisiana, Michigan, Mississippi, New Hampshire, New York, North Carolina, South Carolina, South Dakota, and Virginia.

In the late 1980s and early 1990s, the Justice Department in the first Bush administration interpreted amendments to the VRA adopted in 1982 to require that state legislatures go beyond nondiscrimination to drawing districts designed to maximize minority representation. If a legislature *could* draw a district that would likely elect an African American or Latino candidate, then the legislature *must* draw the district. In other words, state legislatures would have to maximize the number of **majority-minority districts,** which are legislative districts with populations that are more than 50 percent minority.[11]

Why would a Republican administration choose to implement the VRA to increase African American and Latino representation in Congress and state legislatures? After all, most minority lawmakers are Democrats. The reason was simple: The policy also helped the Republican Party gain seats.[12] To construct majority African American and Latino districts, state legislatures redrew district lines to shift minority voters away from adjacent districts into new majority-minority districts. Because most African American and Latino voters are Democrats, the redistricting reduced Democratic voting strength in surrounding districts, threatening the political survival of some white Democratic members of Congress. The Georgia congressional delegation, for example, went from one African American Democrat, eight white Democrats, and one white Republican before redistricting in 1991 to three African American Democrats and eight white Republicans after the 1994 election. Nationwide, the creation of majority-minority districts after the 1990 census helped white Republicans pick up about ten seats in Congress, defeating white Democrats who were stripped of some of their minority voter support.[13]

In the mid-1990s, the U.S. Supreme Court overruled the Justice Department's interpretation of the VRA. Responding to legal challenges filed against majority-minority districts created in Louisiana, Georgia, and other southern states, the Court

"The conception of political equality from the Declaration of Independence to Lincoln's Gettysburg Address, to the Fifteenth, Seventeenth, and Nineteenth Amendments can mean only one thing—one person, one vote."
—Justice William O. Douglas, majority opinion, *Gray v. Sanders*

"Racial redistricting harms the party selected by most black voters."
—David Lublin and D. Stephen Voss, political scientists

declared that state governments cannot use race as the predominant, overriding factor in drawing district lines unless they have a "compelling" reason. The goal of maximizing the number of majority-minority districts was not sufficient to justify race-based redistricting, the Court said, because Congress enacted the VRA to prevent discrimination rather than maximize the number of districts that would elect African American and Latino candidates.[14]

? WHAT IS YOUR OPINION?

Should state legislatures consider race and ethnicity in drawing legislative districts?

The role of the VRA in the redistricting process changed considerably during the 1990s. At the beginning of the decade, the VRA forced legislatures to focus on race and ethnicity during redistricting and legislatures throughout the South created majority-minority districts whenever possible. By the end of the decade, however, the U.S. Supreme Court had made it clear that legislatures could not use race and ethnicity as the primary basis for redistricting unless they had a compelling reason. State legislatures could not regress; that is, they could not legally create legislative districts that would diminish the political influence of minority voters, but they did not need to increase the number of majority-minority districts.

The Politics of Redistricting

Redistricting is a highly political process. Legislative districts can be drawn to advantage one political party over another or one candidate over another. The drawing of legislative district lines for political advantage is known as **gerrymandering.** In the 1991 redistricting, for example, Democratic State Senator (now U.S. Representative) Eddie Bernice Johnson of Dallas used her position as chair of the Texas senate's redistricting committee to enhance her own chances of winning a seat in Congress. The congressional district she created not only included much of her old state senate district, but also excluded the residences of potential opponents.[15]

Gerrymandering can affect election outcomes. After redistricting in 1980, the political parties that drew the lines usually won more seats than they did before redistricting and almost always held the seats created for them throughout the decade. Furthermore, they generally won a higher percentage of seats than votes.[16] On average, a political party with complete control of the redistricting process can gerrymander legislative districts to allow the party's candidates to win 54 percent of legislative seats while only capturing 50 percent of the total vote.[17]

Democrats controlled the redistricting process in Texas following the 1990 census because they held a majority in both chambers of the Texas legislature and Democrat Ann Richards was governor. Republicans accused the Democrats of using their power to create congressional and legislative districts that were unfair to Republican candidates. In 1992, Democratic candidates for the U.S. house won 21 of the state's 30 congressional seats even though they received only 50 percent of the votes cast. Two years later, Republican congressional candidates carried the popular

"Never be surprised by how quickly self-interest can inspire a politician to rise above principle."
—Common wisdom

More than 50 Democratic legislators spent several days in Ardmore, Oklahoma in May 2003 in hopes of defeating a congressional redistricting plan that would favor the Republicans.

vote 56 percent to 42 percent, but Democrats still won 19 of 30 seats. Similarly, Democrats captured 17 of the 30 seats at stake in 1996 despite once again losing the popular vote, this time by 54 percent to 44 percent.[18]

The political landscape in Texas after the 2000 census was considerably different than it was ten years earlier because neither party enjoyed clear control of the redistricting process. Although Democrats still held a majority of seats in the Texas house, Republicans enjoyed a 16 to 15 advantage in the Texas senate and the governor, Rick Perry, was a Republican. The result was a legislative stalemate. The 2001 session of the Texas legislature ended without passage of a redistricting plan for either the two houses of the legislature or the Congress.

When the legislature and the governor failed to adopt redistricting plans, the responsibility for drawing new district lines for the Texas legislature fell to the **Legislative Redistricting Board (LRB),** which is an agency composed of the Speaker, lieutenant governor, comptroller, land commissioner, and attorney general

LEARNING EXERCISE

Do-It-Yourself Gerrymandering

The year is 2001 and you are a staff member to an aide for one of the Republican members of the Legislative Redistricting Board (LRB). You have been assigned to draft a redistricting plan for the Texas house for a county of roughly 420,000 people, a large enough population for three house districts. The only instructions you have been given are the following: Maximize the number of districts that will elect Republicans while adhering to the one-person, one-vote principle.

Assume that the grid below represents the county. Each letter is an area of similar population size. The **R**'s stand for areas that normally vote Republican by large margins and the **D**'s represent areas of comparable Democratic strength. Use a pencil to draw three house legislative districts.

Once you have completed the assignment, answer the following questions.

QUESTIONS TO CONSIDER

1. What did you do to ensure that you followed the one-person, one-vote requirement?
2. Number your districts 1 through 3 and then discuss which party is the likely winner in each district in the next election. Do you think your boss will be pleased with the districts you have drawn? Why or why not?
3. Your instructions did not mention the VRA. Under what circumstances would your redistricting plan likely violate the VRA?

R	R	R	D	D	D
R	R	R	D	D	D
R	R	R	D	D	D
R	R	R	D	D	D

that draws the boundaries of Texas house and senate seats when the legislature is unable to agree on a redistricting plan. In 2001, Republicans held four of the five seats on the LRB. Lieutenant Governor Bill Ratliff, Attorney General John Cornyn, Comptroller Carole Keeton Rylander, and Land Commissioner David Dewhurst were all Republicans. Speaker Pete Laney was the sole Democrat on the panel.

The LRB considered two main alternative redistricting schemes. Speaker Laney and Lieutenant Governor Ratliff proposed a plan that was designed to protect incumbent legislators of both parties. The two legislative leaders were more interested in protecting their friends and colleagues in the legislature than they were in advancing the cause of either political party. The problem for Laney and Ratliff was that the LRB makes decisions by majority vote and none of the other members of the LRB would agree to support their plan.

In the meantime, Attorney General Cornyn presented an alternative plan aimed at increasing Republican strength in the legislature at the expense of incumbent legislators of both parties. Based on voting history, Republicans would win control of the Texas house under Cornyn's proposal and increase their majority in the Texas senate.[19] To improve Republican chances to win seats, Cornyn ignored the interests of incumbents, even Republican incumbents. His plan would force 39 members of the house to run in the same districts, including 27 Democrats.[20] Many other in-

"Just as there are no atheists in foxholes, there are no nonpartisans in redistricting."
—Paul Green, political scientist

cumbent members of the legislature were put in new districts from which it would be difficult to win reelection.

Rylander and Dewhurst joined Cornyn to provide a three to two majority for the Cornyn plan, making it the official redistricting plan for the Texas house and senate. With some minor modifications imposed by a federal court, the districts drawn by the LRB elected the members of the Texas house and senate in 2002. As predicted, the plan enabled the GOP to win a majority of seats in the Texas house for the first time in more than a century and to increase the Republican majority in the senate.

Whereas the Republicans were pleased with the results of legislative redistricting, the Democrats were relieved at the outcome of congressional redistricting. Because the LRB only has jurisdiction over redistricting the legislature, a federal court drew the lines for the state's congressional districts. The court redrew the state's existing 30 congressional districts in such a fashion that incumbent members of Congress from both parties would likely win reelection. It then put one of the state's two new congressional districts in central Texas and the other in the Dallas suburbs. Although Republicans easily captured the two new congressional districts, the Democrats held onto a 17 to 15 majority in the state's congressional delegation because Democratic incumbents were able to retain their seats.

> "They [Texas Democrats] may look at themselves as important. But I look at them as irrelevant."
> —Congressman Tom DeLay, R., Texas

The Republican Party attempted to increase its strength in the U.S. House of Representatives by revisiting the issue of redistricting in 2003. Republican Congressman Tom DeLay of Sugarland, Texas, the house Majority Leader, presented the GOP leadership in the Texas house with a congressional redistricting plan that could lead to the defeat of every white Democratic congressman from Texas, producing a congressional delegation from the Lone Star State of 22 Republicans and 10 Democrats. When Tom Craddick, the Speaker of the Texas house, pushed for a vote on the plan in the closing days of the legislative session, enough Democrats fled to Ardmore to prevent a quorum, therefore preventing the plan from passing the house.

> "Obviously, this was done for political purposes . . . My interest in this was simply to send a few more Republican seats to Washington to hold on to a majority to assist President Bush in his endeavors."
> —State Representative Phil King, R., Weatherford

DeLay's redistricting proposal was highly controversial. Republicans said that redrawing the state's congressional district lines to increase the number of Republicans in Congress was fair because Texas is a Republican state. In 2002, Democrats won 17 of the state's 32 U.S. house seats even though 57 percent of Texas voters supported Republicans for Congress. If most Texans vote Republican, DeLay said, most Texas members of Congress should be Republican as well. In contrast, Democrats pointed out that redistricting anytime other than the session after the census is both unusual and unnecessary. They accused DeLay of a power grab aimed at ensuring continued Republican control of the U.S. House of Representatives. Democrats hold a majority of the state's congressional delegation, they said, because Texas voters in a number of districts split their tickets to vote Republican for statewide office while backing Democrats for Congress.

Shortly after the end of the 2003 regular session of the legislature, Governor Perry called a 30-day special session to consider congressional redistricting. The house quickly passed a redistricting plan and sent the measure to the senate where it ran into trouble. Many senate Republicans disagreed with the plan put forward by the house. In order to maximize the number of Republicans in Congress, the house plan linked most of rural and small town Texas to suburban areas, which vote reliably Republican. Republican senators from east and west Texas opposed the plan because their communities would be placed in congressional districts dominated by the suburbs of Dallas or Houston. Meanwhile, the senate Democrats held together to block consideration of the plan on the floor of the senate. The longstanding practice in the Texas senate is to require a two-thirds' vote before a measure can be considered on the floor. With 11 senate Democrats refusing to agree to debate, the redistricting bill failed. The first special session ended without accomplishing anything.

As the first special session ended, the Republican leadership set a trap for the Democrats. Lieutenant Governor David Dewhurst declared that he would not honor the two-thirds' rule in a second special session, therefore ensuring that the Republican majority would be able to vote a redistricting plan out of the senate. While Democrats caucused in the capital, Governor Perry called a second special session and Dewhurst ordered the doors locked to trap the Democrats inside. Unfortunately for Dewhurst and Perry, the Democrats got word of the scheme just in time and slipped out a side door. They drove to the airport and flew to Albuquerque, New Mexico, out of the reach of Texas authorities. With 11 Democrats in Albuquerque, the senate lacked a quorum necessary to conduct official business. The second special session accomplished nothing.

Before Governor Perry could call a third special session, the senate Democrats in Albuquerque broke ranks. Senator Whitmire returned to Texas, declaring that he and his fellow Democrats had made their point and the next battle would be in the courts. Whitmire said he would be on the senate floor when the governor called the next special session, ensuring a quorum. Although the other Democrats were furious with Whitmire, they had no choice but to end their boycott and return to Texas.

Whitmire's return did not mean a quick end to the redistricting battle because house and senate Republicans could not agree on a new map. After several weeks of wrangling, Congressman DeLay flew to Texas to broker an agreement. The house and senate passed and Governor Perry signed a redistricting plan that many observers believed would increase the number of Republicans in the U.S. house from 15 to at least 20 and maybe 22.

Democrats and minority rights organizations immediately filed a series of lawsuits aimed at preventing the plan from ever taking effect. They charged that the DeLay redistricting map violated the VRA because it diminished the voting power of minority citizens. In order to defeat incumbent Democratic members of Congress, the DeLay plan split communities of African American and Latino voters that typically vote Democratic and placed them in new districts dominated by suburban Republican voters. The Democrats also argued that the legislature and the governor violated the U.S. Constitution by redistricting after a legal redistricting plan following the last census had been adopted and an election had been held under that plan. Because the Constitution requires a census only once every ten years, the Democrats believe that it implies that redistricting should take place only once every ten years as well.[21] The federal courts would ultimately decide the fate of redistricting in Texas.

A special three-judge federal court ruled that the new redistricting plan was legal and constitutional. Although the judges criticized the timing of redistricting and the results of the process, they concluded that the legislature and the governor had violated neither the VRA nor the Texas Constitution. Consequently, the 2004 election would be held using the new district lines.

MONEY

Election campaigns are expensive. The total cost of the campaigns for governor, other statewide executive offices, and the legislature in 2002 was $216 million.[22] Candidates running competitive races for the Texas House of Representatives typically spend $600,000 or more. The cost of a Texas senate seat in rural areas is a million dollars; $2 or $3 million in urban areas.[23] Local contests in large metropolitan areas are expensive as well. The two runoff candidates for mayor of Houston in 2003 spent more than $12 million between them.[24]

Candidates need money to hire a campaign staff, cover overhead expenses, and pay for advertising. They hire consultants to plan strategy, pollsters to assess public reaction to candidates and issues, media consultants to develop a media campaign, field organizers to get out the vote, opposition research experts to dig for dirt on opponents, and fundraisers to raise the cash to pay for it all.[25] Other money goes for campaign literature, office space, postage, telephones, polling, and consulting fees. The largest single item in the big-time campaign budget is media, especially television. In 2002, Democratic gubernatorial candidate Tony Sanchez averaged nearly a million dollars a week in media costs.[26]

Advertising costs vary by medium and market size. The average charge for running a thirty-second television ad during the late night news in Dallas is about $5,000. A sixty-second radio spot during drive time in a major market is much less expensive, only around $600, but the audience for radio is only a fraction of what television reaches.[27] Candidates for statewide office buy advertising on both radio and television throughout the state if they have the money available. In contrast, candidates running for local office or the legislature may focus their efforts on less expensive approaches, such as radio advertising, cable television, and mail.

Candidates who are wealthy can bankroll their own campaigns. Sanchez and his family spent nearly $62.4 million dollars on his unsuccessful campaign to become governor. Similarly, David Dewhurst invested $24.2 million in his successful campaign for lieutenant governor, counting both contributions and personal loans.[28] Candidates who loan money to their campaigns can often raise money after the election to cover their loans, especially if they won the election. State law caps the amount of reimbursement for personal loans to $500,000 for candidates for governor and $250,000 for candidates for other statewide offices. Because the law puts no limit on reimbursement for third-party loans personally guaranteed by candidates, none of Dewhurst's loans were subject to the cap.[29]

> "The only people who can run for office are those who can self-fund, or those who can get money from wealthy special interests."
> —Fred Lewis, campaign finance reform advocate

? WHAT IS YOUR OPINION?

Should wealthy individuals be allowed to finance their own political campaigns?

Campaign money comes from a relatively small number of contributors. In 2002, just 48 wealthy families supplied more than half the money raised by GOP candidates for state office, giving $34 million of the $64 million raised by Republican campaigns. Bob Perry, a Houston homebuilder, was the top donor, contributing $3.8 million to

Republican candidates and campaign committees. Other major donors included James Leininger, a San Antonio businessman, Albert Huddleston, a Dallas real estate and oil investor, and Lonnie "Bo" Pilgrim, an east Texas poultry producer.[30]

Most of the individuals and groups who give money to candidates for office have a financial stake in the operation of state government. For example, Bob Perry and other members of the Texas Association of Builders favor legislation to shelter homebuilders from lawsuits filed by homebuyers. In 2003, the Texas legislature and the governor delivered for Perry by creating the Texas Residential Construction Commission. The nine-member commission, which included four builders, would adopt building standards for home construction and establish a dispute resolution process. Disgruntled homeowners would have to present their disputes with their builder to the commission rather than file a lawsuit.[31]

Even redistricting had a financial angle to it. Congressman DeLay enjoyed influence with house Republican leaders in part because he helped put them in place. DeLay created the Texans for a Republican Majority PAC and used it to raise $1.5 million, much of it from out-of-state corporations concerned with federal legislation, including Phillip Morris, AT&T, and Westar Energy. DeLay funneled the money to Republican candidates for the Texas house, focusing on 22 key races. When the GOP won control of the house for the first time in more than a century, DeLay was in a position to call in his IOUs by asking the Republican leadership to redraw U.S. congressional districts in order to increase the number of Republicans from Texas in Congress.[32]

Some contributors give to both major candidates in a campaign, even if they wait until after the election to open their checkbooks. When individuals and groups guess wrong by backing a losing candidate, they can make amends by giving to the winner after the election is over, a practice known as **catching the late train.** In 2002, for example, the Texas Association of Realtors (TAR) endorsed John Sharp for lieutenant governor and contributed $35,000 to his campaign. After Sharp lost the election, TAR gave $25,000 to Dewhurst, his Republican opponent. Similarly, Governor Perry raised a million dollars in campaign donations after Election Day from people who supported the Sanchez campaign.[33]

Most states restrict the amount of money individuals and groups can contribute to candidates for office, but not Texas. Two-thirds of the states limit campaign contributions and one-third provide public funding for campaigns in exchange for voluntary spending limits.[34] In contrast, Texas law places no limits on campaign contributions or campaign expenditures for candidates for executive or legislative office. Contribution and expenditure limits on judicial races are voluntary. In short, candidates for executive and legislative office in Texas can raise an unlimited amount of money as long as they report the names, occupations, and employers of people who give them $500 or more in campaign contributions.

Money is indispensable to major campaign efforts. In general, candidates who spend the most money get the most votes.[35] Money is especially important for challengers and first-term incumbents who usually are not as well known as long-term officeholders.[36] Raising money early in the campaign is particularly important because it gives candidates credibility with potential contributors, making it easier to raise money later in the campaign season.[37] Candidates who amass campaign war chests often scare away potential serious challengers.

"I don't think the average citizen puts the study, the man-hours into what's good for everybody. Maybe the larger donors may have more influence, but it's not necessarily influence for the wrong thing."
—Lonnie "Bo" Pilgrim, major campaign contributor

"We've now got a government by and for the wealthy few."
—Suzy Woodford, Common Cause of Texas

"You can always buy a ticket on the late train. It's just going to cost a lot more."
—Walter Mischer, Houston business leader

"The federal [fundraising] system is terrible, and the Texas system makes the federal system look like the Golden Rule."
—State Representative John Hirschi

? WHAT IS YOUR OPINION?

Would you support using taxpayer money to finance election campaigns in order to reduce the role of private contributions?

> "Money can buy admission to the arena, but it can't buy the game."
> —Sherry Bebitch Jeffe, political scientist

Nonetheless, money does not guarantee victory. Ask Tony Sanchez, who burned more than $60 million of his family's fortune and barely got 40 percent of the vote. Furthermore, studies suggest that a law of diminishing returns may apply to campaign spending.[38] The marginal difference between spending $15 million and $13 million is not nearly as great as that between spending $2 million and $4 million. After all, if the average Texas voter sees a candidate's commercial 15 times, will it make much difference to see it once or twice more?

The relationship between money and electoral success is complex. Although it is true that well-funded candidates are usually successful, it is perhaps more accurate to say that successful candidates are well funded. Major campaign contributors give money to candidates they believe are likely to win because they hope to gain access to elected officials. Money makes strong candidates stronger; the lack of money makes weak candidates weaker. In 1998, for example, Governor George W. Bush raised more than $25 million for his reelection campaign even though no one believed that his main opponent, Democrat Gary Mauro, had a serious chance of winning the election.[39] Individuals and groups gave generously to Governor Bush because he was almost a sure bet for reelection. Bush was also someone prominently mentioned as a likely presidential candidate in 2000. Major money players were eager to write big checks to the Bush campaign in hopes of gaining influence not just with the governor of Texas but also with someone who might become president of the United States.

TEXAS ONLINE ★ Forces of Change

Follow the Money

The National Institute of Money in State Politics has created a database that can be used to access information showing the names of contributors to candidates for state office. It can be found online at the following URL:

www.followthemoney.org/

Explore the website and answer the following questions.

QUESTIONS TO CONSIDER

1. How much money did your state representative raise in the last election campaign for which data are available? (To find the name of your state representative and state senator, click on "Who Represents Me?" at **www.capitol.state.tx.us/**.)

2. What types of financial interests contributed to your state representative's campaign?

3. How much money did your state senator raise in the last election campaign for which data are available?

4. What types of financial interests contributed to your state senator's campaign?

★ CAMPAIGNS

A **political campaign** is an attempt to get information to voters that will persuade them to elect a candidate or not elect an opponent. Many local contests are modest affairs. The candidates, their families, and a few friends shake some hands, knock on a few doors, put up some signs, and, perhaps, raise enough money to buy a small ad in the local newspaper. The contest may be hard fought, but the stakes are not high enough to support a major-league campaign effort. Not so, however, with statewide races, local elections in big cities, and contests for Congress and the state legislature. These elections feature professional campaign consultants, well-oiled organizations, and big money.

Big-time campaigns are long, drawn-out affairs, beginning years before voters go to the polls. Candidates spend the early months of a race raising money, building organization, and planning strategy. Candidates who successfully raise money and create a professional organization well before Election Day establish a reputation as serious candidates. In contrast, candidates who fail to raise money and create a campaign organization early in the political season will probably never seriously contend.[40]

An important goal for many campaigns is to improve the candidate's name recognition, especially if a candidate is a challenger who is not already well known.

> "Big business, big bucks, and big city slickers buy our elections."
> —Tom Smith, campaign reform activist

Why is Tony Sanchez smiling? He spent more than $60 million of his family fortune running for governor in 2002 but barely got 40 percent of the vote.

Races for low-profile offices may never move beyond the name-recognition stage. It helps if voters are already familiar with the candidate, or at least the candidate's name. In the 1970s, for example, a man named Bruce Wettman ran for state district judge in Harris County by posting billboards picturing his name written on an umbrella; the strategy must have worked because he won easily.

Sometimes candidates borrow name recognition from better-known namesakes. In 1990, a San Antonio attorney named Gene Kelly won the Democratic nomination for a seat on the Texas Supreme Court despite spending almost no money on the race. Primary voters apparently associated Kelly with the famous entertainer of the same name. "If I had been Fred Astaire, I might have won," joked Kelly's defeated opponent. Kelly's luck ran out in the general election when he lost to Republican nominee John Cornyn, who spent heavily on media advertising that attacked Kelly as unqualified. Ten years later, Kelly repeated his primary success by winning the Democratic nomination for the U.S. senate to oppose Senator Kay Bailey Hutchison. Once again, Kelly failed to mount a serious general election campaign and Hutchison easily won reelection.

Besides building name recognition, campaigns attempt to create a favorable image for the candidate. In the fall of 1989, advertising firms hired by Clayton Williams ran a series of political commercials that turned Williams from a virtually unknown candidate into the frontrunner for the Republican nomination for governor. Riding on horseback, wearing a white hat, and bathed in golden light, Williams promised to get tough on illegal drugs by teaching teenagers who use drugs "the joys of bustin' rocks."

> "You don't convert any voters to your side [with attack ads]. What you do is discourage voters from supporting the other side."
> —James Riddlesperger, political scientist

Campaigns also attempt to create unfavorable impressions of their opponents. In 2002, for example, Governor Perry ran radio and television ads that attempted to link Sanchez to the 1985 murder of Enrique "Kiki" Camarena, a federal narcotics officer, because the gang responsible for the murder had earlier done banking business with a savings and loan owned by Sanchez. The ads featured a pair of former drug agents who advised voters to "just say no to Tony Sanchez." Political scientists believe that candidates use negative advertising to discourage their opponent's support from going to the polls.[41]

> "The Latino vote, if it turns out, is going to be Democratic. But the dilemma is to turn them [sic] out."
> —Rodolfo de la Garza, political scientist

The last but perhaps most important task for each campaign is to get supporters to the polls. The most popular candidate will not win if his or her supporters stay home on Election Day. Well-organized campaigns identify likely voters and remind them to vote. The campaign will distribute early voting materials and telephone likely supporters to urge them to cast their ballots. Getting out the vote is usually more important for Democrats than Republicans. GOP voters tend to be better educated and more affluent than are Democratic voters and thus more likely to participate in elections. Turning out likely Democratic voters, especially African Americans and Latinos, often requires an organized effort.

THE VOTERS DECIDE

Why do voters decide as they do? Political scientists identify a number of factors influencing voter choice.

Political Party Identification

Political party identification is closely related to voter choice.[42] Democrats vote for Democratic candidates; Republicans back Republicans. On average, 75 percent of voters cast their ballots for the candidate of the party with which they identify.[43] In 2000, 79 percent of Democratic voters in Texas supported Democrat Al Gore for president while 96 percent of the Republicans cast their ballots for George W. Bush.[44] Nonetheless, party identification is a complex phenomenon. People identify with one party or the other because they agree with its issue positions, have confidence in its leaders, or feel comfortable with groups associated with the party. When citizens decide to vote for Candidate A because Candidate A is a Democrat (or Republican), their choice is more than blind allegiance to a party label but also a response to the perceived issue positions and image of the party.

Issues

Political scientists have long debated the role of issues in election campaigns. Many scholars believe that most Americans are too poorly informed to be issue voters. They note that most Americans lack a detailed knowledge of issues and are unfamiliar with the issue positions of candidates.[45] Nonetheless, other scholars believe that issues are important despite the average citizen's lack of detailed knowledge. Some high profile issues, such as abortion, can influence the choices of a substantial number of voters in races in which the candidates take opposing views.[46] Furthermore, issues are important to party activists who play a disproportionate role in the success of many candidates' campaigns because of their role as campaign volunteers and financial contributors.[47]

Political scientist Samuel L. Popkin uses the concept of low-information rationality to describe the sort of political thinking in which most people actually engage. **Low-information rationality** is the concept that because most voters have a limited understanding of the political world, they decide how to vote by using informational shortcuts about parties, candidate behavior, personal characteristics, and the relationship candidates have with familiar groups and people. Popkin likens low-information rationality to gut reasoning. Voters use their evaluation of a candidate's personal character as a substitute for information about the candidate's political character. They assume that the skill a candidate displays as a campaigner is an indication of the candidate's competence in office. They determine a candidate's issue positions based on the candidate's party affiliation and the individuals and groups who support the candidate. They also rely on the judgment of **opinion leaders,** who are individuals whose views shape the political attitudes of the general public.[48]

Incumbency

In most election contests, an incumbent enjoys a distinct advantage over a challenger. Nationwide, incumbent members of the U.S. Congress win reelection at a rate that typically exceeds 90 percent[49] and incumbent state legislators seeking reelection do nearly as well. The success rate for incumbent governors running for reelection is greater than 80 percent.[50] Furthermore, the advantages of incumbency

Campaign volunteers staff phone banks to get out the vote for their candidate.

are apparently growing. A study of legislative elections in the South finds that the number of incumbents winning reelection has increased and a substantial number of incumbents win without facing opposition in either the party primary or the general election. Many potential candidates decide not to run against an incumbent because they believe the incumbent will be difficult to beat.[51]

Incumbent success rates are based on several factors. Incumbents have more name recognition than most challengers and they are usually able to raise more money than their opponents can. Incumbent officeholders can often use their positions to generate favorable publicity for themselves through press releases. In contrast, most challengers, especially in down-ballot races, are hard pressed to generate any meaningful amount of press coverage. Incumbents can also make friends by providing services to individual constituents or groups of constituents.

> "A campaign is nothing but a machine that creates messages. Money is the conveyance of those messages, and the assembly of it is an essential portion of the game."
> —George Shipley, political consultant

Campaigns

Campaigns matter because they help define the choices for voters. Candidates attempt to raise the visibility of issues that benefit them and weaken their opponents. In 2002, the Sanchez campaign focused on insurance rates. He promised to roll back skyrocketing insurance premiums while branding Governor Perry as too beholden to the insurance industry to effectively address the problem. Perry responded by attacking Sanchez as a poor businessman who was so indifferent to public affairs that he sometimes did not bother to vote. Although Sanchez succeeded in damaging the governor's popularity, he failed to establish himself as a credible alternative to the incumbent.

Candidate Image

Voter perceptions of the personal images of candidates influence candidate choice. This does not mean that most voters are primarily concerned with a candidate's age, hairstyle, and wardrobe, at least not explicitly. Instead, they focus on qualities related to performance in office. One recent study of presidential voting concludes that voters evaluate candidates on the basis on their model of what a president should be like. This study found that voters regard competence, integrity, and reliability as qualities they desire in a president. On Election Day, voters pick the candidate they believe best matches the qualities the office requires.[52] Although political scientists have yet to conduct similar studies on state and local elections, it is reasonable to expect that voters may approach state and local election voting decisions in a similar fashion.

Retrospective and Prospective Voting

Citizens make voting decisions based on their evaluations of the past and expectations for the future. **Retrospective voting** is the concept that voters choose candidates based on their perception of an incumbent candidate's past performance in office or the performance of the incumbent party. If voters perceive that things are going well, incumbent officeholders and their party usually get the credit. In contrast, they get the blame if voters believe that the state or country is on the wrong track.[53] Political science research indicates that the state of the nation's economy is a key element of voters' evaluation of incumbent performance. As economic conditions worsen, citizens are more likely to vote against the incumbent party, and vice versa.[54] Similarly, research shows that rising unemployment rates hurt the reelection chances of an incumbent governor.[55]

Voter evaluations have a prospective as well as a retrospective component. **Prospective voting** is the concept that voters evaluate the incumbent officeholder and the incumbent's party based on their expectations of future developments. One study finds, for example, that voter expectations of economic performance have a strong influence on voter choice.[56]

National Factors

National factors can affect voting decisions in Texas. Presidential popularity and economic conditions can influence the outcome of races in nonpresidential election years.[57] In 1994, for example, incumbent Democratic Governor Ann Richards was hurt by the unpopularity in Texas of Democratic President Bill Clinton. Although Richards herself enjoyed a 55 percent approval rating, Clinton's rating in Texas stood at a puny 38 percent.[58] In contrast, Perry and the entire GOP ticket benefited from the popularity of President Bush in 2002.

Texas candidates can also be helped by popular national figures. In a presidential election year, for example, a popular presidential candidate can sometimes provide coattails to boost candidates of the same party in other races. The **coattail effect** is a political phenomenon in which a strong candidate for one office gives a boost to fellow party members on the same ballot seeking other offices. A study of presidential coattails in U.S. senate elections estimates that a 10 percent gain in a party's presidential vote in a state adds about two percentage points to the vote for its senate candidate.[59]

CONCLUSION: ELECTIONS AND POLICYMAKING

Elections have a significant impact on the policymaking process.

Agenda Building

Election campaigns focus public attention on particular issues. Candidates and parties who raise issues during a campaign often address those issues once in office. The big issues in the 2002 state election were insurance rate regulation, education finance, and medical malpractice insurance reform. The legislature and the governor addressed insurance regulation and medical malpractice insurance in the 2003 regular session and laid the groundwork to tackle education finance later in a special legislative session.

Policy Formulation and Adoption

Political scientists use the concept of electoral mandate to discuss the relationship between elections and public policy. An **electoral mandate** is the expression of popular support for a particular policy demonstrated through the electoral process. The concept of electoral mandate reflects the democratic ideal that elections enable citizens to shape the course of public policy as voters select candidates who endorse policies that the voters favor. On Election Day, voters judge officeholders on how well they followed through with their policy promises. In theory at least, the electoral system makes government responsive to the people.

In America, the relationship between elections and specific public policies is indirect at best. After all, elections are fought over many issues. Homeowners' insurance rates, education funding, medical malpractice insurance, and taxes all played a role in the 2002 governor's race. Furthermore, candidates do not always adopt opposing positions on major issues. Both Perry and Sanchez pledged to do something about insurance rates. Without a dominant issue or a group of dominant issues on which the candidates took opposing positions, the election outcome cannot reflect clear policy preferences on the part of the electorate.

Voter choice is based on more than just issues. Party affiliation, perceptions of the candidates' personal qualities and image, and voter assessments of past and future performance, especially economic performance, affect voter decisions. Perry won and Sanchez lost the 2002 governor's election because of a range of factors, not just issue positions.

Election constituencies overlap. Whereas the president is chosen nationally through the Electoral College, senators and governors are elected in statewide elections; members of the U.S. house and state legislatures are chosen from districts. One group of voters, desiring one set of policy outcomes, selects the governor; other groups of voters, preferring other policy outcomes, elect members of the legislature.

Furthermore, the constitutional system tempers the short-term impact of electoral change. Because of the separation of powers with checks and balances, and the federal system, no newly elected governor can achieve dramatic change without the cooperation of other political actors. Elections are one factor affecting the course of public policy, but they are not the only factor.

Policy Implementation and Evaluation

Elections have an indirect influence on policy adoption. Public officials may interpret an election outcome as an indication that the voters want the government to implement a policy more or less aggressively. Governor Perry took his election victory in 2002 as an endorsement by the voters of the issues they stressed during the campaign, especially his promise not to raise taxes.

Elections are a means for citizens to evaluate the policy performance of government officials. The concept of retrospective voting is that citizens base their election decisions on their evaluation of the performance of incumbent officials. Indeed, the history of elections in America is one of the voters tossing officials out of office when they believe that government policies have failed and reelecting incumbents when times are good.

★ REVIEW QUESTIONS

1. Why did Democratic members of the Texas house go to Ardmore, Oklahoma during the 2003 regular legislative session? Why did Democratic senators go to Albuquerque, New Mexico during a special session? Was their strategy ultimately successful? Why or why not?

2. What are the arguments for and against the long ballot?

3. How are general elections and primary elections conducted in Texas?

4. How do Texans participate in the presidential nominating process for the two major parties?

5. In Texas, which officials are elected at large and which are elected from districts?

6. What legal factors affect the redistricting process in Texas?

7. What is the role of money in Texas election campaigns?

8. What are the goals of an election campaign?

9. What factors influence voter choice?

10. To what extent do election results provide officials with an electoral mandate?

11. How do elections affect the policymaking process?

★ KEY TERMS

at-large election
bond
bond election
catching the late train
caucus method of delegate selection
closed primary
coattail effect
district election
electoral mandate
general election
gerrymandering
initiative process

Legislative Redistricting Board (LRB)
local-option election
long ballot
low-information rationality
majority-minority districts
nonpartisan elections
one person, one vote
open primary
opinion leaders
political campaign
preclearance provision of the VRA

presidential preference primary election
primary election
prospective voting
recall
redistricting
retrospective voting
runoff primary election
special election
split-ticket voting
straight-ticket voting
super delegates
Voting Rights Act (VRA)

★ NOTES

1. Thad L. Beyle, ed., *State Government: CQ's Guide to Current Issues and Activities 1985–1986* (Washington, DC: Congressional Quarterly Press, 1985), p. 93.

2. "A Closer Look at Harris County's Vote," *Houston Chronicle*, November 14, 2002, p. 32A.

3. Carolyn Barta, "Hispanics Credited with Third of Party's Votes," *Dallas Morning News*, March 17, 2002, available at **www.dallasnews.com**.

4. Charles S. Bullock III and Loch K. Johnson, *Runoff Elections in the United States* (Chapel Hill, NC: University of North Carolina Press, 1992), p. 144.

5. Brian F. Schaffner, Matthew Streb, and Gerald Wright, "Teams Without Uniforms: The Nonpartisan Ballot in State and Local Elections," *Political Research Quarterly* 54 (March 2001): 7–30.

6. Steve Bickerstaff, "State Legislative and Congressional Reapportionment in Texas: A Historical Perspective," *Public Affairs Comment* 37 (Winter 1991): 2.

7. *Wesberry v. Sanders*, 376 U.S. 1 (1964) and *Reynolds v. Sims*, 377 U.S. 533 (1964).

8. *Vieth v. Commonwealth of Pennsylvania*, 195 F. Supp. 2d 672 (M.D. Pa. 2002).

9. Victor L. Mote, "The Geographical Consequences of Politics in the United States and Texas," in Kent L. Tedin, Donald S. Lutz, and Edward P. Fuchs, *Perspectives on Texas and American Politics*, 4th ed. (Dubuque, IA: Kendall/Hunt, 1994), p. 10.

10. Mathew D. McCubbins and Thomas Schwartz, "Congress, the Courts, and Public Policy: Consequences of the One Man, One Vote Rule," *American Journal of Political Science* 32 (May 1988): 388–415.

11. Mark Monmonier, *Bushmanders and Bullwinkles: How Politicians Manipulate Electronic Maps and Census Data to Win Elections* (Chicago: University of Chicago Press, 2001), p. 62.

12. David Lublin and D. Stephen Voss, "Racial Redistricting and Realignment in Southern State Legislatures," *American Journal of Political Science* 44 (October 2000): 792–810.

13. David T. Canon, *Race, Redistricting, and Representation: The Unintended Consequences of Black Majority Districts* (Chicago: University of Chicago Press, 1999), p. 257.

14. *Shaw v. Reno*, 509 U.S. 630 (1993) and *Miller v. Johnson*, 515 U.S. 900 (1995).

15. *Texas Government Newsletter*, July 11, 1994, p. 1.

16. Peverill Squire, "The Partisan Consequences of Congressional Redistricting," *American Politics Quarterly* 23 (April 1995): 229–40.

17. Richard G. Niemi and Simon Jackman, "Bias and Responsiveness in State Legislative Districting," *Legislative Studies Quarterly* 16 (May 1991): 183–202.

18. Michael Barone and Grant Ujifusa, *The Almanac of American Politics 1998* (Washington, DC: National Journal, 1997), p. 1339.

19. Sam Attlesey, "Panel OKs Map Favoring GOP," *Dallas Morning News*, November 29, 2001, available at **www.dallasnews.com**.

20. *Capitol Update*, December 14, 2001, p. 1.

21. Edward Walsh, "Redrawing Districts Raises Questions," *Washington Post*, October 26, 2003, p. A04.

22. National Institute on Money in State Politics, available at **www.followthemoney.org**.

23. Sam Kinch, Jr., *Too Much Money Is Not Enough: Big Money and Political Power in Texas* (Austin, TX: Campaign for People, 2000), pp. 5–6.

24. "The Money on the Campaign Trail," *Houston Chronicle*, December 2, 2003, p. 30A.

25. James A. Thurber, *The Battle for Congress: Consultants, Candidates, and Voters* (Washington, DC: Brookings Institution Press, 2001), p. 4.

26. Christy Hoppe, "It's the Attack of the Radio Ads," *Dallas Morning News*, August 25, 2002, available at **www.dallasnews.com**.

27. Hoppe, "It's the Attack of the Radio Ads."

28. R. G. Ratcliffe, "GOP Winners' Coffers Fattened after Election," *Houston Chronicle*, January 16, 2003, available at **www.houstonchronicle.com**.

29. *Capitol Update*, December 13, 2002, p. 1.

30. R. G. Ratcliffe, "Wealthy Few Aided GOP's State Sweep," *Houston Chronicle*, December 22, 2002, pp. 1A, 23A.

31. HB 730, 78th Legislature.

32. Christy Hoppe and Todd J. Gillman, "'Soft' Funds Helped Fuel House Flip," *Dallas Morning News*, June 29, 2003, available at **www.dallasnews.com**.

33. Pete Slover, "Political Checks . . . and Balances," *Dallas Morning News*, January 16, 2003, available at **www. dallasnews.com**.

34. Malcolm E. Jewell and Sarah M. Morehouse, *Political Parties and Elections in American States*, 4th ed. (Washington, DC: CQ Press, 2001), pp. 67–69.

35. Randall W. Partin, "Assessing the Impact of Campaign Spending in Governors' Races," *Political Research Quarterly* 55 (March 2002); 213–33.

36. Anthony Gierzynski and David Breaux, "Money and Votes in State Legislative Elections," *Legislative Studies Quarterly* 16 (May 1991): 203–17; Robert K. Goidel and Donald A. Gross, "A Systems Approach to Campaign Finance in U.S. House Elections," *American Politics Quarterly* 22 (April 1994): 124–53.

37. Robert Siersack, Paul S. Herrnson, and Clyde Wilcox, "Seeds for Success: Early Money in Congressional Elections," *Legislative Studies Quarterly* 18 (November 1993): 535–51.

38. Anthony Gierzynski and David A. Breaux, "Money and the Party Vote in State House Elections," *Legislative Studies Quarterly* 18 (November 1993): 515–33.

39. The National Institute on Money in State Politics, available at **www.followthemoney.org**.

40. Stephen K. Medric, "The Effectiveness of the Political Consultant as a Campaign Resource," *PS: Political Science and Politics* (June 1998): 150–54.

41. Bud Kennedy, "Clever Candidates Use Vitriol to Curb Voting," *Fort Worth Star-Telegram*, October 29, 2002, available at **www.dfw.com**.

42. Warren E. Miller, "Party Identification, Realignment, and Party Voting: Back to the Basics," *American Political Science Review* 85 (June 1991): 557–68.

43. John R. Petrocik, "Reporting Campaigns: Reforming the Press," in James A. Thurber and Candice J. Nelson, eds., *Campaigns and Elections American Style* (Boulder, CO: Westview, 1995), p. 128.

44. Exit poll data, available from **www.cnn.com/election/2000/results/index.epolls.html**.

45. W. Russell Neuman, *The Paradox of Mass Politics: Knowledge and Opinion in the American Electorate* (Cambridge: Harvard University Press, 1986).

46. Elizabeth Adell Cook, Ted G. Jelen, and Clyde Wilcox, "Issue Voting in Gubernatorial Elections: Abortion and Post-*Webster* Politics," *Journal of Politics* 56 (February 1994): 187–99.

47. David P. Baron, "Electoral Competition with Informed and Uninformed Voters," *American Political Science Review* 88 (March 1994): 33–47.

48. Samuel L. Popkin, *The Reasoning Voter: Communication and Persuasion in Presidential Campaigns* (Chicago: University of Chicago Press, 1991), pp. 7–64, 213.

49. John H. Aldrich, "Political Parties in a Critical Era," *American Politics Quarterly* 27 (January 1999): 24.

50. Jewell and Morehouse, *Political Parties and Elections in America*, pp. 183, 202.

51. Thomas A. Kazee, "Ambition and Candidacy: Running as a Strategic Calculation," in Thomas A. Kazee, ed., *Who Runs for Congress: Ambition, Context, and Candidate Emergence* (Washington, DC: Congressional Quarterly, 1994), pp. 175–76.

52. Arthur H. Miller, Martin P. Wattenberg, and Oksana Malachuk, "Schematic Assessments of Presidential Candidates," *American Political Science Review* 80 (June 1986): 521–40.

53. Dennis M. Simon, Charles W. Ostrom, Jr., and Robin F. Marra, "The President, Referendum Voting, and Subnational Elections in the United States," *American Political Science Review* 85 (December 1991): 1177–92.

54. Michael S. Lewis-Beck, *Economics and Elections: The Major Western Democracies* (Ann Arbor, MI: University of Michigan Press, 1988), pp. 155–56.

55. Susan B. Hansen, "Governors' Job Performance Ratings and State Unemployment: The Case of California," *State and Local Government Review* 31 (Winter 1999): 7–17.

56. Brad Lockerbie, "Prospective Voting in Presidential Elections, 1956–1988," *American Politics Quarterly* 20 (July 1992): 308–25.

57. Thomas M. Holbrook-Provow, "National Factors in Gubernatorial Elections," *American Politics Quarterly* 15 (October 1987): 471–83; and Alan I. Abramowitz, "Economic Conditions, Presidential Popularity, and Voting Behavior in Mid-Term Congressional Elections," *Journal of Politics* 47 (February 1985): 31–43.

58. James Cullen, "Sick Yellow Dogs," *Texas Observer*, November 25, 1994, p. 7.

59. James E. Campbell and Joe A. Sumners, "Presidential Coattails in Senate Elections," *American Political Science Review* 84 (June 1990): 513–24.

ONLINE PRACTICE TEST

Test your understanding of this chapter
with interactive review quizzes at

www.ablongman.com/tannahilltexas/chapter7

CHAPTER EIGHT

The Texas Legislature

LEARNING OBJECTIVES

After studying Chapter 8, students should be able to do the following:

★ Describe the role of the Texas legislature in the policymaking process using homeowner insurance reform as an example.
★ Compare and contrast the Texas house and Texas senate.
★ Describe the impact of bicameralism, biennial sessions, and limited session length on legislative policymaking in Texas.
★ List the formal qualifications for membership in the Texas legislature and describe the changes that have taken place in the composition of the legislature since the early 1960s.
★ Evaluate the attractiveness of a seat in the Texas legislature, considering salary and nonsalary compensation as well as turnover rates.
★ Assess the impact of term limits on state legislatures.

★ Describe the organization of the Texas legislature, focusing on leadership selection, the powers and responsibilities of legislative leaders, the committee system, and legislative assistance.
★ Trace the steps of the legislative process, including introduction, committee action, floor action, conference committee action, and action by the governor.
★ Evaluate the impact of the following factors on the legislative process: legislative leadership, interest groups, constituency, the governor and other state officials, political parties, and political ideology.
★ Describe the role of the legislature in the policymaking process.
★ Define the key terms listed on page 216 and explain their significance.

Texas has long had the highest homeowner insurance rates in the country. In 2001, the average Texas homeowner paid $937 for insurance compared to a national average of $530. Insurance rates are relatively high in the Lone Star State because Texas has more weather-related disasters and more weather-related insurance claims than other states. Hurricanes, tornadoes, hailstorms, floods, and high winds all drive up the cost of insurance.[1]

In 2002, the Texas insurance market became much more difficult for the state's homeowners. The average premium rose by 38 percent between early 2001 and early 2002.[2] Almost every insurance company doing business in Texas increased its premiums well above the benchmark rate set by the Texas Department of Insurance (TDI), which is the rate determined by regulators as sufficient to allow companies to make a reasonable profit. Companies could charge as much as 30 percent more or less than the benchmark rate. Because of a loophole in the law, however, 95 percent of the state's insurance companies escaped regulation.[3] Furthermore, two major insurance companies announced that they would reduce their exposure in the state. Farmers Insurance declared that it would end coverage for its 700,000 customers in Texas as their homeowner policies expired while State Farm announced that it would stop selling new policies. Many Texas homeowners worried not just about the cost of insurance but about obtaining coverage at all.[4]

What caused the Texas insurance crisis? The insurance industry blamed a rash of insurance claims for toxic mold remediation. Although mold is common in the Texas heat and humidity and most molds are harmless, some molds cause allergic reactions in some people. In 2001, press coverage of the dangers of toxic mold produced an onslaught of mold insurance claims. Between 2001 and 2002, mold-related insurance claims in Texas jumped from 7,082 to 37,202.[5] Insurance companies stopped selling policies that included mold coverage and asked the state to crack down on unregulated mold remediation companies. They opposed state regulation of insurance rates, arguing that competition would eventually stabilize the market. In contrast, consumer groups warned that unregulated insurance companies were using mold claims as an excuse to gouge consumers. They called on state government to close the loophole that allowed most insurance companies to escape regulation.

The controversy over insurance regulation illustrates the role of the Texas legislature in the policymaking process. Insurance reform was a hot-button issue in the 2002 election campaign, with candidates for governor, lieutenant governor, and the legislature promising to take action. Consequently, insurance reform was on everyone's agenda when the Texas legislature met for its 78th regular session in 2003. We discuss what the legislature did about insurance reform below as we examine the Texas legislature and its role in the policymaking process.

This chapter on the legislature is the first of a series of five chapters dealing with the policymaking institutions of Texas government. The next chapter, Chapter 9, focuses on the executive branch of Texas government; Chapter 10 studies the judicial branch. Chapters 11 and 12 examine local government. Chapter 11 considers city government while Chapter 12 discusses the other units of local government in the state—counties, school districts, and special districts.

"The insurance industry doesn't want any type of rate regulation. We're a very competitive business, and if rates go up, there's a reason for it."

—Mark Hanna, Insurance Council of Texas

"When the [insurance] companies are left to their own devices, they can't be trusted to keep rates stable and ensure availability of coverage."

—Rob Schneider, Consumers Union

STRUCTURE

The Texas Constitution provides for a bicameral legislature to meet in biennial regular sessions of 140 days in length.

Bicameralism

Texas has a **bicameral** (two-chamber) **legislature** consisting of a House of Representatives and a senate. The house has 150 members elected from districts to serve two-year terms while the senate consists of 31 senators elected from districts to serve four-year terms. Senate terms overlap, with about half the senators standing for re-election every two years. The exception to this pattern occurs in the first election after redistricting when the entire senate must stand for election. In 2002, all 31 senate seats were up for election under new district lines drawn after the 2000 census. The newly elected senators then drew lots to determine whether they would have to run for election again in 2004 or 2006.

The Texas Constitution assigns each legislative chamber certain powers and responsibilities. The senate has sole authority to confirm or reject the governor's appointments by a two-thirds' vote. Only the house may initiate legislation to raise taxes, although both chambers must agree before any tax bill can pass. The house alone, by majority vote, has the power of **impeachment,** which is a formal accusation against an executive or judicial officeholder. The senate tries the impeached official, with a two-thirds' vote needed for conviction and removal from office.

The constitution requires that the two legislative chambers share certain responsibilities. Both the house and senate must concur before any measure can pass the legislature. Both must vote by a two-thirds' margin to propose constitutional amendments. Also, two-thirds of the members of each chamber must agree to override a governor's veto.

The Texas house and Texas senate often approach policy issues differently because of structural differences in the two legislative chambers. Compare, for example, Texas house and senate districts. Each house member represents approximately 139,000 people whereas the population of each state senate district is 673,000. Because state senate districts are roughly five times larger than house districts, they will probably be more diverse than the smaller house districts. Needing to please a more diverse constituency, senators may prove more moderate than house members whose districts are more homogeneous. In Texas, the two legislative chambers also differ in the length of the terms of office of members. house members must stand for election every two years, whereas senators serve four-year terms. As a result, senators can evaluate policy issues from a longer-range perspective than house members, whose next reelection campaign is always just around the corner.

Bicameralism has supporters and critics. Its defenders believe that bicameralism allows one house to correct the mistakes of the other. In contrast, the critics of bicameralism believe that a single-house legislature is more economical and efficient. Every state has a bicameral legislature except Nebraska, which has a **unicameral (one-chamber) legislature.** Nebraska adopted a state constitutional amendment in

1937 to create a unicameral legislature whose members would be chosen in **nonpartisan elections,** which are contests in which the names of the candidates appear on the ballot but not their party affiliations. The 49 members of the Nebraska legislature serve four-year overlapping terms.

The conventional wisdom is that bicameralism has a conservative effect on the policymaking process because two chambers must approve it before it can clear the legislature. Nonetheless, Professor James R. Rogers believes that bicameralism is as likely to increase legislative output as to decrease it because both chambers can initiate legislation as well as reject it. Furthermore, he says, the historical evidence from legislative bodies that have switched from unicameral to bicameral or vice versa fails to support the conventional view.[6]

?   WHAT IS YOUR OPINION?

Should Texas replace its bicameral legislature with a unicameral legislature?

Session Frequency

The Texas Constitution provides that the legislature meet in regular session every other year, in odd-calendar years (2003, 2005, etc.), with sessions beginning on the second Tuesday in January. In the late nineteenth century when the Texas Constitution was written, biennial legislative sessions were standard practice in most American states. As recently as 1960, 32 states still had biennial sessions. Today, Texas is one of only seven states whose legislatures do not meet in regular session every year.[7]

The Texas Constitution empowers the governor to call special sessions of the legislature, which may last for a maximum of 30-calendar days. Governor Perry called three consecutive special sessions in the summer of 2003 to consider and finally pass the redistricting legislation that failed during the regular session. Although most state legislatures may call themselves into special session, the Texas legislature has no such power.

Annual legislative sessions are near the top of the list of constitutional reforms proposed by those who would like to see a more streamlined state government. Reformers believe that the affairs of state government are too complex to handle in biennial sessions. Budget issues are particularly difficult to address in biennial sessions because the legislature can neither anticipate state spending needs nor estimate tax revenues over so long a period. Had the Texas legislature met in 2002, for example, it might have curtailed state spending or increased revenues, preventing the $9.9 billion budget shortfall the legislature had to confront in 2003. The most popular proposal for annual sessions would maintain the current 140-day session in odd-numbered years and add a shorter, 60-day session in even years. The 140-day sessions would write a one-year budget and deal with general legislative concerns. Sixty-day sessions would be limited to writing a budget, plus any additional matters the governor wished to submit for legislative consideration.

Nonetheless, biennial legislative sessions have their defenders. Give the legislature more time, they say, and Texas will have more laws, more regulations, more spending, and more taxes. Although observers often blame biennial sessions for leg-

"Biennial sessions are for when Texas was a horse and buggy state."
—Suzy Woodford,
Common Cause
of Texas

islative logjams at the end of a session, research shows that legislatures that have annual sessions have worse logjams than legislatures with biennial sessions.[8] For example, the New York legislature, which meets annually, has been ridiculed for years because of its inability to pass a budget on time. Furthermore, the citizens of Texas have expressed their support for biennial sessions every time they have had a chance to vote on the issue. In 1930, 1949, 1958, 1969, 1973, and 1975, voters rejected constitutional amendments that would have provided for annual legislative sessions.

> "No man's life, liberty, or property is safe while the legislature is in session."
> —Texas proverb

Session Length

Constitutional reformers would also like to increase the length of legislative sessions in the Lone Star State. With sessions limited to 140-calendar days, the legislature may not have time to do the state's business. The legislature often falls behind and has to act on a flood of bills in the last few weeks of the session before time runs out. On the last day of the 1995 session, for example, the senate acted on 72 bills and resolutions in a span of only 90 minutes.[9]

Defenders of the 140-day session point out that legislative session limits are common among the states and a useful device for forcing legislators to get down to business. Political scientist Malcolm Jewell believes that session limits force lawmakers to make decisions because they establish a defined endpoint, a looming deadline, for wrapping up business. "When there's no limit," he says, "it drags on. They [legislators] postpone compromise to the last minute; they bargain; they play games."[10]

Research shows that the legislative workload in Texas is not as congested as conventional wisdom suggests. Legislative activity in Texas tends to concentrate at certain times, such as the deadline for submitting bills and the end of the session, but lawmakers work on legislation throughout the session. Although 80 percent of the votes for final passage of bills comes in the last two weeks of the session, most of the measures passed have been under legislative consideration for months.[11] Furthermore, the Texas house and senate have adopted rules to prevent a last minute rush of legislative activity.

 WHAT IS YOUR OPINION?

Should the Texas legislature meet in annual sessions?

★ MEMBERSHIP

In 2003, the combined membership of the Texas house and senate included 38 Latinos, 16 African Americans, 1 Asian American, and 36 women out of 181 members. Every African American member of the legislature and all but one of the Latinos were Democrats. In contrast, only 2 out of the 107 Republicans in the legislature were minority, a Hispanic and the Asian American member.

Although the Texas legislature is a more diverse body than at any time in its history, it is not a cross-section of the state's population. As Figure 8.1 indicates,

The capitol dome.

Latinos, African Americans, Asian Americans, and women were all underrepresented in the 78th Legislature whereas non-Hispanic whites were overrepresented. Times are changing, though, and the number of women and minorities in the legislature continues to increase. Several recent scholarly studies have found that gender alone is not an insurmountable barrier for women candidates. A more significant problem for female candidates is that few women are **incumbents,** that is, current officeholders. Women challengers have the same difficulties raising money, building campaign organizations, and getting media attention that male challengers face. As more women run for office and some win, those barriers will become less formi-

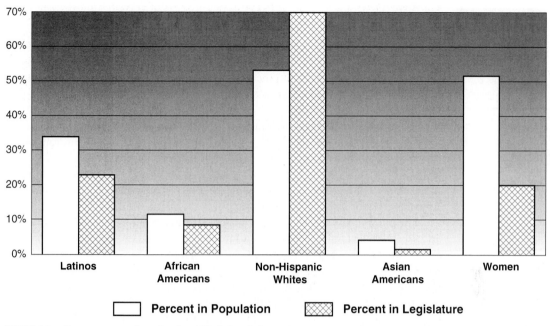

FIGURE 8.1   Representation in the 78th Legislature

dable.[12] Also, a recent poll shows that the percentage of Texans expressing prejudice toward persons of another race has declined significantly over the last 20 years.[13] Greater racial tolerance may lead to the election of more minority candidates to public office.

Compensation

"It's just not reasonable to pay lawmakers only $600 a month to deal with issues of huge importance and multibillion-dollar budgets."
—George Christian, political consultant

The official salary for members of the legislature, whether they serve in the house or senate, is set by the Texas Constitution at $600 a month or $7,200 a year. Compared with other states, this figure is low. Several states, including New York and California have full-time, professional legislatures, and pay their lawmakers accordingly: $57,500 a year in New York, $75,600 in California. Even most states whose legislatures meet for limited periods, as in Texas, pay their lawmakers more than Texas legislators receive. Members of the Oklahoma legislature receive $32,000 a year. The pay for legislators in Louisiana is $16,800 a year. Florida legislators receive $24,912 annually.[14]

Should legislators be paid more? The proponents of higher legislative salaries believe that better pay would allow a wide cross-section of Texans to seek office, not just people who are independently wealthy or have careers that permit them time off to attend legislative sessions. Furthermore, higher salaries would help keep legislators independent of interest groups. In contrast, defenders of the current salary structure argue that low salaries ensure the continuation of a citizen-legislature whose members are relatively immune from outside pressures. Because lawmakers are not dependent on legislative salaries, they are more willing to take political chances to do the right thing than they would if their salaries were higher.

Nonsalary compensation for Texas legislators is relatively generous. When the legislature is in session, lawmakers receive a daily expense allowance of $125. The allowance enables legislators to increase their earnings by $16,660 for each regular session and $3,570 for each 30-day special session. Furthermore, legislators have provided themselves with one of the most generous pension plans in the nation. When Representative Tom Uher lost his race for reelection in 2002 after serving 35 years in the Texas house, he immediately began collecting an $80,000 annual pension. Members who serve a minimum of eight years can qualify for a pension of $18,700 a year at age 60.[15] Members serving 12 or more years can begin collecting at 50 years of age. For each year of legislative service, a member receives an annual pension equal to 2.5 percent of the salary of a state district judge, which was $101,700 in 2002.

Legislators may also use excess campaign funds to supplement their incomes and enrich their families. State law allows legislators to deposit leftover campaign funds into officeholder accounts that can be used to pay for whatever expenses the lawmaker wants to cover.[16] Although legislators use money from their officeholder accounts to help cover the expense of operating a legislative office, some lawmakers divert money for personal and family expenses. In 2001, a state senator from Harris County used his officeholder account to purchase a Jeep Cherokee for more than $37,000. He explained that the vehicle would only be used for campaigning even though he did not have to face reelection for more than a year.[17] During the 2003 legislative session, Speaker Craddick paid his daughter $45,000 from his officeholder account to advise his political campaign about legal issues, fundraising, and, ironically, ethics.[18]

Legislative Turnover

Legislative turnover refers to the replacement of individual members of a legislature from one session to the next. Legislative turnover peaks in the first election after redistricting because the redistricting process changes the geography of legislative districts. Some legislators retire rather than attempt reelection from new, less hospitable districts while others are defeated for reelection. The 78th Legislature, which was the first legislature elected from lines drawn after the 2000 census, included 43 new members, 5 senators and 38 members of the house. In contrast, legislative turnover declines as redistricting approaches. Incumbents have become entrenched and potential challengers often choose to wait until after redistricting before deciding whether to run. The 77th Legislature, the last legislature elected under the lines drawn after the 1990 Census, included only 11 new faces out of 181 members, 1 in the senate and 10 in the house.

Legislative turnover is generally more often the result of voluntary retirement than election defeat. Some members leave because they know they cannot win reelection while others quit out of frustration. They complain about low pay, poor staff support, little public appreciation for their efforts, the hectic pace of legislative sessions, and pressure from interest groups and constituents. house members in particular often grow cynical about their ability to accomplish their goals. Not all reasons

The membership of the Texas legislature is more diverse today than at any time in its history.

for leaving are negative. Some legislators attempt to move up the political ladder by running for higher office. Others choose to leave because their law practice has picked up or they receive a business offer they cannot refuse. Some resign to become lobbyists, who are paid far more generously than legislators are paid. Lobbyist Neal Jones, Jr., an ex-legislator, manages lobby contracts worth $1,875,000, making substantially more money than he earned as a member of the legislature.[19]

Term Limits

Term limitation refers to the movement to restrict the number of terms elected officials may serve. Sixteen states limit the terms of state legislators. Limits for members of the house range from 6 to 12 years. They vary from 8 to 12 years for state senators. The legislature enacted term limits in only one of the states that have legislative term limits.[20] In every other state, the voters adopted term limitation through the **initiative process,** which is a procedure whereby citizens can propose the adoption of a policy measure by gathering a prerequisite number of signatures. State officials then place the measure on the ballot for approval by the voters. Because Texas does not have initiative, most observers think it is unlikely that the state will adopt term limitation. Although polls show that term limits are popular with the voters, many members of the legislature are unwilling to vote themselves out of a job.

The advocates of term limits believe that they will improve the capacity of the legislature to do its work. They offer the following arguments on behalf of term limitation:

- Members who are not career-oriented can focus on solving the state's problems rather than entrenching themselves in office.

- By forcing veteran lawmakers from office, term limits give new people with fresh ideas an opportunity to have an impact on public policy.
- Term limits reduce the power of interest groups by forcing their favorite lawmakers from office.

In contrast, the opponents of term limitation are convinced that term limits make legislatures less effective. Here are some of the arguments that they offer against term limitation:

- Legislators with valuable experience and expertise will be forced from office.
- Bureaucrats and lobbyists will be more powerful because it will be easier for them to outwit inexperienced lawmakers than it was the veteran legislators who were forced to retire.
- Legislators will only concern themselves with short-run problems because they serve for limited periods of time.

In practice, term limits have been neither as beneficial as their advocates have hoped nor as harmful as their opponents have warned. On the positive side, state legislators who are term limited place a greater emphasis on the needs of the state as a whole relative to the interests of the districts they represent. Term-limited legislators are less focused on obtaining special benefits for their districts than are other legislators. On the negative side, term limits strengthen the governor and possibly legislative staffers while weakening legislative leaders. Because term-limited legislators are relatively inexperienced, they have not developed the personal relationships that form the basis for legislative compromise and cooperation. Consequently, influence slips away from the legislature toward other political actors, especially executive branch officials and legislative staffers.[21]

ORGANIZATION

Modern legislatures choose leaders, establish committees, and hire staff assistance in order to facilitate their work.

Leadership

The lieutenant governor and Speaker of the house are the presiding officers and foremost political leaders of the Texas legislature. The lieutenant governor, who presides in the senate, is elected statewide for a four-year term in the same general election year in which the governor is chosen. In contrast to the president and vice president of the United States, the governor and lieutenant governor do not run as a formal ticket. Voters cast ballots for the two offices separately and may choose individuals from different political parties. In 1994 when Republican George W. Bush was initially elected governor, Bob Bullock, a Democrat, was reelected lieutenant governor.

If the office of lieutenant governor becomes vacant, the senate chooses a successor. When Bush resigned as governor to move to the White House in 2001, Lieutenant Governor Rick Perry moved up to become governor, leaving the office

NATIONAL PERSPECTIVE

Repealing Term Limits in Idaho

In 1994, Idaho voters adopted the most sweeping term limits law in the country. The measure, which received nearly 60 percent of the vote, restricted the terms of every elected state official from the governor down to county commissioners and school board members. It limited most state and local officials to 8 years in office over any 15-year period; county commissioners and school board members could serve no more than 6 years out of 11. Because the term limit clock did not begin ticking until 1996, term limits would not apply to officials in major offices until 2004; it would not impact local officeholders until 2002.

Opposition to term limits grew as the date for their implementation approached. The Republican Party, which is the majority party in Idaho, declared its opposition to term limits because many of its officials, including the legislative leadership, would be forced from office. Party leaders worked behind the scenes to convince Republican legislators to vote to repeal term limits. Local officials and business leaders in rural areas opposed term limits as well because of their potential impact on local government. In sparsely populated rural areas, relatively few people may be willing to serve in low-pay or no-pay positions as county officials and school board members. If long-term incumbents were forced from office by term limits, perhaps no one would be willing to take their places.

In 2002, Idaho became the first (and so far only) state to repeal term limits. Early in the year, the legislature voted for repeal, overriding the governor's veto. Term limit supporters gathered sufficient signatures to put the issue on the ballot to give the voters the chance to "repeal the repeal" in the November 2002 election. By the narrow margin of 1,889 votes out of more than 400,000 ballots cast, Idahoans approved the legislature's action and sustained the repeal of term limits, with rural voters providing the margin of victory. The issue of term limits may not be resolved, however, because term limitation proponents vowed to raise the issue again in 2004.*

QUESTIONS TO CONSIDER

1. When the idea of legislative term limits was introduced more than a decade ago, Republicans supported the concept. Now, however, they oppose term limits, at least in Idaho. Why do you think many Republicans switched sides?
2. Do you think that Idaho voters would support term limits if local governments were exempted?
3. For which level of government are term limits the most appropriate (if any)?

*Daniel A. Smith, "Overturning Term limits: The Legislature's Own Private Idaho?" *P.S. Political Science and Politics* (April 2003): 215–20.

of lieutenant governor vacant. The 31 members of the Texas senate selected fellow Senator Bill Ratliff to replace Perry by majority vote. Ratliff served the remainder of Perry's term as lieutenant governor without resigning his senate seat. He chose not to stand for election as lieutenant governor in 2002, preferring to run for reelection to the senate.

The Speaker, who presides in the house, is a state representative who is selected by the members of the house to serve as Speaker. Because the Speaker's powers are extraordinary, the race for the position may be intense. State representatives who hope to become Speaker gather signed pledges of support from other house members in hopes of obtaining majority backing well ahead of the actual vote. Usually one candidate wraps up the race early, months or even years ahead of the vote. Because representatives do not want to be on the Speaker's bad side, members quickly climb on the bandwagon as soon as it becomes clear that one candidate has the edge. Voting for the Speaker is done publicly rather than by secret ballot, so members who vote against the Speaker may fear retaliation. Consequently, the actual vote for Speaker is usually lopsided. In 2003, Republican Tom Craddick won election as Speaker with only one dissenting vote.

The race for Speaker in 2003 illustrates the dynamics of the process. Incumbent Speaker Pete Laney, a Democrat, hoped to hold onto the office despite the adoption of a redistricting plan that would almost certainly give the Republican Party a majority of seats in the Texas house. Because he enjoyed a close personal relationship with a number of veteran Republican legislators, Laney figured he could win reelection as Speaker as long as the seat margin between the two parties was relatively close. Craddick was Laney's main Republican opponent, but several other GOP lawmakers announced their candidacies as well, hoping to become the compromise alternative choice if neither Laney nor Craddick could line up majority support. When the Republicans won 88 out of 150 house seats in the 2002 election, most political analysts figured that Laney would not have enough support to keep his job. The day after the election, a group of Democratic house members announced their support for Craddick as Speaker and before long almost every member of the house had signed onto the Craddick bandwagon.

> "Anybody with any common sense would try to catch that train with the Republican label on it before it left town."
>
> —State Representative Al Edwards, D., Houston, explaining his support for Republican Tom Craddick as House Speaker

The Speaker and lieutenant governor are two of the most powerful public officials in the state, exercising extraordinary authority in their respective chambers. The Speaker and lieutenant governor control many of the legislative procedures of the house and senate. They assign bills to committee and, once committees have done their work, they have considerable influence over which bills are scheduled for debate. As presiding officers in their respective chambers, the Speaker and lieutenant governor recognize members for debate, rule on points of order, and interpret rules.

The Speaker and lieutenant governor rarely participate directly in the official deliberations of their respective chambers. As an elected member of the house, the Speaker is entitled to participate in debate and vote on every issue before the chamber. In practice, though, the Speaker seldom engages in floor discussions and only votes on those matters for which he or she wishes to register strong support. With the exception of Ratliff, who was a state senator, the lieutenant governor is technically not a member of the senate and may vote only to break a tie.

The Speaker and lieutenant governor serve on and make appointments to some of the state's most important policymaking bodies, including the Legislative Budget Board (LBB) and the Legislative Redistricting Board (LRB). The **Legislative Budget Board (LBB)** is an agency created by the legislature to study state revenue and budgetary needs between legislative sessions and prepare budget and appropriations bills to submit to the legislature. The **Legislative Redistricting Board (LRB),** which is composed of the Speaker, lieutenant governor, comptroller, land commissioner, and attorney general, is responsible for redrawing the boundaries of Texas house and senate seats when the legislature is unable to agree on a redistricting plan.

Finally, the Speaker and lieutenant governor exercise considerable control over committee membership. They appoint legislative committee chairs, vice chairs, subcommittee chairs, most committee members, and some subcommittee members. We discuss this procedure in more detail in the section below.

Although the lieutenant governor and the Speaker have extraordinary powers, they seldom act in an arbitrary or dictatorial fashion. For the most part, the powers of the Speaker and lieutenant governor are not spelled out in the state constitution and as recently as the 1930s their authority extended little beyond presiding. The powers of the leadership have grown because of changes in house and senate rules adopted by majority vote in each chamber that could just as easily be withdrawn. The offices of Speaker and lieutenant governor have acquired and maintained such broad authority because the people who have held the posts have generally exercised power in a fashion that a majority of legislators approve.

The Speaker and lieutenant governor base their authority in their ability to keep most of the members of the legislature happy. Both the Speaker and the lieutenant governor are in a position to bestow favors on their friends. These favors can be as small as giving a legislator a larger office or as great as appointing a legislator to chair a prestigious committee. In either case, the legislator owes a favor that the Speaker or lieutenant governor can cash in when the time is right.

> "I've been given more responsibility in this session than I've ever been given before."
>
> —State Representative Ron Wilson, D., Houston, an early supporter of Speaker Craddick

The leadership of the Speaker and lieutenant governor is collective rather than individual. Each official heads a leadership team made up of supporters in the chamber. This is especially true in the house where the Speaker must first win the backing of a majority of members of the chamber. Both the Speaker and the lieutenant governor have a corps of supporters in the chamber that makes up their leadership team. The members of the leadership team advise the Speaker or lieutenant governor and work to organize the full chamber to support the leadership's position. The Speaker and lieutenant governor reward their team leaders by appointing them to chair the most important committees.[22] In 2003, for example, Republican Speaker Craddick named several of the Democrats who backed him for speaker to leadership positions in the house.

Committees

Some of the legislature's most important work takes place in committee. A **standing committee** is a permanent committee established to handle legislation in a certain field. Table 8.1 lists the standing committees in the Texas house and senate during the 78th Legislature. The Texas house had 40 committees in 2003, ranging in size from 5 to 29 members. The most common size for house committees was 9 members. The Texas senate had 15 committees, ranging from 5 to 15 members.

Committees are important because they enable members to divide the legislative workload. More than 5,000 bills may be introduced in a regular session, far too many for each member to consider in depth. Committees allow small groups of legislators to examine a bill in detail and then report their evaluation to the full chamber. Committees also permit members to specialize in particular policy areas. Most committees deal with particular substantive policy areas, such as higher education, criminal justice, or agriculture.

Legislators usually have strong preferences regarding committee assignments. In the house, the most coveted committee assignments are the Appropriations, State

TABLE 8.1   Standing Committees in the 78th Legislature

House Committees	Senate Committees
Agriculture and Livestock	Administration
Appropriations	Business and Commerce
Border and International Affairs	Criminal Justice
Business and Industry	Education
Calendars	Finance
Civil Practices	Government Organization
Corrections	Health and Human Services
County Affairs	Infrastructure Development and Security
Criminal Jurisprudence	Intergovernmental Relations
Defense Affairs and State-Federal Relations	International Relations and Trade
Economic Development	Jurisprudence
Elections	Natural Resources
Energy Resources	Nominations
Environmental Regulation	State Affairs
Financial Institutions	Veterans Affairs and Military Installations
General Investigating	
Government Reform	
Higher Education	
House Administration	
Human Services	
Insurance	
Judicial Affairs	
Juvenile Justice and Family Issues	
Land and Resource Management	
Law Enforcement	
Licensing and Administrative Procedures	
Local and Consent Calendars	
Local Government Ways and Means	
Natural Resources	
Pensions and Investments	
Public Education	
Public Health	
Redistricting	
Regulated Industries	
Rules and Resolutions	
State Affairs	
State Cultural and Recreational Resources	
Transportation	
Urban Affairs	
Ways and Means	

Affairs, and Ways and Means Committees. The committees of choice in the senate are the Finance, State Affairs, and Jurisprudence Committees. The committees dealing with business interests (Business and Industry in the house, Business and Commerce in the senate) are popular as well. Legislators may also prefer a particular committee assignment because of personal preference or constituency interest. A state representative from Houston or Dallas, for example, may favor service on the Urban Affairs Committee.

House and senate rules limit the number of standing committees on which legislators may serve to three. Senators are restricted to membership on no more than two of the three most influential committees: Finance, State Affairs, and Jurisprudence. No house member may serve on more than two of the following three committees: Ways and Means, Appropriations, and State Affairs. No legislator may chair more than one committee.

State senators typically serve on more committees than do state representatives. Because the senate has only 31 members, individual members typically serve on 3 or 4 committees. In 2003, for example, State Senator Gonzalo Barrientos of Austin was the vice chair of the Infrastructure Development and Security Committee and a member of the Natural Resources Committee and the Nominations Committee. Because the house is larger with 150 members, individual representatives have more opportunity to specialize on committee assignments. In 2003, most house members served on only one or two committees. Representative Dianne White Delisi of Temple, for example, served on the Defense Affairs and State-Federal Relations Committee and the Energy Resources Committee.

The lieutenant governor and Speaker make most committee assignments. In the senate, the lieutenant governor appoints all committee chairs, vice chairs, and committee members at the beginning of each legislative session. The only restriction on the lieutenant governor's assignment power is that three members of each committee with ten of fewer members, and four members of each committee with more than ten members, must be senators who served on the committee during the last regular session.

In the house, the Speaker appoints committee chairs, vice chairs, and all of the members of the Appropriations Committee and the Calendars Committee. The Speaker also names at least half of the members of each of the other standing committees. House rules allow representatives, in order of seniority, to select one committee assignment, provided that the committee is not already half staffed. **Seniority** refers to the length of continuous service a member has with a legislative body.

Compared with the U.S. Congress and some other state legislatures, seniority is relatively unimportant in the Texas legislature. Although the members of the majority party in each chamber of Congress elect committee chairs, the lawmakers selected are usually the individuals from the majority party with the most seniority on the committee. In contrast, seniority is at best a secondary consideration in the selection of committee chairs by the Speaker and lieutenant governor.

An **interim committee** is a committee established to study a particular policy issue between legislative sessions, such as higher education or public school finance. Frequently, an interim committee is also a **select** or **special committee,** which is a committee that is established for a limited period of time to address a specific problem.

Interim committees may include private citizens as well as legislators. The Speaker, lieutenant governor, and the governor may appoint interim committees. Legislative leaders use interim committees as a way to compensate for biennial legislative sessions of limited duration. Because interim committees have more time to study issues and formulate policies than do standing committees they can lay the groundwork for legislation before the regular session begins.

Legislative Assistance

Staff assistance is important to members of the Texas legislature because they are essentially part-time employees asked to perform a monumental legislative task in a limited period of time. Legislative staff members improve the quantity and quality of information available to legislators, bring insight to issues, and help solve constituent problems. Texas legislators have sufficient funds to employ staff assistance in Austin and their home districts.

The legislature provides members with some institutional assistance as well. Before each session, the Legislative Council conducts a brief orientation for new legislators. During sessions, the staff of the Legislative Council helps members draft bills and assists committees. The Legislative Reference Library fulfills routine requests for research assistance. The House Research Organization (HRO) and Senate Research Center (SRC) research issues, help draft legislation, and prepare technical analyses of bills pending in the legislature. The HRO and SRC also publish daily floor reports explaining and presenting arguments for and against proposed legislation. Standing committees have permanent staffs as well, ranging in size from 1 to 15 staff members in the senate and from 1 to 6 in the House.[23]

THE LEGISLATIVE PROCESS

The legislative process in the Texas legislature resembles that of the U.S. Congress but with differences that affect policy.

Introduction

Each legislative session, members introduce thousands of bills and hundreds of resolutions. A **bill** is a proposed law, such as a proposal to prohibit small children from riding in the open bed of a pickup truck. A **resolution** is a legislative statement of opinion on a certain matter, such as a measure congratulating a Texas sports team for winning a championship. An amendment to the Texas Constitution takes the form of a **joint resolution,** which is a resolution that must be passed by a two-thirds' vote of each chamber.

Introducing bills and resolutions into the legislative process is fairly straightforward. Members of the house or senate may officially introduce legislation by filing copies in their own chamber with the secretary of the senate or the chief clerk of the house during a period that begins on the first Monday after the November general election. State Senator Mike Jackson of La Porte filed the insurance reform bill that eventually became law in November 2002, two months before the beginning of the regular session of the 78th Legislature. After the first 60 days of a session, members can only introduce local bills or measures declared an emergency by the governor unless they obtain the approval of four-fifths of the members of their chamber. Once a bill is introduced, the secretary of the senate or the chief clerk of the house assigns the measure a number, indicating the chamber of origin and order of introduction. HB 45, for example, indicates House Bill number 45. SR 102 stands for Senate Resolution 102. Senator Jackson's insurance reform bill was SB 14.

Committee Action

The lieutenant governor and the Speaker, in consultation with the chamber parliamentarian, assign newly introduced measures to committee. With important exceptions, the legislative leadership matches a bill with the committee that specializes in the subject matter it addresses. The lieutenant governor assigned SB 14 to the Senate Business and Commerce Committee. After the measure passed the senate and went to the house, the Speaker referred it to the House Insurance Committee. The exception to the general practice of matching legislation to the committee that deals with its subject matter involves the House State Affairs Committee and the Senate State Affairs Committee, which are general-purpose committees to which the Speaker and lieutenant governor regularly assign major pieces of legislation regardless of their subject matter.

Committees begin their consideration of proposed legislation by holding public hearings. The Senate Business and Commerce Committee and the House Insurance Committee separately conducted hearings on SB 14, taking testimony from spokespersons for consumer organizations, insurance companies, homeowners associations, and the TDI. A total of 72 people testified on SB 72, including 33 from the insurance industry.

After the hearings are complete, the committee meets for **mark up,** which is the process in which legislators go over a piece of legislation line-by-line, revising, amending, or rewriting it. Major legislation is almost always rewritten in committee, with the final product reflecting a compromise among the various groups and interests involved. Eventually, committee members vote whether to recommend the revised measure to the entire house or senate for passage. The Senate Business and Commerce Committee passed SB 14 by a 6–2 vote; the House Insurance Committee approved it 6–0. If a majority on the committee votes in the affirmative, the measure leaves committee with a favorable report. The report includes the revised text of the measure, a detailed analysis of the bill, and a **fiscal note,** which is an analysis of a legislative measure indicating its cost to state government if any. If the majority on the committee votes against the measure, the legislation is probably dead.

Floor Action

The procedure by which legislation moves from committee to the floor differs in the two chambers of the Texas legislature. In the house, measures recommended favorably by a standing committee go to the Calendars Committee for assignment to a

The detailed work of the legislature takes place in committees.

house calendar, which sets the order of priority for considering legislation. In 2003, the house calendars were, in order of priority, the following:

- **Emergency Calendar** This calendar is reserved for legislation declared an emergency by the governor and other measures deemed by the Calendars Committee to merit immediate attention. Tax bills and the **appropriation bill,** which is a legislative authorization to spend money for particular purposes, are usually assigned to the emergency calendar as well.
- **Major State Calendar** This calendar includes measures of statewide effect that do not merit emergency designation. The Calendars Committee placed SB 14 on this calendar.
- **Constitutional Amendment Calendar** This calendar is for proposed amendments to the Texas Constitution or ratification of amendments to the U.S. Constitution.
- **General State Calendar** This calendar is for bills of statewide impact, but of secondary significance.
- **Local, Consent, and Resolution Calendar** This calendar includes bills and resolutions that are not controversial as well as **local bills,** which are proposed laws that affect only a single unit of local government.
- **Resolutions Calendar** This calendar is reserved for resolutions.
- **Congratulatory and Memorial Resolutions Calendar** This calendar contains resolutions congratulating people, places, and organizations for various accomplishments or honoring individuals who have died.

Although house rules provide for the consideration of measures in order of priority as set by the calendar system, the house may vote by a two-thirds' margin to consider a measure outside the sequence established by the calendar system. On Mondays, which are known as Calendar Mondays, members can suspend the rules by a simple majority vote. House members may also suspend the rules on other days to sandwich time for items on the last three calendars between other measures.

The house calendar system becomes more important as a legislative session wears on. During the early months of a session, relatively few bills pass committee for assignment to a calendar and the house typically considers every measure before ending its legislative day. Toward the end of the session, however, the legislative pace quickens and the number of measures on the calendar grows. By the end of the session, measures placed on low-priority calendars risk failure for lack of action.

In the senate, suspending the rules to consider legislation out of order is standard practice. Although senate rules require that bills emerging from committee be placed on a single calendar for consideration in order, the procedure is almost never followed. The first bill reported out of committee at the beginning of a session is invariably a "blocking bill," introduced not to be passed but to rest atop the senate calendar, blocking consideration of other measures. In 2003, the blocking bill, SB 220, proposed the creation of a county park beautification and improvement program. Except for local bills and other noncontroversial measures, which are scheduled for debate by the Senate Committee on Administration, bills require a two-thirds' vote to be considered on the floor of the senate. An important feature of this practice is that 11 senators (one-third plus one) can block senate action on a bill they oppose. Consequently, measures without the support of at least two-thirds of the members of the senate do not even come to a vote in that chamber. In the 2003 special session on redistricting, the key question was not whether the senate would pass the measure, but whether enough votes could be found to bring the bill to the floor for consideration.

> "[The two-thirds' rule] protects the conservatives from wacky liberal bills and it protects the liberals from wacky conservative bills."
> —State Sen. Jeff Wentworth, R., San Antonio

Once a bill reaches the floor of either chamber, members debate its merits and, perhaps, offer amendments. Because house rules limit debate, the measure eventually comes to a vote unless the session ends before action can be taken. In the senate, members may speak as long as they please, and occasionally senators attempt to defeat a bill through prolonged debate, a practice that is known as a **filibuster.** Because debate can be ended by majority vote, the filibuster is not the weapon in the Texas senate that it is in the U.S. Senate where 60 of 100 votes are needed to shut off debate.

Both the senate and house set deadlines for consideration of measures several days in advance of the constitutional end of the session. Senate rules declare that no bill can be considered unless it is reported from committee at least 15 days before final adjournment. No votes can be taken on the last day of the session except to correct errors. The house has comparable rules.

Voting procedures differ between the two chambers. Members of the house vote electronically and a scoreboard displays each member's vote. In the smaller senate, the clerk calls the roll and members shout out their vote. In each chamber, a simple majority (50 percent plus one) of the members voting is sufficient to pass legislation. In the house, members sometimes cast votes for absent colleagues, even though house rules prohibit the practice. In 1991, for example, a legislator who was found dead in his apartment was recorded as having cast several votes after his death but before word of his passing reached the chamber. Nonetheless, ghost voting is unlikely to affect the fate of a bill because members who suspect funny business can ask for a verification of the vote in which the clerk calls the roll. Only members who answer "present" have their votes counted.

Conference Committee Action

A measure has not cleared the legislature until it has passed both the house and the senate in identical form. Sometimes legislation will pass one chamber and then go to the other for consideration. SB 14 passed the senate and then went to the house for consideration by that chamber. At other times, legislators will introduce similar or identical measures simultaneously in both the house and senate. Legislation that passes one house of the legislature may be rewritten in the other chamber, either during committee markup or on the floor. By the time a measure that has passed the house has made its way through the senate (or vice versa), it may well differ considerably from the measure originally passed by the other chamber.

What happens when the house and senate pass similar, but not identical measures? Frequently, the chamber that initially passed the legislation agrees to the changes adopted by the other chamber. When agreement cannot be reached, and this is often true with major pieces of legislation, the house and senate form a conference committee to work out differences. A **conference committee** is a special committee created to negotiate differences on similar pieces of legislation passed by the house and senate. Separate conference committees are formed to deal with each bill in dispute. In the Texas legislature, conference committees include five members from each chamber appointed by the presiding officers. A majority of conference members from each house must concur before the conference committee has finished its work. A conference committee drafted the final version of SB 14.

Once conference committee members have reached an agreement, the conference committee returns it to the floor of the house and the senate for another vote. Each chamber has the option of voting the legislation up or down, or returning it to conference committee for further negotiation. The house and senate may not amend the measure at this point; legislators must accept or reject the piece of legislation in its entirety.

All told, the legislature passes about a fourth of the measures introduced during a session. In the 2003 regular session, the legislature approved 1,384 bills of 5,592 measures that were introduced for a passage rate of 25 percent.[24] Many of the measures that passed were local bills or other noncontroversial pieces of legislation.

Action by the Governor

Once a bill passes the legislature, it goes to the governor, who has three options. The first option is to do nothing. If the legislature remains in session, the bill becomes

TEXAS ONLINE ★ Forces of Change

Tracking Legislation Online

The Texas legislature maintains a website to enable citizens to track the progress of legislation online: **www.capitol.state.tx.us/**
By entering the number of a bill, a citizen can follow the progress of the measure through the legislative process. The site can also be used to review the actions taken on a particular piece of legislation in a past legislative session.

Go to the website and enter SB 1317 for the 78th regular session of the legislature, which took place in 2003. Review the history of SB 1317 and answer the following questions.

QUESTIONS TO CONSIDER
1. What was the purpose of the bill?
2. Who was the bill's author (that is, the legislator who files a bill and guides it through the legislative process)?
3. Did the bill become law? Why or why not?

law after 10 days. If the measure reaches the governor's desk within 10 days of adjournment, it becomes law 20 days after the legislative session has ended. Governors generally use this option for bills about which they have mixed feelings. Although they are willing for the measures to become law, they do not want to go on record in favor of them. The governor's second option is to sign the bill into law. Governors often sign politically popular bills, such as insurance reform legislation, with great fanfare, staging televised bill signing ceremonies. Finally, the governor can issue a **veto,** which is an action by the chief executive of a state or nation refusing to approve a bill passed by the legislature. In 2003, Governor Perry vetoed 48 bills.[25] Except for appropriation bills, the governor must choose to veto all of a bill or none of it. For appropriation bills, the governor has the **line-item veto,** which is the power of the governor to veto sections or items of an appropriation bill while signing the remainder of the bill into law. In 2003, Governor Perry used the line-item veto to cut $81 million from the state budget of $117 billion, mostly targeting higher education.[26]

If the legislature is still in session, it can override the governor's veto by a two-thirds' vote of each chamber and the bill becomes law despite the governor's opposition. Nonetheless, overrides are rare in Texas. Because most bills that clear the legislature pass in the last two weeks of the session, the governor can wait until the legislature has adjourned before casting a veto and the veto stands unchallenged.

Laws take effect at different times. The Texas Constitution declares that all laws except the appropriation bill go into effect 90 days after the legislature adjourns unless the legislature by a two-thirds' vote stipulates another date. The appropriation bill takes effect on October 1, the beginning of the state budget year. The 2003 insurance reform measure took effect immediately because the legislature voted by a two-thirds' margin for its immediate application.

LEGISLATIVE POLICYMAKING

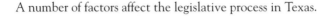

A number of factors affect the legislative process in Texas.

Legislative Leadership

> "A speaker who uses the office fully can virtually determine what does and what does not become law in Texas."
>
> —Ben Barnes, Former Speaker of the Texas House

The Speaker of the house and the lieutenant governor are the most powerful figures in the Texas legislature. They appoint members of their leadership team to chair committees and stack key standing committees and conference committees with members who share their political perspectives. They have the power to reward their friends in the legislature and punish their enemies. Their support greatly enhances any measure's chances for passage; their opposition almost certainly dooms a bill to defeat.

The centralization of legislative power in the hands of the leadership offers both advantages and disadvantages for the policymaking process in the legislature. On one hand, the centralization of legislative power enables the legislature to act on a fair amount of legislation in a relatively short period of time. Leaders with power are in position to make things happen. On the other hand, the disadvantage of a centralized power structure is that members who are not part of the leadership team may be left out of the legislative policymaking process. Texas is a diverse state, but that diversity has not always been represented in the outcomes of the legislative process. Historically, the poor, minorities, organized labor, consumers, and other groups not part of the conservative legislative majority have often had little impact on the outcome of policy debates.

Nonetheless, it would be a mistake to regard the Speaker and lieutenant governor as legislative dictators. Their considerable powers have been freely given to them by the members of the legislature and could as easily be withdrawn by majority vote of the membership. The Speaker and lieutenant governor hold power because they have usually exercised their authority in a fashion that most members consider fair. Most important, they have generally used their power to promote public policies acceptable to the majority in their chambers. In sum, the legislative leaders work to meet the expectations of their followers and help them attain their goals.[27]

> "Leaders these days are no stronger than the members want them to be."
>
> —Alan Rosenthal, political scientist

The support of the Speaker and lieutenant governor helped ensure passage of insurance reform in 2003. Because the conference committee did not agree on a bill until May 31, the house and senate had to act quickly to pass the measure before adjournment. The leadership moved the bill through its final stages just in time to go to the governor before the session ended on June 2.

Interest Groups

Interest groups lay the groundwork for influencing the legislative process by contributing money to candidates. Groups give money to legislative candidates because they want **legislative access,** which is an open door through which an interest group hopes to influence the details of policy. Consequently, interest groups target their contributions to the legislature's most powerful members, including the leadership and members of key committees.[28] During the 2002 election campaign, insurance interests contributed $1.3 million to candidates for the Texas legislature. Farmer's Insurance, which was then under indictment for price gouging, was the largest contributor, giving more than $339,000 through its political action committee (PAC). Rep. Craddick was the single biggest beneficiary of insurance money, receiving more than $186,000 in campaign contributions. Members of the Senate Business and Commerce Committee and the House Insurance Committee collectively recorded more than $200,000 in contributions from insurance interests.[29] Insurance groups also helped fund the Perry and Dewhurst campaigns, giving $542,000 to Perry and $102,000 to Dewhurst.[30]

Interest groups attempt to affect the legislative process through **lobbying,** which is the communication of information by a representative of an interest group to a government official for the purpose of influencing a policy decision. Some lobbyists represent a single firm or organization whereas others contract to lobby on behalf of several clients. In 2003, for example, former state senator David Sibley was a registered lobbyist for 34 interests. Sibley's clients included AT&T, Cap Rock Energy, the City of Waco, Entergy Services, Inc., Texas Association of Builders, Texas Medical Association, Universal Insurance Exchange, Wholesale Beer Distributors of Texas, and Zurich American Insurance.[31]

The debate over homeowner insurance reform pitted insurance industry lobbyists against consumer groups. The insurance industry enjoyed the advantage of a professional lobby effort backed by generous campaign contributions that targeted key members of the legislature. Industry lobbyists could call on thousands of insurance agents scattered throughout the state to contact their legislators on behalf of the industry's position. The industry also benefited in that the Republican Party, the political party most closely tied to business interests, had just won control of both chambers of the legislature. In contrast, consumer groups lacked the money either to back candidates in the 2002 election or mount a lobby campaign comparable to that of the insurance industry. Meanwhile, the Democratic Party, the party most closely allied with consumer organizations, had just suffered its worst defeat in the history of the state. Nonetheless, consumer groups did enjoy some advantages. Public opinion strongly favored insurance reform and almost every member of the legislature won office in 2002 promising to take action to address the problem of rising homeowner insurance premiums.

Constituency

To what extent do the actions of legislators reflect the wishes of their constituents? Political scientists identify three approaches legislators take to representation. The **delegate approach to representation** is an approach to representation in which legislators attempt to reflect the views of their constituents in a mirror-like fashion. They try to learn the majority consensus of their constituents on policy issues and vote accordingly. The **trustee approach to representation** is an approach to representation in which legislators do what they believe is in the best interests of their constituents. Legislators assume that their knowledge of policy matters is greater than that of most of their constituents. Consequently, they do what they believe is best for their districts. Finally, the **politico approach to representation** is an approach to representation in which legislators behave as delegates on issues that are highly visible to their constituents, while acting as trustees on other questions. Legislators vote their districts on matters of greatest concern to their constituents, but use their own judgment to decide those issues about which constituents have little knowledge or interest. In this way, legislators can protect their reelection chances while still exercising their own wisdom on most policy matters.

?   WHAT IS YOUR OPINION?

If you were a member of the legislature, would you act based on your own judgment of what was best or would you try to vote the way a majority of your constituents would want you to act?

Studies of legislative decision making have generally found that legislators take the politico approach to representation. Constituency is an important influence on legislators, especially on issues that are visible to voters, but other factors influence legislative decision making as well. A study of congressional decision making concluded that members of the U.S. Congress decide issues based on their own values and preferences in addition to their perceptions of constituent values.[32] Research on decision making in state legislatures has found that when asked to name the factors that affect their voting decisions, legislators identify constituents along with other factors, such as interest groups, fellow legislators, committee reports, party leadership, and their personal values.[33]

The most ambitious study of constituency influence in the Texas legislature is an examination of the congruence between the votes of legislators and constituents on two proposed state constitutional amendments in 1967. One amendment involved repeal of the statewide prohibition against the sale of mixed drinks in restaurants while the other would have required annual sessions of the legislature. Both amendments cleared the legislature by the required two-thirds' margin but only the liquor-sale amendment won voter approval. The study compared the votes of individual legislators on each of the measures with the votes of their constituents. It found 85 percent congruence between legislators and their districts on the liquor-by-the-drink amendment, but only 45 percent agreement on the annual sessions amendment. The authors of the study concluded that issue salience might have been the key factor accounting for this difference. Legislators are more likely to vote the views of their constituents on issues of high visibility than on lower visibility issues. The fight over liquor-by-the-drink was hot and heavy, but the discussion about annual legislative sessions was relatively subdued. As a result, legislators were better able to identify the preferences of their constituents on liquor-by-the-drink and, probably, more fearful of electoral retaliation if they did not vote the position of their constituents on the issue.[34]

Some of the most important constituency-based legislative divisions in the Texas legislature reflect whether a district is predominantly inner city, suburban, or rural. Inner-city residents worry about crime, public school quality, neighborhood restoration,

"A legislator is going to listen to his own constituents any day over me."
—Guy Spearman, lobbyist

Insurance industry lobbyists at work in the Texas capitol.

and opportunities for minorities. Suburban voters are concerned about property taxes, crime, annexation, and neighborhood preservation. Rural residents focus on agricultural issues, natural-resource development, and property rights. Consider how a legislator's approach to the issue of transportation varies depending on whether the lawmaker represents an inner-city, suburban, or rural district. Legislators representing inner-city districts are interested in state support for public transportation because many of their constituents depend on local bus systems to get around. Rural lawmakers focus on the construction and maintenance of highways and farm-to-market (FM) roads. Suburban legislators are interested in highways and public transportation alternatives that would enable their constituents to get from their homes to the downtown business district.

Public outrage over rising homeowner insurance premiums ensured the passage of some sort of reform legislation. Governor Perry, Lieutenant Governor Dewhurst, and virtually every member of the legislature promised their constituents that the legislature would address the issue during the 2002 election campaign. Nonetheless, the general public offered legislators little guidance as to the details of the legislation. After all, insurance regulation is a complex subject. The state's elected officials could claim to have kept their promise as long as the legislature passed a bill that could plausibly lower insurance rates.

Know Your Legislators

What do you know about the people who represent you in the Texas legislature? If you don't know the names of your state senator and state representative, you can find them online at the following Internet address: **www.capitol.state.tx.us/**. You can then get information about your legislators at **www.house.state.tx.us** and **www.senate.state.tx.us**. Read about your state legislators and answer the questions below.

QUESTIONS TO CONSIDER

1. What is the number of the state house district in which you live?
2. Who is your state representative?
3. Describe your state representative in terms of party affiliation, age, occupational background, political experience, and years in the legislature.
4. On which committees did your representative serve in the last session of the legislature? Were any of these among the more powerful committees in the house? Did your representative chair a committee?
5. Based on your state representative's committee assignments, do you believe that he or she is one of the more powerful members of the house? Why or why not?
6. What is the number of your state senate district?
7. Who is your state senator?
8. Describe your state senator in terms of party affiliation, age, occupational background, political experience, and years in the legislature.
9. On which committees did your senator serve in the last session of the legislature? Were any of these among the more powerful committees in the senate? Did your senator chair a committee?
10. Based on your state senator's committee assignments, do you believe that he or she is one of the more powerful members of the senate? Why or why not?

Political Parties

For most of the state's history, political parties played relatively little role in legislative policymaking because nearly every legislator was a Democrat. As recently as 1970, only two Republicans served in the senate while ten Republicans sat in the house. Neither the Democrats nor the Republicans in the Texas legislature organized formally nor did they elect party leaders or meet regularly as party groups. Even as the Republican contingent in the legislature grew, partisanship generally remained in the background. The Speaker and lieutenant governor included both Republicans and Democrats in their leadership teams and appointed legislators of both parties to chair important committees. In 2001, for example, Republican Lieutenant Governor Bill Ratliff appointed a Democrat, Rodney Ellis of Houston, to chair the important Finance Committee and Democratic House Speaker Pete Laney named a Republican, Delwin Jones of Lubbock, to chair the critical Redistricting Committee.

The 78th Legislature may well mark the beginning of a more partisan legislature, especially in the house. Many Democrats regarded Craddick as a polarizing figure because he was the longtime leader of the movement to elect a Republican majority in the Texas house. Even though Speaker Craddick appointed Democrats to chair a number of legislative committees, many Democratic legislators remained bitter. The atmosphere in the house worsened in the battle over the budget with many

"We [Republicans] went out there and argued our point [when we were in the minority]. And we lost, but at least we expressed our wishes publicly and we didn't run and hide."
—Speaker Tom Craddick

votes breaking down almost along party lines. The battle over redistricting left the house deeply divided along party lines. Democrats charged the Republican leadership with backing a power grab by U.S. Congressman Tom DeLay by scheduling a vote on redistricting outside the normal redistricting timeline. In contrast, Republicans accused the Democrats, who blocked a vote in the regular session by leaving town for Ardmore, Oklahoma, of failing to accept that they no longer controlled the legislative process.

The success of the Republicans in the 2002 election benefited the insurance industry in the battle over homeowner insurance reform. Although almost every candidate for the legislature promised to address the homeowner insurance rate crisis, Republican legislators are typically more sympathetic to industry concerns than are their Democratic counterparts. Because the Republican Party controlled the legislature and held the governor's mansion in 2003, it was probable that the insurance reform measure adopted by the legislature and the governor would be at least minimally acceptable to the insurance industry.

Political Ideology

Political ideology (liberalism/conservatism) influences the legislative process. **Liberalism** is the political view that seeks to change the political, economic, or social institutions of society to foster the development and well-being of the individual. Liberals believe that government should foster social progress by promoting social justice, political equality, and economic prosperity. Liberals usually favor government regulation and high levels of spending for social programs. On social issues, such as abortion and pornography regulation, liberals tend to support the right of adult free choice against government interference. In contrast, **conservatism** is the political view that seeks to preserve the political, economic, and social institutions of society against abrupt change. Conservatives generally oppose most government economic regulation and heavy government spending while favoring low taxes and traditional values.

Historically, conservatives have dominated the Texas legislature and legislative policies have reflected their political values. The legislature has enacted regulatory and tax policies designed to promote business expansion while adopting social welfare policies that stress personal responsibility. Few states spend less money on welfare than Texas. The legislature has been tough on crime, building the nation's largest prison system. The legislature has also created the nation's most prolific capital punishment system, executing more convicted murderers than any other state.

Liberals and conservatives disagreed on the best approach to addressing the problem of rising homeowner insurance premiums. Liberals demanded the enactment of government regulations designed to rollback rates to more affordable levels while conservatives argued in favor of relying on competition to control rates. Considering the historic dominance of conservative views in the legislature, it was likely that the legislature would adopt a market-based solution to insurance reform rather than tight regulation.

CONCLUSION: THE LEGISLATURE AND THE POLICYMAKING PROCESS

The legislature is the central policymaking institution of state government.

Agenda Building

Forces outside the legislature and institutional responsibilities set the agenda for the legislature. Interest groups, the media, political parties, the federal government, local governments, public opinion, election campaigns, and state officials in other branches of government all raise issues for legislative consideration. The legislature addressed homeowner insurance regulation because of the public outcry over rapidly rising premiums. With 86 percent of the respondents to the Texas Poll calling homeowner insurance premiums a serious problem, lawmakers had little choice but to address the issue.[35]

"It's hard to find a state representative in an election contest that [wasn't] having to talk about mold in front of citizens groups and town hall meetings. It [was] a constant theme throughout the whole state."
—Harvey Kornberg, Texas political analyst

Policy Formulation and Adoption

The legislature formulates policy by drafting legislation and proposing constitutional amendments. Individual members of the house and senate introduce measures that may be revised during committee mark up, amended on the floor of each chamber, and then rewritten in conference committee. The policy formulation process in the legislature usually involves competition among political interests. The outcome of that process may reflect compromise among interests or the triumph of one set of interests over other interests, depending on the relative political strength of competing groups.

In 2003, the Texas legislature adopted insurance reform legislation that empowered the Texas Department of Insurance (TDI) to regulate homeowner insurance rates but did not ensure that consumers would necessarily pay lower premiums. Insurance companies had to file their rate structure with the TDI 30 days after the law went into effect, disclosing the factors they used to set premiums. The TDI would then have 70 days to review each company's rate structure and order a rollback if it could not be justified. Insurance companies that were unhappy with the decision of the TDI could appeal first to the insurance commissioner and then to a state district court.

The TDI implemented the new legislation by ordering most of the insurance companies doing business in the state to lower their rates by an average of 13.4 percent. The three largest companies—State Farm, Allstate, and Farmers—had to reduce their premiums by 12 percent, 18.2 percent, and 17.5 percent, respectively. Homeowners would not get refunds, but would pay lower rates when their policies were renewed. In the meantime, most insurance companies filed appeals to overturn the decision of the TDI.[36]

Neither the insurance industry nor consumer interests were happy with insurance reform or its implementation. The insurance industry criticized the legislation because it imposed state regulation on insurance rates. The industry favored a system that would rely on competition to keep rates affordable for consumers. In the meantime, consumer groups argued that the legislation did not go far enough. They wanted the state to rollback the rate increases of the previous two years in their entirety.

Policy Implementation and Evaluation

The legislature plays an indirect, informal role in policy implementation. Individual legislators may contact the heads of state agencies concerning the implementation of a policy. Becuase agency heads want to stay on the good side of legislators, the respond positively to most requests.

The legislature is also involved in policy evaluation. The legislature as a whole evaluates programs when problems persist or when the media publicize scandals in administration. Six months after the adoption of insurance reform, the TDI reported that homeowner insurance rates were continuing to increase although not as rapidly as they had risen in the previous two years.[37] Consumer groups declared insurance reform a failure. If legislators agree, the issue of insurance reform would likely appear again on the legislative agenda in its next session.

★ REVIEW QUESTIONS

1. What impact does bicameralism have on the legislative process in Texas?

2. Is the Texas legislature representative of the state's population?

3. Are the members of the Texas legislature adequately compensated?

4. How have term limits affected state legislatures nationwide?

5. How are the lieutenant governor and Speaker chosen?

6. How are committees structured in the Texas legislature?

7. How does the legislative process in Texas compare with that in Congress?

8. What role do the Speaker and lieutenant governor play in the legislative process?

9. How did the passage of homeowner insurance reform in 2003 illustrate the nature of legislative policymaking in Texas?

10. Why have political parties historically played a relatively small role in the legislative process in Texas?

11. What role does the legislature play in the policymaking process?

★ KEY TERMS

appropriation bill

bicameral legislature

bill

conference committee

conservatism

delegate approach to
representation

filibuster

fiscal note

impeachment

incumbents

initiative process

interim committee

joint resolution

legislative access

Legislative Budget Board (LBB)

legislative oversight

Legislative Redistricting Board
(LRB)

legislative turnover

liberalism

line-item veto

lobbying

local bills

mark up

nonpartisan election

politico approach to
representation

resolution

select or special committee

seniority

standing committee

term limitation

trustee approach to
representation

unicameral legislature

veto

★ NOTES

1. Bruce Wright, "Home Sweet Home—Without Insurance?" *Fiscal Notes* (March 2003): 6.
2. Wright, "Home Sweet Home—Without Insurance?" p. 7.
3. Terrence Stutz, "Homeowner Premiums Skyrocket," *Dallas Morning News*, June 2, 2002, available at **www.dallasnews.com**.
4. Jim Yardley, "Texas Home Insurance Crisis Roils Residents and Top Race," *New York Times*, October 3, 2002, available at **www.nytimes.com**.
5. Wright, "Home Sweet Home—Without Insurance?" p. 6.
6. James R. Rogers, "The Impact of Bicameralism on Legislative Production," *Legislative Studies Quarterly* 28 (November 2003): 509–528.
7. Ken S. Chi, "Legislative Reform," *State Government News*, April 2000, p. 38.
8. Harvey J. Tucker, "Legislative Logjams: A Comparative State Analysis," *Western Political Quarterly* 38 (September 1985): 432–46.
9. Ross Ramsey and Kathy Walt, "Fast to the Finish Line," *Houston Chronicle*, May 30, 1995, pp. 13A, 15A.
10. Quoted in Ellen Perlman, "The Gold-Plated Legislature," *Governing* (February 1998): 40.
11. Harvey J. Tucker, "Legislative Workload Congestion in Texas," *Journal of Politics* 49 (May 1987): 565–78.
12. Susan Welch, et. al., "The Effect of Candidate Gender on Electoral Outcomes in State Legislative Races," *Western Political Quarterly* 38 (September 1985): 464–75; James G. Benze, Jr. and Eugene R. DeClercq, "The Importance of Gender in Congressional and Statewide Elections," *Social Science Quarterly* 66 (December 1985): 954–63.
13. *The Texas Poll*, Fall 1986, pp. 14–15.
14. Karen Hansen, "Legislator Pay: Baseball It Ain't," *State Legislatures* (July/August 1997): 22.
15. Jay Root, "Lawmakers' Perks Raise Eyebrows," *Fort Worth Star-Telegram*, February 6, 2003, available at **www.dfw.com**.
16. Sam Kinch, Jr., *Too Much Money Is Not Enough: Big Money and Political Power in Texas* (Austin: Campaign for People, 2000), p. 95.
17. Eric Berger, "Campaign Funds Are a Regularly Milked Cash Cow," *Houston Chronicle*, April 2, 2001, p. 1A.
18. Janet Elliott, "Critics Question $45,000 Salary for Political Work for Father," *Houston Chronicle*, July 16, 2003, available at **www.houstonchronicle.com**.
19. "Million Dollar Monsters," *Texas Observer*, June 21, 2002, p. 32.
20. U.S. Term Limits, "State Legislative Term Limits," available at **www.termlimits.org**.
21. John M. Carey, Richard G. Niemi, and Lynda W. Powell, *Term Limits in the State Legislatures* (Ann Arbor, MI: University of Michigan Press, 2000), pp. 123–27.
22. *Texas Government Newsletter*, January 26, 1987, p. 2.
23. Johanna M. Donlin and Brian J. Weberg, *Legislative Staff Services: Profiles of the 50 States and Territories* (Washington, DC: National Conference of State Legislatures, 1999), p. 167.
24. Texas Legislature Online, "Legislative Reports for the 78th Legislature," available at **www.capitol.state.tx.us**.
25. Texas Legislature Online, "Legislative Reports for the 78th Legislature," available at **www.capitol.state.tx.us**.

26. Jim Vertuno, "Gov. Perry Signs $117 Billion, 2-Year Spending Plan," *Houston Chronicle*, June 25, 2003, available at **www.houstonchronicle.com**.

27. Richard A. Clucas, "Principal-Agent Theory and the Power of the State House Speakers," *Legislative Studies Quarterly* 26 (May 2001): 334.

28. Gregory S. Thielemann and Donald R. Dixon, "Explaining Contributions: Rational Contributors and the Election for the 71st Texas House," *Legislative Studies Quarterly* 19 (November 1994): 495–505.

29. *Capitol Update*, March 14, 2003, p. 3.

30. R. A. Dyer, "Insurers Donated $1.3 Million to Lawmakers," *Fort Worth Star-Telegram*, February 27, 2003, available at **www.dfw.com**.

31. "Lobby Lists," Texas Ethics Commission, available at **www.ethics.state.tx.us**.

32. Warren E. Miller and Donald E. Stokes, "Constituency Influence in Congress," *American Political Science Review* 57 (March 1963): 45–56.

33. David Ray, "The Sources of Voting Cues in Three State Legislatures," *Journal of Politics* 44 (November 1982): 1074–87; Donald R. Songer, et. al., "Voting Cues in Two State Legislatures," *Social Science Quarterly* 66 (December 1985): 983–90.

34. William C. Adams and Paul H. Ferber, "Measuring Legislator-Constituency Congruence: Liquor, Legislators and Linkage," *Journal of Politics* 42 (February 1980): 202–208.

35. Shannon Buggs, "Many Cite Insurance as Big Issue," *Houston Chronicle*, September 19, 2002, available at **www.houstonchronicle.com**.

36. Bill Hensel, Jr., "Texas Tells Insurers to Shave Rates," *Houston Chronicle*, August 9, 2003, available at **www.houstonchronicle.com**.

37. Terrence Stutz, "Home Insurance Rates See Rise," *Dallas Morning News*, December 10, 2003, available at **www.dallasnews.com**.

ONLINE PRACTICE TEST

Test your understanding of this chapter
with interactive review quizzes at

www.ablongman.com/tannahilltexas/chapter8

Executive Branch

LEARNING OBJECTIVES

After studying Chapter 9, students should be able to do the following:

★ Assess the impact of the plural executive on administrative policymaking in Texas.

★ Describe the background and socioeconomic characteristics of the typical governor of Texas and evaluate how closely recent office holders have fit the image.

★ Outline the constitutional/legal office of governor, including formal qualifications, length of term, removal, compensation, and staff assistance.

★ Describe the powers and responsibilities of the office of governor, focusing on legislative powers, appointive powers, judicial powers, budgetary powers, law enforcement and military powers, ceremonial powers, political party leadership, and administrative authority.

★ Evaluate the power of the Texas office of governor in comparison with governors of other states and in light of scholarly efforts to measure gubernatorial power.

★ Describe the role of the governor in the policymaking process.

★ Compare and contrast the experiences of Governor Bush and Governor Perry with the Texas legislature.

★ List the powers and responsibilities of each of the following elected executive officials: lieutenant governor, attorney general, comptroller of public accounts, commissioner of agriculture, and commissioner of the General Land Office.

★ Describe the powers and responsibilities of the Texas secretary of state, Texas Railroad Commission, and the State Board of Education.

★ Describe the organization of the appointed boards and commissions.

★ Identify the perspectives and political resources each of the following political actors has to influence the state's administrative process: the legislature, governor, interest groups, and the executive-branch bureaucracy.

★ Describe the role of the executive branch in the state's policymaking process.

★ Define the key terms listed on page 247 and explain their significance.

The 78th Legislature faced a budget crisis. When lawmakers gathered in Austin in January 2003, Comptroller Carole Keeton Strayhorn estimated that state revenues would fall $9.9 billion short of the amount needed to cover current budget expenditures and then fully fund state services for the next **biennium** (two-year budget period).[1] Texas was in a financial hole because of a sluggish economy coupled with the rising cost of state services, especially health care. Slow economic growth caused sales tax receipts to lag because people had less money to purchase taxable items. Meanwhile, the cost of government health programs climbed more rapidly than expected, especially expenditures for the **Medicaid program,** which is a federal program designed to provide health insurance coverage to poor people, the disabled, and elderly Americans who are impoverished.

A crisis is an opportunity for leadership. When Governor Rick Perry made his State of the State Address to the legislature in February 2003, he made clear how he wanted the state to respond to the budget crisis. "When ends don't meet," he said, "our families prioritize. Why shouldn't government?"[2] The legislature should address the budget shortfall by cutting spending, declared the governor. It should not raise taxes.

The governor ultimately got his wish. The legislature passed and the governor signed a budget for the 2004–2005 biennium that included no new taxes. To be sure, the budget reflected some difficult choices. The legislature cut state funding for textbooks, teachers' health insurance, higher education, state prisons, and health care for low-income children and poor families. Although the legislature did not increase taxes, it raised fees for many government services, including college tuition. Furthermore, the legislature transferred the costs of some services to other units of governments, forcing cities, counties, and school districts to raise their own tax rates.

Governor Perry achieved his budget goals because a majority of legislators and public opinion supported his position. During the 2002 election campaign, most candidates for the legislature and state executive positions promised to oppose any tax increases. No major candidate even discussed the possibility that a tax increase might be necessary, certainly not Perry and not even Tony Sanchez, the Democratic nominee for governor. Governor Perry's promise to hold the line on taxes reflected the point of view of the legislative leadership and most members of the legislature. Critics, including many Democratic legislators and some Republican lawmakers as well, charged that reducing expenditures for social services was the wrong policy choice for a state that already ranked 50th in state government spending per capita.[3] Nonetheless, the critics lacked the public visibility necessary to compete with the governor to influence public opinion. Consequently, few observers were surprised by opinion surveys indicating that 50 percent of Texans believed that the best way to balance the budget was by cutting spending. Only 4 percent favored tax and fee increases while 35 percent supported a combination of spending cuts and tax increases.[4] Finally, the governor had the constitutional authority to back up his promise on taxes because of the veto. As long as Perry held firm to his opposition to any tax increases, his position would prevail because of the veto. The chances of the legislature overriding a veto of a tax bill were zero.

What does Governor Perry's success in preventing a tax increase in 2003 indicate about the powers of the office of governor of Texas? We will discuss that question as we study the role of the governor in the policymaking process. This chapter focuses on the executive branch of state government. The first part of the chapter examines the office of governor. It considers the qualifications and background of the state's chief executive. The chapter identifies the powers and responsibilities of the governor and assesses the power of the Texas governor compared with governors in other states. The chapter then studies the role of the governor in the policymaking process. The second part of the chapter describes the various agencies and departments that comprise the executive branch of state government. It discusses the elected executive officials other than the governor, appointed executive officials, elected boards and commissions, and appointed boards and commissions. The chapter then identifies the various political actors involved in administrative policymaking. Finally, the chapter concludes with a discussion of the role of the executive branch of state government in the policymaking process.

This chapter is the second in a series of five chapters dealing with the policymaking institutions of state and local government. The first three chapters in the series—Chapters 8, 9, and 10—examine the legislative, executive, and judicial branches of state government. The final two chapters in the series focus on units of local government. Chapter 11 discusses city government whereas Chapter 12 studies counties, school districts, and special districts.

> "No government has ever taxed and spent its way to greater prosperity."
> —Governor Rick Perry

THE GOVERNOR

The governor is the chief executive officer of the state with important powers to influence the policymaking process.

Qualifications and Background

The Texas Constitution declares that the governor must be an American citizen, a resident of Texas for 5 years preceding election, and at least 30 years of age. In practice, most of the state's chief executives have come from narrow social circles. All governors have been White, Anglo-Saxon Protestants. Only two (Miriam Ferguson and Ann Richards) were women. Most governors have been well-to-do, middle-aged lawyers or business executives with prior experience in public affairs. They have also had fairly common, easy-to-pronounce names, such as Perry, Bush, Richards, White, Clements, Briscoe, Smith, and Connally.

Although most recent governors have conformed fairly closely to the traditional image, the election of Ann Richards showed that Texas voters are willing to consider candidates who do not fit the mold in all respects. Not only is Richards a woman, but also her political career is based on her own efforts rather than those of her husband. Richards is a divorcee who was a schoolteacher before winning election as county commissioner in Travis County (which includes the city of Austin). In 1982, Richards was elected state treasurer, holding that post until her election as governor in 1990.

Term of Office, Selection, and Removal

The governor's term of office is four years, increased from two years by a constitutional amendment adopted in 1972. Today, only 2 of the 50 states elect their governors for terms of 2 years instead of 4 years.[5] Elections for governor and other elective state executive officials are held in even-numbered years, timed so they will not coincide with national presidential elections (e.g., 2002, 2006). The Texas Constitution sets no limit on the number of terms a governor may serve. Bill Clements, who held office for two nonconsecutive four-year terms (1979–1983 and 1987–1991), holds the record for longest service.

A governor can be removed from office before a term is ended through the process of impeachment and removal by the legislature. **Impeachment** is the formal process through which the house accuses an executive or judicial branch official of misconduct serious enough to warrant removal from office. The house votes to impeach the governor by majority vote. The senate conducts a trial and may vote to remove by a two-thirds margin. In 1917, the house impeached Governor James Ferguson and the senate removed him from office over the alleged misuse of public funds.[6] Ferguson is the only governor to be impeached in the history of the state. Many of the state's voters apparently did not share the legislature's opinion of Ferguson, twice electing his wife, Miriam Ferguson, to serve as the state's chief executive.

Staff Support

The governor enjoys the support of 184 full-time professional staff members,[7] who are appointed without need of senate confirmation and serve at the governor's pleasure. The governor has a chief of staff, general counsel, and a press secretary. The governor's office also includes administrative units dealing with legislative matters, communications, budgeting and planning, and criminal justice. The size of the governor's staff has grown over the years because state government is larger and more complex, and today's governor has become a more visible and active participant in the state policy process. Furthermore, federal grant programs often require gubernatorial participation in and coordination of program planning and implementation.[8]

G E T T I N G   I N V O L V E D

Forming a Study Group

A study group is an excellent way for students to learn and retain course material. Studying in a group is more efficient than individual study because the collective knowledge of the group almost always exceeds the knowledge of even the best prepared student in the class. Consequently, students are less likely to be stumped for an answer to a question and have to waste time looking it up. Study groups are also more fun than studying alone and they motivate students to succeed.

Take the initiative to organize a study group for this course. Identify students who seem serious about their education based on their class attendance and participation and schedule a group study session at a mutually agreed time and place. Coffee shops are a traditional hangout for students preparing for exams. Use the materials in the study guide or the various learning resources in the textbook (review questions, key terms, etc.) to organize your session.

It's your education—get involved!

Powers and Responsibilities

Although the Texas Constitution grants the governor authority to act in a broad range of policy areas, most of the governor's powers are coupled with limitations.

"The Governor shall, at the commencement of each session of the Legislature . . . give to the Legislature information, by message, of the condition of the State; and he shall recommend to the Legislature such measures as he may deem expedient."
—Texas Constitution, Article 4, Section 9

Legislative Powers   The strongest constitutional powers of the governor are those used for influencing the legislature. The Texas Constitution requires that the governor deliver a message to the legislature at the beginning of each legislative session on the condition of the state. The State of the State address, which is comparable to the State of the Union speech the president gives to Congress, enables the governor to focus attention on issues the governor considers the state's most serious policy needs and offer proposals to meet those needs. In 2003, Governor Perry used the address to make clear his opposition to any tax increases. The governor can send messages to the legislature at other times as well, both formally and informally. Of course, any legislative measure that the governor proposes must be introduced by a member of the legislature and passed by the Texas house and senate before it can become a law.

The governor can also influence legislative priorities by declaring certain pieces of legislation emergency measures. In the house, emergency measures receive priority attention on the floor. Furthermore, members of the legislature can introduce legislation after the deadline for bill filing if the governor designates the measure as emergency legislation. In 2003, the governor labeled both homeowner insurance reform and medical malpractice reform as emergencies.

The governor has the power of the **veto,** which is an action by the chief executive of a state or nation refusing to approve a measure passed by the legislature. If the governor objects to a bill passed by the legislature, the governor has 10 days to act unless the legislature adjourns during that time. In that case, the governor has 20 days from adjournment in which to decide to issue a veto.

The governor also enjoys the power of the **line-item veto,** which is the authority of the governor to veto sections or items of an appropriation bill while signing the remainder of the bill into law. Keep in mind that the authority of the governor to issue the line-item veto is limited to the **appropriation bill,** which is a legislative authorization to spend money for particular purposes. In 2003, Governor Perry used the line-item veto to cut $81 million from the state budget of $117 billion.[9] On other pieces of legislation, the governor's options are limited to either accepting or rejecting the measure in its entirety.

The Texas legislature can override the governor's veto by a two-thirds vote of each chamber, voting separately. Nationwide, state legislatures override about 10 percent of governors' vetoes.[10] Since Texas became a state, the legislature has successfully overridden only 52 of more than 1,600 gubernatorial vetoes (not counting item vetoes), for an override rate of 3 percent. Furthermore, since 1941 the legislature has overridden only one veto—a veto cast by Governor Bill Clements in 1979 of a local bill exempting Comal County from the state's game laws.

Why has the legislature so seldom reversed the governor's vetoes? Two-thirds majorities are difficult to attain, of course. More important, most gubernatorial vetoes in Texas come after adjournment when overriding is impossible. Because much of the legislation introduced during a regular session does not pass until the session's final days, the governor can simply wait until adjournment to issue a veto. Governor Perry vetoed 48 bills passed by the 78th Legislature, but every veto came after adjournment.[11] With the legislature gone home, a veto stands unchallenged. Although a number of state constitutions allow the legislature to call itself back into session to consider overriding vetoes, the Texas Constitution does not.

A final legislative power the governor enjoys is the authority to call special sessions. The state constitution empowers the governor to convene the legislature in special sessions that may last no longer than 30 days. It places no limit on the number of special sessions a governor can call. The constitution declares that in a special session the "legislature may consider only those matters that the governor specifies in the call or subsequently presents to the legislature." The governor can use the power to set the agenda for special sessions as a bargaining tool in negotiations with legislators. In exchange for support on other matters, the governor can offer to expand the call to include issues of particular interest to individual legislators or groups of lawmakers.

Appointive Powers   The governor has extensive powers of appointment. The governor is responsible for staffing positions on more than 200 state administrative boards and commissions that set policy for state agencies under their authority. Furthermore, the Texas Constitution empowers the governor to fill vacancies in many otherwise elective positions, including district and appellate judgeships, should openings occur between elections. All told, a governor makes about 3,000 appointments during a four-year term.[12]

The power of appointment gives the governor the opportunity to influence policy and score political points. As the state's population has grown more diverse, governors of both political parties have sought a diverse set of appointees. Governor Richards named more women and minorities to office than any governor in the history of the state. Forty-one percent of her appointees were women, 32 percent Latino, and 12 percent African American. Governor Bush and Governor Perry continued to diversify state government. Nine percent of Bush's appointees were African American, 13 percent Latino, and 37 percent women. During Perry's first 4 years in office, his list of appointments was 11 percent African American, 16 percent Latino, and 36 percent female.[13]

The appointive powers of the governor are limited. Because most administrative board members serve six-year overlapping terms, new governors must work with an administrative structure that was put in place by a predecessor. Although new governors can fill about a third of administrative positions when they first assume office, they do not have the opportunity to name their own people to a majority of posts for another two years.

The governor has little official removal power. An incoming governor cannot force the resignation of holdover administrators unless they are found guilty of gross mismanagement. The Texas Constitution gives governors authority to remove their *own* appointees (but not those of a predecessor) with a two-thirds vote of approval by the state senate, but this limited procedure has not been used.

The governor's appointive powers are often restricted by technical, legal requirements. Consider the make up of the Texas Racing Commission, which oversees the operation of pari-mutuel wagering on horse and dog racing in the state. The leg-

"We are always on the lookout for strong leaders who share Governor Perry's philosophies, especially from the minority community."
—Ray Sullivan, governor's staff

After the 2003 legislative session, Governor Rick Perry vetoed 48 bills.

islature reserved two of the eight positions on the commission for the state comptroller and the chair of the Texas Public Safety Commission. The governor can appoint the other six members but only within certain strict guidelines. Two members of the commission must be experienced in horse racing and two others must be experienced at racing greyhounds. The other two commission members must be veterinarians, one specializing in large animals and the other in small animals. Furthermore, the legislature specified that all members of the commission be residents of Texas for at least 10 years and must file detailed financial statements. Persons with a financial interest in a racetrack or closely related to someone with such as interest would be ineligible to serve.

Finally, the governor's appointees must be confirmed by a two-thirds vote of the state senate. In contrast, presidential appointees require only a majority vote of approval in the U.S. Senate. Furthermore, the tradition of senatorial courtesy ensures that the governor's appointees must pass political inspection by their home-area senator or face rejection. **Senatorial courtesy** is a custom of the Texas senate that allows individual senators a veto over nominees who live in their districts. By tradition, senators will vote against a nominee if the senator from the district in which the nominee lives declares opposition to the nomination.

Judicial Powers   The Texas Constitution gives the governor some authority in the judicial process. On the recommendation of the Board of Pardons and Paroles, the governor may grant reprieves, commutations, and pardons. A **reprieve** is the postponement of the implementation of punishment for a criminal offense; a **commutation** is the reduction of punishment for a criminal offense. A **pardon** is the exemption from punishment for a criminal offense. In a **capital punishment** (death penalty) case, the governor has authority to grant one 30-day reprieve independently, without recommendation by Pardons and Paroles, thus postponing a condemned person's execution.

Probably the most effective tool the governor has for influencing judicial policy is the power of appointment. Texas state judges are elected, but when appellate and district judges die, retire, or resign during the midst of a term, the state constitution empowers the governor to appoint a new judge to serve until the next election. In 2002, 44 percent of the state's appellate judges and 42 percent of district judges initially took office through gubernatorial appointment rather than election.[14]

Budgetary Powers   The president of the United States and the governors of 47 states enjoy budget making authority, preparing a budget to submit to the legislative branch.[15] Although the final budget is invariably a negotiated document between the legislative and executive branches of government, the chief executive has the advantage of proposing the initial document. Consequently, the budget debate in the legislature at least begins with the governor's budgetary priorities and policy proposals.

The governor of Texas has no such advantage. Although the Texas Constitution requires the governor to submit budget proposals to the legislature, the Legislative Budget Board (LBB) prepares a budget as well, and its ideas generally carry more weight. The **Legislative Budget Board (LBB)** is an agency created by the legislature to study state revenue and budgetary needs between legislative sessions and prepare budget and appropriation bills to submit to the legislature. As the legislature debates the budget, the point of departure is not the governor's budget, but the budget proposed by the LBB. As a result, the governor begins on the defensive.

The most important power the governor of Texas has for influencing budget priorities is the line-item veto. In contrast to the president, whose only option on an appropriation bill is to accept or reject the measure in its entirety, most state governors can selectively eliminate items while signing the rest into law. This veto and the threat of its use allow a politically skilled governor the opportunity to exercise considerable influence over the final budget document.

Budget execution authority refers to the power to cut agency spending or transfer money between agencies during the period when the legislature is not in session. Much can happen in the two-year interval between legislative sessions. Because of unforeseen events, such as a hurricane striking the coast or declining welfare rolls, some budget categories may run short of money whereas others may have excess cash. Budget execution authority is the power to transfer funds among accounts between legislative sessions. The Texas Constitution allows either the governor or the LBB to propose a reduction in spending or a shift in state funds. Both the governor and LBB must concur in proposed spending reductions or money transfers before they can take place.

Law Enforcement and Military Powers   The governor has some peripheral authority in law enforcement. The governor appoints the three-member board that heads the Department of Public Safety and is empowered to assume command of the Texas Rangers should circumstances warrant, which is rare. The governor is also commander in chief of the Texas National Guard, which the governor may call out to assist in situations beyond the control of local law enforcement agencies, such as a natural disaster or civil disorder. The primary responsibilities for law enforcement in the state are in the hands of the county sheriff and city police departments.

Ceremonial Powers   In addition to official powers, the governor is the ceremonial leader of the state. The governor greets foreign leaders, speaks at local chamber of commerce luncheons, issues proclamations on state holidays, and shakes hands with visiting scout troops. Although some observers may view these sorts of activities as somewhat trivial, they allow the governor the opportunity to give the appearance of leadership, which can be helpful for a governor to influence the policy process. Leadership depends on the perceptions of the public and other political leaders as much as it depends on official powers.

Governors sometimes use their leadership position to recruit out-of-state companies to relocate to the state. Governor Perry, for example, helped convince Toyota to select San Antonio as the site of a new auto-assembly plant. The legislature did its part by approving the expenditure of state funds to build rail tracks to connect the plant to major rail lines. State and local governments are also paid to train 2,000 full-time workers for the plant.[16] Research indicates that governors recruit out-of-state firms to relocate to counties that opposed them in the last election in hopes of increasing job growth and income before the next election, but that the governor's efforts typically fail to increase political support.[17]

Political Party Leadership   The governor is the unofficial leader of his or her political party in the state. When Texas was a one-party Democratic state, the governor traditionally headed the state's delegation to the Democratic National Convention. In 1964 and 1968, for instance, Democratic Governor John Connally used his influence at the head of the Texas delegation to become a major force in national party politics.

Since Texas has become more competitive politically, the governor's role as a party leader has grown. Recent governors frequently speak out on partisan controversies and campaign for their party's candidates in state and national elections. Furthermore, as the most visible elected official in a large state, the governor of Texas is

President George W. Bush at his ranch in Crawford, Texas.

often a national political figure. Governor Richards was a prominent figure in Democratic national politics. Her successor, Governor Bush, was elected president of the United States in 2000.

Administrative Powers   The governor of Texas is probably weakest in the area of administration because of the **plural executive,** which is the division of executive power among several elected officials. Because the land commissioner, attorney general, comptroller, lieutenant governor, and commissioner of agriculture are all elected, they answer not to the governor, but to the voters. Elected executive officials may not share the governor's party affiliation and may be political rivals, even when they share the same political party affiliation.

The governor also has relatively little power to manage the various state boards and agencies that are headed by appointed administrators. Because board members are appointed to serve six-year terms, a new governor takes office facing an executive branch staffed by the previous governor. The governor cannot remove a predecessor's appointees and can remove his or her own appointees only with the approval of the state senate. In sum, the governor has few direct controls over the administration of state programs in such important policy areas as education, agriculture, insurance regulation, corrections, welfare, highway construction, and utility regulation.

Measuring Gubernatorial Powers

Observers have long held that the constitutional/legal powers of the governor of Texas are among the weakest in the nation. Political scientist Thomas M. Holbrook has created an index to measure the official powers of state governors based on the following factors: appointive power, veto power, staff resources, organizational power, tenure potential, and control over the state budget. According to this measure, the official powers of the governor of Texas rank 49th, ahead only of the powers of the governor of South Carolina.[18]

But are indexes of constitutional/legal powers an accurate assessment of a governor's policymaking influence? Many political scientists believe that they are not. One scholar thinks that the power of the contemporary governor is too complex to be measured by an index.[19] Other political scientists believe that official powers are overrated. One study concludes that the importance of removal authority is exaggerated because governors are often restricted from removing other executive branch officials by political considerations and, in some circumstances, court rulings.[20]

A number of political scientists believe that a governor's unofficial, informal powers are at least as important to a governor's policymaking influence as the governor's official constitutional/legal authority. One study finds, for example, that official powers must be translated into influence through the mechanism of the governor's informal political resources, such as communication and political bargaining skills.[21] Another scholar believes that the official powers of the governor or the number of orders the governor can give have relatively little impact on the success of the governor as a policy leader. Instead, a governor's influence hinges on how the governor chooses to spend time, what resources the governor can bring to achieve goals, whose advice the governor takes, and whose pleas for support the governor heeds.[22]

The experience of Governor Bush in dealing with the legislature illustrates the ability of a governor to use unofficial, informal powers to achieve policy influence. In 1995, when Bush first took office, he targeted four policy areas—public education, juvenile justice, welfare, and tort reform. The legislature passed measures enacting major reforms in each of these areas. With the exception of welfare policy, the legislature adopted policies that closely reflected the policy preferences of the governor.

Governor Bush succeeded in 1995 because he set limited goals for himself and communicated regularly with legislators. Bush targeted policy areas already high on the official policy agenda because of media attention, the efforts of interest groups, and the recent election campaign. He staked out policy positions on these issues that already enjoyed a good deal of support in the legislature and were popular with the electorate. Bush and his staff communicated directly with individual members of the house and senate, and the governor spoke regularly with speaker of the house Pete Laney and Lieutenant Governor Bob Bullock.

In 1997, Governor Bush used his political skills to survive the defeat of his primary legislative goal and emerge from the session with his reputation as a leader in tact. At the beginning of the session, Bush proposed a sweeping reform of the state's tax system. The governor asked the legislature to reduce local school property taxes by $6 billion over the next two years and replace the lost revenues by broadening the sales tax base and increasing taxes on business. The Texas house passed a modified version of Bush's plan, but it died in the Texas senate. Ironically, the main opposition to Bush's proposal came from Republican legislators who did not want to go on record voting in favor of a tax increase on business. Instead of accepting defeat, Governor Bush scaled back his goals and asked for a $1 billion property tax cut to be funded out of a budget surplus left over from the previous budget cycle. The legislature agreed and the governor declared victory even though the final product was considerably less than what he had initially requested.

The chief goals of Governor Bush in the 1999 session of the legislature were to pass a tax cut bill and avoid controversies that could damage his planned campaign for the presidency. The legislature passed a tax cut, enabling Bush to run for the White House as a governor who signed tax cut legislation in two consecutive legislative sessions. Bush also succeeded in avoiding controversy by persuading the Texas senate to kill **hate-crimes legislation,** which is a legislative measure that increases penalties for persons convicted of criminal offenses motivated by prejudice based on race, religion, national origin, gender, or sexual orientation. On one hand, Bush did not want to sign the measure because of the opposition of conservative Republicans who disagreed with the concept of hate-crimes legislation in general and opposed the inclusion of sexual orientation in particular. On the other hand, Bush did not want to veto the hate-crimes bill because Democrats would use the veto against him in his presidential campaign. Texas is the site of several well-publicized hate crimes and a veto would make Bush appear insensitive to the concerns of minority populations.

Governor Perry's experience with the Texas legislature in 2001 contrasted sharply with the work of his predecessor. Perry did not establish the personal relationships with individual legislators as Bush had done. Whereas Bush worked closely with Speaker Laney and Lieutenant Governor Bullock, Perry had poor relationships with Laney and Lieutenant Governor Bill Ratliff. By and large, Perry ignored the legislative process until bills reached his desk. Consequently, the governor had little influence on the details of legislation. Perry also had to take public stands on a number of controversial measures, including hate-crimes legislation and a bill that would have made it more difficult for the state to execute convicted murderers who are mentally retarded. Perry signed the former and vetoed the latter. Furthermore, Perry's numerous vetoes angered legislators and lobbyists who were blindsided by the governor's opposition.[23]

"People say the Texas Governor is a weak position. Only a weak person makes it a weak position."
—Governor George W. Bush

Governor Perry's chief legislative goal in 2003 was to keep his campaign promise to avoid a tax increase. He stressed the theme in his State of the State Address and even presented lawmakers with a budget document that consisted of line after line of zeros. Perry said that he offered the zero-filled budget to emphasize that lawmakers should start from scratch in setting budget priorities. In contrast, critics

"He [Perry] is a big-
picture guy. His lead-
ership style is to offer
the vision. The
specifics he is leaving
to the representatives
elected by the
people."
—Carole Keeton
Strayhorn,
Comptroller

belittled the governor's budget as a failure to offer policy guidance to legislators; it was an example of "zero-based leadership," they sneered. The governor told lawmakers what he did not want—a tax increase—but he gave little direction in how legislators should reach the goal. Nonetheless, Governor Perry achieved his goal of holding the line on taxes while leaving the politically difficult decisions on spending cuts and fee increases to the legislature. Furthermore, the governor and his staff stayed in close enough communication with legislators during the 2003 session to avoid the controversial series of vetoes he issued after the 2001 session.

The Governor of Texas and the Policymaking Process

Theodore Roosevelt once said that the presidency was a "bully pulpit." By that phrase he meant that the office provided its occupants with an excellent platform for making their views widely known. In today's age of modern communications, the phrase "big microphone" might be a more appropriate metaphor.

Similar to the president, the governor is well positioned to influence the official policy agenda. Texas governors are required by the state constitution to make recommendations to the legislature and are empowered to call the legislature into special session for the sole purpose of considering gubernatorial proposals. The governor is the most visible public official in the state and today's mass media provide the governor ample opportunity to get messages across to the people.

The governor's powers to affect policy formulation and adoption are considerable as well. The governor presents a budget to the legislature and may offer policy initiatives on any subject. As the legislature debates policy proposals, the governor can be an effective lobbyist. The governor's veto power, especially the item veto for appropriation measures, puts the governor in a powerful position to bargain on behalf of his or her program. At the very least, the veto virtually ensures that the governor can defeat legislation he or she opposes.

The governor is weakest in the areas of policy implementation and evaluation. In Texas, public policies are implemented by departments headed by elected executives or appointed boards, all of which are largely independent of direct gubernatorial control. Although the state constitution calls the governor the state's "chief executive," it offers the governor little power to fulfill that role. Furthermore, the governor has no formal mechanism for policy evaluation. Instead, the governor must rely on policy analyses conducted by others, including legislative committees, the LBB, the comptroller, the Sunset Advisory Commission, and the press.

Although scholars have frequently described the office of governor of Texas as politically weak, the governor has sufficient power to play an important policymaking role. Governors who set realistic policy goals can often achieve them if they are willing to use the resources at their disposal. Governor Bush demonstrated that a politically skillful governor could have influence on at least a range of policy issues. Governor Perry successfully blocked a policy option he opposed. The governor lacks the official powers to coordinate policy implementation effectively, but he or she has ample tools to be a successful leader in agenda setting, policy formulation, and policy adoption.

"The governor's office
is what you make
of it."
—Bill Clements,
former governor
of Texas

THE EXECUTIVE BUREAUCRACY

The executive bureaucracy of Texas government includes more than 200 boards, agencies, offices, departments, committees, councils, and commissions. Some parts of the bureaucracy, such as the Office of the Attorney General and the Railroad Commission, are constitutionally established. The legislature and the governor have created the rest of the state bureaucracy through the legislative process. The executive branch of state government employs nearly 350,000 people.[24]

The executive bureaucracy in Texas is decentralized. No one official is in charge of the entire structure. Agencies directed by elected executives or elected boards are virtually independent of direction by the governor or other state officials. They respond to the voters, not other officials. Agencies directed by appointed boards operate with a good deal of autonomy as well.

Bureaucratic fragmentation in Texas is a legacy of Jacksonian democracy and the post-Reconstruction distrust of central authority. **Jacksonian democracy** is the view (associated with President Andrew Jackson) that the right to vote should be extended to all adult male citizens and that all government offices of any importance should be filled by election. The influence of Jacksonian democracy in the South led to the creation of the plural executive in which state executive power was divided among several elected executive branch officials. The framers of the Texas Constitution distrusted central control of government because of their experience with it during Reconstruction. They created a decentralized executive branch to guard against the excessive concentration of power in any one person or department.

Elected Executive Officials

In addition to the governor, voters elect five other state executive officials: the lieutenant governor, attorney general, comptroller of public accounts, commissioner of agriculture, and commissioner of the General Land Office. These officials are elected simultaneously with the governor to serve four-year terms. Only four states elect more executive officials than Texas. Every state elects a governor and a majority of states also elect an attorney general, lieutenant governor, and treasurer. Only about a fourth of the states elect agriculture commissioners or comptrollers; a tenth elect land commissioners.[25]

Lieutenant Governor   The lieutenant governor is first in line of succession to the governor's office should the governor die, resign, or be removed from office. When Governor George W. Bush resigned to become president, Lieutenant Governor Perry moved up to the office of governor. The lieutenant governor also becomes temporary governor whenever the governor is absent from the state. In practice, the foremost responsibilities of the office lie in the state senate, where the lieutenant governor presides, votes in case of a tie, appoints members of standing and conference committees, helps determine the order of business on the floor, and enforces senate rules. In addition, the lieutenant governor is a member of several boards and councils, including the LBB and the Legislative Redistricting Board. The **Legislative Redistricting Board (LRB)** is an agency composed of the speaker, lieutenant governor, comptroller, land commissioner, and attorney general, and is responsible for redrawing the boundaries of Texas house and senate seats when the legislature is unable to agree on a redistricting plan. These responsibilities make the lieutenant governor one of the most visible and important figures in state government. When the legislature is in town, the lieutenant governor is arguably the most powerful official in the state, more powerful even than the governor.

? WHAT IS YOUR OPINION?

Who is more powerful, the governor or lieutenant governor?

Attorney General   In recent election campaigns, candidates for attorney general have broadcast political advertisements touting their law-and-order credentials and their determination to get tough on crime. Although these kinds of advertisements may be politically effective, they are factually misleading. Other than representing Texas in lawsuits challenging the constitutionality of state criminal laws, the attorney general has relatively little to do with fighting crime. That job is primarily the responsibility of city and county law enforcement agencies and county district attorneys.

The attorney general is the state's lawyer, representing state government and its various components in court. In recent years, the attorney general's office has defended the state in federal court against lawsuits over bilingual education, prison overcrowding, the death penalty, and congressional redistricting. The attorney general has broad authority to initiate legal action on behalf of the state. In the late 1990s, for example, Texas Attorney General Dan Morales filed a lawsuit against the tobacco industry to recover the cost of smoking-related illnesses covered by Medicaid program. Before the case could go to trial, the tobacco industry and the attorney general agreed on a $17.3 billion settlement to be paid out over the next 25 years. The industry also agreed to remove all tobacco billboards in Texas as well as tobacco advertising on buses, bus stops, taxis, and taxi stands.[26]

? WHAT IS YOUR OPINION?

Should the attorney general file suit against the gun industry to recover the cost to the Medicaid program of caring for people injured in the misuse of firearms?

The attorney general gives legal advice to state and local officials and agencies in the form of opinions. Usually opinions are restricted to questions of law connected to the performance of official duties. For example, the attorney general issued an opinion holding that the legalization of casino gambling in the state would require an amendment to the state constitution rather than just the enactment of a state law. This was a particularly important opinion because the adoption of a constitutional amendment requires a two-thirds vote in both the state house and senate

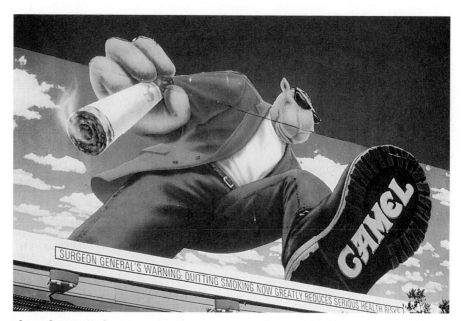

SURGEON GENERAL'S WARNING: QUITTING SMOKING NOW GREATLY REDUCES SERIOUS HEALTH RISKS

The tobacco industry agreed to remove all tobacco billboards in Texas as part of the lawsuit settlement.

as well as voter approval, whereas the enactment of a state law requires only a majority vote of each legislative chamber and the governor's signature. The attorney general's opinion is not binding on the court system, but in the absence of a court ruling it stands as the highest existing interpretation of law or the Texas Constitution.

Comptroller of Public Accounts　The comptroller is the state's chief tax administrator and accountant. The comptroller monitors compliance with state tax laws and collects taxes on behalf of the state. Texans who operate retail businesses work closely with the comptroller's office to collect the state sales tax from their customers and remit tax receipts to the state. If a retailer fails to pass along sales tax receipts to the state, the comptroller has the power to shut it down and sell off its assets to pay back taxes.

In 1995, the voters approved a constitutional amendment abolishing the office of state treasurer and turning over the treasurer's duties to the comptroller. Consequently, the comptroller is now the state's banker, receiving funds, assuming responsibility for their safekeeping, and paying the state's bills. When tax revenues flow in more rapidly than the state expends funds, the comptroller deposits the money in interest bearing accounts to generate additional revenue for the state. In contrast, when the rate of revenue collection lags behind the rate of expenditure, the comptroller borrows money on a short-term basis to ensure that the state will have enough cash on hand to pay its bills.

The comptroller's most publicized task involves the state budget. The Texas Constitution requires the comptroller to estimate state revenues for the next biennium at the beginning of each legislative session. The comptroller may update the revenue estimate during a session to take account of revisions in state tax laws and changing economic conditions. The constitution specifies that no appropriation bill may become law without the comptroller's certification that it falls within the revenue estimate unless the legislature votes by a four-fifths margin to adopt an unbalanced budget.

Commissioner of Agriculture   The commissioner of agriculture administers all statutes relating to agriculture and enforces the state's weights and measures law. The agency inspects and regulates a variety of items, including seeds, gasoline pumps, meat market scales, flower and plant nurseries, and the use of pesticides. The commissioner of agriculture also promotes the sale of Texas agricultural products.

Commissioner of the General Land Office   The treaty of annexation that added Texas to the Union in 1845 allowed the Lone Star State to retain its state lands. Although much of that land was eventually sold, the state still owns at least the mineral rights on more than 20 million acres. The land commissioner is responsible for managing the land, leasing it for mineral exploration and production and for agricultural purposes. In recent years, leasing revenues have averaged roughly $500 million dollars a year. That money goes into the **Permanent School Fund (PSF),** which is a fund established in the Texas Constitution as an endowment to finance public elementary and secondary education. The Texas Board of Education invests the money in the PSF to generate investment income known as the Available School Fund (ASF), which is distributed annually to Texas school districts on a per-student basis under laws passed by the legislature. The land commissioner also manages the Veterans' Land Program, which provides low-interest loans to the state's military veterans to purchase land.

Appointed Executives

One measure of a governor's power over administration is the number of officials he or she can appoint. In Texas, the most important executive officials are elected, leaving only a handful of executive positions to be filled by the governor, subject, of course, to a two-thirds senate confirmation. The most significant of these officials is the Texas secretary of state who is the state's chief election officer, responsible for the uniform application, operation, and interpretation of election laws. On election night, the office of the secretary of state gathers election returns from around the state, compiles them, and releases running vote totals to the press. Later, the office tabulates and releases final, official returns. In addition to its electoral responsibilities, the secretary of state's office serves as a depository of various agreements, reports, and records of state agencies.

Elected Boards and Commissions

The Railroad Commission and the State Board of Education are executive agencies headed by elected boards.

The Railroad Commission   The Texas Railroad Commission was originally established to enforce state laws concerning railroads, but its duties have expanded to include

L E A R N I N G   E X E R C I S E

Profile of a State Agency

Your assignment is to research an agency of state government. The agency assigned to you depends on the last digit of your Social Security number. If, for example, your Social Security number is 346-70-1379, your assignment is number 9 below.

0. Racing Commission
1. Parks and Wildlife Commission
2. Board of Pardons and Paroles
3. Commission on Environmental Quality
4. Department of Public Safety
5. Department of Insurance
6. Department of Criminal Justice
7. Alcoholic Beverage Commission
8. Funeral Service Commission
9. State Board of Barber Examiners

You can find out a good deal about the agency online. Begin your research at the following website:
wwwz.tsl.state.tx.us.trail/agencies.jsp

Once you have read about the agency and reviewed its homepage, answer the following questions.

QUESTIONS TO CONSIDER

1. Your textbook classifies state agencies. In which category would you place the agency you have been assigned?
2. What is the title of the person (or persons) who heads the agency? What is that person's name?
3. How is the head of the agency chosen? Does the agency head serve a fixed term?
4. What does the agency do? Answer in your own words. Do not copy the agency's mission statement.
5. What (if any) are the major administrative units of the agency?
6. What current issues or events are affecting the agency?
7. What power does the legislature have to influence the operation of the agency?
8. What power does the governor have to influence the operation of the agency?
9. Give an example of an interest group that would be concerned with the activities of the agency.
10. How do the activities of this agency affect ordinary citizens?

"The [Railroad] Commission is the most powerful state agency there is."
—Phillip Robinson, lobbyist

the regulation of commercial vehicle transportation, gas utilities, liquefied petroleum gas, and oil and gas exploration. The Railroad Commission is composed of three members elected for six-year overlapping terms. In practice, most commission members initially assume office through gubernatorial appointment. When a commission member resigns before the end of a six-year term, the governor names a replacement subject to a two-thirds confirmation vote by the Texas senate. Appointed railroad commissioners must face the voters at the next general election, but their initial appointment gives them a significant advantage in name recognition and fundraising capability.

The Railroad Commission's regulatory policies fall into three broad categories. First, the commission is a conservation agency. To prevent the waste of natural resources, the commission establishes what is called an allowable for each oil and gas well in the state. The **allowable** is the maximum permissible rate of production for oil and gas wells in Texas as set by the Railroad Commission. This rate, which is determined by technical engineering and geological considerations, maximizes current production without jeopardizing long-term output. The Railroad Commission also regulates the drilling, storage, and pipeline transmission of oil and gas to protect the natural environment.

The Railroad Commission regulates the Texas oil industry.

Second, the commission historically has prorated oil production to conform to market demand. Every month, the commission establishes a percentage of allowable that each well may produce. For example, if a well's allowable were 100 barrels a day and the commission prorated production to 80 percent of allowable, the well could pump only 80 barrels a day for that month. From the 1930s to the 1970s, the Railroad Commission used this method to limit the supply of oil to an amount sufficient to fill market demand *at the current price*. If a new oil field were to come on line, the commission prevented oversupply by reducing the percentage allowable for wells across Texas. Because Texas oil was such a big proportion of the national and world oil supply, the commission effectively controlled oil supplies and, consequently, oil prices worldwide. Since the early 1970s, the worldwide demand for petroleum has been so great that the Railroad Commission no longer prorates oil production below the 100 percent allowable.

Third, the Railroad Commission has protected the rights of producers and royalty owners, particularly smaller operators. In the early years, the commission established rules on well spacing, transportation, and oil production quotas that generally benefited small producers at the expense of major oil companies. More recently, however, hostile court decisions and personnel changes have led the commission to adopt more evenhanded rules.[27]

State Board of Education (SBOE)   The SBOE coordinates education activities and services below the college level. A 15-member elected board heads the agency. Each member of the board runs for election from a district to serve a four-year term. The terms of the board members are staggered, with roughly half the members facing the voters each general election year. The SBOE oversees the investment of the money in the Permanent School Fund to generate income for the Available School Fund. It sets standards for teacher certification and school accreditation. The SBOE also approves curricula and selects textbooks for use in the state's public schools.

The textbook approval process has been the board's most publicized and controversial activity. For years, conservative political activists, such as Norma and Mel Gabler of Longview, dominated the textbook selection process by attacking books for what they considered to be threats to traditional family values. The SBOE once required that high school biology texts carry a disclaimer that evolution was just a theory and told publishers to delete all references to venereal disease in textbooks for junior high school students.

In 1995, the legislature passed and Governor Bush signed legislation to limit the ability of the SBOE to order textbooks rewritten to reflect political values. The measure limited SBOE oversight to ensuring that textbooks cover at least 50 percent of the state's curriculum standards, contain no factual errors, and meet physical manufacturing specifications. Textbooks that satisfied these minimum standards would be available for possible adoption by local school districts.

Nonetheless, the battle over textbooks has not subsided. Conservative groups such as the Texas Public Policy Foundation argue that the inclusion of political bias or the omission of certain information in a textbook constitutes factual inaccuracy. They also based their textbook critiques on a provision in the Texas Education Code that declares that texts should "present positive aspects of the United States and its heritage." In the face of the conservative criticism, publishing companies have rewritten textbooks to tone down references to pollution, equivocate about the threat of global warming, avoid discussions of sexuality, limit references to evolution, and remove critical discussions of American society.[28] Liberal groups such as the Texas Freedom Network worry that self-censorship by publishers trying to meet conservative objections and satisfy the SBOE will impact the quality of education not just in Texas but nationwide. Because Texas represents a substantial share of the national textbook market, publishers sell textbooks developed for the Texas market nationwide.

> "I think it is really dangerous that the Texas Public Policy Foundation has so much influence that you have publishers writing to please the conservative right at the risk of suppressing alternative views and critically examining the issues."
>
> —Dean DeChambeau, Jones & Bartlett Publishers

> "We citizens are truly the clients [of the textbook publishers]. It is our children's education and future at stake, and our tax dollars are paying for the books. If people in Texas are more conservative than people in Massachusetts or New York, so be it."
>
> —Peggy Venable, Texas chapter of Citizens for a Sound Economy

? WHAT IS YOUR OPINION?

Should textbooks reflect the political values of a majority of Texans?

Appointed Commissions

Appointed commissions comprise a substantial part of the executive branch of state government. An unpaid board of 3, 6, 9, or 18 members heads most of the commissions (which may also be called a department, board, council, or authority). The governor appoints board members with two-thirds senate approval to serve fixed, overlapping terms of six years. Boards meet periodically to set policy. An executive director, who is either appointed by the governor or hired by the board, depending on the agency, manages the professional staff, which does the day-to-day work of the agency. The nine-member board of the Texas Department of Parks and Wildlife, for example, hires an executive director who heads a professional staff that carries out the work of the agency.

Agencies perform such a wide variety of functions that they are a challenge to classify. Nonetheless, it is possible to group many of the agencies by form or function.

Administrative Departments The executive branch of Texas government includes a number of administrative departments that are responsible for implementing policy and carrying out basic state functions. The Texas Department of Criminal Justice operates the state prison system. The General Land Office manages state lands. The Texas Department of Agriculture implements state agricultural policy. The Lottery Commission operates the state lottery. The Texas Department of Transportation is responsible for the financing, construction, regulation, and use of highways, rail stations, airports, and other facilities of public transportation. Other state administrative departments include Parks and Wildlife, Health, Public Safety, and Mental Health and Mental Retardation.

College and University Boards Appointed boards of regents oversee each of the state's public colleges and university systems. University boards consist of nine members appointed by the governor with senate concurrence to serve overlapping six-year terms. University regents are considered prestige appointments, eagerly sought by well-to-do alumni and often awarded to the governor's major financial backers during the last election campaign. The members of the board of regents of the University of Texas and the Texas A&M University systems in particular read like a Who's Who of major political supporters of recent governors. During his tenure as governor, Governor Bush appointed ten people to the Board of Regents of the University of Texas. These ten appointees collectively gave Bush more than $400,000 in his

TEXAS ONLINE ★ Forces of Change

The Textbook Debate

The Texas Public Policy Foundation and Texas Freedom Network are fighting the textbook battle online as well as at the SBOE. The Texas Public Policy Foundation posts its textbook reports at the following Internet address:

www.texaspolicy.com/research_reports.php

Click on "Textbooks" under "Research and Reports." You can find the response of the Texas Freedom Network linked from its main website:

www.tfn.org/

Study the materials posted by both sides and answer the following questions.

QUESTIONS TO CONSIDER

1. To whom is each side addressing the materials on its website? What is the target audience?
2. How would you summarize each side's point of view?
3. In your opinion, which group is more persuasive? Why?

two campaigns for governor.[29] In general, the board of regents sets basic university policy while leaving daily management to professional administrators on campus.

Licensing Boards   A number of boards and commissions are responsible for licensing and regulating various professions. Some of these include the Board of Barber Examiners, Advisory Board of Athletic Trainers, Board of Chiropractic Examiners, Cosmetology Commission, Polygraph Examiners Board, and the Funeral Service Commission. State law generally requires that licensing boards include members of the professions they are charged with regulating as well as lay members. The Board of Barber Examiners, for example, is composed primarily of barbers.

> "It's a time-honored tradition in Texas politics that if you expect to receive one of the plum appointed positions, you should expect to be a hefty contributor."
>
> —John Hildreth, Common Cause

N A T I O N A L   P E R S P E C T I V E

Electricity Deregulation in California

In the late 1990s, nearly half the states adopted legislation to deregulate their electric utilities, including Texas. The goal of deregulation was lower electric rates for consumers. Without the government setting rates, firms would compete for customers by offering low rates and reliable service.

California began implementing electricity deregulation in 1998 and the result was a disaster. Between the spring of 1999 and spring 2000, electric rates more than tripled and electricity supplies were so low that the state's electric utilities had to resort to rolling blackouts to conserve energy. Electric retailers faced bankruptcy, losing more than $12 billion. To keep the system running, state government borrowed $10 billion to purchase electricity from regional energy suppliers.*

Electricity deregulation in California failed because of bad luck and poor planning. When the legislature and governor adopted deregulation in 1996, California had a surplus of power. The surplus evaporated in the latter years of the decade because rapid economic growth in the state drove up the demand for electricity. In the meantime, the supply of electricity was flat. Unsure of the effect of deregulation on the industry, investors did not put up the money to build new power plants. No new power plants were built in California in the late 1990s. By the end of the decade, the demand for

electricity in California exceeded the supply and the state's consumers faced rate hikes and blackouts.†

Most economists believe that the implementation of electricity deregulation in Texas will be much smoother than it was in California. In contrast to California, the supply of electricity has been growing in Texas. Utility companies have built more than 20 new power plants since 1995 and over 12 more are under construction.‡ Furthermore, Texas has its own power grid. Consequently, it is less vulnerable to bottlenecks in power transmission than California and most other states.§

QUESTIONS TO CONSIDER

1. Did you and your family switch energy providers when Texas implemented electricity deregulation?

2. Has electricity deregulation had a positive or negative impact on your life (if any)?

3. Do you think the Texas legislature should repeal electricity deregulation?

---

*Matthew H. Brown, "The Electricity Market Mess," *State Legislatures* (March 2001): 15–19.

†Elaine Stuart, "Watt Went Wrong?" *State Government News* (March 2001): 14–17, 36.
‡John Greenwald, "The New Energy Crunch," *Time* (January 29, 2001): 42.
§Daniel Eisenberg, "Which State is Next?" *Time* (January 29, 2001): 46.

Regulatory Boards   Other state agencies regulate various areas of business and industry. The Public Utility Commission (PUC) regulates telephone and electric utilities. The Texas Department of Insurance (TDI) licenses and regulates insurance companies. The Finance Commission regulates banks and savings and loan institutions. The Texas Alcoholic Beverage Commission regulates the manufacture, transportation, and sale of alcoholic beverages in the state. The Texas Racing Commission oversees horse and dog racing. Most regulatory boards are led by officials appointed by the governor with senate approval.

State regulatory agencies make **rules,** which are legally binding regulations adopted by a regulatory agency. Whenever the PUC sets telephone rates, for example, it does so through **rulemaking,** which is a regulatory process used by government agencies to enact legally binding regulations. In Texas, the formal rulemaking process has several steps. When a board or commission considers the adoption of a rule, it must first publish the text of that rule in the *Texas Register.* Interested parties may then file comments on the rule. State law requires regulatory agencies to hold public hearings if as many as 25 people request one. After a hearing (if one is held), the board votes to adopt or reject the proposed rule. If the rule is adopted, it goes into effect no sooner than 20 days after the agency files 2 certified copies with the Texas secretary of state.

The rulemaking process in Texas often involves only a minimal amount of public input. Although some regulatory agency actions, such as the adoption of new telephone rates, receive a great deal of media attention, most rulemaking decisions escape notice of all but those parties most directly involved with the particular agency's action. In practice, most proposed rules generate little comment and public hearings are rare.[30]

Agencies have no inherent constitutional power to make rules. Instead, the legislature delegates authority to agencies to make regulations to implement legislative policy. If the legislature is unhappy with an agency's actions, it can enact legislation to restrict or even eliminate the agency's rulemaking authority.

Social Service Agencies   The legislature has created a number of agencies to facilitate the receipt of federal funds and promote the interests of particular groups in society. The Texas Commission on Alcohol and Drug Abuse administers federal grant programs dealing with substance abuse. The Governor's Committee on People with Disabilities advises state government on disability issues. Other social service agencies include the Texas Department on Aging, Commission for the Blind, Cancer Council, and the Commission for the Deaf and Hard of Hearing. Appointed boards head social service agencies. Board members are appointed by the governor pending senate confirmation to serve fixed terms.

Promotional and Preservation Agencies   Several state agencies are charged either with promoting economic development or preserving the state's historical heritage. The Food and Fiber Commission works to find new uses and markets for Texas farm products, especially cotton, wool, mohair, and other textiles. The Texas Historical Commission works to preserve the state's architectural, archeological, and cultural landmarks.

★
POLITICS AND ADMINISTRATION

Administrative policymaking in Texas is a complex process involving the governor, legislature, interest groups, and the executive-branch bureaucracy. Each participant has its own perspectives and set of political resources for achieving influence.

The Legislature

In theory, the legislature has ultimate authority over most administrative agencies. Except for state agencies established by the Texas Constitution such as the Railroad Commission, the administrative bureaucracy is a creature of the legislature. The legislature can restructure or eliminate a state agency if it chooses or adopt legislation directing an agency to take or refrain from taking particular actions. In practice, however, the legislature sometimes struggles to exert control because of its brief, infrequent sessions. Consequently, the legislature has adopted a number of procedures to provide ongoing oversight and administrative control, including sunset review, committee oversight, and LBB supervision.

Sunset review is the periodic evaluation of state agencies by the legislature to determine whether they should be reauthorized. Approximately 150 state agencies are subject to sunset review. Each agency undergoes sunset review every 12 years, with 20 to 30 agencies facing review each legislative session. The list of state agencies facing sunset review in 2003 included the Lottery Commission, Department of Health, Department of Human Services, Higher Education Coordinating Board, and Funeral Service Commission.[31]

The sunset review process involves the agency facing review, the Sunset Advisory Commission, the legislature, and, to a lesser degree, the governor. The Sunset Advisory Commission includes four members of the house, four members of the senate, and two citizens. The speaker of the house appoints the house members and one citizen representative while the lieutenant governor names the state senators and the other citizen representative.

Both the agency under review and the staff of the Sunset Advisory Commission evaluate the agency's operation and performance. The agency conducts a self-study while the Commission staff prepares an independent evaluation. Commission members review the two documents and hold hearings at which agency officials, interest group spokespersons, and interested parties present testimony. After the hearings are complete, the commission recommends whether the agency should be kept as it is, reformed, or abolished. These steps take place before the legislature meets in regular session.

Once the legislative session convenes, lawmakers consider the Sunset Advisory Commission's recommendations and decide the agency's fate. The key feature of the process is that the legislature must reauthorize each agency under review. The reauthorization legislation then goes to the governor for signature or veto. If the legislature fails to act or the governor vetoes the reauthorization measure, the agency dies: The sun sets on it. Since the legislature began the sunset process in 1979, it has eliminated 44 agencies and consolidated 11 others.[32] In practice, the legislature

The State Board of Barber Examiners licenses barbers and barbershops.

reauthorizes most state agencies while mandating reforms in their procedures. The legislature has added public representation to governing boards, provided for more public input into agency decision making, imposed conflict-of-interest restrictions on board members, and mandated closer legislative review of agency expenditures.

In addition to the sunset process, the legislature uses the committee system and the Legislative Budget Board (LBB) to oversee the executive bureaucracy. During legislative sessions, standing committees may evaluate agency operations and hold hearings to investigate agency performance. Interim committees may oversee agency operations between sessions. An **interim committee** is a committee that is established to study a particular policy issue between legislative sessions. The LBB influences agency operations through its role in budget execution. Between legislative sessions, the LBB may propose moving funds from one budget category to another, pending the governor's approval. In practice, budget execution authority gives the LBB power to act like a board of directors for the state bureaucracy. The LBB sets goals for agencies, reviews whether the goals are met, and fine-tunes the budget between legislative sessions to reward (or punish) agencies based on their support of LBB goals.

The Governor

The legal/constitutional powers of the governor of Texas for influencing administrative policymaking are relatively weak. Although the line-item veto (and the threat of its use) can be an effective weapon at times, the governor's powers over administration are otherwise limited. The heads of a number of state agencies are independently elected and thus immune from direct gubernatorial control. The governor appoints the members of most state boards, but because members serve fixed, multiyear terms, a new governor does not usually get to name a majority of the members of any particular agency for several years. Furthermore, board members are not legally obliged to consult with the governor on policy matters or necessarily follow the governor's lead.

Nonetheless, a determined governor who picks fights carefully can have influence over executive branch agencies. Ann Richards made insurance reform an issue during her successful campaign for governor in 1990. When Richards took office in 1991, she faced a state insurance agency dominated by members appointed by her predecessor who were openly hostile to her position on insurance rates. Governor Richards demanded that the holdover board members resign and threatened to invoke an obscure, never-used law allowing state agencies to be placed under the control of the state Conservatorship Board. Richards said that she would ask the Legislative Audit Committee to declare the insurance agency guilty of "gross fiscal mismanagement." Before the Legislative Audit Committee could act, one of the holdover board members resigned and Richards was able to name a replacement, giving her appointees a majority on the three-member board. Richards won the fight because she succeeded in framing the issue as a battle between overcharged consumers and greedy insurance companies and placing herself on the side of the consumers.

Over time, a governor can influence the administrative bureaucracy through the appointment process. A governor can shape an agency's policy perspectives by appointing men and women to agency boards that share a particular point of view. Governor Bush and Governor Perry both tended to name business-oriented conservatives to serve on most boards, especially boards that directly impact business interests. For example, Governor Perry appointed businessman Bob Perry (no relation), an executive with Perry Homes, one of the state's largest homebuilders, to serve on the Residential Construction Commission. The legislature created the commission to develop home building performance standards and establish a dispute resolution process that disgruntled purchasers would have to complete before they could file a lawsuit. Perry, who had an obvious personal interest in the work of the commission, was also the single most generous campaign contributor to the governor, giving Perry $580,000 since 1997 when Perry was still agriculture commissioner.[33]

Interest Groups

Every state agency has several and perhaps dozens of interest groups vitally concerned about the programs it administers. Teachers' unions, textbook publishers, and a range of conservative and liberal social issue groups focus on the actions of the SBOE. Doctors are concerned about the Board of Medical Examiners. Insurance companies and consumer groups are interested in the work of the Texas Department of Insurance.

Interest groups use a number of approaches to influence the state bureaucracy. Groups seek access to decision makers by contributing to the campaigns of candidates for statewide executive office. Campaign funding for Railroad Commission candidates typically comes from oil companies, trucking firms, and railroads regulated by the commission. Agricultural interests back candidates for Commissioner of Agriculture. Groups lobby agencies directly. Farm groups lobby the Department of Agriculture over the enforcement of agricultural rules and regulations. The American Association of Retired Persons (AARP) pressures the Public Utility Commission (PUC) over utility rates. Interest groups try to influence agencies indirectly by lobbying the legislature to pressure the state bureaucracy on their behalf. Financial institutions, such as banks and savings and loans, lobby the legislature concerning the state Finance Commission. Groups file lawsuits to block or reverse agency decisions. In general, lawsuits taken against state agencies allege that the agency did not follow proper procedures in arriving at some decision. After the Texas Department of Parks and Wildlife issued an emergency order that banned oyster fishing, for example, the Texas Oyster Association filed suit, arguing that the agency had acted improperly. Finally, interest groups have influence in bureaucratic policymaking through the exchange of personnel. Both elected and appointed administrators often come from the industry their agencies oversee. In fact, state laws sometimes require that a majority of the members of occupational licensing boards be members of the profession involved. A majority of the members of the Funeral Service Commission, for example, must be morticians.

Bureaucrats

State bureaucrats have goals of their own. State employees are primarily concerned with their own jobs in their own departments in their own agencies. They want to preserve and enhance their positions, programs, and budgets. Consequently, bureaucrats rally to protect their departments and programs against proposed budget cuts or reorganizations.

Bureaucrats have resources with which to defend their interests. Sometimes career employees resort to subtle, behind-the-scenes resistance to policy changes they oppose. Changes may be delayed. Bureaucrats may follow the letter but not the spirit of directives. Officials may "forget" to pass along orders to subordinates. News of mistakes or internal bickering can be leaked to the press. Expertise is another weapon bureaucrats have for fighting policy battles. Today's policy problems are often so complex that the bureaucracy's knowledge, technical expertise, and experience are virtually indispensable. Therein lies power. In such fields as education, hazardous waste disposal, oil and gas regulation, health care, agriculture, and pollution control, the professional knowledge and expertise of state employees is fundamental to the implementation of public policy.

Bureaucracy also finds power in alliances with legislative leaders and interest groups. State agencies are some of the legislature's most vigorous and effective lobbyists. Frequently, state agencies are the main or even the only source of information on an issue for legislators. Furthermore, most state agencies have interest allies that are willing to use their political muscle on behalf of the agency. Highway contractors support the Texas Department of Transportation. Racing interests pushed for the creation of the Texas Racing Commission.

CONCLUSION: THE EXECUTIVE BRANCH AND THE POLICYMAKING PROCESS

The governor and the various agencies and departments of the executive branch of Texas government play an important role in the policymaking process.

Agenda Building

Executive branch officials help set the policy agenda. The governor enjoys the public visibility to focus public attention on an issue. By declaring an issue an emergency or calling a special session, the governor can set the agenda for the legislature. Governor Richards made insurance reform a major state issue when she was governor. Other executive officials can take action that put items on the official policy agenda as well. Attorney General Morales's lawsuit against the tobacco industry pushed the issue of industry liability for state health costs to the forefront of the policy agenda.

Policy Formulation and Adoption

The officials and departments of the executive branch participate in policy formulation. Executive branch officials and their staffs testify before legislative committees and advise individual legislators on how best to address policy problems. Furthermore, the governor and other state executives participate in policy formulation by supporting one particular policy approach over alternatives. Governor Perry's role in budget policy formulation in 2003 was to take the option of a tax increase off the table.

The executive branch plays a key role in policy adoption. The governor may sign, veto, or allow measures passed by the legislature to become law without signature. A number of state agencies also adopt policy through the rulemaking process. The Railroad Commission, for example, makes state energy policy.

Policy Implementation and Evaluation

Executive branch agencies and departments implement policy. The comptroller's office collects taxes. The Department of Agriculture enforces state laws dealing with agriculture. The Texas Department of Parks and Wildlife carries out state policy concerning game laws, conservation, and park management. The Texas Commission on Environmental Quality implements the state's environmental laws.

Finally, the executive branch evaluates policy. State agencies, departments, and bureaus regularly compile data on the operation of state programs and occasionally conduct formal evaluation reports. The comptroller, in particular, gathers data and conducts performance reviews of state agencies. Executive branch officials, legislators, political activists, and the media sometimes use the data and reports as feedback to promote new agendas and policy initiatives.

★ REVIEW QUESTIONS

1. How effectively did Governor Perry influence budgetary policymaking in the 2003 session of the legislature?

2. How does the plural executive affect administrative policymaking in Texas?

3. How do the powers and responsibilities of the governor of Texas compare and contrast with those of the president of the United States?

4. How do the official powers of the governor of Texas compare with those of other state governors?

5. What do the experiences of Governors Bush and Perry reveal about the policymaking influence of the governor of Texas?

6. What are the powers and responsibilities of the lieutenant governor, attorney general,

land commissioner, comptroller, and agriculture commissioner?

7. What are the powers and responsibilities of the secretary of state, Railroad Commission, and State Board of Education?

8. What are the most common structures in the executive branch of Texas government?

9. What tools does the legislature have for influencing administrative policymaking?

10. How much influence does the governor have over administrative policymaking?

11. What tools do interest groups have for influencing administrative policymaking?

12. How do state employees affect administrative policymaking?

13. What role does the executive branch of state government play in the policymaking process?

★ KEY TERMS

allowable

appropriation bill

biennium

budget execution authority

capital punishment

commutation

hate-crimes legislation

impeachment

interim committee

Jacksonian democracy

Legislative Budget Board (LBB)

Legislative Redistricting Board (LRB)

line-item veto

Medicaid program

pardon

Permanent School Fund (PSF)

plural executive

reprieve

rulemaking

rules

senatorial courtesy

sunset review

veto

★ NOTES

1. Texas Comptroller of Public Accounts, *Biennial Revenue Estimate 2004–2005*, available at **www.window .state.tx.us**.

2. 2003 State of the State Address, available at **www.governor.state.tx.us/divisions/press/speeches/ speech_2003-02-11**.

3. Eva DeLuna Castro and Dick Lavine, *The Texas Budget and Tax Primer* (Austin: Center for Public Policy Priorities, 2002), p. 9.

4. University of Houston Center for Public Policy, quoted in "Poll: Most Texans Oblivious to State Budget Deficit," *Houston Business Journal*, February 10, 2003, available at **www.bizjournals.com**.

5. David M. Hedge, *Governance and the Changing American States* (Boulder, CO: Westview, 1998), p. 93.

6. Jack Keever, "Impeachment Winds Stir Memories of Ferguson," *Houston Post*, July 5, 1987, p. 8A.

7. Personal communication with J. Kevin Patterson, Assistant General Counsel, Office of the Governor, July 22, 2003.

8. Susan A. MacManus, "Playing a New Game: Governors and the Job Training Partnership Act (JTPA)," *American Politics Quarterly* 14 (July 1986): 131–49.

9. House Research Organization, available at **www.capitol .state.tx.us/hrofr/**.

10. David C. Saffell, *State and Local Government: Politics and Public Policies*, 4th ed. (New York: McGraw-Hill, 1990), p. 154.

11. Legislative Reports for the Seventy-Eighth Legislature, available at **www.capitol.state.tx.us**.

12. Governor's Appointment Office, available at **www .governor.state.tx.us**.

13. Kelly Shannon, "27% of Perry Appointees are Minorities," *Houston Chronicle*, November 28, 2003, p. 1A.

14. "Profile of Appellate and Trial Judges," *Texas Judicial System Annual Report—Fiscal Year 2002*, available at **www.courts.state.tx.us/publicinfo/**.

15. Glen Abney and Thomas P. Lauth, "The Executive Budget in the States: Normative Idea and Empirical Observation," *Policy Studies Journal* 17 (Summer 1989): 829–62.

16. "Perry Signs Toyota Rail Legislation," *San Antonio Business Journal*, April 11, 2003, available at **www .bizjournals.com/sanantonio**.

17. Robert C. Turner, "The Political Economy of Gubernatorial Smokestack Chasing: Bad Policy and Bad Politics?" *State Politics and Policy Quarterly* 3 (Fall 2003): 270–93.

18. Thomas M. Holbrook, "Institutional Strength and Gubernatorial Elections," *American Politics Quarterly* 21 (July 1993): 261–71.

19. Nelson C. Dometrius, "Changing Gubernatorial Power: The Measure vs. Reality," *Western Political Quarterly* 40 (June 1987): 319–28.

20. Thad L. Beyle and Scott Mouw, "Governors: The Power of Removal," *Policy Studies Journal* 17 (Summer 1989): 804–28.

21. Lee Sigelman and Nelson C. Dometrius, "Governors as Chief Administrators," *American Politics Quarterly* 16 (April 1988): 157–70.

22. Martha Wagner Weinberg, "Gubernatorial Style in Managing the State," in *Subnational Politics: Readings in State and Local Government*, David C. Saffell and Terry Gilbreth, eds. (Reading, MA: Addison-Wesley, 1982), pp. 137–56.

23. *Texas Weekly*, June 25, 2001, pp. 1–2.

24. "State Government Employees," *Governing State and Local Source Book 2003*, September 2003, p. 51.

25. Council of State Governments, *The Book of the States*, 1984–1985 (Lexington, KY: Council of State Governments, 1984), pp. 72–73.

26. *Texas Weekly*, February 2, 1998, p. 6.

27. David F. Prindle, *Petroleum, Politics, and the Texas Railroad Commission* (Austin: University of Texas Press, 1981), ch. 1.

28. Alexander Stille, "Textbook Publishers Learn to Avoid Messing with Texas," *New York Times*, June 29, 2002, available at **www.nytimes.com**.

29. "Well-Appointed Officials," Texans for Public Justice, available at **www.tpj.org**.

30. Edwin S. Davis, "Rule Making Activity of Selected Texas Regulatory Agencies," *Texas Journal of Political Studies* 8 (Fall/Winter 1985–1986): 26–36.

31. Sunset Advisory Commission, available at **www.sunset .state.tx.us**.

32. "General Information," Sunset Advisory Commission, available at **www.sunset.state.tx.us**.

33. Janet Elliott, "Perry Homes Executive Named to Commission," *Houston Chronicle*, September 30, 2003, p. 15A.

ONLINE PRACTICE TEST

Test your understanding of this chapter
with interactive review quizzes at
www.ablongman.com/tannahilltexas/chapter9

Judicial Branch

LEARNING OBJECTIVES

After studying Chapter 10, students should be able to do the following:

★ Distinguish between criminal and civil cases and among the types of cases within each classification.

★ Compare and contrast trial court and appellate court procedures.

★ Outline the organization of the judicial branch of Texas government, identifying the various courts and describing the types of cases they hear.

★ List the terms of office, method of selection, and qualifications for judges in Texas.

★ Describe the process of judicial selection in Texas.

★ Evaluate the arguments for and against the state's system of selecting judges.

★ Evaluate the various proposals for reforming the judicial selection process in the state.

★ Describe the process of judicial retirement and removal.

★ Describe the role of the judicial branch in the state's policymaking process.

★ Define the key terms listed on pages 273–274 and explain their significance.

Should the government cover the cost of medically necessary abortions for low-income women? **Medicaid** is a federal program designed to provide health insurance coverage to poor people, the disabled, and elderly Americans who are impoverished. Although the U.S. Supreme Court has long held that women have the constitutional right to terminate a pregnancy until the fetus has achieved viability, Congress has prohibited the use of federal Medicaid money to pay for an abortion except when the life of the women is at stake or in the case of rape or incest. States may choose to include abortion services in their Medicaid programs and fund them with state money, but Texas does not. Poor women in Texas who are advised by a physician to terminate a pregnancy because of a medical condition, such as epilepsy, cancer, or asthma, must either cover the $400–$500 cost themselves or carry the pregnancy to term.

Abortion rights advocates filed suit in Texas court against the state's refusal to cover medically necessary abortions in its Medicaid program, charging that the policy amounted to illegal sex discrimination. They based their lawsuit on the **Texas Equal Rights Amendment (ERA),** which is a provision in the Texas Constitution that states the following: "Equality under the law shall not be denied or abridged because of sex, race, color, creed, or national origin." Although the Texas Medicaid program covers all medically necessary procedures for men, they argued, it does not fund all medically necessary procedures for women because it does not cover abortion services.

> "They [the Texas Supreme Court justices] have found it constitutional for the state to prefer child-bearing over abortion even if the result is to jeopardize the woman's health and ultimately harm her ability to care for her family."
> —Kae McLaughlin, Texas Abortion and Reproductive Rights Action League

The Texas Supreme Court rejected the argument. The purpose of the policy, the court said, was not to discriminate against women, but to promote childbirth. Because Texas has a legitimate interest in favoring childbirth over abortion, the state is not constitutionally required to fund medically necessary abortions.[1]

The judicial branch is an important part of the policymaking process. The courts are primarily involved in policy implementation through the administration of justice. They try criminal defendants and hear lawsuits among private parties. As the lawsuit over the state's refusal to cover medically necessary abortions in its Medicaid program demonstrates, Texas courts sometimes participate in policy adoption. In this example, the Texas Supreme Court confirmed a policy decision made by the legislature and executive branches of government.

This chapter is the third in a series of five chapters examining the policymaking units of state and local government in Texas. Chapter 8 focused on the Texas legislature and Chapter 9 examined the executive branch while the next two chapters deal with the units of local government. Chapter 11 studies city government. Chapter 12 considers counties, school districts, and special districts.

TYPES OF LEGAL DISPUTES

The courts administer justice by settling criminal and civil disputes.

Criminal Cases

A **criminal case** is a legal dispute dealing with an alleged violation of a penal law. A **criminal defendant** is the party charged with a criminal offense whereas the

prosecutor is the attorney who tries a criminal case on behalf of the government. The role of the court in a criminal case is to guide and referee the dispute. Ultimately, a judge or jury rules on the defendant's guilt or innocence and, if the verdict is guilty, assesses punishment.

? WHAT IS YOUR OPINION?

Should the Texas Medicaid program cover the cost of medically necessary abortions for low-income women?

The **burden of proof** is the legal obligation of one party in a lawsuit to prove its position to a court. The prosecutor has the burden of proof in a criminal case. In other words, the prosecutor must show that the defendant is guilty; the defendant need not demonstrate innocence. Texas law requires that the government must prove the defendant's guilt "beyond a reasonable doubt." Unless the evidence clearly points to the defendant's guilt, the law requires that the defendant be found not guilty.

The penal code classifies criminal cases according to their severity. A **misdemeanor** is a relatively minor criminal offense, such as a traffic violation. Texas law classifies misdemeanor offenses as Class A, B, or C. Class A misdemeanors are the most serious; Class C, the least serious. Class A misdemeanors can be punishable by a fine not to exceed $3,000 and/or a jail term of a year or less. In contrast, the maximum punishment for a Class C misdemeanor is a fine of $500.

A **felony** is a serious criminal offense, such as murder, sexual assault, or burglary. Texas law divides felony offenses into five categories—capital, first-, second-, third-, and fourth-degree (state jail) felonies—with fourth degree being the least serious category of offenses. Convicted felons may be fined heavily and sentenced to as many as 99 years in prison. In Texas and 37 other states, convicted capital murderers may be sentenced to death. The death penalty is known as **capital punishment.**

Civil Disputes

Courts also settle civil disputes. A **civil case** is a legal dispute concerning a private conflict between two or more parties—individuals, corporations, or government agencies. In this type of legal dispute, the party initiating the lawsuit is called the **plaintiff;** the **civil defendant** is the responding party. The plaintiff feels wronged by the defendant and files suit to ask a court to award monetary damages or order the defendant to remedy the wrong.

The burden of proof in civil cases is on the plaintiff, but it is not as heavy as it is in criminal disputes. With the exception of lawsuits filed to terminate parental rights, the plaintiff is required to prove the case "by a preponderance of the evidence." For the plaintiff's side to win a lawsuit, it need only demonstrate that the weight of evidence in the case is slightly more in its favor. If a judge or jury believes that the evidence is evenly balanced between the plaintiff and the defendant, the defendant prevails because the plaintiff has the burden of proof. A lawsuit to terminate parental rights is a civil action filed by the Texas Department of Protective and Regulatory Services to ask a court to end a parent-child relationship. The plaintiff

The Texas Supreme Court ruled that the Texas Constitution does not require the state to cover medically necessary abortions for poor women in its Medicaid program.

has the burden of proof to show by clear and convincing evidence that an individual's parental rights should be terminated because he or she is not a fit parent.

Civil disputes include property, probate, domestic relations, contract, and tort cases. A **property case** is a civil suit over the ownership of real estate or personal possessions, such as land, jewelry, or an automobile. A **probate case** is a civil suit dealing with the disposition of the property of a deceased individual. A **domestic-relations case** is a civil suit based on the law involving the relationships between husband and wife, and between parents and children, such as divorce and child custody cases. A **contract case** is a civil suit dealing with disputes over written or implied legal agreements, such as a suit over a faulty roof repair job. Finally, a **tort case** is a civil suit involving personal injury or damage to property, such as a lawsuit stemming from an automobile accident.

COURT PROCEDURES

The typical image of a court at work is that of a trial with judge, jury, witnesses, and evidence. The parties in the lawsuit, the **litigants,** are represented by counsel engaging in an **adversary proceeding,** which is a legal procedure in which each side presents evidence and arguments to bolster its position while rebutting evidence that might support the other side. Theoretically, the process helps the judge or jury determine the facts in a case.

In practice, most legal disputes are settled not by trials but through a process of negotiation and compromise between the parties involved. In civil cases, litigants usually decide that it is quicker and less costly to settle out of court than to go through the trial process. They agree on a settlement either before the case goes to trial or during the early stages of the trial. Similarly, most criminal cases are resolved through a **plea bargain,** which is a procedure in which a defendant agrees to plead guilty in order to receive punishment less than the maximum for an offense. On occasion, defendants may plead guilty to lesser offenses than the offense with which they were originally charged.

Judicial procedures are divided into trials and appeals. A **trial** is the formal examination of a civil or criminal action in accordance with law before a single judge who has jurisdiction to hear the dispute. Trials involve attorneys, witnesses, testimony, evidence, judges, and, occasionally, juries. In civil cases, the verdict determines which party in the lawsuit prevails. A criminal verdict decides whether the defendant is guilty or not guilty as charged. In general, the outcome of a trial can be appealed to a higher court for review.

Criminal defendants have a constitutional right to trial by jury. The U.S. Supreme Court has held that the U.S. Constitution obliges state governments to offer jury trials to persons charged with felony offenses.[2] The Texas Constitution goes further, granting accused persons the right to trial by jury in *all* cases, misdemeanor and felony, although defendants may waive the right to a jury trial and be tried by a judge alone. Litigants in civil cases have the option of having their case heard by a judge alone or by a jury.

Prospective trial jurors are selected from county voter registration rolls and lists of persons holding Texas driver's licenses and DPS identification cards. Persons who are convicted felons or under felony indictment are ineligible to serve on a jury. Some groups of people are exempt from jury service if they wish, including full-time students, individuals over 70 years of age, and persons with custody of small children whose absence would leave children without proper supervision.

An **appeal** is the taking of a case from a lower court to a higher court by the losing party in a lower court decision. Civil litigants argue that the trial court failed to follow proper procedures or incorrectly applied the law. They hope that an appellate court will reverse or at least temper the decision of the trial court. Parties who lose tort cases, for example, may ask an appellate court to reduce the amount of damages awarded. Criminal defendants who appeal their convictions contend that the trial court committed **reversible error,** which is a mistake committed by a trial court that is serious enough to warrant a new trial because the mistake could have affected the outcome of the original trial. In contrast, **harmless error** is a mistake committed by a trial court that is not serious enough to warrant a new trial because it could not have affected the outcome of the original trial. The right to appeal criminal court decisions extends only to the defendant; the prosecution does not have the right to appeal an acquittal. The constitutional principle that an individual may not be tried a second time by the same unit of government for a single offense if acquitted in the first trial is known as the prohibition against **double jeopardy.**

The procedures of appeals courts differ notably from those of trial courts. In general, trial courts are concerned with questions of fact and the law as it applies to those facts. In contrast, appeals are based on issues of law and procedure. Appellate courts do not retry cases appealed to them. Instead, appeals court justices (juries do not participate in appellate proceedings) make decisions based on the law and the constitution, the written and oral arguments presented by attorneys for the litigants in the lawsuit, and the written record of the lower-court proceedings. Also, appellate court justices usually make decisions collectively in panels of three or more judges rather than singly, as do trial court judges.

Appeals court decisions are themselves subject to appeal. The Texas Courts of Appeals hear all appellate cases in the state except for death penalty cases, which go to the Texas Court of Criminal Appeals. Civil litigants can file appeals with the Texas Supreme Court; criminal cases can be appealed to the Texas Court of Criminal Appeals. Both the prosecution and the defendant have the right to appeal the decisions of appellate courts in criminal cases. The constitutional protection against double jeopardy applies only to trial proceedings.

Appeals courts may uphold, reverse, or modify lower court decisions. Appeals courts may direct a trial court to reconsider a case in light of the appellate court's ruling on certain legal issues. If an appeals court overturns a criminal conviction, the defendant does not necessarily go free. The district attorney who initially prosecuted the case has the option either to retry the case or release the defendant. In practice, many defendants are retried, convicted, and sentenced once again. Ignacio Cuevas, for example, was tried three times for capital murder, convicted three times, and sentenced to death three times. Twice the Texas Court of Criminal Appeals overturned Cuevas's conviction, but not a third time. Cuevas was executed.

> "A jury consists of twelve persons chosen to decide who has the better lawyer."
> —Robert Frost, poet

THE TEXAS COURT SYSTEM

The Texas court system has three levels:

- **Local Courts** Municipal courts, justice of the peace (JP) courts, and county courts hear relatively minor civil and misdemeanor criminal disputes.
- **District Courts** State district courts are the general trial courts of the state, hearing major civil disputes and trying felony criminal cases.
- **Appellate Courts** The Texas Courts of Appeals, Texas Court of Criminal Appeals, and Texas Supreme Court comprise the state's appellate court system.

Local Courts

Municipal, JP, and county courts are local courts operated by cities and county governments.

Municipal Courts   The Texas legislature has created municipal courts in every incorporated city in the state. Municipal courts operate in 877 cities, staffed by more than

SHOE

Source: Reprinted by permission of Tribune Media Services.

1,250 judges.[3] Smaller cities have one municipal court with a single judge; larger cities operate several courtrooms, each with its own judge.

Most municipal court cases involve relatively minor criminal matters. Municipal courts have exclusive jurisdiction over cases involving violations of **city ordinances,** which are laws enacted by the governing body of a municipality. In general, persons convicted of violating city ordinances may be fined no more than $500, although violators of ordinances relating to litter, fire safety, zoning, public health, and sanitation may be fined as much as $2,000. Municipal courts share jurisdiction with justice of the peace courts in misdemeanor cases involving violations of Class C misdemeanors within city limits. The maximum fine for a Class C misdemeanor is $500. Municipal courts also have the power to award limited civil monetary penalties in cases involving dangerous dogs.

Cases involving traffic tickets account for nearly 85 percent of the workload of municipal courts. Most defendants plead guilty and pay a relatively small fine. Only about a fourth of municipal court cases go to trial with most of those resulting in guilty verdicts. Only 1.2 percent of municipal court defendants found guilty file an appeal of their convictions.[4] Under state law, municipal court proceedings in all but a handful of the state's largest cities (including Houston, Dallas, Fort Worth, San Antonio, and Austin) are not recorded. Consequently, municipal court defendants in most cities are entitled to a new trial called trial *de novo*, usually in county court, if they appeal a conviction. In cities whose municipal courts are courts of record, the appeal is done by the record only and is not a trial *de novo*. Relatively few defendants appeal a conviction because the cost of hiring an attorney to handle the appeal usually exceeds the amount of the fine.

Municipal court judges serve as **magistrates** (judicial officers) for the state in a range of proceedings involving both misdemeanor and felony offenses. They may issue search and arrest warrants, set bail for criminal defendants, and hold preliminary hearings. Municipal court judges may also conduct driver's license suspension hearings and emergency mental commitment hearings.

Justice of the Peace (JP) Courts   The Texas Constitution requires each county to operate at least one JP court and allows larger counties to have as many as 16. In 2002, 834 JP courts operated statewide.

JP courts hear both criminal and civil cases, with criminal disputes comprising more than 90 percent of their caseloads. They hear criminal cases involving Class C misdemeanor offenses. Almost three-fourths of these cases involve traffic offenses, with the rest concerning nontraffic misdemeanors, such as game law violations and arrests for public intoxication, disorderly conduct, and some thefts. Justice of the peace courts have a civil jurisdiction, hearing small claims civil cases of $5,000 or less and conducting a number of civil actions. Individuals with civil disputes over relatively small amounts of money can file suit in JP court and present their case to the justice of the peace without aid of an attorney. JP courts also conduct civil proceedings dealing with mortgage foreclosures, property liens, and forcible entry and detainer suits. A **property lien** is a financial claim against property for payment of debt. A **forcible entry and detainer suit** is an effort by a landlord to evict a tenant (usually for failure to pay rent).

JP court proceedings, similar to most municipal court proceedings, are not recorded. As a result, a person who files an appeal of a JP court decision is entitled to a new trial, generally in county court. In practice, most cases appealed from JP courts are settled by plea bargains or dismissed by county court judges. Appeals of justice court decisions are rare, involving less than 1 percent of the cases disposed by trial in a JP court.[5]

Similar to municipal court judges, justices of the peace are state magistrates. They may issue search and arrest warrants in both misdemeanor and felony cases, set bail for criminal defendants, and conduct preliminary hearings. They also hold driver's license suspension hearings and conduct emergency mental commitment hearings.

County Courts　Each of the state's 254 counties has a constitutional county court, so called because it is required by the Texas Constitution. These courts have both criminal and civil jurisdiction. County courts try criminal cases involving violations of Class A and Class B misdemeanors. In practice, criminal cases constitute almost three-fourths of the cases heard by county courts, with theft, worthless checks, and driving while intoxicated or under the influence of drugs (DWI/DUID) the most common offenses. County courts also try Class C misdemeanor cases appealed from JP or municipal courts.[6]

The civil jurisdiction of the constitutional county courts extends to disputes in which the amount of money at stake is between $200 and $5,000, although these courts may also hear cases involving lesser amounts that are appealed from JP court. The constitutional county courts share their civil jurisdiction with both JP and district courts. An individual suing for $1,000, for example, could legally file in JP, district, or county court. Suits over debts, personal injury or damage, and divorce are the most commonly heard civil cases in constitutional county courts.

In addition to their basic civil and criminal jurisdictions, the constitutional county courts fulfill a number of other functions. They probate uncontested wills, appoint guardians for minors, and conduct mental health competency/commitment hearings. County court decisions on mental competency and probate may be appealed to district courts, but all other appeals from county court are taken to the courts of appeals.

The Texas legislature has created 200 additional county courts known as statutory county courts (because they are established by statute) and 16 statutory probate courts

LEARNING EXERCISE

Small Claims Court in Action

Small claims courts allow citizens access to the judicial system for disputes that are too small to justify a full-blown judicial proceeding. Suppose your former landlord refuses to refund your $600 apartment rent deposit or that the $50 watch you bought at the flea market quit running after two days and the merchant will not give you back your money. These are examples of the kinds of legal controversies that citizens can resolve in small claims court without hiring an attorney and having to pay expensive court costs.

Your assignment in this learning exercise is to visit a local small claims court and then write a short first-person essay discussing your experience. Begin by consulting the government pages of the telephone book to locate a JP court in your area. Visit the court for at least an hour. (You should call ahead to learn when the court is in session.) Then, write an essay describing and discussing your experience. In your essay, answer the following questions.

QUESTIONS TO CONSIDER

1. Which court did you visit?
2. When did you visit?
3. How long did you stay?
4. Who was the presiding judge?
5. How did the judge get his/her position, by election or appointment?
6. How many cases did you witness?
7. What issue(s) did the case(s) involve?
8. What procedures did the court follow?
9. How many people were in the courtroom and who were they (defendants, lawyers, law officers, etc.)?
10. Did the court run smoothly? Why do you say so?
11. Do you think the court ran fairly? Why do you say so?
12. If you could make one change in the manner in which the court was run, what would it be?
13. Would you advise a friend involved in a dispute to use a small claims court to settle it? Why or why not?
14. Did you have a good time? Discuss.

to supplement the constitutional county courts. These courts operate primarily in urban areas where the caseload of the constitutional county court is overwhelming, and the county judge, who presides in the constitutional county court, is busy with the affairs of county government. Some statutory county courts concentrate on civil matters and some handle only criminal cases. The legislature allows many of the statutory county courts to hear civil cases involving as much as $100,000. Appeals from the statutory county courts proceed in the same manner as appeals from constitutional county courts.

District Courts

Texas has 418 district courts. Each court serves a specific geographic area, which, in rural areas, may encompass several counties. In urban counties, the legislature has created multiple courts, many of which specialize in particular areas of the law. Harris County alone has nearly 60 district courts, including civil, criminal, family, and juvenile district courts.

District courts are the basic trial courts of the state of Texas. They hear all felony cases and have jurisdiction in civil matters involving $200 or more, sharing jurisdiction on smaller sums with JP and county courts. Civil cases comprise two-thirds of the caseload for district courts. Family law disputes, including divorce and

In civil trials, the plaintiff must prove the case by a preponderance of the evidence.

child custody cases, are the civil matters most frequently handled by district courts. Personal injury cases, tax cases, and disputes over debts are important as well. The most frequently heard criminal cases are drug offenses, theft, assault, and burglary.[7] District courts may also issue a number of **legal writs,** which are written orders issued by a court directing the performance of an act or prohibiting some act. The constitutional challenge to the state's Medicaid program involved a district court suit filed by abortion rights advocates asking the judge to issue a legal writ to permanently prevent the state from enforcing its policy against funding medically necessary abortions because the policy violated the Texas ERA. Appeals from district court decisions are taken to the courts of appeals, except capital murder cases in which the death penalty is assessed. These cases are appealed directly and automatically to the Texas Court of Criminal Appeals. After the district court ruled against the plaintiffs in the abortion funding case, they appealed to the 3rd Court of Appeals.

Appellate Courts

The Courts of Appeals, Texas Court of Criminal Appeals, and Texas Supreme Court comprise the state's appellate court system, considering appeals filed by litigants who lose in lower courts. With the exception of capital murder cases in which the death penalty has been assessed, appellate courts need not hold hearings in every case. After reading **legal briefs,** which are written legal arguments, and reviewing the trial-court record, appeals court justices may simply **affirm** (uphold) the lower court ruling without holding a hearing to consider formal arguments. In practice, appellate courts reject the overwhelming majority of appeals based solely on the legal briefs filed in the case.

When an appeals court decides to accept a case on appeal, the court generally schedules a hearing at which attorneys for the two sides in the dispute present oral arguments and answer questions posed by the justices. Appeals courts do not retry cases. Instead, they review the trial court record and consider legal arguments raised by the attorneys in the case. After hearing oral arguments and studying legal briefs, appeals court justices discuss the case and eventually vote on a decision, with a majority vote of the justices required to decide a case. The court may affirm the lower court decision, reverse it, modify it, or affirm part of the lower court ruling while reversing or modifying the rest. Frequently, an appeals court will **remand** (return) a case to the trial court for reconsideration in light of the appeals court decision.

When the court announces its decision, it may issue a **majority** *or* **deciding opinion,** which is the official written statement of a court that explains and justifies its ruling and serves as a guideline for lower courts when similar legal issues arise in the future. Associate Supreme Court Justice Harriett O'Neill wrote the opinion of the court in the Medicaid abortion funding case. In addition to the court's majority opinion, members of an appellate court may release dissenting or concurring opinions. A **dissenting opinion** is a written judicial statement that disagrees with the decision of the court's majority. It presents the viewpoint of one or more justices who disagree with the court's decision. A **concurring opinion** is a written judicial statement that agrees with the majority opinion's ruling but disagrees with its reasoning. Justices who voted in favor of the court's decision for reasons other than those stated in the majority opinion may file concurring opinions. No justices wrote dissenting or concurring opinions in the Medicaid abortion funding case.

Courts of Appeals   Texas has 14 Courts of Appeals, each serving a specific geographic area called a Court of Appeals District. The 3rd Court of Appeals, which sits in Austin, heard the appeal of the challenge to the state's ban on Medicaid funding for medically necessary abortions. The number of justices in each court varies from 3 to 13, depending on the workload. Altogether, 80 justices staff the 14 Courts of Appeals. The justices on each court hear cases in panels of at least 3 justices, with decisions made by majority vote. A panel of the 3rd Court of Appeals voted 2 to 1 in favor of the plaintiffs in the abortion funding case.

Each of the Courts of Appeals has jurisdiction on appeals from trial courts located in its district. The Courts of Appeals hear both civil and criminal appeals, except death penalty appeals, which are considered by the Texas Court of Criminal Appeals. The Courts of Appeals dealt with more than 12,000 cases in 2002, with criminal cases outnumbering civil cases by a 3 to 2 margin.[8] The Courts of Appeals reversed the decision of the trial court in whole or in part in 9.4 percent of the cases it heard.[9] The rulings of the Courts of Appeals may be appealed either to the Texas Court of Criminal Appeals for criminal matters or the Texas Supreme Court for civil cases. After the 3rd Court of Appeals ruled against it in the Medicaid abortion funding case, the state appealed to the Texas Supreme Court.

Texas Court of Criminal Appeals   Texas is one of two states (Oklahoma is the other) with two supreme courts—the Texas Supreme Court for civil disputes and the Texas Court of Criminal Appeals for criminal matters. The Texas Court of Criminal Appeals, which meets in Austin, is the court of last resort for all criminal cases in the state. It has nine judges, one presiding judge and eight additional judges. They sit *en banc* (as a

"The judicial power of this State shall be vested in one Supreme Court, in one Court of Criminal Appeals, in Courts of Appeals, in District Courts, in County Courts, in Commissioners Courts, in Courts of Justices of the Peace, and in such other courts as may be provided by law."
—Texas Constitution, Art. 5, Sec. 1

TEXAS ONLINE ★ Forces of Change

The Texas Court of Criminal Appeals

The Texas Court of Criminal Appeals has its own website:
www.cca.courts.state.tx.us/
   Click on the opinions link and find the text of a recent court decision. Read the decision and answer the following questions.

QUESTIONS TO CONSIDER

1. What is the factual background of the case?
2. How did the court rule in the case?
3. Did the court rule in favor of the prosecution or the defendant?

group), with all nine judges hearing a case. As in other appellate courts, the judges of the Texas Court of Criminal Appeals decide cases by majority vote. Decisions of the Texas Court of Criminal Appeals may be appealed to the U.S. Supreme Court when they involve matters of federal law or the U.S. Constitution. The Texas Court of Criminal Appeals is the highest court on issues of state criminal law and the state constitution. The U.S. Supreme Court will not accept appeals on state matters unless they involve federal issues.

   The Texas Court of Criminal Appeals considers appeals brought from the Courts of Appeals and death penalty cases appealed directly from district courts. In 2002, the Texas Court of Criminal Appeals disposed of more than 2,000 cases, including 17 death penalty appeals. Although the court is required to review death-penalty cases, other appeals are discretionary—the justices have the option to review the lower-court decision or to allow it to stand without review. In practice, the Texas Court of Criminal Appeals agrees to consider about 7 percent of the cases appealed to it. The court reverses the decision of the lower court in 60 percent of the cases it reviews.[10]

   The Texas Court of Criminal Appeals is empowered to issue a number of writs. The most important of these is the **writ of *habeas corpus,*** which is a court order requiring a government official to show cause why a person is being held in custody. Persons serving sentences in the state's prisons who believe that their rights have been violated may petition the Texas Court of Criminal Appeals for a writ of *habeas corpus* as a means of reopening their case. If the court grants the petition, the state must respond to the prisoner's charges in court. In 2002, the Texas Court of Criminal Appeals granted 39 writs of *habeas corpus* out of 6,868 petitions filed.[11]

Texas Supreme Court   The Texas Supreme Court, which sits in Austin, has nine members—one chief justice and eight associate justices—who decide cases by majority vote *en banc*. The Texas Supreme Court decided the Medicaid abortion funding case by an 8 to 0 vote, with one justice not participating. The Texas Supreme Court is the civil court of highest authority on matters of state law, although losers in cases decided by the Texas Supreme Court may appeal to the U.S. Supreme Court *if* they can demonstrate that an issue under federal law or the U.S.

Constitution is involved. The U.S. Supreme Court will not review state court interpretations of state law or the state constitution. The Texas Supreme Court was probably the end of the line for the plaintiffs in the Medicaid abortion funding case because they based their argument on the Texas ERA, a provision of the Texas Constitution.

The Texas Supreme Court hears civil matters only. Most of its cases come from the Courts of Appeals, although appeals may be taken directly to the Texas Supreme Court whenever any state court rules on the validity of a state law or administrative action under the Texas Constitution. The court is also empowered to issue writs of *mandamus* to compel public officials to fulfill their duties and/or follow the law. A **writ of *mandamus*** is a court order directing a public official to perform a specific act or duty. In 2002, the court acted on 3,230 matters.[12]

The Texas Supreme Court reviews lower court decisions on a discretionary basis—the justices pick and choose which cases they will consider. In practice, the Texas Supreme Court grants review to 11 percent of the cases appealed to it. If the court refuses to grant review, the lower court decision stands. The Texas Supreme Court reverses the decision of the lower court in whole or in part in two-thirds of the cases it agrees to hear.[13]

In addition to its judicial functions, the Texas Supreme Court plays an important role in administering the judicial branch of state government. It sets the rules of administration and civil procedure for the state court system (as long as those rules do not conflict with state law). It has authority to approve law schools in the state and appoints the Board of Law Examiners, which administers the bar exam to prospective attorneys. The court also has final authority over the involuntary retirement or removal of all judges in the state.

JUDGES

Table 10.1 summarizes the length of term, method of selection, and qualifications for the more than 3,100 judges who staff Texas courts. As the table shows, the term of office for Texas judges ranges from two to six years. Although municipal court judges in some cities serve two-year terms, most trial court judges are elected for four years. Appellate court judges serve six-year terms.

Except for some municipal court judges who are appointed, Texas judges are chosen by **partisan election,** which is an election contest in which both the names of the candidates and their party affiliations appear on the ballot. Elected municipal court judges run citywide, generally in nonpartisan city elections. Justices of the peace are elected from JP precincts. Counties with a population of 18,000 to 30,000 people have 2 to 5 JP precincts; larger counties have between 4 and 8 JP precincts. Each JP precinct elects either 1 or 2 justices of the peace, depending on the size of the county. County court judges are elected countywide. District court judges and Courts of Appeals justices run from districts ranging in size from countywide for district courts in metropolitan areas to geographically

TABLE 10.1   Texas Judges

Court	Length of Term	Method of Selection	Qualifications
Municipal courts	2 or 4 years, depending on the city	Election or appointment, depending on the city	Set by city government
Justice of the peace courts	4 years	Partisan election from precincts	Qualified voter
Constitutional county courts	4 years	Partisan election countywide	"Well-informed in the law of the state"
Statutory county courts	4 years	Partisan election countywide	Must be licensed to practice law, other qualifications vary
District courts	4 years	Partisan election countywide or from multicounty districts, with vacancies filled by gubernatorial appointment	Citizen, resident of district for 2 years, licensed to practice law in Texas, and a practicing attorney or judge for 4 years
Courts of Appeals	6 years overlapping terms	Partisan election from a court of appeals district, with vacancies filled by gubernatorial appointment	Citizen, 35 years of age, practicing attorney or judge of a court of record for 10 years
Texas Court of Criminal Appeals	6 years overlapping terms	Partisan election statewide, with vacancies filled by gubernatorial appointment	Citizen, 35 years of age, practicing attorney or judge of a court of record for 10 years
Texas Supreme Court	6 years overlapping terms	Partisan election statewide, with vacancies filled by gubernatorial appointment	Citizen, 35 years of age, practicing attorney or judge of a court of record for 10 years

large multicounty districts for Courts of Appeals and district court judges in rural areas. Judges on the Texas Court of Criminal Appeals and the Texas Supreme Court are elected statewide.

The qualifications of judges in Texas depend on the court. The requirements to serve as a municipal court judge vary from city to city, with many municipalities requiring prospective judges to be experienced attorneys. The qualifications of JPs and constitutional county court judges are set in the state constitution. Justices of the peace and constitutional county court judges must be qualified voters, but they need not be attorneys, and many are not. Although the Texas Constitution requires that constitutional county court judges "shall be well-informed in the law of the state," it gives no standard for measuring that requirement. State law does require, however, that individuals who are elected as judges but who are not attorneys must complete a course in legal training before they can serve. The qualifications of statutory county court judges vary, with many courts requiring two to five years of experience as a practicing attorney.

The Texas Constitution establishes the requirements for judges serving on district and appellate courts. District court judges must be citizens and residents of the district for two years. They must be licensed to practice law in Texas and have at least four years experience as a practicing attorney or a judge in a court of record. Appellate court judges are required to be citizens at least 35 years of age and must be practicing lawyers or judges in a court of record for at least 10 years.

"[Judicial] campaign strategy is based entirely on experience and name identification."
—Anne Whittington, political consultant

JUDICIAL SELECTION

"Our electoral system is deeply flawed because it requires judges to raise large amounts of money. There is a danger in our system that judges will be forced to take too much money from special interests."

—Harry Reasoner, partner, Vinson & Elkins law firm

Texas and eight other states elect judges on the partisan ballot.[14] Except for municipal court judges, Texas judges are chosen in a fashion that is formally the same as that for electing officials to the legislative and executive branches of government. People who want to become judges run in either the Democratic or Republican primary, with the primary election winners representing their party on the general election ballot. The candidate with the most votes in November becomes judge.

Despite the formality of an election system, a substantial number of the state's district and appellate judges first reach the bench through appointment. The Texas Constitution empowers the governor (with senate confirmation) to staff newly created courts at the appellate and district levels and fill judicial vacancies on those courts caused by deaths, retirements, or resignations. In 2002, 42 percent of appellate judges and 43 percent of district judges initially took office through gubernatorial appointment rather than election.[15] When a vacancy occurs on a county or JP court, the commissioners court of that county fills the vacancy. Although appointed judges must face the voters at the next election, they then enjoy the advantage of incumbency.

Is Justice for Sale in Texas?

"The way Texas elects partisan judges and allows those who practice before them to supply the campaign money will always fuel suspicion that justice is for sale here."

—Chief Justice Thomas Phillips, Texas Supreme Court

Critics of the judicial selection system in Texas believe that money plays too prominent a role in the process. Sitting judges and candidates for judicial office raise and spend money in amounts comparable to candidates for other down-ballot statewide and local offices. Successful candidates for the Texas Supreme Court must raise and spend $1 million or more. Even candidates for district judgeships may raise and spend sums well in excess of $30,000 on their campaigns.

Although Texas law limits campaign expenditures in judicial elections, the limits are ineffective. Candidates for statewide judicial office may spend no more than $2 million for each election. Candidates seeking seats on the Courts of Appeals or district court judgeships have lower spending limits. In practice, however, the spending limits are too high to have a meaningful impact on judicial elections. Supreme court candidates, for example, can raise $2 million for the primary election, $2 million more for the primary runoff (if there is one), and yet another $2 million for the general election. The limits are voluntary. Furthermore, candidates who pledge to adhere to the spending limits are also not bound if an opponent exceeds the limits.[16]

The critics of Texas's judicial selection system believe that campaign contributions have undermined the integrity of the state's court system. In 2002, the ten major party candidates for the five Texas Supreme Court seats on the ballot raised more than $1 million apiece, with most of the money coming from major law firms and frequent litigants before the court. The biggest contributors were Vinson & Elkins and Baker Botts, two of the state's more prominent law firms.[17] Frequent litigants are also generous contributors. Consider the relationship between David Weekley Homes and the members of the Texas Supreme Court. In 2003, David Weekley Homes filed an appeal with the Texas Supreme Court over a lower court ruling in a lawsuit filed against the homebuilder by the Richardson family who alleged that their $238,000 David Weekley Home was a mold-filled lemon that poisoned the whole family. The nine Texas Supreme Court justices who decided the case had taken more than $120,000 in campaign contributions from Texans for Lawsuit Reform (TLR), the PAC founded by David and Richard Weekley, and from Weekley family members.[18] Critics suggested that the relationship between David Weekley Homes and the members of the Texas Supreme Court gave at least the appearance that the court would be biased in favor of its financial benefactor.

? WHAT IS YOUR OPINION?

If you were a member of the Richardson family, would you expect that the Texas Supreme Court would treat you fairly?

Do Voters Know the Candidates?

Critics also charge that many voters are unable to intelligently evaluate the qualifications of judicial candidates. This problem has worsened, they say, as the number of judgeships has increased. In November 2002, for example, the election ballot in Harris County included 34 contested judicial races. As former Lieutenant Governor Bill Hobby phrased it:

> There is almost no way the most dedicated, public-spirited citizens can learn the qualifications of the candidates in races ranging from justice of the peace to the (Texas) Supreme Court. . . . It's not the fault of the voters, who try to be responsible. It's not the fault of the media, which tries [*sic*] to inform the public. It's just a fact. . . . The results are an unstable judiciary and an increasingly inexperienced one.[19]

"If I never took money from a lawyer with a pending case, I probably wouldn't have any money."
—District Court Judge Kathy Stone

The election of Steve Mansfield in 1994 to the Texas Court of Criminal Appeals suggests that voters are often uninformed about judicial candidates. Mansfield admitted having lied in his campaign literature about his place of birth, legal experience, and political background. Nonetheless, the message apparently did not reach many of the voters who chose Republican Mansfield over incumbent Democratic Judge Chuck Campbell. After the election, the press discovered that Mansfield had been charged with using marijuana in Massachusetts and the unauthorized practice of law in Florida.[20]

Is the Texas Judiciary Representative of the State's Population?

Critics of Texas's system of judicial selection note that it has produced a judiciary that does not reflect the ethnic and racial diversity of the state's population. As Figure 10.1 shows, non-Hispanic Whites are overrepresented on the Texas bench whereas Latinos, African Americans, and people of other ethnicities are underrepresented. Almost three-fourths of Texas judges are men and the average age is in the mid-fifties. [21]

Reforming the Judicial Selection Process

Observers offer a number of policy options for reforming the state's method for choosing judges. Some reformers propose that the state adopt the so-called merit selection (or Missouri Plan) system of judicial selection that originated in the state of Missouri

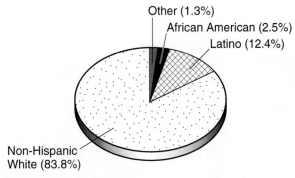

Other (1.3%)
African American (2.5%)
Latino (12.4%)
Non-Hispanic
White (83.8%)

FIGURE 10.1 Profile of Texas Judges
Source: Office of Court Administration

in 1941. **Merit selection (or the Missouri Plan)** is a method for selecting judges that combines gubernatorial appointment with voter approval in a retention election. Eighteen states use merit selection to fill a significant number of judgeships.[22]

? WHAT IS YOUR OPINION?

How important is it that Texas judges reflect the racial and ethnic diversity of the state?

Former Chief Justice John Hill offers the most detailed proposal for implementing merit selection in Texas. Under Hill's plan, the governor, lieutenant governor, speaker of the house, president of the state Bar Association, and the chairs of the state Democratic and Republican Parties would each choose one or more individuals to serve on a 15-member nominating commission. These 15 individuals would include 9 lawyers and 6 nonlawyers who would serve 6-year staggered terms. When an opening would occur on one of the state's appellate or trial courts, the commission would draw up a list of three to five qualified persons from which the governor would fill the vacancy on the bench. The governor's choice would be subject to a two-thirds confirmation vote by the state senate. The newly appointed judge would face the voters in a retention (or confirmation) election in the next general election. The ballot would read as follows: "Should Judge _____ be retained in office?" If a majority of voters approved, the judge would continue in office for a full multiyear term before facing another retention election. Judges failing to win majority support at a retention election would lose their seats. Replacements would be selected through the initial procedure of nomination by commission and gubernatorial appointment.

? WHAT IS YOUR OPINION?

Should judges be allowed to raise campaign money from people with an interest in the decisions they make?

In Texas, judges campaign for election just like members of the legislative and executive branches of government.

Merit selection can be used to choose all or part of a state's judges. Hill proposes separate nominating commissions for appellate and trial courts. He would also permit individual counties to opt out of the plan and continue electing local trial judges if they wish. Other proposals would limit merit selection to appellate justices.

The proponents of merit selection believe that it is an ideal compromise between a system of appointing judges and the election method. Although the governor is able to select the state's judges under merit selection, the bipartisan nominating commission limits the governor's choices to qualified individuals rather than political cronies. Retention (or confirmation) elections allow voters to participate in the process while removing judicial selection from party politics.

Not all Texans favor merit selection. Critics note that research shows no appreciable difference in the qualifications of judges chosen through merit selection and judges selected through other methods.[23] Furthermore, retention elections are generally meaningless in that voters almost never turn incumbent judges out of office.[24]

The strongest attack on merit selection is that it is an elitist system that produces a judiciary unrepresentative of the state's population. Critics say that merit selection takes the control of judicial selection away from the people and gives it to lawyers who will ensure that judgeships go to attorneys from the best families who went to the most prestigious law schools and now work for the most prominent law firms.[25] Merit selection, critics warn, leads to the appointment of judges simply because they are technically well qualified, without regard to their basic values, philosophy, or life experience. William Garrett, a voting rights attorney for the **League of United Latin American Citizens (LULAC),** a Latino interest group, goes so far as to argue that merit selection is racist:

> Merit selection is a scheme by those in power to stay in power. What you end up with is this elitist club. The idea of merit selection brought up at this point is rooted in racism: It was fine to elect judges so long as they were white, but as soon as it became possible for blacks and Hispanics to get elected, they want to stop elections. Why the hell weren't they crying about it in 1955 or '65? It's only now . . . that they're complaining.[26]

Many minority rights advocates prefer the election of district judges from relatively small subcounty districts, perhaps even single-member districts. A **district election** is a method for choosing public officials in which a political subdivision, such as a state or county, is divided into districts, with each district electing one official. The proponents of district elections believe they increase representation for ethnic/racial minorities, make judges more responsive to citizens, and lessen the importance of money in judicial elections. In contrast, opponents of district elections warn that judges chosen from relatively small districts might be partial to litigants from their districts. Furthermore, they point out that many minority judges who now hold office would be defeated under a district system because they live in upper-income neighborhoods that would be unlikely to elect African American or Latino judicial candidates.

? WHAT IS YOUR OPINION?

Should the current system of judicial selection replaced?

Other proposed reforms of the judicial selection process in Texas involve ballot modifications. Some reformers believe that judges should be chosen through **nonpartisan election,** an election in which candidates run without party labels. Other reformers propose preventing voters from casting a straight-ticket ballot for judicial races. **Straight-ticket voting** refers to citizens casting their ballots only for the candidates of one party. The advocates of these ballot reforms argue that they reduce the likelihood of partisan sweeps. Furthermore, some research indicates that African American and Latino judicial candidates lose not because of their race but because they usually run as Democrats in counties that are leaning Republican.[27] If party labels are removed from the ballot or straight-ticket voting is made more difficult, minority candidates may have more success. In contrast, other observers point out that these limited reforms do little to lessen the role of money in judicial elections and do nothing to solve the problem of poorly informed voters. In fact, nonpartisan elections reduce the amount of information readily available to voters about the candidates because they remove party labels from the ballot.

Not all Texans oppose the current system of electing judges. Many political leaders, elected officials, and judges (including many of the justices on the state supreme court) favor retaining the current system of partisan election of judges. Texans who want to preserve the state's current system of judicial selection argue that election is the democratic way for choosing public officials. Elected judges are more likely to reflect the will of the community than appointed judges. Furthermore, most of the criticisms made against the election of judges could also be made against the election of legislators and executive branch officials. The best way to improve the judicial election process (and the election process in general) is better voter education.

Judicial Retirement and Removal

Judges leave the bench for a variety of reasons. Some die, some lose reelection, and some retire. State law requires district and appellate judges to retire at age 75. Judges can qualify for an increased pension if they retire before reaching 70.

Judges may be disciplined and removed from office for incompetence or unethical conduct. The Texas Constitution empowers the Commission on Judicial Conduct, a body composed of judges, lawyers, and lay persons, to investigate complaints against judges and recommend discipline. The Commission may take any of the following disciplinary actions:

- **An admonition** is the least serious sanction the commission can impose. It consists of a letter to a judge suggesting that a given action was inappropriate or that another action might have been better. Admonitions may be either private or public.

- **A warning** is stronger than an admonition. It may be issued privately or publicly.

- **A reprimand** is more serious than either an admonition or a warning. The Commission on Judicial Conduct issues a reprimand, either publicly or privately, when it believes a judge has committed serious misconduct.

- **Recommendation to remove from office** is the strongest action the commission may take. When this happens, the chief justice of the Texas Supreme Court selects a seven-judge panel chosen by lot from justices sitting on the various Courts of Appeals. The panel reviews the report and makes a recommendation to the supreme court, which may then remove the offending judge from office.

In addition to removal by the state supreme court, Texas judges may be removed through the impeachment process or by a procedure known as address from office. Judges may be impeached by majority vote in the state house and removed by a two-thirds' vote of the senate. **Address from office** is a procedure for removing judicial officials that is initiated by the governor and requires a two-thirds' vote by the legislature. Neither impeachment nor address from office is used with any frequency. In general, judges in trouble choose to resign rather than undergo the public humiliation of removal.

NATIONAL PERSPECTIVE

Drug Courts in Florida

Over the last decade, states around the nation have been creating a new type of court called a problem-solving court to deal with criminal offenses such as drug use and possession, prostitution, shoplifting, and domestic violence. In contrast to a traditional court, which focuses on facts and legal issues, a **problem-solving court** is a judicial body that attempts to change the future behavior of litigants and promote the welfare of the community. The goal of a problem-solving court is not just to punish offenders but also to prevent future harm.[*]

The oldest problem-solving court in the nation is the drug court of Dade County (Miami), Florida. The Florida legislature created the drug court in 1989 because of the ineffectiveness of traditional judicial approaches to drug crime. The legislature hoped that the drug court would achieve better results for victims, defendants, and the community than traditional courts had achieved. The drug court sentences addicted defendants to long-term drug treatment instead of prison. The judge monitors the defendant's drug treatment and responds to progress or failure with a system of rewards or punishments, including short-term jail sentences. If a defendant completes treatment successfully, the judge reduces the charges or even dismisses the case altogether.

Research shows that the Florida drug court is effective. Defendants who go through drug court are less likely to be rearrested than are defendants whose cases are heard by a traditional court. Drug court defendants are also more likely to complete treatment than defendants who enter drug rehabilitation voluntarily.[†]

Texas has begun using drug courts as well. In 2001, the Texas legislature passed and the governor signed a measure requiring counties of more than 550,000 people to set up drug courts and meet minimum enrollment figures in treatment programs. Texas officials hope not only to reduce drug offenses but also to save the state money because it is less expensive to sentence drug defendants to drug rehabilitation than it is to send them to prison.[‡]

QUESTIONS TO CONSIDER

1. Are drug courts soft on crime?
2. Would you favor the use of a problem-solving court for other sorts of crimes, such as robbery and assault? Why or why not?
3. Are you for or against using drug courts in Texas?

[†]Greg Berman and John Feinblatt, "Problem-Solving Courts: A Brief Primer", *Law & Policy* 23 (April 2001): 125–32.
[‡]Pam Wagner, "Drug Courts on Trial", *Fiscal Notes* (June 2002): 8–9.

[*]Jeffrey A. Butts, "Introduction: Problem-Solving Courts," *Law & Policy* 23 (April 2001): 121–24.

Visiting Judges

Retirement or election defeat does not necessarily spell the end of a Texas judge's career on the bench. Many judges who have retired or been defeated for reelection continue working as visiting judges, the judicial equivalent of temporary workers. Visiting judges are especially in demand in the state's rapidly growing urban areas where the number of district courts has not increased rapidly enough to keep pace with growing caseloads. Visiting judges now hear about a fourth of district court cases in the state and participate in a tenth of appellate court decisions.[28]

The visiting judge system is controversial. The defenders of the practice declare that temporary judges are needed to keep up with crowded court dockets. Unless the legislature is willing to create dozens of new courts with their own full-time judges, the only alternative to visiting judges would be a hopelessly overloaded court system. In contrast, critics charge that visiting judges are unaccountable to the voters, especially visiting judges who were defeated for reelection.

★ CONCLUSION: THE JUDICIAL BRANCH AND THE POLICYMAKING PROCESS

The judicial branch of Texas government plays an important role in the policymaking process in a broad range of policy areas. The courts have been prominent participants in death penalty appeals and tort reform because both of these issues involve access to the courts. (**Tort reform** refers to the revision of state laws to limit the ability of plaintiffs in personal injury lawsuits to recover damages in court.) State policy in both of these areas reflects the interplay of legislative action and judicial decisions.

The courts participate in other policy areas because of their role in interpreting state law and the Texas Constitution. Parties unhappy with the outcome of the policy process in the executive and legislative branches of government often turn to the courts for relief. Abortion rights advocates, critical of the state's refusal to fund medically necessary abortions in its Medicaid program, sued the state, asking the courts to overturn the policy on the basis of the Texas Constitution.

Agenda Building

Litigants set the agenda of the state's courts by filing cases that raise policy issues. Abortion rights activists raised the issue of Medicaid abortion funding by filing suit against the current state policy. Similarly, property poor school districts filed *Edgewood* v. *Kirby* to attack the state's school finance system.[29] Both sets of plaintiffs turned to the courts to raise their issue because they had failed to achieve their policy goals in the legislative and executive branches. The Texas Supreme Court's decision in *Edgewood* then set the agenda for the legislature and the governor by forcing them to devise a school funding system that would be constitutional. Although legislators had been debating the school funding system for years, the legislature and the governor had only taken half steps toward funding equalization. The *Edgewood* decision forced the legislature and the governor to adopt a major overhaul of the school finance system.

The *Edgewood* case is the exception rather than the rule. Relatively few state court rulings in Texas have raised major issues that were subsequently addressed by the other branches of state government. To some degree, this situation reflects the style of the Texas Constitution. The detailed nature of the state constitution leaves relatively little room for judicial interpretation. Furthermore, Texas judges may be

Volunteer to Become a Court Appointed Special Advocate

A court appointed special advocate is a trained volunteer appointed by a juvenile or family court judge to represent the interests of children who appear before the court. A majority of cases with an advocate involve children who are removed from their home because of abuse or neglect. The advocate meets with the child, the child's parents, prospective foster parents, social service caseworkers, and other people involved in the child's life to determine what course of action is in the best interest of the child. The advocate makes recommendations to the court and assists the child in making a transition to a new living situation.

Although the court appointed special advocacy program is extremely rewarding, it requires a major time commitment and should not be taken lightly.

Volunteers must be at least 21 years old, mature enough to handle difficult situations, and willing to complete a 30-hour training course. They must have their own transportation and be willing to commit to a year or more of volunteer work to see a case through to its resolution.

You can learn more about the Texas child advocacy program at the following website: **www.texascasa.org/volunteer.asp.** The website discusses the program and provides contact information for potential volunteers in most of the state's counties. Contact the local organization in your community and inquire about participating in the program. It is your opportunity to play a positive role in the life of a child who needs help.

It's your community—get involved!

reluctant to raise policy issues that have not been addressed by the other branches of government because they must periodically face the voters. Unlike federal judges who are appointed for life, state judges in Texas serve no more than six years before they must stand for election. Finally, Texas judges may have little incentive to raise policy issues because their policy values are similar to those of executive and legislative branch officials. Most Texas judges are conservative Republicans and so are most of the members of the Texas legislature and the executive branch of state government. Few observers were surprised by the Texas Supreme Court's ruling on the constitutionality of the state's Medicaid abortion funding policy in light of the stridently antiabortion position of the Texas Republican Party. Any Republican supreme court justice who ruled in favor of Medicaid funding for medically necessary abortions would almost certainly face a prolife opponent in the Republican primary.

Policy Formulation and Adoption

The judicial branch of Texas government participates in policy formulation and adoption in selected policy areas. Consider the role of the Texas Supreme Court in reforming the school finance system. The majority opinion in *Edgewood* gave legislators some guidance on how the school-finance system should be revised in order for it to satisfy the Texas Constitution. Subsequently, the court rejected legislative efforts to fix the problem until finally approving a solution that included the transfer of funds from wealthy school districts to poor school districts, the so-called Robin

Hood Plan. The supreme court did not exactly formulate and adopt the policy itself, but it set the parameters for the other branches of government.

Tort reform is another policy area that bears the imprint of the judicial branch. In the early 1980s, the Texas Supreme Court issued a series of rulings that expanded the opportunities for individuals to recover damages from insurance companies and other business defendants in personal injury lawsuits. In 1986, for example, the court ruled that the relatives of a man killed by a drunken driver could sue the restaurant that served alcohol to the intoxicated driver.[30] Subsequently, the legislature and the governor adopted tort reform measures to limit access to the courts and reduce damage awards to plaintiffs in personal injury cases. Although courts in a number of states overturned tort reform laws as unconstitutional, the Texas Supreme Court embraced tort reform by interpreting state laws to limit the ability of plaintiffs to file suit and recover damages in civil cases.[31] In recent years, for example, the court has made it difficult to file **class action lawsuits,** which are suits brought on behalf of a group of people wronged in the same way, even though some potential clients may not know that a suit has been filed.[32]

Courts participate in policy adoption by exercising the power of **judicial review,** which is the authority of courts to declare unconstitutional the actions of the other branches and units of government. If a court believes that a state law, regulatory rule, city ordinance, or another policy of state or local government violates the constitution, the court declares it unconstitutional. An unconstitutional policy is null and void.

The scope of a court's authority to exercise judicial review depends on the level of the court. Although Texas district courts may declare policies unconstitutional, the impact of their rulings is limited to the case at hand. In 1998, for example, a district court in El Paso declared unconstitutional a state law prohibiting the sale of automobiles on consecutive Saturdays and Sundays.[33] The ruling only affected the case before the court and had no impact statewide. A decision by the courts of appeals is binding only on the particular courts of appeal district. The Texas Supreme Court and the Texas Court of Criminal Appeals are the only state courts whose decisions have statewide applicability.

Texas courts rule on both the Texas and the U.S. Constitution. *Edgewood* v. *Kirby,* for example, was based on the Texas Constitution. On issues of state constitutional law, the Texas Supreme Court is the final authority for civil issues whereas the Texas Court of Criminal Appeals is the court of last resort for criminal matters. The only recourse for litigants who lose on state constitutional grounds in either of the state's highest appellate courts is either to ask the court to rehear the case or to lobby the legislature to propose a constitutional amendment.

The state's courts also base their rulings on the U.S. Constitution. In 1996, for example, the Texas Supreme Court held that a police officer's constitutional rights had not been violated when the city of Sherman denied him a promotion because he had had an affair with the wife of another officer. The court declared that neither the Texas Constitution nor the Constitution of the United States includes a right to privacy that encompasses adultery.[34] The police officer could not file an appeal of the Court's interpretation of the Texas Constitution because the Texas Supreme Court is the final authority on issues of state constitutional law. He could, however, file an appeal of the court's interpretation of the U.S. Constitution to the U.S. Supreme Court. Although Texas courts may base their rulings on the U.S. Constitution, their decisions may be appealed to the federal courts.

Policy Implementation and Evaluation

The judicial branch of Texas government plays a key role in implementing the state's criminal and civil justice systems. The state courts enforce the criminal law by hearing cases filed against people accused of violating the law. They apply the civil law by settling disputes among litigants over personal injuries, property, domestic relations, and other matters. Although the importance of most court decisions is limited to the case at hand, the courts occasionally make decisions that have a significant impact on the implementation of the law. In 1997, for example, the Texas Court of Criminal Appeals ruled that convicted child molesters were eligible for the prison early release program. When the legislature wrote the law, it inadvertently left the crime of indecency with a child off the list of crimes for which offenders were ineligible for early release. The Texas Court of Criminal Appeals declared that the state had no choice but to implement the law as it was written.[35]

The judicial branch plays a limited role in policy evaluation. In contrast to legislative committees and executive branch agencies, courts do not conduct performance audits of state agencies or issue reports on the effectiveness of government programs. Courts do, however, evaluate government programs on the basis of their consistency with the constitution. *Edgewood* v. *Kirby* represented an evaluation of the state's school finance system.

★ REVIEW QUESTIONS

1. What was the basis for the constitutional challenge to the Texas Medicaid program? How did the Texas Supreme Court rule on the challenge?

2. How are legal disputes classified?

3. How do appeals procedures differ from trials?

4. How is the court system in Texas organized?

5. How are judges chosen in Texas?

6. What are the most important criticisms of the Texas system of judicial selection?

7. What are some of the proposals for reforming the state's system of judicial selection?

8. What are the arguments for and against the reform proposals?

9. What role does the judicial branch play in the state's policymaking process?

★ KEY TERMS

address from office
adversary proceeding
affirm
appeal
burden of proof

capital punishment
city ordinances
civil case
civil defendant
class action lawsuits

concurring opinion
contract case
criminal case
criminal defendant
dissenting opinion

district election

domestic-relations case

double jeopardy

felony

forcible entry and detainer suit

habeas corpus, writ of

harmless error

judicial review

League of United Latin American Citizens (LULAC)

legal briefs

legal writs

litigants

magistrates

majority *or* deciding opinion

mandamus, writ of

Medicaid

merit selection (the Missouri Plan)

misdemeanor

nonpartisan election

partisan election

plaintiff

plea bargain

probate case

problem-solving court

property case

property lien

prosecutor

remand

reversible error

straight-ticket voting

Texas Equal Rights Amendment (ERA)

tort case

tort reform

trial

★ NOTES

1. *Bell v. Low Income Women of Texas*, Texas Supreme Court, No. 01-0061 (December 2002).
2. *Duncan v. Louisiana*, 391 U.S. 145 (1968).
3. Texas Judiciary Online, available at **www.courts.state .tx.us.**
4. Texas Judicial System, "Caseload Trends in Municipal Courts," *2002 Annual Report*, available at **www.courts .state.tx.us.**
5. Texas Judicial System, "Caseload Trends in the Justice of the Peace Courts," *2002 Annual Report.*
6. Texas Judicial System, "Caseload Trends in the County-Level Courts," *2002 Annual Report.*
7. Texas Judicial System, "Caseload Trends in the District Courts," *2002 Annual Report.*
8. Texas Judicial System, "Caseload Trends in the Courts of Appeals," *2002 Annual Report.*
9. Texas Judicial System, "Activity for the Year Ended August 31, 2002," *2002 Annual Report.*
10. Texas Judicial System, "Court of Criminal Appeals, Docket Activity: FY 2002," *2002 Annual Report.*
11. Texas Judicial System, "Court of Criminal Appeals, Docket Activity: FY 2002," *2002 Annual Report.*
12. Texas Judicial System, "Supreme Court Docket Activity: 1998–2002," *2002 Annual Report.*
13. Texas Judicial System, "Supreme Court Docket Activity: 1998–2002," *2002 Annual Report.*
14. Charles Mahtesian, "Bench Press," *Governing*, (August 1998): 20.
15. "Profile of Appellate and Trial Judges as of September 1, 2002," Office of Court Administration, available at **www .courts.state.tx.us.**
16. Sam Kinch, Jr., *Too Much Money Is Not Enough: Big Money and Political Power in Texas* (Austin: Campaign for People, 2000), p. 14.
17. "High Court Candidates Raise $1 Million a Seat," Texans for Public Justice, November 1, 2002, available at **www .tpj.com.**
18. "Weekley Homes Comes on Home," Texans for Public Justice, May 19, 2003, available at **www.tpj.org/ index.jsp.**
19. Quoted in Pete Brewton, "Hobby Joins Hill in Call for Appointment of Judges," *Houston Post*, June 21, 1986, p. 3A.
20. *Texas Weekly*, December 12, 1994, p. 4.
21. "Profile of Appellate and Trial Judges as of September 1, 2002."
22. Kenyon D. Bunch and Gregory Casey, "Political Controversy on Missouri's Supreme Court: The Case of Merit vs. Politics," *State and Local Government Review* 22 (Winter 1990): 5–16.
23. Craig F. Emmert and Henry R. Glick, "The Selection of State Supreme Court Justices," *American Politics Quarterly* 16 (October 1988): 445–65.
24. Robert C. Luskin, Christoper N. Bratcher, Christopher B. Jordan, and Kris S. Seago, "How Minority Judges Fare in Retention Elections," *Judicature* 71 (1994): 316–21.
25. Amy Johnson, "Court Reform? The Case Against the Appointment of Judges," *Texas Observer*, February 6, 1987, pp. 8–10.
26. Quoted in Brett Campbell, "Courting Inequality," *Texas Observer*, March 9, 1990, p. 17.

27. Delbert A. Taebel, "On the Way to Midland: Race or Partisanship? A Research Note on Comparative Voting in Urban Counties in Judicial Elections," *Texas Journal of Political Studies* 12 (Fall/Winter 1989/90): 5–23.

28. Mark Smith, "Business Good for Visiting Judges," *Houston Chronicle*, September 20, 1998, p. 23A.

29. *Edgewood v. Kirby,* 777 S.W.2d 391 (1989).

30. *Poole v. El Chico Corp.*, 713 S.W.2nd 959 Tex. (1986).

31. Sarah Whitmire, "Torts Pit Lawmakers vs. Courts," *State Government News* (February 2000): 14–17.

32. Mary Flood, "Court's Year One of Discord," *Houston Chronicle*, July 7, 2000, p. 1A.

33. *Texas Weekly*, September 14, 1998, p. 5.

34. Peggy Fikac, "Court Concludes Right to Privacy Doesn't Apply to Adultery," *Houston Chronicle*, July 9, 1996, p. 15A.

35. "Many Child Molesters May Walk Free Under Appeals Court Ruling," *Houston Chronicle*, November 28, 1997, p. 43A.

ONLINE PRACTICE TEST

Test your understanding of this chapter
with interactive review quizzes at

www.ablongman.com/tannahilltexas/chapter10

CHAPTER ELEVEN

City Government

LEARNING OBJECTIVES

After studying Chapter 11, students should be able to do the following:

★ Describe the debate over urban planning.

★ Distinguish between general law and home rule cities.

★ Compare and contrast the strong- and weak-mayor variations of the mayor-council form of city government.

★ Compare and contrast the mayor-council and council-manager forms of city government.

★ Evaluate the various types of city election systems, tracing the history of their use in Texas.

★ Compare and contrast developmental, redistributive, and allocational policies, giving examples of each type of policy.

★ Identify the major expenditure items and revenue sources for the budgets of city governments in Texas.

★ Explain how property taxes are assessed and collected.

★ Assess the arguments for and against tax increment financing, tax abatements, and enterprise zones.

★ Describe annexation policies.

★ Describe land use policies in Texas cities.

★ Evaluate the arguments for and against zoning and other land use regulations.

★ Compare and contrast zoning with deed restrictions.

★ Compare and contrast the elite approach to urban politics with the pluralist approach.

★ Describe the evolution of big-city politics in the state from the 1950s through the early 2000s.

★ Define the key terms listed on pages 305–306 and explain their significance.

Texas cities are spread out, too spread out in the opinion of some people. The concept of **urban sprawl** refers to the excessive geographic expansion of cities. As urban centers grow, middle- and upper-income residents move to ever-distant suburbs, leaving behind a decaying inner city populated primarily by low-income African American and Latino residents. Many of the people who live in the suburbs spend hours a day commuting to work downtown on crowded freeways, isolated from each other and estranged from the city in which they work. Urban sprawl also increases the cost of government because it is more expensive to provide basic services such as streets, sidewalks, water, sewer service, flood control, and police and fire protection to people living in a larger geographic area than it is to provide services to people living closer together.

The critics of urban sprawl believe that it threatens the health of urban areas. Although the lifestyles of the business executives who commute from the suburbs depend on a healthy metropolis, they pay taxes to suburban developments located well outside the central city. Consequently, the city may lack the resources to provide the basic city services and amenities essential to the quality of life for the entire area. If the central city decays, everyone suffers, including people living in the suburbs.

Some urban policy analysts believe that government policies promote urban sprawl. Highway construction and mass transit systems enable business executives who work downtown to live in the distant suburbs. Federally backed home loans and home mortgage interest tax deductions help middle-class people buy homes in the suburbs.[1]

The critics of urban sprawl advocate the adoption of public policies designed to control sprawl and improve the health of the inner city. They favor **urban planning,** which is the formulation, adoption, and implementation of public policies designed to promote the orderly development of metropolitan areas.[2] They believe that government and the private sector should work together to plan urban development to enhance the quality of life for urban residents and provide for the efficient delivery of public services. Planned development, for example, can be designed to maximize the utility of public transportation and take advantage of existing water and sewer lines.

Not everyone agrees that urban sprawl is necessarily bad. The opponents of urban planning argue that urban sprawl reflects the preferences of consumers. Americans choose to live in the suburbs because they want large homes with big yards. They tolerate the long commute as an acceptable tradeoff for the suburban lifestyles they prefer. The critics of urban planning believe that it is inappropriate for government to adopt policy decisions aimed at controlling where people live.[3]

The debate over urban planning underlies many of the policy issues facing urban policymakers today, including election systems, budgetary policy, annexation, and land use regulation. (**Annexation** is the authority of a city to increase its geographic size by extending its boundaries to take in adjacent unincorporated areas.) Should city government adopt policies designed to promote the orderly redevelopment of inner-city neighborhoods or focus its resources instead on improving transportation between the downtown business district and the suburbs where many people prefer to live? Should suburban developments be added to the city tax rolls so that people living outside the urban core can share in the cost of maintaining the health of the inner city?

"You can drive anywhere in Houston and see that development is out of control."

—Peter Brown, Houston architect

"People should be permitted to live and work where they like."

—Wendell Cox, Heritage Foundation

Many Texans spend hours a week commuting from their homes in the suburbs to their jobs downtown.

Urban policy issues are particularly difficult to resolve because they divide people based not just on location but also along the lines of race and ethnicity, social class, and partisanship. Many inner-city residents are relatively poor members of racial and ethnic minority groups, especially African Americans and Latinos. In contrast, most people living in the suburbs are middle-income non-Hispanic White Texans. The inner city is also home to gay men and lesbians, single adults, and childless couples in greater proportion than in the suburbs. Inner-city areas tend to vote Democratic whereas the suburbs generally vote Republican. Resolving individual issues, such as annexation, is sometimes difficult for policymakers because other differences overlap.

This chapter is the fourth of five chapters examining the policymaking institutions of state and local government. Chapters 8, 9, and 10 considered the legislative, executive, and judicial branches of state government and Chapter 12 focuses on counties, school districts, and special districts. This chapter deals with the role of cities in the policymaking process. It examines the legal status of Texas cities and describes their political structures and election systems. The chapter discusses three areas of urban policymaking: budgetary policy, annexation and suburban development, and land use regulation. The chapter examines politics in big-city Texas.

LEGAL STATUS OF TEXAS CITIES

City governments in Texas have broad authority to provide public services, enact regulations, and levy taxes. Texas cities may provide hospitals, libraries, parks, paved streets, police protection, airports, water and sewer service, health clinics, and fire protection for their residents. They may adopt **city ordinances,** which are laws enacted by the governing body of a municipality to regulate such matters as building construction procedures, land use practices, and driving habits. Cities fund their operations by levying property taxes, sales taxes, and a variety of other taxes, fees, and service charges.

Nonetheless, cities and other units of local government are subordinate units of government, subject to the constitutions and laws of the United States and the state of Texas. Federal laws take precedence over city ordinances and regulations. Furthermore, cities are dependent on state constitutions and state laws for their creation, organization, and authority. State law controls such matters as city tax rates and exemptions; wages, hours, benefits, and promotion policies for city employees; and annexation procedures.

The Texas legislature and the governor frequently adopt legislation designed to define and limit the policymaking authority of city government. State law, for example, prohibits cities from suing the firearms industry. More than 20 cities nationwide have sued gun manufacturers to hold them accountable for manufacturing guns with inadequate safety features that would prevent unauthorized and unintentional shootings, and for negligent distribution and marketing practices that contribute to a massive illegal gun market.[4] The legislature and the governor have also adopted legislation prohibiting city governments from establishing their own **minimum wage,** which is the lowest hourly wage that an employer can pay covered workers. No Texas city has its own minimum wage, but Houston voters rejected a ballot initiative that would have raised the minimum wage in Houston to $6.50, well above the federal minimum wage of $5.15.

> "People get elected mayor because citizens think they have a good vision for the city, not because they're Democrats. That's what I like about the job. It doesn't have anything to do with party politics."
> —Mayor Laura Miller, Dallas

The legislature and the governor have grown increasingly willing to override the policy decisions of city governments because of a shift in partisanship. Even though most city elections are officially nonpartisan (party labels are not on the ballot), most officials in the state's major cities are Democrats. In 2002, Ron Kirk, the Democratic nominee for the U.S. Senate was the former Mayor of Dallas while Kirk Watson, the Democratic candidate for Texas attorney general, was the former mayor of Austin. In contrast, the Republican Party now controls both chambers of the Texas legislature and the governorship. On issues such as annexation, which pit city governments against interests usually aligned with the Republican Party, such as suburban residents and developers, the legislature and the governor more often than not intervene against the city.

Incorporation

State law sets the requirements and procedures under which an unincorporated urban area in Texas may become an **incorporated municipality,** which is a city under the laws of the state. An **unincorporated area,** which is territory not part of a legal city, must have a population of at least 200 people to form a municipality. It must also be outside the legal jurisdiction of other incorporated municipalities unless it receives permission to incorporate from the established city. The proponents of incorporation begin the process by collecting signatures on an incorporation petition. After they have gathered the required number of names, perhaps as many as 10 percent of the registered voters in the prospective municipality, they present their petition to the county judge, who calls an election in which the area's voters may choose either to incorporate or remain unincorporated. The residents of an incorporated city can follow the same procedure if they wish to disincorporate. The voters of a newly incorporated municipality must also approve a **city charter,** which is the basic law of a city that defines its powers, responsibilities, and organization. Changes in a city charter must receive voter approval as well.

General Law and Home Rule Cities

Texas cities are classified as either general law or home rule cities. A **general law city** is a municipality that is limited to those governmental structures and powers specifically granted by state law. State law requires that municipalities with fewer than 5,000 people must be general law cities.

General law cities are bound by **Dillon's rule,** which is the legal principle that a city can exercise only those powers expressly allowed by state law. Dillon's rule is named after Judge J. F. Dillon, a member of the Iowa Supreme Court who wrote an opinion in 1868 concerning the legal status of cities. Dillon concluded that municipalities owe their origins to and derive their power from the state legislature. Therefore, they are totally dependent on and subservient to the legislature. Courts in Texas and in states around the nation have followed Dillon's rule in defining the authority of general law cities. If a general law city wants to offer a service or adopt a structure of government not provided in state law, it must first obtain specific authorization from the legislature.

In 1913, the Texas legislature proposed and the voters approved an amendment to the state constitution to allow a municipality with 5,000 or more people to become a **home rule city,** which is a municipality that can take any actions not prohibited by state or federal law or the constitutions of the United States or the state of Texas. In contrast to general law cities, home rule cities are not burdened by the limitations of Dillon's rule. A home rule city can do anything that qualifies as a "public purpose" that does not violate the Texas Constitution or the laws of the state. Compared with general law cities, home rule cities enjoy more freedom in the following areas:

- *Organizational Structure* Home rule cities can adopt any structure of municipal government they choose whereas general law cities are limited to a narrow range of options.
- *Annexation* Home rule cities can annex without the approval of the people living in the annexed area. General law cities cannot annex unless the residents of the targeted area vote to accept annexation.

- *Ordinance-Making Authority* Home rule cities have broader authority to adopt ordinances than do general law municipalities.

- *Election Processes* Home rule cities may include both recall and the initiative process in their charters. More than 90 percent of home rule cities allow citizens the power of **recall,** which is a procedure for allowing voters to remove elected officials from office before the expiration of their terms. Eighty-five percent of home rule cities have the **initiative process,** a procedure available in some states and cities whereby citizens can propose the adoption of a policy measure by gathering a prerequisite number of signatures. Voters must then approve the measure before it can take effect.[5]

Nearly 300 Texas cities are home rule, including all of the state's big cities. Only 19 cities larger than 5,000 people have chosen to remain general law cities. If a home rule city falls below the 5,000-population threshold, it maintains its home rule status.[6]

The legislature has the power to pass laws limiting home rule authority. For example, the legislature has established uniform election dates, limiting most local elections to four dates—the first Saturday in February, first Saturday in May, second Saturday in September, and first Tuesday after the first Monday in November. Although the Texas Constitution prevents the legislature from passing local laws regulating the affairs of individual cities, the legislature gets around the restriction by enacting **population bracket laws,** which are state laws designed to target particular cities based on their population. Houston and Austin are the most frequent targets of population bracket legislation. For example, the legislature could pass a measure that applies to all Texas cities with a population larger than 1.9 million. It so happens that only one city meets that criterion—Houston. If the legislature wanted to target Austin, it could adopt a bill aimed at cities with populations between 650,000 and 660,000 in 2000. That description applies only to Austin.

FORMS OF CITY GOVERNMENT

The mayor-council and council-manager forms of city government are the basic structures of municipal government in Texas.

Mayor-Council Form

The **mayor-council form of city government** is a structure of municipal government in which the voters elect a mayor as the chief executive officer of the city and a council that serves as a legislative body. In the mayor-council form of city government, the mayor and council together make policy for the city. They are responsible for raising and spending city revenue, passing local ordinances, and supervising the city's administrative departments.

Being mayor or serving on city council is a full-time job in big cities using the mayor-council form of government, but not in small towns. In Houston, for example, the mayor devotes full-time to running city government and earns a salary of

$187,000 a year. Although most members of the Houston city council have other jobs, they, too, spend many hours a week on city business, making $50,000 a year. In contrast, mayors and council members in small towns using the mayor-council form of city government usually earn only a small salary for a job that normally takes just a few hours a week.

Cities using the mayor-council form of city government differ in the amount of power the mayor enjoys. Figures 11.1 and 11.2 diagram the strong mayor and weak mayor variations of the mayor-council form of city government. In the strong mayor variation (Figure 11.1), the mayor is the foremost figure in city government, acting as both a political leader and the city's chief administrator. The mayor prepares the budget, vetoes council actions (with or without the possibility of council override), hires and fires department heads, and essentially runs city government. Although the city council must approve (and thus may reject) many of the mayor's actions, politically skillful mayors can usually win approval of most of their initiatives and appointments. Council members elected from districts will want to stay in the mayor's favor because the mayor oversees the provision of public services to their districts. Furthermore, the mayor and the mayor's financial backers may get involved in council races to elect individuals to council who will be part of the "mayor's team" and to defeat the mayor's opponents on council. Bob Lanier, who was mayor of Houston in the 1990s, only lost three council votes

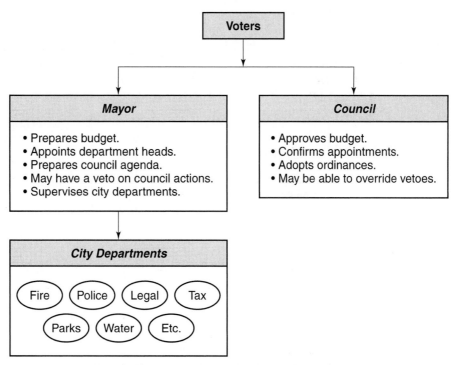

FIGURE 11.1   Strong Mayor-Council Form of City Government

during his six years in office.[7] Former Houston City Council Member Vince Ryan described the strong mayor system in Houston as "King Kong and the 14 chimps" because of the relative imbalance of power between the mayor and the 14 council members.[8]

The advocates of the strong mayor variation of the mayor-council form of city government believe that the system provides for efficient city government because it concentrates power and responsibility for policy leadership and policy implementation in the hands of a single official, the mayor. The mayor can take the lead in agenda setting, policy formulation, policy adoption, and policy implementation. The voters can then evaluate the mayor on performance. In contrast, the critics of the mayor-council form of city government argue that the strong mayor variation gives the mayor too much power. They worry that the mayor will build a personal empire and become a political boss. Although the voters elect council members to represent neighborhoods and communities, they have relatively little influence on major policy decisions in the strong mayor variation. Instead, council members focus on the most mundane details of urban policy implementation, such as abandoned houses, overgrown vacant lots, potholes, and stray dogs.[9]

In contrast to the strong mayor system, the weak mayor variation of the mayor-council form of city government (Figure 11.2) fragments political authority by forcing the mayor to share power with council and other elected officials, including, perhaps, a tax assessor, treasurer, and even a police chief. The mayor and council together appoint administrative officials, supervise city administration, and adopt

> "I think city councils have been neutered in most cases. They are engaging in the most trivial aspects of urban government, rather than the most important aspects."
> —Professor Dennis Judd, urban affairs specialist

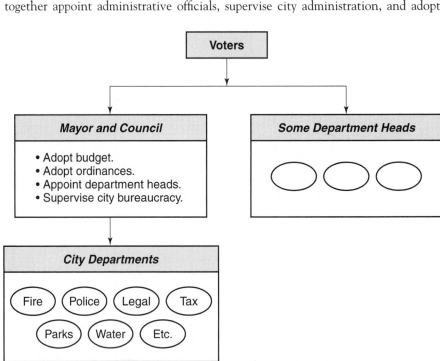

FIGURE 11.2 Weak Mayor-Council Form of City Government

the budget. The proponents of the weak mayor system contend that it prevents the mayor from becoming too powerful by creating a check and balance system. Critics of the weak mayor variation say that it invites corruption and dilutes accountability because it fails to assign policymaking authority to any single official.

The mayor-council system is the traditional form of city government in America and it is still found in most of the nation's largest cities. It is also the most common form of city government among general law municipalities in Texas, which are required by state law to adopt either the mayor-council or council-manager structure of city government. Most general law cities prefer the mayor-council form because it is less expensive to operate than the council-manager form, which would require the city to hire a full-time city manager. In contrast, only 39 of the state's home rule cities use the mayor-council form of city government.[10] Houston is the only big city to use the mayor-council form. Texas's other large cities, including Dallas, San Antonio, El Paso, Fort Worth, Austin, and Corpus Christi, have adopted the council-manager form instead.

> "There are some terrific mayors out there, but unfortunately they don't have the strong mayor form. You've got to have someone who is accountable."
> —Buddy Cianci, former mayor of Providence, RI

Council-Manager Form

The **council-manager form of city government** is a structure of municipal government in which the city council/mayor appoints a professional administrator called a city manager to act as the chief executive of the municipality. In this form of city government, the power of the mayor is limited to performing ceremonial duties and presiding at council meetings. In fact, in some council-manager cities, voters do not directly choose a mayor at all. Instead, the office may go to the at-large council member receiving the most votes. Alternatively, the council may choose one of its members to serve as mayor. In such cases, the mayor's ability to act as a policy leader depends on personal leadership skills rather than official powers.

The major difference between the mayor-council and council-manager forms of city government concerns the implementation of policy. In both systems, the mayor and council make basic policy decisions, but in the council-manager form, policy implementation is the responsibility of a professional administrator hired by the city council—a **city manager.** Figure 11.3 diagrams this form of city government. The city manager is the chief administrative official of the city and is generally responsible for hiring and firing department heads, preparing the budget, and overseeing policy administration. In council-manager cities, the mayor and council members are usually considered part-time officials and they are paid accordingly. In Fort Worth, for example, the mayor and council members each receive $75 for every week they attend one or more official meetings. In the meantime, the Fort Worth city manager earns $186,513 a year.[11]

The council-manager form is the most common type of city government among the state's home rule cities. Its advocates believe that it is an efficient system that keeps politics out of administration and administrators out of politics. They argue that a professional city manager can provide more efficient policy administration than a mayor with no administrative experience. Nonetheless, most political scientists believe that city managers inevitably become involved in politics, even in the sense of participating extensively in policy formulation and adoption. Furthermore, policy implementation is inherently political because it determines how the power of government is exercised. City managers act politically when they make recommendations to elected officials and seek to develop support for their positions among public officials and interest groups influential in city politics.[12]

? WHAT IS YOUR OPINION?

If you were one of the founders of a new city in Texas, what form of city government would you favor for the new city? Why?

Critics of the council-manager form of city government argue that it may work fine for midsize, uncomplicated cities but not for larger cities. They believe that big cities with diverse populations need the policy leadership of a strong mayor. The city manager system is designed to ensure the efficient implementation of policy. What happens, they ask, when city residents and the city council are deeply divided over policy alternatives? Neither the city manager nor the mayor in the council-manager form of government has the political strength to forge a consensus among competing

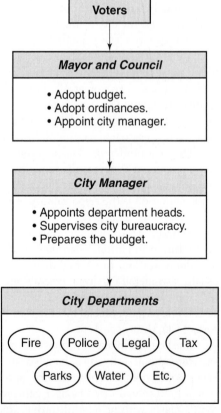

FIGURE 11.3   Council-Manager Form of City Government

political forces.[13] Critics of city government in Dallas, for example, charge that the city suffers from a council that is divided along ethnic, ideological, and geographic lines, and that the mayor has too little power to provide leadership.[14]

Hybrid Structures

Not every city government structure matches the classic mayor-council or council-manager form of municipal government. Home rule cities have the flexibility to adopt features of either basic system. Some strong mayor cities employ a city manager or chief administrative officer, for example, while some council-manager cities allow the mayor veto power and budget preparation authority.[15]

★ ELECTION SYSTEMS

The most popular system for choosing council members in Texas is the **at-large election,** which is a method for choosing public officials in which every citizen of a political subdivision, such as a state or county, votes to select a public official. As Table 11.1 indicates, 131 cities use a place system. Candidates must declare for particular seats (or places) on council and voters then select among the candidates for each council seat. Thirty-six cities elect council members at large without the use of a place system. On Election Day, voters select as many candidates as seats on council. If the city has five council members, for example, a voter chooses five candidates from among the list of people running for council.

In contrast to the at-large election method, a **district election** is a method for choosing public officials in which a political subdivision, such as a state or city, is divided into districts, with each district electing one official. Seventy-four cities use district election systems. El Paso, for example, elects eight council members from districts.

Not all Texas cities use either at-large or district election systems. Forty-eight cities have a combination of at-large and district seats. The Houston city council, for example, has 14 members—9 members chosen from districts and 5 elected at

TABLE 11.1   Methods of Council Election in Texas Home Rule Cities

Method of Election	No. of Cities Using System
At-large election by place	131
At-large election	36
District election	74
Combination of district and at-large seats	48
Cumulative voting	1
Total	**290**

Source: Terrell Blodget, "Municipal Home Rule Charters in Texas," *Public Affairs Comment* 41 (1996): 4.

large. Finally, one Texas home rule city has a **cumulative voting system,** which is an election system that allows individual voters to cast more than one ballot in the simultaneous election of several officials. The difference between at-large and cumulative voting is that the cumulative system allows voters to cast all of their votes for a single candidate.

Both district and at-large election systems have their proponents. Supporters of district elections believe that they make government more responsive to citizens and increase participation. District elections reduce the role of money in city politics, they say, because candidates need less money to campaign in a district than they would to run a campaign citywide. Furthermore, the advocates of district elections argue that they produce a council that more closely reflects the racial and ethnic diversity of the city because they enable geographically concentrated minorities to elect group members to public office.

In contrast, defenders of at-large elections believe that council members chosen at large consider policy issues from a broader perspective than district council members. Whereas district representatives focus on the particular concerns of their districts, at-large council members must consider what is best for the city as a whole. Furthermore, the supporters of at-large elections believe that citywide campaigns produce better quality officials than district elections.

Historically, district (or ward) election systems were associated with big-city **political machines,** which were entrenched political organizations headed by a boss or small group of leaders who held power through such techniques as patronage, control over nominations, and bribery. **Political patronage** is the power of an officeholder to award favors, such as government jobs, to political allies. In the late nineteenth century, machine politicians in New York City, St. Louis, Cleveland, Chicago, and other big cities won election from districts with the support of geographically concentrated White ethnic minorities, especially Italian, Irish, and Polish Americans.

"I just want to help my friends and shaft my enemies."
—Vito Marzullo, former Chicago politician

Well-to-do White Anglo-Saxon business groups who opposed the political machines attacked district elections as corrupt, proposing instead the adoption of nonpartisan at-large council election systems. A **nonpartisan election** is an election in which candidates run without party labels. The business groups packaged their proposal as a "good government" reform, but in fact it was designed to favor the interests of affluent business groups who would have more money to fund candidates for citywide seats than would the working-class ethnic minority groups who supported the political machine.

Although most large industrialized cities, including Chicago, St. Louis, and Cleveland, did not adopt nonpartisan at-large election systems, many of the new cities in the South and West did, including most cities in Texas. Dallas, for example, created a nine-member city council with each member elected at large. Houston's eight-member council was chosen at large as well.

The adoption of at-large council elections in Texas cities limited the political influence of ethnic and racial minorities, primarily African Americans and Latinos. Under the at-large council system in Dallas, no African Americans and only one Latino won election to council, and the successful Latino candidate was a north Dallas businessman who was endorsed and financed by wealthy business groups led by non-Hispanic Whites.[16] Similarly, the only minority candidate

NATIONAL   PERSPECTIVE

Municipal Elections in New York City

Voters in New York City elect the mayor, city council, and other city officials in a partisan election system similar to the state's method of electing a governor and members of the state legislature. Candidates compete in a primary election for the right to represent their party on the general-election ballot—Democrats against other Democrats, Republicans against Republicans. The candidates with the most votes in each party's primary election face off in the general election and the person with the most votes wins the office.

New York Mayor Michael Bloomberg wants to replace party primaries with a nonpartisan election system. Bloomberg and other proponents of the electoral reform argue that the current system excludes a third of the city's electorate from the first round of voting because they are not registered as either Democrats or Republicans. New York uses the **closed primary,** which is an election system that limits primary election participation to registered party members. Only Democrats can vote in the Democratic Primary and only Republicans can participate in the Republican Primary. Independents and people registered as supporters of other parties cannot vote until the general election. Bloomberg wants to open the primary to participation by candidates and voters without regard for their party affiliation. The top two candidates in the primary then face one another in a general election regardless of their party affiliation. All voters would be able to participate in both rounds of voting.

Many party leaders in New York City prefer the current election method to Bloomberg's proposed reform. They argue that party labels help voters to intelligently choose among candidates because party affiliation often indicates a candidate's political alliances and policy preferences. Some party leaders also believe that nonpartisan elections would reduce the opportunities of African American and Latino candidates to win office. Because most minority voters are Democrats, African American and Latino candidates frequently win Democratic primary contests for municipal office and then win election as the Democratic candidate in the general election. The elimination of party primary elections would diminish the impact of minority votes in the first round of voting. Finally, many critics of the mayor's proposal declare that it is nothing more than a political ploy to help the mayor win reelection. Bloomberg, a lifelong Democrat, ran for mayor in 2001 as a Republican and won after spending $75 million of his personal fortune on the campaign. Critics charge that the mayor wants the city to adopt a nonpartisan election system because he is too unpopular to win either party's primary and a nonpartisan system would be his best shot at winning reelection.*

QUESTIONS TO CONSIDER

1. Are nonpartisan elections unfair to minorities? Why or why not?
2. Would elections for governor and the legislature be improved if they were nonpartisan instead of party contests?
3. How much effect do election systems have on the outcome of elections?

*Jonathan P. Hicks, "Charter Panel Defends Push for Nonpartisan Election," The New York Times, August 14, 2003, available at **www.nytimes.com**.

elected to the Houston city council under that city's at-large election system was an African-American real estate investor who had the support of downtown business interests.

The federal Voting Rights Act provided a means for minority-rights groups to attack election systems they considered discriminatory. The **Voting Rights Act (VRA)** is federal law designed to protect the voting rights of racial and ethnic minorities. The act allows voters to file lawsuits in federal court challenging local election laws and procedures they believe discriminate against minority voters.

In the late 1970s and early 1980s, minority-rights groups used the VRA to force Dallas, Houston, San Antonio, El Paso, Fort Worth, and other cities in the state to abandon at-large election systems. Some cities, such as San Antonio, El Paso, and Fort Worth, began electing all council members from districts; other cities adopted mixed systems that combined district seats with at-large positions. Dallas adopted a system with eight district seats and two at-large positions, with the mayor elected at large. In 1991, the city of Dallas settled a voting rights lawsuit by changing its city election to provide for a 14-member council, all chosen from districts with only the mayor elected at large.

The introduction of district election systems led to the selection of city councils in most of the state's big cities that were more ethnically and racially diverse than ever before. In the first election after the implementation of single-member districts, Houston voters chose three African Americans and one Latino to serve on council. In San Antonio, Latinos and African Americans together won a majority on that city's ten-member council. A study of ten Texas cities found that the change from at-large to district election systems led to increases in the number of Latino council candidates, Latinos elected to office, and Latino council members living in Latino neighborhoods.[17]

 WHAT IS YOUR OPINION?

What sort of city election system is the best—district, at-large, or a mixed system?

The Dallas City Council has 14 members, all chosen from districts.

PUBLIC POLICIES IN TEXAS CITIES

Political scientist Paul E. Peterson divides urban public policies into three categories: developmental, redistributive, and allocational. **Developmental urban policies** are local programs that enhance the economic position of a community in its competition with other communities. They strengthen the local economy, expand the tax base, and generate additional tax revenues for the city. For example, Houston, Dallas, and San Antonio municipal governments have all recently built new sports arenas to keep or attract professional sports teams. City leaders justified the expenditure of public funds as an investment in the economic vitality of their community. The decision of a city government to offer a tax break to business to relocate to their area is another example of a developmental urban policy.

Redistributive urban policies are local programs that benefit low-income residents of an area. These include such programs as the provision of low-income housing and food assistance to poor families. Although redistributive programs may be desirable from a humanitarian point of view, Peterson says that they retard economic development. Consider the provision of city health clinics for low-income families. City-funded health clinics may discourage businesses and middle-income taxpayers from relocating to the city because they will have to pay more in taxes for this particular service than they will receive in benefits. Health clinics may encourage the migration of low-income families to the city to take advantage of the service, especially if neighboring ("competing") cities choose not to provide their residents health clinics, instead keeping their tax rates low.

Allocational urban policies are local programs that are more or less neutral in their impact on the local economy. The best examples of allocational policies are urban housekeeping programs such as police and fire protection, garbage pickup, and routine street maintenance. Allocational programs are neither developmental nor redistributive in nature because all members of the community benefit from them without regard for economic status.[18]

Economic factors influence the adoption of urban public policies. Cities concentrate on developmental and allocational programs in order to enhance their tax bases and protect the local economy. Research shows that levels of municipal services and tax rates tend to be lower in cities bordered by other municipalities than they are in cities that are relatively isolated. The study concludes that city officials are forced to keep taxes down and, of course, services low as well because businesses and middle-income taxpayers have the option of moving to a neighboring municipality with lower tax rates.[19]

City governments frequently adopt developmental policies that entail building entertainment centers such as sports stadiums and convention centers designed to attract visitors from out of town and the suburbs.[20] Although city officials promise that expensive new sports and entertainment facilities generate tax revenue and increase employment, research indicates that most projects never pay for themselves.[21] New stadiums may be symbols of mayoral leadership, but they seldom contribute to economic development.

Political factors also play an important role in urban policymaking. Developmental and allocational policies are often characterized by conflict as political

"Any locality making a serious attempt to tax the rich and give to the poor will attract poor citizens and dine away the rich."

—Paul E. Peterson, political scientist

"Sure, sports are important to a city's image, but in my judgment it's more important to have parks, police, water, and youth programs."

—Bob Lanier, former mayor of Houston

L E A R N I N G   E X E R C I S E

Profile of a City Government

What are the issues on the agenda of big-city governments in Texas today? The homepages of the state's largest cities can be found at the following Internet addresses:

Austin: **www.ci.austin.tx.us/**
Houston: **www.cityofhouston.gov/**
Dallas: **www.dallascityhall.com**
El Paso: **www.ci.elpaso.tx.us/**
Fort Worth: **www.ci.fort-worth.tx.us/**
San Antonio: **www.ci.sat.tx.us/**

Identify the city nearest you, study its website, and answer the following questions.

QUESTIONS TO CONSIDER

1. What form of city government does the city have?
2. Who is the mayor of the city?
3. How many members does the city council have? Are they elected from districts or at large?
4. What is the city's property tax rate?
5. What would be the annual tax bill for a piece of business property valued at $500,000?

forces compete over policy alternatives. In Houston, for example, two sets of business groups opposed one another over the location of a new convention center, whether it would be built east or west of the downtown business district. Similarly, neighborhoods fought over the timing of the construction of new decentralized police command stations, with each region of town wanting its command station built first.

City officials must balance economic concerns with political demands. Groups representing the interests of disadvantaged constituents in the state's big cities call for the adoption of redistributive programs. They demand home rehabilitation loans, low-interest mortgage loans, small business loans, technical assistance to new businesses, public housing, affirmative action, and hiring goals for women and minorities. Research shows that cities become more responsive to the concerns of minority residents as minorities increase their elected representation in city government. One study finds that after city councils experience an increase in minority representation, city governments hire more minorities, award more contracts to minority-owned businesses, and enact programs favored by minority groups.[22]

Budgetary Policy

The state's largest cities are big enterprises with annual budgets greater than a billion dollars. In fiscal (budget) year 2004, the total budget for the city of Houston was $2.6 billion.[23] It was $1.9 billion for the city of Dallas[24] and $1.5 billion for San Antonio.[25] The state's largest cities offer their residents a broad range of services, including police protection, street repair, garbage pickup, libraries, recreational facilities, health clinics, fire protection, emergency medical services (EMS), water and sewer service, airports, sidewalks, and street lighting. In contrast, small towns may only provide a limited number of basic services. Public safety—police and fire protection—is typically the largest item in all city budgets because it is labor intensive.

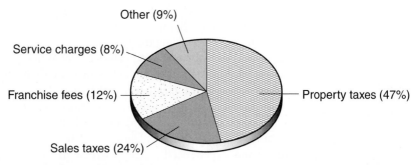

FIGURE 11.4   General Fund Revenues, Houston 2004
Source: City of Houston, Fiscal Year 2004 Budget

Texas cities generate revenue from property taxes, sales taxes, franchise revenues, charges for services, and fines. Figure 11.4shows the relative importance of the various revenue sources for the city of Houston. Property and sales taxes combined accounted for more than 70 percent of city revenue with franchise fees and service charges providing most of the rest.

The **property tax,** which is also known as the *ad valorem* **property tax,** is a levy assessed on real property, such as houses, land, business inventory, and industrial plants. State law sets a maximum property tax rate of $1.50 per $100 of valuation for general law cities and $2.50 per $100 for home rule cities. In practice, the property tax rates in most cities are well below the maximum. In 2003, the property tax rate for Dallas was $0.6998. It was $0.655 for Houston, $0.57854 for San Antonio, $0.865 for Fort Worth, and $0.4597 for Austin.[26]

City governments may grant property tax breaks called exemptions to certain categories of taxpayers, such as homeowners, elderly residents, or disabled veterans. Fort Worth, for example, grants exemptions for homeowners, senior citizens, disabled persons, property that is a historic site, and transitional housing for indigent persons. The most common exemption is the **homestead exemption,** which is a property tax reduction granted homeowners on their principal residence. State law stipulates that property tax exemptions must be at least $5,000 but not more than 20 percent of property value (unless that figure is less than $5,000).

Figuring a property tax bill is relatively easy. Assume, for example, that a home is assessed at $150,000, the city tax rate is $0.60 per $100 valuation, and the city grants a $5,000 homestead exemption. The homeowner's annual property tax bill to the city would be figured as follows:

$150,000   Assessed value
−$5,000   Homestead exemption
$145,000   Taxable value
× .60 per $100   Municipal tax rate
$870   Municipal tax due

A property owner's tax bill depends on both the tax rate and the valuation of the property. Property taxes go up (and down), of course, when the local government raises (or lowers) tax rates. Taxes also change when property values change. Texas is not one of the 22 states that have **truth in taxation laws,** which are laws that block local governments from raising the total amount of property taxes they collect from one year to the next when assessed values go up. When property values increase in these states, local officials have to vote to increase their total tax revenues and advertise their action in the newspaper. Otherwise, the tax rate falls automatically to compensate for rising property values.[27] In contrast, local governments in Texas benefit from rising property values without elected officials having to go on record in favor of raising additional revenue. During the late 1990s and early 2000s, many Texas property owners experienced a steep increase in their property taxes because the value of their property increased.

The sales tax is the other major tax source for municipal government in Texas. A **sales tax** is a levy on the retail sale of taxable items. State law allows cities to piggyback an extra 1 percent onto the state's general sales tax rate of 6.25 percent. All of the state's larger cities and many smaller towns take advantage of the sales tax option. Furthermore, cities without transit authorities may seek voter approval to levy a 0.5 percent additional sales tax to reduce city or county property taxes or help fund law enforcement. Cities of 56,000 or more population that do not want to swap property taxes for sales taxes can ask voter approval for a 0.25 percent sales tax to use for mass transit.

In addition to property and sales taxes, city governments in Texas raise revenue from franchise fees, service charges, and fines. Telephone, gas, cable TV, and electric utility companies pay cities annual franchise fees for the right to use public right-of-ways to string wires or lay cable. Cities generate revenue from service charges, such as fees for water and sewerage service. Fines for traffic infractions and violations of city ordinances provide cities with revenues as well. Cities also raise money from hotel and motel occupancy taxes, rental car taxes, and federal grant money. Federal grant programs offer assistance to municipalities to build sewerage treatment plants, acquire parkland, construct airports, treat drug addiction, rehabilitate economically depressed neighborhoods, and provide housing to low-income families.

City governments borrow money by issuing bonds to cover the cost of capital improvements, such as the construction of buildings, airports, roads, and utility plants. A **bond** is a certificate of indebtedness. A **capital expenditure** is the purchase by government of a permanent, fixed asset, such as a new city hall or highway overpass. City governments levy property taxes to pay back the money they borrow plus interest. In 2004, for example, the property tax rate for the city of Houston was $0.47459 for general purposes and $0.18041 for debt service.[28]

Budgetary policies in urban Texas have historically been allocational and developmental. Police and fire protection, sanitation, and street maintenance—the largest expenditure items for municipal government in the state—are allocational programs. Other allocational expenditures include money for libraries, parkland acquisition, and traffic management. In the meantime, capital expenditures for street construction, sewer trunk line replacement, and new police and fire stations are developmental because they provide infrastructure improvements essential to economic growth.

City governments use tax incentives to promote economic growth as well, including tax increment financing, tax abatements, and enterprise zones. **Tax increment financing** is a program in which a local government promises to earmark increased property tax revenues generated by development in a designated area called a tax increment financing district to fund improvements in the area, such as roads, parks, sidewalks, and street lighting. A city hopes to encourage private investment by promising that any additional tax revenues generated from higher property values resulting from private development in the district will be spent by the city in the area under development. **Tax abatement** is a program that exempts property owners from local property taxes on new construction and improvements in a designated tax abatement district for a set period of time. **Enterprise zones** is a state program that allows local governments to designate certain areas called enterprise zones in which private investors can receive property tax abatements, local sales tax rebates (refunds), and government-backed low-interest loans.

> "We are in a competitive world, and it's important to retain jobs."
> —Bob Lanier, former mayor of Houston

Local officials argue that tax incentives are an important economic development tool. They believe that tax breaks may make the difference between a company deciding to build a plant in Texas or locate it in another state. When businesses establish new facilities in the state, they create new jobs that fuel economic growth because their employees purchase goods and services from established businesses. Local governments benefit as well because the increased economic activity generates added tax revenues that may be sufficient to make up for the revenues lost by the tax incentives.

? WHAT IS YOUR OPINION?

Should city governments use tax increment financing, tax abatements, and enterprise zones to promote economic development?

The critics of tax incentives charge that they are unnecessary and unfair. Tax breaks are unnecessary, they say, because business managers seldom, if ever, base their relocation decisions on taxes. Businesses decide to expand expansion or relocate based primarily on such factors as transportation and the availability of an educated workforce. Critics charge that tax breaks for new firms are unfair because they shift the cost of government to other taxpayers, including homeowners and established businesses. As of December 2002, the city of Houston had granted tax abatements to 49 businesses worth more than a billion dollars over the lifetime of the tax break, money that had to be made up by other taxpayers.[29] Business people in particular strongly oppose the use of tax incentives to attract potential competitors.

> "If I'm paying taxes, these big companies should, too."
> —Lillie Walker, Houstonian

Furthermore, research shows that the developmental policies of city government have little if any impact on the location decisions of investors and business managers. One study of the factors influencing the location of manufacturing plants in Texas found that local taxes had little effect on plant location decisions. The research discovered that the availability of skilled labor and the presence of strong colleges and universities were important to **high technology industries,** which are industries based on the latest in modern technology. Some of the other factors important to economic development were the presence of port facilities and the concentration in the area of firms in a similar line of work.[30] Some scholars believe that local officials grant tax incentives because of the political pressure to create jobs.[31] Tax incentive programs give the *appearance* that local officials are doing something to help the economy even if they have little real impact on economic development. Businesses that accept economic development money typically exaggerate the number of jobs they plan to create and actually expand more slowly than companies that do not accept government subsidies.[32]

Annexation and Suburban Development

Annexation is the power of a city to increase its geographic size by extending its boundaries to take in adjacent unincorporated areas. Traditionally, cities have annexed in order to protect their tax bases. Big cities across America have been caught in a financial squeeze as revenues have fallen while demand for services has risen. For decades, the tax bases of the nation's largest cities have declined. Middle-class taxpayers and business establishments have moved to the suburbs in search of safer streets, better schools, and more desirable housing. In contrast, poor people, seriously ill persons who do not have health insurance, and people without places to live have moved into the city to take advantage of health clinics, shelters, and other social services not available in the suburbs. Texas cities have used their power to annex to maintain their tax bases and financial health.

Another reason for annexation involves the desire of city officials to prevent encirclement by other incorporated municipalities. Because state law prohibits cities from annexing other cities without their consent, a big city surrounded by smaller incorporated municipalities cannot grow. Many cities located in the northeast and midwest find themselves in just such a position. Dallas allowed itself to become ringed by small towns during the early years of its development. In 1976, Dallas broke out of its encirclement by convincing the town of Renner to agree to become part of Dallas. Since the Renner annexation, Dallas has pushed its city limits to the north into Collin and Denton Counties. Other Texas cities have avoided Dallas's predicament by annexing adjacent unincorporated areas before they could incorporate and by annexing the land around neighboring small towns to prevent their expansion. In Harris County, for example, the municipalities of Bellaire and West University Place are completely surrounded by Houston.

Finally, cities annex in order to reap the political benefits of a larger population. Federal grant money is often awarded on the basis of formulas that include population. More people means more money. Furthermore, because legislative districts are drawn on the basis of population size, increased population leads to additional representation in Congress and the Texas legislature.

State law permits a city to increase its total land area by as much as 10 percent in any one year. A city that does not annex its full allotment of land in a year may carry the remaining amount forward to be used in later years as long as the city does

Most city governments provide garbage collection services for their residents.

"Right now, we don't have the right to vote on something that is as simple and fundamental as where we choose to live."
—Stephanie Pivec,
Citizens Against
Forced Annexation

not increase its geographic size by more than 30 percent in any one year. A city of 100 square miles, for example, could add another 10 square miles to its land area this year. Because state law allows municipalities to carry forward unused annexation authority, the city of 100 square miles could wait a few years and then annex up to 30 square miles.

A city government typically annexes an entire **utility district,** which is a special district that provides utilities such as water and sewer service to residents living in unincorporated urban areas. When a city annexes a subdivision, it annexes the utility district that services the subdivision rather than the development itself. The annexing city takes over the operation of the utility district similar to a large corporation taking over a small corporation. The city takes possession of the utility district's physical assets, such as its water and sewer facilities, and assumes its financial assets and liabilities. The city will bring in its police, fire, solid waste, and emergency medical services (EMS) to the area while contracting with a private company to operate the old utility district's water and sewer system.

Historically, Texas cities have annexed aggressively. Between 1950 and 1980, Houston added more than 370 square miles, Dallas more than 230, San Antonio nearly 200, El Paso over 200, Fort Worth nearly 150, Corpus Christi more than 150, and Austin more than 80. During the 1970s alone, Texas cities annexed 1,472 square miles containing 456,000 people. That is an area bigger than Rhode Island and a population almost as large as Wyoming.[33]

Since the early 1980s, the pace of annexation by Texas cities has slowed. The annexations of the 1970s produced a political backlash from newly annexed residents who were determined to do their best to vote incumbent mayors and council members out of office. Subsequently, local officeholders grew cautious about adding more angry constituents to their cities. Furthermore, the Texas legislature and the governor have responded to complaints from people living in unincorporated areas near major cities by adopting legislation forcing cities to better accommodate the interests of suburban residents living in unincorporated areas.

In 1999, the legislature passed and the governor signed a measure overhauling annexation policy to require that cities adopt an annexation plan that specifically identifies the areas to be annexed and details how the city will provide those areas with services. The county government may appoint a panel of citizens to negotiate with the city on behalf of area residents. The city cannot complete the actual annexation until the 3rd anniversary of the adoption of the annexation plan and then it must act within 31 days or lose the opportunity to annex the identified areas for 5 years. The city must provide police, fire, EMS, solid waste, street repair, water and sewer, and park maintenance services immediately. It has two and a half years to provide full services comparable to those offered to other city residents. If a majority of residents in the newly annexed area believe that the city has failed to provide them with full services, they may petition the city to be disannexed. If the city fails to act, residents may file suit in district court to ask a judge to order disannexation.

❓ WHAT IS YOUR OPINION?

Do you favor changing state law to require that the people in an area to be annexed must approve before the annexation can take place?

The legislation also gave cities and utility districts the authority to negotiate Strategic Partnership Agreements (SPAs) to provide for limited purpose annexation. The utility district gives the city permission to collect sales taxes at retail businesses within the district but not property taxes. In exchange, the city provides the district with some city services, such as police and fire service, and a portion of the sales tax revenues collected within its borders. The city also pledges to postpone annexing the district during the period of the partnership.[34] Both units of government benefit from additional tax revenues while utility district residents avoid annexation at least in the short run.

In addition to reforming annexation procedures, the legislature and the governor have revised state laws dealing with **extraterritorial jurisdiction (ETJ),** which is the authority of a city to require conformity with city ordinances and regulations affecting streets, parks, alleys, utility easements, sanitary sewers, and the like in a ring of land extending from one-half to five miles beyond the city-limits line. The width of an ETJ depends on the population of the city. Within the extraterritorial area, no new cities may be incorporated without the consent of the existing city. The ETJ is

TEXAS ONLINE ★ Forces of Change

Texas Cities

Most Texas cities have their own homepages. The URLs for some of the state's midsize cities are listed below.

Amarillo: **www.ci.amarillo.tx.us/**
Beaumont: **www.cityofbeaumont.com/**
Corpus Christi: **www.ci.corpus-christi.tx.us/**
Garland: **www.ci.garland.tx.us/**
Laredo: **www.cityoflaredo.com**
Midland: **www.ci.midland.tx.us/**
Plano: **www.ci.plano.tx.us/**
Waco: **www.waco-texas.com/**

Browse the websites and answer the following questions.

QUESTIONS TO CONSIDER

1. Which city has the more interesting homepage? Why?
2. Which city would you most want to visit? Why?
3. In which city would you most enjoy living? Why?

not part of the city; its residents do not pay property or sales taxes to city government, and they receive no services.

The original purpose of extraterritoriality was to enable a city to control development within the ETJ, thus preparing it for future annexation. When the city eventually annexed subdivisions in the ETJ, they would already conform to city building standards. If the ETJs of two cities overlapped, the cities generally apportioned the area between them.

In 2001, the legislature passed and the governor signed legislation requiring cities and counties to create a single office for dealing with development in the ETJ that would be run by the city, the county, or cooperatively by both units of local government. The legislature acted in response to complaints from developers that they were sometimes caught between conflicting county and city regulations. In practice, most cities and counties have created a joint office, with a city office the next most popular option.[35]

Land Use Regulation

Historically, land use policies in Texas cities have been developmental. Instead of regulating land use, municipalities in the Lone Star State have promoted private development through street construction and the provision of streetlights, drainage, and water and sewer services in undeveloped areas. In the process, city governments have left decisions about land use policy to private interests—developers, investors, builders, realtors, and architects.

Land use policy in Texas cities is undergoing a transformation. The introduction of single-member districts has increased the political strength of neighborhood groups concerned about quality-of-life issues, such as traffic congestion, air pollution, and neighborhood revitalization. Neighborhood groups in low-income areas have demanded that city government focus on land use policies affecting their neighborhoods, such as low-cost housing and urban redevelopment.

Building and Housing Codes   Building and housing codes are established by city ordinance to set minimum standards for the construction and maintenance of buildings. **Building codes** are municipal ordinances that set minimum standards for the types of materials used in construction, building design, and construction methods employed in all building within the city. Building permits are required for all construction covered by the code. Violators of housing codes may be fined.

Housing codes are local ordinances requiring all dwelling places in a city to meet certain standards of upkeep and structural integrity. City officials enforce the housing codes by making systematic inspections and investigating complaints. Property owners are responsible for structural integrity. Owners and occupants share responsibility for upkeep. Violators of housing codes may be fined.

Building and housing codes are designed to promote the health, safety, and welfare of the community, but the results often fall short of the ideal. Critics say that codes are frequently outdated and inconsistent across cities. They believe that enforcement is often lax and too frequently accompanied by graft. The opponents of building codes also charge that they increase building costs, thus encouraging construction outside a city's ETJ, beyond the reach of city authority. Furthermore, the opponents of building and housing codes argue that property owners sometimes fail to repair old, run-down structures because improvements would place them under the building codes, thus forcing owners to undertake more expensive work than they desire and can afford.

Compared with cities in other states, Texas municipalities have been slow to establish code standards. Many Texas cities did not adopt building codes until after 1954 when the federal government made them a condition for obtaining federal funds for public housing, FHA, and urban renewal programs. Houston did not even adopt fire codes until the 1970s.

Zoning and Planning   The governmental designation of tracts of land for industrial, commercial, or residential use is known as **zoning.** In 1927, the Texas legislature authorized municipalities to adopt zoning ordinances to restrict the use of privately owned land. Subsequently, many Texas cities adopted local zoning ordinances.

How does zoning work? Once a city decides it wishes to control land use within its boundaries, it creates a zoning commission. The commission studies land use in the area and makes recommendations concerning appropriate uses of land and the location of commercial and residential districts. After public hearings, the city council considers the proposal and adopts a zoning ordinance based on the commission's proposal. After the ordinance goes into effect, property owners may not build any structure or put property to any use that conflicts with the zoning ordinance applicable to their district.

In addition to zoning, cities may adopt other measures designed to manage development, including setback ordinances, off-street parking requirements, and height limitations for buildings. A **setback ordinance** is a city requirement that construction take place at least a specified minimum distance from the street right-of-way. An **off-street parking requirement** is a city regulation that business owners provide off-street parking for clients and customers. A **height limitation** is a city regulation restricting the height of buildings within the city.

> "Planning and zoning must be embraced if Houstonians are to take part in defining their destiny as a great city rather than simply reacting to the shock waves generated by unplanned growth."
> —Jim Greenwood, former Houston city council member

> "There is no such thing as zoning. There are just deals."
> —zoning opponent

Proponents of zoning and other types of land use regulation believe that they help create an orderly city. They say that zoning enables city government to separate districts for residential, commercial, and industrial uses, thus preventing nuisances from developing in residential areas, such as strip shopping centers and trailer parks. Careful planning, they argue, can prevent street congestion, overcrowding of land, and overconcentration of population by allowing city officials adequately to plan for the provision of transportation, water, sewage, schools, parks, drainage, and other public requirements.

Opponents of zoning and other types of land use restrictions believe that city planning is inefficient and potentially corrupt because it substitutes the judgment of government bureaucrats for free-enterprise development. Without government controls, they say, cities develop and change in accordance with the dictates of the marketplace. Zoning shifts the basis for deciding how land will be used from economics to politics. As a result, land use decisions become political, with decisions made on the basis of which developers made the largest campaign contributions.

Urban land use policies reflect political conflict between the owners of developed land and the owners of undeveloped property. Homeowners and commercial property owners favor the imposition of strict land use controls to manage further development in their neighborhoods in order to maintain and enhance their property values. In contrast, persons who own undeveloped tracts of land prefer few land use restrictions so they can develop their property unhindered. Throughout much of the twentieth century, developers held the upper hand politically in big-city Texas and used their influence to limit land use controls. Over the last decade or so, however, the political balance has changed in most of the state's large cities. As cities have matured and development has slowed, the owners of developed land have gained political influence. Furthermore, the introduction of single-member districts has enhanced the political influence of neighborhood civic associations concerned about property values.

? WHAT IS YOUR OPINION?

Are you in favor of zoning?

Deed Restrictions   The opponents of zoning sometimes argue that deed restrictions are preferable to government regulation. **Deed restrictions** are private contractual agreements that limit what residential property owners can do with their houses and land. Almost every modern residential subdivision in the state has deed restrictions. Developers and sometimes the mortgage company draw up deed restrictions to spell out in detail what lot owners may or may not do. Deed restrictions differ from zoning in that they are the result of voluntary contractual agreements between private parties whereas zoning involves the enactment of city ordinances.

Deed restrictions typically allow owners to use their property only for specified purposes. They force property owners to observe certain standards and refrain from altering their property without the written approval of the neighborhood civic association's architectural control committee. Deed restrictions cover such issues as

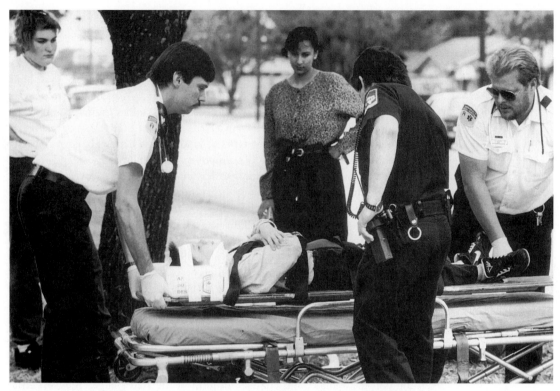

Emergency medical services are also provided by city governments.

where residents can park their vehicles, the color they can paint their homes, and the type of shingles they can put on their roofs. If someone violates the restrictions, the civic association can get a court order commanding the offender to stop the violation. Property owners who disobey a court order can be fined or jailed for contempt of court. Deed restrictions that are not enforced may terminate or become unenforceable. This is most likely to occur, of course, in older neighborhoods.

Deed restrictions accomplish some but not all of the goals of zoning. At its best, zoning represents an attempt by government to ensure orderly development. In contrast, deed restrictions provide piecemeal zoning by private developers without resorting to a comprehensive plan. People who live in the suburbs benefit while the residents of older neighborhoods without zoning must live with changes wrought by market forces.

CITY POLITICS IN TEXAS

Before the mid-1970s, political power in big-city Texas was in the hands of an elite. **Elite theory** (or **elitism**) is the view that political power is held by a small group of people who dominate politics by controlling economic resources. Growth-oriented business leaders in each of the state's major cities used their economic power to dominate the local policymaking process. In Houston, the elite was a small group of busi-

Contacting City Officials

City governments deal with issues that are close to home—police and fire protection, street repair, garbage pickup, water and sewer service, EMS, parks, libraries, airports, animal control, and local taxes. You can find the name and contact information for the mayor and council members of your city at the city's homepage, which can be found at the following website: **www.tded.state.tx.us/tx-city/tx-city .htm**. Contact the people who represent you at city hall and let them know how you feel about city services, taxes, and regulations.

It's your city—get involved!

ness leaders called the 8-F Crowd because of their practice of meeting informally in Suite 8-F of a downtown hotel. The members of the 8-F Crowd were all wealthy businessmen with interests in real estate, construction, oil and gas, banking, law, and insurance.

The overriding goal of the business groups who dominated city politics was economic growth and development. They were **boosters** (people who promote local economic development) who believed that whatever was good for business was also good for their city. The business leaders favored low tax rates, rapid annexation, and few restrictions on land use. When the occasion arose, they did what was necessary to boost their cities. During the 1930s, for example, Dallas business leaders convinced the legislature to make their city the site for the official celebration of the Texas Centennial, even though Dallas did not exist during the Texas Revolution. In Houston, business leaders promoted the construction of the Ship Channel and the creation of the Johnson Spacecraft Center (JSC).

Business leaders frequently exerted their influence through the vehicle of nonpartisan "good government" groups such as the Citizens' Charter Association (CCA) in Dallas, Good Government League (GGL) in San Antonio, Seventh Street in Fort Worth, Citizens for Better Government in Abilene, and Citizens' Committee for Good Government in Wichita Falls. These groups recruited slates of candidates sympathetic with their goals and backed them financially in the at-large nonpartisan elections that were then the norm in most Texas cities. In San Antonio, the GGL won 85 of 97 contested council races between 1955 and 1975. In Dallas, the CCA captured 181 out of 211 seats between 1931 and 1975.[36]

Candidates supported by business groups were nearly all non-Hispanic White businessmen. In Fort Worth, no African Americans were elected to city council before 1967; no Hispanics were chosen before 1977. In fact, most Fort Worth council members lived within blocks of one another on the city's affluent southwest side.[37] In Houston, no women, no Latinos, and only one African American were elected to council before 1981.

Texas cities grew rapidly, but the growth came with certain social costs. Texas cities developed serious air and water pollution problems. The **Environmental Protection Agency (EPA),** the federal agency responsible for enforcing the nation's environmental laws, identified four major areas of the state that failed to meet federal air-quality standards for ozone: Dallas-Fort Worth, Houston-Galveston, Beaumont-Port Arthur, and El Paso.[38] In the meantime, air quality in Austin, San Antonio, and Tyler barely met the standard. Texas cities also suffered from traffic congestion, overcrowded schools, and flooding brought on by **subsidence,** which is the sinking of the surface of the land caused by the too-rapid extraction of subsurface water.

The costs of growth mobilized opposition to the growth-oriented business groups that had long dominated city politics. The business community split between those industries that benefit from growth and those that were more concerned with quality of life issues. Real estate developers, construction contractors, and other firms that depend on growth favored continuing growth-oriented public policies. In contrast, the tourist industry and high-technology firms that employed middle-class professionals were more concerned with the quality of urban life. Neighborhood groups and minority interests demanded that city governments respond to their needs. For example, the **Communities Organized for Public Service (COPS),** a predominantly Latino neighborhood reform organization in San Antonio, demanded better city services for low-income communities.[39]

By the mid-1970s, the rules of the political game had changed sufficiently to allow these new forces to have an impact on the policy process. The elimination of the poll tax and liberalization of Texas's once highly restrictive voter registration procedures opened the door to greater political participation by African Americans and Latinos. Furthermore, the extension of the VRA in 1975 to include Texas led to the introduction of single-member districts in most of the state's largest cities, including Houston, Dallas, San Antonio, El Paso, Lubbock, Corpus Christi, and Waco.

The new voter registration procedures and single-member district elections enabled minority and neighborhood groups to gain a real share of political power in big-city Texas. More African Americans and Latinos won city council seats than ever before, and some Asian Americans have won seats on councils as well. The number of women serving on city councils has increased and both Houston and Dallas have elected city council members who were openly gay or lesbian. African Americans, Latinos, and women have served as mayor in the state's major cities.

The nature of business groups in big-city Texas had also changed. During the 1950s, each city's business establishment was dominated by a fairly small group of strong-willed, fiercely independent, wealthy entrepreneurs such as Eric Jonsson in Dallas and George Brown in Houston. By the 1980s, the business community in big-city Texas had grown too diverse for any one individual or small group of individuals to speak on its behalf. Furthermore, the days of the individual entrepreneur were past, as management teams now run the state's major corporations. Before local managers could agree to support a local development project, they would have to obtain approval from a corporate board of directors based in New York, San Francisco, or Tokyo.

Contemporary urban politics in Texas can best be described as pluralist. **Pluralist theory (or pluralism)** is the view that diverse groups of elites with differing interests compete with one another to control policy in various issue areas. In big-city Texas today, different groups are active on different issues, but no one group is able to dominate policymaking across issue areas. Business groups may control policymaking in one issue area while neighborhood or minority-rights groups may have more influence in another issue area.

★ CONCLUSION: CITY GOVERNMENT AND POLICYMAKING

We discuss the role of city government in the policymaking process in the conclusion of the next chapter as part of a general discussion of local government in Texas.

★ REVIEW QUESTIONS

1. Why are some people critical of urban sprawl and what is their solution to the problem?

2. What is the legal status of cities in America's system of government?

3. In what areas do home rule cities have more freedom to act than general law cities have?

4. What are the advantages and disadvantages of the most commonly found forms of city government in Texas?

5. What are the different types of election systems used to choose city councils in Texas?

6. What are the three types of public policies adopted by Texas cities?

7. What are the most important expenditure categories and revenue sources for Texas cities?

8. How do cities use budgetary policy to promote economic development?

9. Why do large cities annex their suburbs?

10. What is the difference between zoning and deed restrictions?

11. How has big-city politics in Texas changed since the 1950s?

★ KEY TERMS

allocational urban policies
annexation
at-large election
bond
boosters
building codes
capital expenditure
city charter
city manager
city ordinances
closed primary

Communities Organized for Public Service (COPS)
council-manager form of city government
cumulative voting system
deed restrictions
developmental urban policies
Dillon's rule
district election
elite theory (elitism)
enterprise zones

Environmental Protection Agency (EPA)
extraterritorial jurisdiction (ETJ)
general law city
height limitation
high technology industries
home rule city
homestead exemption
housing codes
incorporated municipality
initiative process

mayor-council form of city
    government

minimum wage

nonpartisan election

off-street parking requirement

pluralist theory (pluralism)

political machines

political patronage

population bracket laws

property tax (*ad valorem*
    property tax)

recall

redistributive urban policies

sales tax

setback ordinance

subsidence

tax abatement

tax increment financing

truth in taxation laws

unincorporated area

urban planning

urban sprawl

utility district

Voting Rights Act (VRA)

zoning

★ NOTES

1. Alan Altshuler, William Merrill, Harold Wolman, and Faith Mitchell, eds., *Governance and Opportunity in Metropolitan America* (Washington, DC: National Academy Press, 1999), p. 8.

2. Jan K. Brueckner, "Urban Sprawl: Diagnosis and Remedies," *Texas Town & City* (February 2000): 13–19.

3. Christopher R. Conte, "The Boys of Sprawl," *Governing* (May 2000): 28–33.

4. "Should Cities Be Allowed to Sue Gun Manufacturers?" *Spectrum* 72 (Summer 1999): 20.

5. Terrell Blodget, "Municipal Home Rule Charters in Texas," *Public Affairs Comment* 41 (1996): 2.

6. Blodget, "Municipal Home Rule Charters in Texas," p. 2.

7. Rachel Graves, "In Need of Repairs," *Houston Chronicle*, July 8, 2001, p. 23A.

8. Quoted in T. J. Milling, "King Kong, 14 Chimps," *Houston Chronicle*, October 8, 1995, p. 38A.

9. Rob Gurwitt, "Are City Councils a Relic of the Past?" *Governing* (April 2003): 20–24.

10. Blodget, "Municipal Home Rule Charters in Texas," p. 3.

11. Wayne Lee Gay, "The Salary Survey," *Fort Worth Star-Telegram*, September 12, 2002, available at **www.dfw.com**.

12. Alan Ehrenhalt, "The City Manager Myth," *Governing* (September 1990): 41–46.

13. Rob Gurwitt, "The Lure of the Strong Mayor," *Governing* (July 1993): 36–41.

14. Rob Gurwitt, "Nobody in Charge," *Governing* (September 1997): 24.

15. Victor S. DeSantis and Tari Renner, "City Government Structures: An Attempt at Classification," *State and Local Government Review* 34 (Spring 2002): 99–103.

16. Steven R. Reed, "Dallas: A City at a Crucial Crossroads," *Houston Chronicle,* December 3, 1990, p. 11A.

17. Jerry L. Polinard, Robert D. Wrinkle, and Tomás Longoria, Jr., "The Impact of District Elections on the Mexican American Community: The Electoral Perspective," *Social Science Quarterly* 72 (September 1991): 608–14.

18. Paul E. Peterson, *City Limits* (Chicago: University of Chicago Press, 1981), ch. 3.

19. Kenneth K. Wong, "Economic Constraint and Political Choice in Urban Policymaking," *American Journal of Political Science* 32 (February 1988): 1–18.

20. Peter Eisinger, "The Politics of Bread and Circuses: Building the City for the Visitor Class," in Dennis R. Judd and Paul Kantor, eds., *The Politics of Urban America*, 3rd ed. (New York: Longman, 2002), pp. 252–266.

21. David Swindell and Mark Rosentraub, "Who Benefits from the Presence of Professional Sports Teams? The Implications for Public Funding of Stadiums and Arenas," *Public Administration Review* 58 (January 1998): 11–20.

22. *Texas Town and City* (March 1990): 17–35.

23. City of Houston, "Houston City Council Approves 2004 Budget," June 26, 2003, available at **www.ci.houston .tx.us/citydesk/budget.html**.

24. City of Dallas, "2003–2004 Budget," available at **www.dallascityhall.com**.

25. City of San Antonio, "Budget Highlights," available at **www.ci.sat.tx.us/**.

26. Various municipal websites.

27. Alan Greenblatt, "The Loathsome Local Levy," *Governing* (October 2001): 36.

28. "General Obligation Debt Service Summary," Fiscal Year 2004 Budget, City of Houston, **www.cityofhouston.gov**.

29. Department of Planning and Development, "Tax Abatement Status Report," City of Houston, available at **www .ci.houston.tx.us/departme/finance/mfr/dec02/38.pdf**.

30. Helen F. Ladd and John Yinger, *America's Ailing Cities: Fiscal Health and the Design of Urban Policy* (Baltimore: Johns Hopkins University Press, 1989), pp. 287–93.

31. David Brunori, "Principles of Tax Policy and Targeted Tax Incentives," *State and Local Government Review* 29 (Winter 1997): 59.

32. Todd M. Gabe and David S. Kraybill, "The Effect of State Economic Development Incentives on Employment Growth of Establishments," *Journal of Regional Science* 42 (November 2002): 703–30.

33. Arnold P. Fleischmann, "Balancing New Skylines," *Texas Humanist* 6 (January/February 1984): 28–31.

34. Terry Kliewer, "Anxiety Over Annexation," *Houston Chronicle*, July 15, 2002, pp. A13–A14.

35. Jeremy Schwartz, "Cities, Counties Grapple with New Law," *Austin American-Statesman*, April 29, 2002, available at **www.statesman.com**.

36. Chandler Davidson and Luis Ricardo Fraga, "Slating Groups as Parties in a 'Nonpartisan' Setting," *Western Political Quarterly* 41 (June 1988): 373–90.

37. Judy Fitzgerald and Melanie Miller, "Fort Worth," in Robert Stewart, ed., *Local Government Election Systems*, Vol. II (Austin: Lyndon B. Johnson School of Public Affairs, 1984), pp. 12–21.

38. Cindy Skrzycki, "A Brand of Compassionate Cooperation?" *Washington Post National Weekly Edition*, January 29–February 4, 2001, p. 16.

39. Dennis R. Judd and Todd Swanstrom, *City Politics: Private Power and Public Policy*, 2nd ed. (New York: Longman, 1998), pp. 280–83.

ONLINE PRACTICE TEST

Test your understanding of this chapter
with interactive review quizzes at
www.ablongman.com/tannahilltexas/chapter11

CHAPTER TWELVE

Counties, School Districts, and Special Districts

LEARNING OBJECTIVES

After studying Chapter 12, students should be able to do the following:

★ Describe the legal/constitutional status of county government.

★ List the responsibilities of county government.

★ Outline the structures of county government, identifying the most important county officials and describing the duties of their offices.

★ Identify the most important revenue sources and expenditure categories for county government.

★ Compare and contrast county government in rural areas with county government in urban counties.

★ Discuss the most important issues facing county government.

★ Describe the organization of independent school districts, discussing the roles of boards of trustees and school superintendents.

★ Identify the funding sources for public education in Texas and assess their relative importance.

★ Evaluate the controversy over education funding.

★ Discuss each of the following educational policy issues: charter schools, parental choice, class size, bilingual education, and basic skills testing.

★ Identify the role special districts play in the provision of local government services.

★ Describe the creation, organization, and operation of the various types of special districts in Texas.

★ Identify the funding sources for special districts.

★ Evaluate the benefits and liabilities of special districts.

★ Assess the role of cities, counties, school districts, and special districts in the policymaking process.

★ Define the key terms listed on page 338 and explain their significance.

Texas is a national leader in basic skills testing. Between 1990 and 2003, Texas public schools administered the **Texas Assessment of Academic Skills (TAAS),** which was a state-mandated basic skills test used to measure student progress and assess school performance. Students in grades three through eight took exams in reading, writing, math, science, and social studies. The high school TAAS test covered reading, writing, and math. High school students had to pass TAAS, which was given in tenth grade, in order to graduate. In 2003–2004, the **Texas Assessment of Knowledge and Skills (TAKS)** replaced TAAS as the state's new basic skills test. The TAKS, which will be given to students in grades three through eleven, is a more challenging test than TAAS because it covers more subjects. The high school TAKS is especially more difficult than its TAAS counterpart, which was generally regarded as a tenth grade basic skills test. For example, the high school exit exam includes both Algebra I and Geometry, which were not on the TAAS exit exam.[1]

The proponents of basic skills testing believe that it improves the quality of public education by holding students, teachers, and school administrators accountable. Students in elementary and middle school must pass TAKS before they can be promoted to higher grades. High school students must pass TAKS in order to graduate. Teachers may face reassignment and school administrators may lose their jobs if their students do poorly on the test. President George W. Bush, who was governor of Texas from 1995 until he resigned to move to the White House in 2001, made basic skills testing the centerpiece of his education reform plan for the nation.

The critics of basic skills testing argue that tests actually undermine educational quality because they force schools to focus on the test rather than student learning. Schools neglect other subjects for weeks before the test is given so they can prepare. Much of their work focuses not on basic skills, but on test-taking techniques. Instead of learning to read, write, and do math, students learn how to take multiple-choice exams. Furthermore, basic-skills testing may actually decrease the high school graduation rate. Some students leave school because they are discouraged about their performance on the test. Meanwhile, school administrators, responsible for district test scores, occasionally pressure weak students to drop out.[2]

The controversy over basic-skills testing illustrates the sort of issues facing local governments in Texas. Local issues are important issues. The quality of education is critical to students, parents, and business leaders who need an educated workforce to grow their companies. Local issues are often controversial. The debate over basic-skills testing involves students, teachers, parents, school administrators, and businesspersons. The controversy over basic-skills testing also demonstrates that local issues are not just local in scope. The Texas legislature and the governor adopted TAAS and TAKS and the state board of education and school districts implement the tests. Because of President Bush's educational reform initiative basic skills testing is now national policy.

This is the last in a series of chapters dealing with the institutions of state and local government in Texas. Chapters 8, 9, and 10 dealt with the legislative, executive, and judicial branches of state government. Chapter 11 focused on city government. This chapter considers county, school district, and special district government.

? WHAT IS YOUR OPINION?

Have TAAS and TAKS improved the quality of public education in Texas?

COUNTY GOVERNMENT

Texas has 254 counties, ranging in population size from Harris County with more than 3.4 million people in 2000 to tiny Loving County with a population of only 67.[3] Some counties are dominated by large cities, such as Harris (Houston), Bexar (San Antonio), Travis (Austin), Tarrant (Fort Worth), El Paso, and Dallas Counties. Other counties are predominantly rural, with only a few small towns and no large cities.

Legal Status

Texas counties are **general-law units of local government,** that is, units of local government that are limited to those structures and powers specifically granted by state law. In contrast to Texas cites and the counties in most other states, Texas counties may not adopt home-rule status, which would allow them greater discretion in choosing governmental structures, functions, and tax systems. **Home rule** refers to the authority of a unit of local government to take actions not prohibited by the laws or constitutions of the United States or the state. If county officials want to respond to local problems by taking an action not specifically allowed by state law, they must first obtain authorization from the Texas legislature.

Edwards County Courthouse in Rocksprings, Texas.

Responsibilities

County governments in Texas play a dual role of implementing state policies and providing local services to their residents.

- **Law enforcement:** Counties enforce state laws. The county sheriff's office is the primary law enforcement agency for Texans living in unincorporated areas. Counties also operate county jails that house people who are awaiting trial and persons convicted of misdemeanor offenses.

- **Courts:** Counties operate justice of the peace, county, and district courts. With the exception of cases tried in municipal court, every state trial that takes place in Texas, both criminal and civil, is held in a court operated by county government.

- **Health:** Counties enforce the state's health laws. Many urban counties provide charity hospitals for indigent residents.

- **Records:** County governments collect and maintain records of births, deaths, marriages, divorces, and deeds.

- **Tax collection:** County governments collect a number of taxes and fees on behalf of the state, including charges for license plates and certificates-of-title for motor vehicles.

- **Elections:** County governments register voters and conduct both primary and general elections for the state.

- **Roads and bridges:** Counties build and maintain roads and bridges.

- **Other services:** State law allows counties to provide a range of additional services. Some counties operate airports or seaports. Counties may also provide their residents with libraries, parks, and recreational facilities.

"It is the forgotten government. Very few people know anything about the workings of county government."
—Robert Thomas, political scientist

Organization

Figure 12.1 is the organizational chart of county government in Texas. In many respects, county government is a miniature version of state government because no single official is in charge. Instead, executive functions are divided among a sizable number of elected and appointed officials.

Commissioners Court   The **commissioners court** is the board of directors for county government composed of four county commissioners and the county judge. The members are chosen in partisan elections that are held concurrently with the biennial statewide general elections. A **partisan election** is an election contest in which both the candidates' names and their party affiliation appear on the ballot. County voters elect the four commissioners, one each from four districts called county commissioners' precincts, to serve four-year staggered terms; they elect the county judge to serve a four-year term as well.

Individual commissioners essentially run county government within their precincts. In most counties, the commissioners oversee road repair and construction in their particular precincts. In fact, roadwork is such an important part of the job of county commissioners in rural counties that residents often refer to them as road

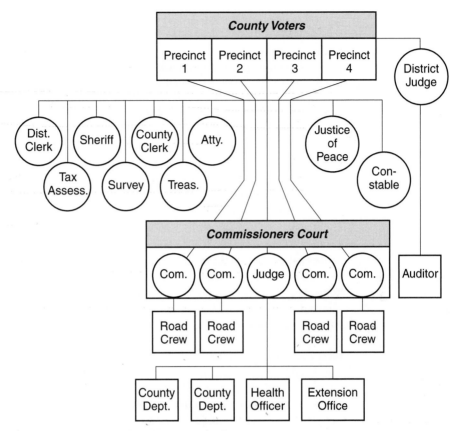

FIGURE 12.1 **County Government in Texas**

commissioners. The commissioners control large road budgets and pick contractors to do county work. Meanwhile, they hire their own crews to do routine maintenance on county roads and in county facilities, such as parks and recreation centers. The commissioners also select vendors for the purchase of equipment and supplies.

The responsibilities of the county judge vary, depending on the size of the county. In rural counties, the county judge is the presiding judge in the constitutional county court. In urban counties, the county judge devotes most, if not all, of his or her time to county business and leaves the work of trying cases to the county courts at law. In smaller counties, those with less than 225,000 people, the judge is also the county's chief budget officer. In larger counties, an auditor appointed by the district court judge(s) drafts the budget and oversees county finances.

The powers of the county judge more closely resemble those of a mayor in the council-manager form of city government than a mayor in the mayor-council form of city government with the strong mayor variation. The county judge presides in commissioners court, but has only one vote and no veto. As the most visible figure in county government, the county judge often serves as the spokesperson for county government. The ability of the county judge to provide policy leadership, however, depends more on political skill than official power because the judge lacks the authority to run the commissioners court and has no executive power to manage county government.

The commissioners court has limited authority because its structure and most of the functions it may perform are established by law and the state constitution. The commissioners court can set the county property tax rate, but it does not have general ordinance-making power. An **ordinance** is a law enacted by the governing body of a unit of local government. Most of the power of the commissioners court comes from its budget-making authority and its power to choose among the optional services available for county government to provide to county residents. The commissioners court is empowered to adopt the county budget. This authority gives it an important tool to influence policy in county departments not directly under the court's supervision. Also, state law gives the commissioners court authority to determine whether the county will offer residents such local programs/services as parks, libraries, airports, hospitals, and recreation facilities. In counties that choose to implement these optional programs, the commissioners court appoints administrators to head them. These appointed officials may include a county agricultural agent, home demonstration agent, fire marshal, county health officer, county welfare officer, medical examiner, librarian, county engineer, and, in more populous counties, a county purchasing agent.

Other Elected County Officials

The county courthouse contains numerous elected officials in addition to the members of the commissioners court. These officials are chosen in partisan elections to serve staggered four-year terms. All but justices of the peace and constables are elected countywide.

After the county judge, the most visible official is the county sheriff who is the chief law enforcement officer for the county. The sheriff's department has jurisdiction over the entire county, but in urban areas, city governments and the county usually agree on a division of labor. City police departments patrol within their cities while the sheriff enforces the law in unincorporated areas. The sheriff also operates the county jail, which holds prisoners awaiting trial for felony offenses and people serving sentences for misdemeanor convictions. In urban counties in particular, managing the jail consumes a significant proportion of the sheriff department's budget and personnel. Finally, the sheriff assists county courts and state district courts within the county by serving arrest warrants and subpoenas, and providing deputies to serve as bailiffs. A **subpoena** is a legal order compelling the attendance of a person at an official proceeding, such as a trial.

Larger counties elect both a district attorney and a county attorney. In smaller counties and in Bexar County (San Antonio), the district attorney performs both roles. In counties with both officials, the district attorney's office prosecutes felony criminal cases in state district courts. The county attorney advises the commissioners court and other county officials on legal issues and represents the county in court on civil matters, mostly lawsuits to collect delinquent property taxes. The county attorney's office also prosecutes misdemeanor cases in JP and county court except in Harris County where the district attorney prosecutes both felony and misdemeanor cases.

> "You have a twofold purpose: You want to enforce the law, yet you want to do it in such a manner that you keep on everyone's good side. If you're a county sheriff, you have to have everybody as your friend, or you'll get voted out."
>
> —Truman Maddox, former sheriff, Austin County

Two other offices whose titles frequently confuse voters are those of county clerk and district clerk. The county clerk records legal documents, such as deeds, mortgages, and contracts, and keeps vital statistics on births, deaths, marriages, and divorce. The county clerk is also the county election official. He or she conducts absentee balloting, instructs precinct election workers, certifies election returns, and forwards election results to the office of the Texas Secretary of State. In a few counties, the county clerk registers voters. The district clerk, meanwhile, maintains legal records for the district courts. In small counties, the county clerk performs the functions of the district clerk.

Justices of the peace try Class C misdemeanor cases and hear small claims civil suits. Depending on its population, a county may be divided into as many as eight JP precincts with each precinct electing one or two JPs. In addition to their judicial duties, JPs in small counties may assume the responsibilities of the county clerk. The JP may also serve as county coroner (although few justices of the peace have medical backgrounds).

Each county elects as many constables as it elects justices of the peace. Although constables are certified law-enforcement officers, their primary chore in most counties is to assist the JP court(s) by serving legal papers such as subpoenas and warrants. Constables also handle evictions, execute judgments, and provide bailiffs for the justice courts. In some urban counties, particularly Harris County, constables provide for-hire law-enforcement services to subdivisions located in unincorporated areas through contract deputy programs.

The tax assessor-collector is the county's chief tax official. The tax assessor collects the county's property taxes, collects fees for automobile license plates, and issues certificates-of-title for motor vehicles. Despite the title of the office, the tax assessor-collector no longer assesses the value of county property for tax purposes. The legislature has assigned that duty to a county tax appraisal district in each county. In small counties, those with fewer than 10,000 people, the sheriff performs the duties of the tax assessor.

In most counties, the tax assessor-collector directs voter registration. This duty is a holdover from the era of the **poll tax,** which was a tax that prospective voters had to pay in order to register to vote. State law allows the commissioners court to transfer voter registration and/or election administration duties to another official and a number of urban counties have assigned those responsibilities to the county clerk or to an appointed election administrator.

The county treasurer is responsible for receiving funds and making authorized expenditures. In recent years, the state legislature has proposed and voters have passed constitutional amendments to allow several counties to abolish the office of county treasurer and transfer its duties to the auditor, who is appointed by the district judge(s) in the county.

Two counties, Harris and Dallas, still have county departments of education. These agencies are governed by five-member boards of trustees, with one trustee elected countywide and the other four trustees chosen from the four commissioners court precincts. Historically, county departments of education coordinated relations among the common school districts within the county. Common school districts have now been replaced by independent school districts and in 1978 the legislature

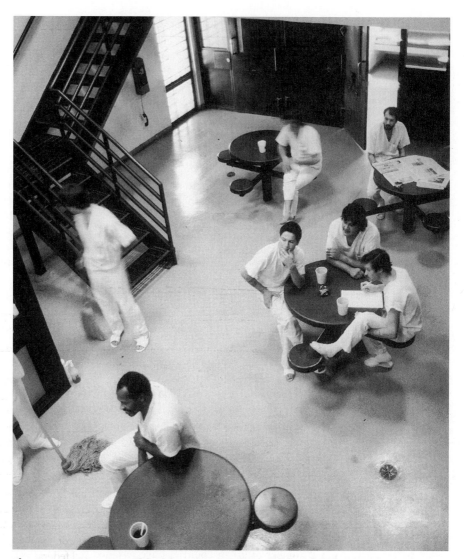

The Travis County Jail holds prisoners awaiting trial for felony offenses and people serving sentences for misdemeanor convictions.

abolished all county education departments except those in Harris and Dallas Counties, which successfully argued that they provided important services to county residents. Critics charge that these agencies are expensive bureaucracies whose services could and should be provided by independent school districts.

Some elected county officials no longer play a substantive policymaking role. The county surveyor was needed to provide accurate land surveys when counties were first settled, but the office is now inactive in most counties. Similarly, the public weigher and the inspector of hides and animals are offices without duties. From time to time, would-

TABLE 12.1 Tax Rates in Selected Counties, 2003

County	Tax Rate per $100 Valuation
Bexar (San Antonio)	$0.337
Dallas	$0.196
El Paso	$0.361434
Harris (Houston)	$0.38814
Tarrant (Fort Worth)	$0.2725
Travis (Austin)	$0.4660

Source: Various county appraisal district websites.

be reformers of county government attempt to have these inactive offices abolished, but their efforts have so far failed. The offices are vacant in most counties although citizens occasionally file for the positions in urban counties, primarily for amusement purposes. People holding the positions have no salaries, no staff, and no office space.

County Revenues and Expenditures

Property taxes are the main source of tax revenue for county government. The county tax rate is limited to 80 cents per $100 of valuation although state law allows county voters to approve as much as 15 cents more for road and bridge operations and up to 30 cents more to build and maintain farm-to-market (FM) roads. Table 12.1 compares the property tax rates of the five largest counties in Texas.

County governments can expand their taxing authority by creating separate but closely allied special districts to provide such costly services as health care, flood control, and toll road construction and maintenance. In Harris County, for example, the commissioners court controls three special districts—the Harris County Flood Control District, Hospital District, and Port of Houston Authority. If the property tax rates for these districts were added to the Harris County tax rate, it would jump from $0.38814 to $0.64627.

Property taxes are not the only revenue source for county governments. Counties that do not have transit authorities or incorporated cities within their boundaries can levy sales taxes. Other revenue sources for county governments include fees for motor vehicle licenses, service charges, and federal aid.

The relative importance of county expenditures varies considerably among counties. Road and bridge construction and maintenance is a major budget item for all counties, but it is particularly prominent in geographically large counties. Rural, sparsely populated counties do little more than maintain the roads, enforce the law, operate a county court, and carry out the basic administrative functions of county government, such as recording deeds and registering voters. In contrast, county governments in metropolitan areas provide a wide range of services, especially if the county has a large population living in unincorporated areas. Although the largest single item in the budget for Harris County is road and bridge construction and maintenance, Harris County government and its related special districts also spend millions of dollars for law enforcement, jail operation, indigent health care, the operation of county and district courts, flood control, and parks.

TEXAS ONLINE ★ Forces of Change

Counties Online

Is your county government online? Although most of the state's cities have homepages, relatively few counties do. Learn about county government by studying the following county homepages and answering the questions below:

Bexar County (San Antonio): **www.co.bexar.tx.us/**
Brazoria County (Angleton): **www.bchm.org/**
Galveston: **www.co.galveston.tx. us/**
Harris County (Houston): **www.co.harris.tx.us/**
Jefferson County (Beaumont): **co.jefferson.tx.us/**
McLennon County (Waco): **www.co.mclennan.tx.us/**
Montgomery County (Conroe): **www.co.montgomery.tx.us/**

Tarrant County (Fort Worth): **www.tarrantcounty.com/**
Travis County (Austin): **www.co.travis.tx.us/**
Williamson County (Georgetown): **www.williamson-county.org/**

QUESTIONS TO CONSIDER

1. Which county has the most attractive website? Why do you like it?
2. Which county has the least attractive website? Why do you not like it?
3. Which site seemed most oriented toward attracting tourists? Why do you think that?

Issues in County Government

County government has both staunch defenders and harsh critics. The proponents of county government declare that counties are the unit of local government that is closest and most responsive to the people. Counties provide basic government services that citizens want and need. In contrast, critics charge that county government is a relic of the nineteenth century. They believe that county government is inefficient and often corrupt.

To a substantial degree, the validity of the criticism against county government depends on the size of the county. For the most part, county government functions satisfactorily in rural and small town Texas. In rural areas, counties are the primary units of local government. Citizens are aware of county services and know county officials well. In contrast, county governments are almost invisible governments in urban Texas despite employing thousands of people and spending millions of dollars. Counties operate with little accountability because the media and most citizens are focused primarily on other units and levels of government.

The Long Ballot and Responsibility of the Voters   The critics of county government believe that the long ballot makes it difficult for county voters to intelligently choose qualified officeholders, at least in urban areas. The **long ballot** is an election system that provides for the election of nearly every public official of any significance. County elections coincide with state and national primary and general elections held in even-numbered years. Considering all the other races on the ballot in those years, especially in urban counties, it is unlikely that many voters are informed of the relative merits of candidates for county clerk, district clerk, or many other county offices. For that matter, most urban voters probably cannot even distinguish between the county clerk and the district clerk.

The theory of democracy is that elections make public officials responsive to the citizens. Public officials do what the voters want because if they do not, they face defeat at the ballot box. Democracy does not work, or at least does not work well, if the voters are unaware of public officials. Furthermore, elected officials have no incentive to serve the public if the public is unaware of their work. The danger is that public officials who are not likely to be held accountable to the voters will act instead to further their own personal interests and the interests of the individuals and groups who support them politically.

The critics of county government would like to reform the system to make county officials more accountable, at least in urban areas. Reformers would like to reduce the number of elected county officials, either consolidating positions into a smaller number of offices or providing for the appointment of officials by a single county executive who would be accountable to the voters. Reformers would also like to minimize the role of organized interests in county policymaking.

? WHAT IS YOUR OPINION?

Are too many county officials elected for voters to keep track of the offices and the candidates?

Hiring, Purchasing, Contracting, and Conflict of Interest   The phrase **conflict of interest** refers to a circumstance in which the personal interests of a public official may clash with that official's professional responsibilities. For example, a public official would face a conflict of interest in determining whether to award a government contract to a firm owned by members of the official's family as opposed to companies whose management had no personal connection to the official. Public policy analysts generally believe that government works better when public officials avoid decisions in which their personal interests are at stake.

The critics of county government believe that county operations make conflict of interest inevitable. In general, county commissioners and elected department heads hire and fire employees as they see fit. County governments lack a merit hiring system and county employees do not enjoy civil service protection. Critics say that county officials often hire and fire employees for political reasons. Furthermore, county employees have an incentive to become campaign workers for their bosses at election time, perhaps even on county time.

Another problem is the absence of centralized purchasing in most counties. Each department contracts for goods and services on its own, often without the benefit of competitive bids. At the least, this practice prevents the county from taking advantage of quantity discounts. More seriously, it increases opportunities for corruption by county officials who may be tempted to do business with their friends and political supporters.

The contracting process presents similar problems. County governments contract for services from engineers, accountants, surveyors, architects, and attorneys. Most of these services are provided in connection with road construction projects. Although rural counties are small businesses, urban counties are big businesses. In 2003, general fund expenditures for Harris County, the state's largest county, totaled $890 million.[4]

Because state law prohibits competitive bidding, individual commissioners decide which firms receive the contracts for work in their precincts while the commissioners court as a whole awards contracts for the entire county. In practice, the firms who win the contracts are also the major election campaign supporters of the members of the commissioners court. Between 1994 and 1998, 14 of the 15 largest political contributions to Harris County elected officials came from individuals and political action committees (PACs) connected to firms that received no-bid professional services contracts from the county. The only contributing firm that did not receive a no-bid contract was NYLCare, the county's insurance provider, which submitted a cost proposal to county officials.[5]

The contracting process is highly controversial. County commissioners declare that they select the firms best able to provide the services to their constituents. Political contributions have no impact on their decisions, they say, because state law makes it illegal for public officials to accept campaign contributions or anything else of value in return for a contract. In contrast, critics charge that the contracting process is inherently corrupt. Furthermore, they say, the system helps insulate county commissioners from electoral accountability. County commissioners receive so much campaign money from firms doing business with the county that incumbent commissioners are virtually impossible to defeat for reelection, at least in urban areas.

Some counties use a unit road system, which is a centralized system for maintaining county roads and bridges under the authority of the county engineer. The proponents of the unit road system argue that it allows county government to operate more efficiently and less politically. In contrast, county commissioners, who would suffer a loss of political influence under a unit road system, contend that it would weaken local control of road and bridge maintenance.

Decentralization and Accountability   Critics believe that the decentralization of county government makes it difficult for county officials to fulfill the responsibilities of their offices and impossible for voters to accurately evaluate their performance. In many instances, the people who raise revenue and write the budget—the commissioners court—have no direct control over the people who administer county programs—the elected department heads. The sheriff, for example, is the county's chief law-enforcement official, but does not control the budget for law enforcement. If county residents are unhappy with the operation of the county jail, whom do they blame—the commissioners court for not putting enough money in the budget or the sheriff for being a poor administrator?

❓ WHAT IS YOUR OPINION?

Is county government too decentralized to operate efficiently?

> "All things being equal, you give the business to your friends. It is human nature to want to work with people you know and trust."
> —Steve Radack, Harris County Commissioner

> "You can call it anything you want, but it is a bribe."
> —Richard Bean, economist

> "When confronted by changing socioeconomic, demographic, and governmental conditions, county officials often face critical problems without authority to legislate locally, raise sufficient revenues, or engage in areawide or neighborhood planning and land use management."
> —Robert Thomas, political scientist

Structural Inflexibility and the Twenty-First Century Is county government able to respond to contemporary policy problems, especially in urban areas? Anyone driving through an urban county can easily distinguish where a city's jurisdiction ends and the county jurisdiction begins by the proliferation of roadside vendors, fireworks stands, outsized billboards, portable signs, and automobile junkyards. Cities can pass ordinances to regulate such matters, but counties cannot. Some reformers favor granting county government ordinance making power, especially county governments in urban areas. If counties could make ordinances, they could better address issues of development in unincorporated areas, such as land use, flood control, environmental protection, and neighborhood integrity. In contrast, the opponents of ordinance making power for county government are against allowing yet another unit of government the power to regulate peoples' lives.

County Politics

The nature of county politics depends on the nature of the county. In rural and small-town Texas, county government is high profile because counties are the primary units of local government. The population is small enough so that public officials and county residents often know one another personally. Officials in some counties hold office for decades without facing electoral challenge, sometimes because they are personally popular and sometimes because no one else wants the job. In other counties, political factions form, often on the basis of personalities, and compete for control, usually in the Democratic Party primary. (Despite the growth of the Republican Party in state politics, most rural county courthouses remain staunchly Democratic.) The issues of county government in rural Texas are relatively minor, but nonetheless important to the people involved. Fixing potholes and paving country roads may not be the most important policy issues facing government in Texas, but they are important issues to people who live in the region.

In urban areas, county governments are big business but low profile. Most residents of the state's big cities are unaware of county issues and ignorant of county government. The local media typically ignore county issues, preferring instead to cover crime, accidents, and natural disasters. When local media outlets do cover local government, they typically focus on city government and, occasionally, school-district politics, but seldom cover county issues.

County government in urban areas is important, especially to selected segments of the population. People without health insurance rely on county health clinics and charity hospitals for health care. Residents of unincorporated areas depend on the county sheriff for police protection. Land developers benefit from road construction that provides access to their property. Engineers, contractors, attorneys, surveyors, and other professionals do substantial business with county government.

County politics in urban Texas involves conflict between downtown and the suburbs, with undercurrents of race and ethnicity, class, and party politics. Consider the long-simmering dispute between the hospital district and the commissioners

NATIONAL PERSPECTIVE

Local Government Consolidation in Indiana

More than 30 years ago, the city of Indianapolis and Marion County Government, where Indianapolis is located, merged to form a consolidated government known as Unigov. The consolidated government was given authority for economic development, public works, parks, transportation, and some elements of public safety. More than 50 other units of local government remained in the same geographic area, including cities, school districts, and special districts. These units of government were responsible for other basic public services, including education, water and sewer, street repair, libraries, and most aspects of public safety.*

Unigov succeeded in its primary goal, which was the revitalization of downtown Indianapolis. Because it covered a substantially larger taxing area than did the city of Indianapolis, the consolidated government enjoyed a bigger tax base to support redevelopment efforts than just the city alone. Unigov funded the development of a new shopping mall downtown as well as the construction of sports facilities to house the Indianapolis Colts National Football League (NFL) team and the Indiana Pacers of the National Basketball Association (NBA).

The success of Unigov in promoting redevelopment in downtown Indianapolis came at the cost of higher taxes and fewer services for inner-city residents. Unigov frequently used tax increment financing to fund downtown revitalization. **Tax increment financing** is a program in which a local government promises to earmark increased property tax revenues generated by development in a designated area called a tax increment financing district to fund improvements in the area, such as roads, parks, sidewalks, and street lighting. This approach reduced the tax revenues available for inner-city school districts and other local governments, forcing them to raise taxes on property owners that had not benefited from development and reduce the services they were able to provide their constituents.†

QUESTIONS TO CONSIDER

1. Would Unigov be more effective if it assumed all the functions of local government in the region rather than just a limited set of functions?
2. Which individuals and groups would be most likely to support city-county consolidation in Texas?
3. Which individuals and groups would most likely oppose city-county consolidation?

*Andrew Sancton, *Merger Mania: The Assault on Local Government* (Montreal, Canada: McGill-Queen's University Press, 2000), pp. 71–72.

†Mark S. Ronsentraub, "City-County Consolidation and the Rebuilding of Image: The Fiscal Lessons from Indianapolis's UniGov Program," *State and Local Government Review* 32 (Fall 2000): 180–91.

court in Harris County. Although the Harris County Hospital District is technically a separate unit of government, it is not really independent because the commissioners court controls its board of directors. For years, some of the members of the commissioners court have been unhappy with the management of the district, charging it with inefficient and wasteful operating procedures. The commissioners court has diverted money from the hospital district to other county activities and shuffled district management. The underlying tension between the commissioners court and the district is that the charity hospital serves a different constituency than the constituency that supports a majority of the members of the commissioners court. The large majority of patients served by the hospital district are low-income African

American and Latino residents of inner-city Houston. In contrast, a majority of the members of the commissioners court have their political bases in the predominantly non-Hispanic White, middle-income suburbs. Their constituents benefit relatively little from the hospital district.

SCHOOL DISTRICTS

Many Texans consider school districts the most important unit of local government. Public education is the single largest budget expenditure for state and local government in Texas. In fact, many homeowners pay more money in school property taxes than they do in county and city property taxes combined. School districts are major employers while school activities, especially high school football, are the focus of social life in many communities. Good schools are the foundation for economic growth in a community and the instrument for training young people for success in college and the workforce.

Public School Administration

Independent school districts (ISDs) are units of local government that provide public education services to district residents from kindergarten through the twelfth grade. The state has 1,041 school districts, ranging in size from the Houston ISD with more than 210,000 students to several hundred districts that have fewer than 500 students. In 2002, more than 4.1 million students attended public schools in Texas.[6]

The governing body for ISDs is the board of trustees, generally composed of seven members (although some of the larger districts have nine members). Trustees may be elected either at large or from districts to serve terms of two, three, four, or six years. Terms of two years are the most common. School trustee elections, which are nonpartisan, are usually held at times that do not coincide with statewide spring primaries and general elections. A **nonpartisan election** is an election in which candidates run without party labels. In many urban areas, city elections and school trustee elections take place on the same day, usually the first Saturday in April in odd-numbered years.

The board of trustees is a body of ordinary citizens that meets periodically to set policy for the district. The members of the board of trustees receive no salary for their services; they are lay people rather than professional educators. The board approves the budget, sets the property tax rate, and arranges financial audits. It makes personnel decisions, involving such matters as setting the salary schedule and approving contracts. Other board decisions concern the letting of contracts for the expansion and repair of the district's physical plant.

Perhaps the board's most important decision is the hiring of a superintendent. The superintendent is a professional school administrator who manages the day-to-day operation of the district and ensures that the board's policy decisions are implemented effectively. Research shows that board members tend to defer to the superintendent on the basic outline of education policy.[7] Nonetheless, board members,

More than four million students attend public schools in Texas.

especially in urban districts, frequently make political demands on a superintendent regarding contracts, jobs, and responding to the needs of particular ethnic groups or constituencies. In large urban districts, boards of trustees are sometimes split along racial and ethnic lines, and between members representing inner-city areas and the suburbs. Consequently, superintendents of urban districts may find themselves caught in the crossfire of a divided board. Nationwide, the average tenure for urban superintendents is less than three years.[8] Texas is no exception to the pattern of conflict between school boards and superintendents. The Dallas ISD, for example, has had five superintendents since 1996.[9]

Education Finance

The federal government, state government, and local taxpayers fund public education in Texas. Figure 12.2 shows the relative importance of the three revenue sources for school districts. In 2002, the average ISD received 55 percent of its funds from local tax sources, 42 percent from the state, and 3 percent in federal grant money.

The relative importance of funding sources varies dramatically among school districts. Figure 12.3 compares funding sources for two large, big-city school districts, Houston Independent School District (HISD) and El Paso Independent School District (EPISD). The HISD raises most of its money from local property taxes whereas

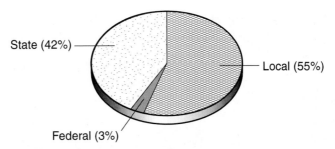

FIGURE 12.2 **Education Funding Sources, 2002**
Source: Texas Education Agency

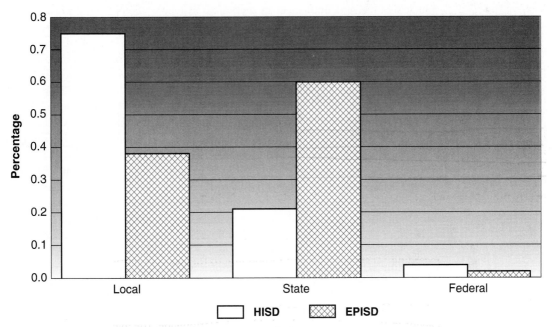

FIGURE 12.3 **Funding Comparison, Houston and El Paso**
Source: Texas Education Agency

the EPISD gets a majority of its funding from the state. Both districts receive some money from the federal government, although federal funding is more important to the HISD than the EPISD.

District funding reflects differences in the way the money is raised or awarded. The federal government gives money to school districts through **federal grant-in-aid programs,** which are programs through which the national government gives money to state and local governments to spend in accordance with set standards and conditions. Federal grant money targets economically disadvantaged students and students with disabilities. Federal dollars also support the **School Lunch Program,** which is a federal program that provides free or inexpensive lunches to children from poor families, and **bilingual education,** which is the teaching of academic subjects in both English and a student's native language, usually Spanish. The amount of federal money a school district receives depends on such factors as the number of district students who are economically disadvantaged or who have limited English-language proficiency. Although both the HISD and the EPISD qualify for substantial amounts of federal money under those criteria, the Houston district qualifies for more money because a larger proportion of its students are poor, have limited English-language proficiency, or need special education. In contrast to the HISD and EPISD, school districts that serve an affluent population, such as the Highland Park ISD in Dallas, receive almost no federal grant money.

The **Foundation School Program** is the basic funding program for public education in the state of Texas. The legislature establishes certain minimum standards that school districts must meet in such areas as teacher compensation and student transportation. The actual amount of money a district receives depends on district wealth, local property tax rates, and a host of other factors. In general, poorer districts receive more money from the state than wealthier districts. Wealthy districts, such as Highland Park ISD, receive relatively little state money, whereas poor districts, such as the Edgewood ISD in San Antonio, receive most of their money from the state. Because the El Paso ISD is relatively poorer than the Houston ISD, it receives a greater share of its funding from the state than does the HISD.

The state distributes other money to school districts from the Available School Fund. In the 1850s, the legislature set aside a large block of state land to create a trust fund for public education. Income from the sale and lease of that land and from royalties earned from oil and gas production on it goes into the **Permanent School Fund (PSF),** which is a fund constitutionally established as an endowment to finance public elementary and secondary education. The PSF principal of more than $17 billion cannot be spent.[10] Instead, it must be invested to earn interest and dividends, which go into the Available School Fund (ASF). The ASF is also supported by one-fourth of the taxes collected on motor fuels and natural resources. The state distributes ASF money to school districts based on the number of students in average daily attendance.

Public education in Texas is also funded through local property taxes. School districts use local tax money to participate in the Foundation School Program and for "local enrichment," that is, to pay for services that go beyond the state-mandated minimum standards. Local money is also spent for building construction and maintenance and to pay off debts, activities for which state funds may not be applied.

School tax rates tend to be higher than the property tax rates assessed by counties and cities. Most districts have tax rates between $1 and $2 per $100 valuation. In 2002, the tax rate for the Dallas ISD was $1.548. It was $1.722 for the San Antonio ISD, $1.641 for Fort Worth ISD, $1.57 for El Paso ISD, and $1.58 for Houston ISD.[11] Property tax rates may have a combined maintenance and operations (M & O) rate and an interest and sinking fund (I & S) rate. The M & O rate applies to the district's general operating expenses whereas the I & S rate is used to pay off the district's bond debt. The legislature limits the M & O rate for most districts to $1.50 per $100 valuation and caps the I & S rate at $0.50 for debt incurred since 1992 plus whatever rate is needed to pay off debts incurred before 1992.[12]

School districts grant property tax breaks to homeowners and people over 65 years of age. The Texas Constitution provides for a $15,000 homestead exemption, reducing the taxable value of a home for school tax purposes. Most school districts grant additional exemptions for disabled persons and people over 65 years of age. Furthermore, a homeowner's school property taxes are frozen at age 65. Regardless of increases in tax rates, elderly Texans are assessed the same tax rate they were charged on their current home when they reached their 65th birthday.

The state's system of financing public education has long been controversial because districts with wealthy property tax bases can raise more money than districts that are less affluent, even with lower property tax rates. The Glen Rose ISD in Somervell County benefits from having a nuclear power plant in its taxing district. The taxable value of property in Glen Rose ISD is $1,340,728 per student. With a relatively modest tax rate of $0.969, Glen Rose ISD generates $7,546 a year per student. In contrast, Crystal City ISD in Zavala County includes no refineries or power plants within its boundaries. The taxable value of property in Crystal City ISD is only $58,043 per student. Even with a relatively hefty property tax rate of $1.62, Crystal City ISD raises just $1,068 per pupil. Left to their own financial resources, the Glen Rose ISD would have substantially more money to spend to provide a quality education to its 1,700 students than Crystal City ISD would have to support the education of its 2,055 students.[13]

"Nobody likes Robin Hood. I didn't like it when I passed it; the people who voted for it didn't like it."
—State Senator Bill Ratliff, R., Mt. Pleasant, legislative sponsor of the Robin Hood Plan

In 1989, the Texas Supreme Court ruled in the case of *Edgewood* v. *Kirby* that the state's system of financing public education violated the Texas Constitution. The court ordered the legislature to create a system whereby districts with the same tax rate would have roughly the same amount of money to spend per student.[14] The court focused on equality of tax revenues rather than equality of expenditures. It ordered the state to adopt a system of school funding that ensured that districts would have the same ability to generate similar revenues per student at similar levels of tax effort. If Glen Rose ISD and Crystal City ISD had the same property tax rate, then they would be able to raise the same amount of money per student. The court did not require expenditure equality because it did not force districts to have the same tax rate. The citizens of Crystal City ISD (or Glen Rose ISD) could choose to fund their schools more (or less) generously by adopting a higher (or lower) tax rate than most other districts.

The legislature responded to *Edgewood* v. *Kirby* by adopting the **Robin Hood Plan,** which was a reform of the state's school finance system designed to increase funding for poor school districts by redistributing money from wealthy districts. The plan requires the state's wealthiest school districts to reduce their property wealth to no more than $295,000 per student. To reach this goal, districts have several choices, but most wealthy districts have complied with the law by either sending money to the state or transferring it to one of the state's poor school districts. In 2003, 118 wealthy school districts including Glen Rose ISD sent more than $700 million of local tax money to the state for redistribution to poor districts.[15]

? WHAT IS YOUR OPINION?

Is the Robin Hood school-finance reform plan fair?

TABLE 12.2   Financial Information, Highland Park ISD and Edgewood ISD, 2001–2002

Financial Criterion	Highland Park ISD	Edgewood ISD
Taxable value per student	$1,116,216	$38,150
Property tax rate per $100	$1.61	$1.631
Percentage total revenue from the state	3 percent	82 percent
Instructional expenditures per pupil	$3,945	$3,252

Source: Texas Education Agency, **www.tea.state.tx.us.**

Because of the Robin Hood Plan poor districts have more money to spend while wealthy districts have less money. Table 12.2 compares the Highland Park ISD in Dallas, one of the state's wealthiest school districts, with the Edgewood ISD in San Antonio, one of the state's poorest school districts and the lead plaintiff in *Edgewood* v. *Kirby*. Highland Park ISD has nearly 30 times the taxable value per student than Edgewood ISD, $1,116,216 per student to just $38,150 per student in Edgewood ISD. Nonetheless, Edgewood ISD is now able to spend almost as much per pupil on instruction as Highland Park ISD, $3,252 per student for Edgewood compared to $3,945 for Highland Park, primarily because of differences in state funding. Edgewood receives 82 percent of its revenue from the state while Highland Park ISD gets only 3 percent of its money from the state. Highland Park ISD no longer has such a lopsided financial advantage because the Robin Hood Plan forces it to reduce its revenue.

"Many districts are looking at deficit budgets. We will have to severely cut programs or go into deficit spending and eventually use up our fund reserve. Those at the cap are on a crisis cruise."

—John Wilson, Clear Creek ISD

Education finance remains controversial. Many parents and school officials in poor districts believe that funding equality is not enough because the needs of their students are greater. Although the state has achieved funding equality, they believe that it has not achieved funding adequacy. In their view, the state needs to substantially increase education funding and target students most at risk for failure. Parents and school administrators in property rich school districts argue that the Robin Hood Plan prevents them from providing a quality education for the youngsters living in their districts. If wealthy districts raise local taxes to improve their schools, most of the money goes to the state. Furthermore, more than 250 districts have increased their property tax rates to the state maximum of $1.50. They lack the ability to raise additional money to support their schools regardless of the need and the wishes of local taxpayers.[16]

The Texas senate passed a measure overhauling the state's school finance system in the 2003 regular session of the legislature. Although the proposal did not pass the house, it could serve as a model for future legislative action. The senate plan would replace most local property taxes with a state property tax of $0.75 per $100. The state would raise additional money for education by increasing and expanding the state sales tax. School district voters would have the option of adopting a $0.10 per $100 local property tax to provide additional money for local schools.[17]

Issues in Education Policy

Education issues are an important part of the official policy agenda of the state of Texas. We will discuss five of the more prominent contemporary educational issues: charter schools, parental choice, class size, bilingual education, and basic skills testing.

Charter Schools   Texas is one of 39 states that have charter schools.[18] A **charter school** is a publicly funded but privately managed school that operates under the terms of a formal contract or charter with the state. Parents, teachers, private companies, and nonprofit organizations may petition the state for a charter to create a school. The charter spells out the school's educational programs, targets the student population the school hopes to serve, defines the school's management style, and identifies its educational goals. Each charter school is independent in that it is not part of an independent school district. Parents from any district may voluntarily choose to send their children to a charter school. Charter schools are open enrollment because they can accept students from any district. Charter schools may not discriminate on the basis of race, ethnicity, gender, disability, or educational need, but they may refuse to accept a student who has a history of misbehavior. A charter school may not charge tuition or levy taxes. Instead, its funding comes from the state through the Foundation School Program. In 2002, 181 charter schools serving more than 47,000 students operated in the state.[19]

Charter schools are exempt from most state education regulations. They must conform to health and safety codes and teach the state-required curriculum, but they do not have to conform to state regulations concerning class sizes, teacher qualifications, and the school calendar. Nonetheless, the state evaluates charter schools on the same basis as other schools, including TAKS, and on the basis of the goals the schools set for themselves. If a charter school performs poorly and fails to meet its goals, it risks losing its charter and having to close its doors.

Charter schools are controversial. Their supporters believe that each charter school is an opportunity for educational innovation. Teachers can do their jobs better when free of red tape, they say. In contrast, the critics of charter schools argue that they are a back-door method for funneling public money from the public schools to private schools. State funds should be used to improve the existing schools rather than support an untested educational experiment.

The charter school experiment in Texas has had mixed results so far. Although the students in some charter schools show excellent academic progress, charter school students as a whole have not performed as well on the TAAS and TAKS as their public school counterparts. In 2002, nearly a fourth of the state's low-performing schools were charters.[20] The defenders of charter schools point out that many of the students who attend charter schools have a history of failure in public schools, so it would be unfair to expect them to catch up in only a few years. As charter schools establish themselves in their communities, they say, the performance of their students will improve.[21]

"The world of charter schools in Texas . . . shows the full range from those doing brilliantly to those that are embarrassments and probably will be closed."
—Chase Untermeyer, State Board of Education

Parental Choice   The educational concept that allowing parents to choose which school their children attend will lead to an improvement in educational quality because schools will compete for students is known as **parental choice.** Under a parental choice program, the state would give parents a voucher that would provide a type of scholarship to be paid to the school that the parents select for their child to attend. Some proponents of parental choice would allow parents to choose not only among public schools but also among private schools.

Parental choice is controversial. The proponents of parental choice believe that competition for funding would force schools to improve. If low-quality public schools did not upgrade the quality of their educational programs, they would have to shut down for lack of funding. In contrast, the opponents of parental choice question whether lack of competition is the main problem with public schools, believing instead that poverty, lack of parental involvement, and inadequate funding are the primary causes of poor school performance. They fear that vouchers would enable middle-class parents to take their children from public schools, leaving the children of poor families behind in public schools with even less funding. Public schools would get worse, they say, not better.

The Texas legislature has created a limited program of parental choice. The parents of students in schools that are rated "Low Performing" in two of the last three years can transfer their children to any other public school that will agree to receive them, including charter schools. In 2001, Texas had 100 low-performing schools with more than 46,000 students. Students who transfer bring with them their state funding.[22]

? WHAT IS YOUR OPINION?

If you were a parent of a student in a low-performing public school, would you transfer your child to another school?

Class Size   Does size matter? Some advocates of education reform believe that the key to improving education is to have smaller classes. The concept is fairly simple: teachers can do a better job if they have fewer students in a class. In recent years, some state legislatures have mandated smaller class sizes, especially in the early grades.

Critics argue that the movement to reduce class size may not be a good use of resources. Reducing class size is an expensive reform because it requires school districts to hire additional teachers. Furthermore, the research on the effect of smaller class sizes is unclear. Studies show that class sizes must drop to 15–17 students to make much difference and even then smaller classes only seem to make a difference in student performance in the lower grades. Critics of the smaller class movement believe that the money could be better spent on teacher training.

Bilingual Education   Bilingual education is the teaching of academic subjects in both English and the student's native language, usually Spanish. Almost an eighth of the

GETTING INVOLVED

Helping a Child Learn

Nothing is more rewarding than helping a child learn. Most school districts have tutoring programs where volunteers assist students trying to learn to read or understand mathematics. Call your local school district (the number is in the telephone book) and volunteer to tutor.

It's your community—get involved!

state's 4.1 million public-school children have limited proficiency in the English language, including 29 percent in Dallas ISD, 26 percent in Houston ISD, and 23 percent in El Paso ISD.[23] Spanish is by far the most common language spoken by Texas children who have limited English-language skills, although Texas youngsters speak more than 50 languages at home.[24]

Bilingual education is a controversial education policy issue. The advocates of bilingual education believe that it enables students whose primary language is not English to learn academic subjects in their own language while they work on their English. Otherwise, they would fall behind, grow frustrated with school, and potentially drop out. Students enrolled in bilingual education programs typically take several years to learn to read, write, and speak English well enough to enter mainstream classes. In contrast, the opponents of bilingual education argue that it retards the English language development of non-English speaking students. They believe that students with limited English-language proficiency are better served by a period of intensive English instruction after which they enter regular academic classes.

The battle over bilingual education in California led to the passage of **Proposition 227,** which was a California state ballot measure passed in 1998 which was designed to outlaw bilingual education in the state. Non-English speaking students would be given no more than a year of English-language immersion after which they would be moved to regular classes. Proposition 227 was adopted through the **initiative process,** which is a procedure whereby citizens can propose the adoption of a policy measure by gathering a prerequisite number of signatures. Election officials then place the measure on the ballot for approval by the voters.

Texas schools use a mixture of bilingual education and English-language immersion programs. The legislature has neither mandated bilingual education nor prohibited its use. Instead, each district decides how it can best meet the educational needs of students with limited English-language proficiency. Furthermore, bilingual education has not become as much a political football in Texas as it did in California when Republican Governor Pete Wilson used the issue to advance his presidential ambitions. In contrast, most Texas officials have taken a moderate position on the issue.

> "We've got a lot of first-generation Spanish-speaking students who come in, and the bilingual program may be just what's needed to help them transition to the English language."
> —George W. Bush, former governor of Texas

Basic Skills Testing Texas is the model for the **No Child Left Behind Act** of 2001, which is the federal law that requires state governments and local school districts to

LEARNING EXERCISE

Comparing School Districts

The largest school districts in the state are Aldine ISD (Harris County), Arlington ISD, Austin ISD, Cypress-Fairbanks ISD (Harris County), Dallas ISD, El Paso ISD, Fort Bend ISD, Fort Worth ISD, Garland ISD, Houston ISD, North East ISD (Bexar), Northside ISD (Bexar County), and San Antonio ISD. Each of these districts has 50,000 or more students. Your assignment is to select two of the state's largest school districts and write an essay in which you compare and contrast the two districts. You can find a great deal of data about the state's school districts in a feature called Snapshot, which can be found at the website of the Texas Education Agency (TEA): **www.tea.state.tx.us/perfreport/snapshot/index.html.**

Your essay should cover the following topics:

- **A demographic profile of each district:** How do the two districts compare in terms of size? What is each district's racial/ethnic profile? What proportion of each district's students has special needs of one sort or another?

- **A funding profile of each district:** How do the districts compare in terms of tax base? What are their tax rates? How much revenue does each district raise per student? How much state aid does each district receive?

- **A profile of each district's teachers:** How experienced are the two faculties? Does each district have a diverse group of faculty? How well paid are each district's teachers?

- **A performance evaluation:** How well do the students of each district perform on TAAS and other tests? What is each district's accountability rating?

Conclude your essay with a discussion of the strengths and weaknesses of each district. Consider whether it is possible to determine which district is more effective. Keep in mind that the challenges facing the two districts are not the same and the resources available may not be identical either.

---

institute basic skills testing as a condition for receiving federal aid. The law requires state governments and local school districts to institute basic skills testing in reading and mathematics for students in grades three through eight as a condition for receiving federal aid. The results of the tests must be used to assess school performance and track the progress of individual students. Poor performing schools that fail to improve will eventually lose federal aid money.

President Bush and other advocates of basic skills testing believe that the success of TAAS demonstrates the value of mandating a similar approach nationwide. They point to a steady improvement in TAAS scores as evidence that the system is working. In 2002, 82.3 percent of students passed TAAS, the highest passing rate ever. Test scores for African American and Latino students in particular have increased significantly since TAAS testing began in 1994.[25] Testing advocates believe that Texas students will continue to improve their academic performance because the state has introduced a new, more challenging curriculum and a new test, TAKS, to measure student mastery of it.

The critics of basic skills testing believe that higher TAAS scores show that school administrators have learned to game the system rather than demonstrate true academic achievement. TAAS scores have gone up, they say, because schools "teach the test" and assign growing numbers of marginal students to special education

> "We're testing more students and the passing rate is rising. That's a clear sign that performance is improving in our schools."
>
> —Jim Nelson, Texas Education Commissioner

The Texas Education Agency uses test scores and other factors to rate schools as exemplary, recognized, acceptable, or low performing.

classes where they escape testing. Between 1994 and 1998, the number of special education students in Texas increased by 60 percent.[26]

Independent assessments of the performance of Texas are less positive than a decade of rising TAAS scores would suggest. Texas students lag behind their counterparts in other states in their performance on the Scholastic Assessment Test (SAT), which is a standardized exam taken by students planning to apply for admission to a university. In 2002, the average SAT score in Texas was 991, ranking the Lone Star State 48th among the 50 states, and Texas is falling further behind. Over the last decade, the average SAT score in the United States has gone up by 19 points compared to an increase of only 12 points in Texas.[27] In the meantime, the dropout rate in Texas is apparently much higher than the state's official data indicate. Whereas the Houston ISD reports an annual dropout rate of 1.5 percent, an independent study estimates that nearly half of the students entering Houston high schools as freshmen quit before graduation. In fact, three of the worst school districts in the nation for high school graduation are in Texas—Houston, Dallas, and Fort Worth.[28] The state dropout rate is 39 percent.[29]

Texas does an average job at best in preparing students for college. The National Center for Public Policy and Higher Education graded states in five areas: preparing schoolchildren for college, participation of state residents in higher education, affordability of college, how promptly students finish degrees, and the economic and social benefits to a state of an educated population. Texas got a C in

"The Texas miracle in education is a myth."
—Walter Haney,
Boston College
education researcher

preparation, affordability, and benefits. It earned a D in participation and a D+ in completion of degrees. Poor people and minorities fared worse in getting a higher education than did non-Hispanic Whites.[30]

SPECIAL DISTRICTS

A **special district** is a unit of local government created to perform specific functions. Soil and water conservation districts, for example, work to prevent soil erosion and preserve water resources. Levee improvement districts build and maintain levees. Coastal subsidence districts regulate the use of subsurface water resources in order to minimize **subsidence,** which is the sinking of the surface of the land caused by the too-rapid extraction of subsurface water. Mosquito control districts spray for mosquitoes to control annoying pests and reduce the danger of encephalitis and other diseases spread by mosquitoes.

Special districts provide important governmental services to millions of Texans. A **utility district** is a special district that provides utilities such as water and sewer service to residents living in unincorporated urban areas. Texas has more than 1,100 utility districts, going by such names as Fresh Water Supply Districts (FWSDs), Water Control and Improvement Districts (WCIDs), and Municipal Utility Districts (MUDs). The latter are the most numerous. In addition to water and sewer services, utility districts may also provide their residents with solid waste collection, fire protection, drainage, parks, and recreation facilities. A **hospital district** is a special district that provides emergency medical services, indigent health care, and community health services. The Harris County Hospital District is the primary medical provider for nearly a million residents in Harris County who do not have health insurance. The largest hospital districts in the state (in Harris, Dallas, and Tarrant Counties) all have budgets well in excess of $100 million a year.[31] Community/junior college districts enroll more students in higher education than do the state's public universities. Flood control districts are responsible for flood control in many areas of the state.

Reasons for Special Districts

Special districts are created to provide services that other units of local government cannot or will not provide. For example, state law specifies a maximum property tax rate for counties and cities. Local governments can overcome the property tax ceiling by creating special districts with their own taxing authority. Harris County has a flood control district, hospital district, and port authority. Although they are separate units of government with their own taxing authority, Harris County Commissioners Court controls them. Transit authorities and port authorities are other big-budget special districts whose operations could not easily be financed within the budget constraints of existing city and county governments.

Sometimes special districts are an advantageous approach to solving problems that transcend the boundaries of existing units of local government. Flooding is seldom confined to a single county or city. A countywide or areawide flood control district offers a regional approach to a regional problem. Similarly, transportation problems may affect several cities and counties. In each of these cases, it is often easier to create a special district that includes the whole area affected by the problem than it is to coordinate the efforts of existing governments.

Other motivations for the establishment of special districts include political expediency and financial gain. At times, existing units of local government refuse to provide certain services because of the opposition of individual officeholders. Special districts can be an effective means of outflanking that opposition. Some problems, such as flood control or mass transit, may become so difficult or controversial that local officials may choose to ignore them. The creation of a special district allows officials to pass the buck while taking credit for having taken the problem "out of politics."

Utility districts enable developers to build subdivisions in rural areas, outside of the coverage of municipal water and sewer services. The utility district borrows money to build water and sewer systems for the development. Homeowners pay off the debt over time through service charges and property taxes. By using a utility district to defer the construction cost of a water and sewer system, developers are able to reduce their upfront construction expenditures while consumers can buy new homes less expensively than if the utility costs were built into the purchase price.[32]

Creation, Organization, and Operation

Special districts are created through a variety of procedures. Hospital districts require the adoption of a constitutional amendment. The State Soil and Water Conservation Board creates soil and water conservation districts. The legislature, Texas Commission on Enviromental Quality (TCEQ), or a county commissioners court can establish utility districts. Utility districts that are to be located in a city's extraterritorial jurisdiction must first be approved by that city. The Texas legislature authorizes community/junior college districts, transit authorities, port authorities, and sports authorities.

Most districts require voter approval of area residents before they can go into operation. After the legislature authorizes the creation of a utility district, for example, the measure goes on the ballot for approval by voters living within the boundaries of the proposed district. At the same election, voters may also be asked to grant the district authority to sell bonds (i.e., borrow money) and to tax. Utility districts generally issue bonds to finance the construction of sewage treatment plants. Flood control districts use them to pay for drainage improvements. Airport authorities use bond money to build runways and terminals. Sports authorities issue bonds to finance the construction of stadiums for football and baseball and arenas for hockey and basketball.

A board of directors, usually consisting of five members, is the governing body for most special districts. The board may be either appointed or elected. District voters elect most water district and community/junior college boards. City mayors appoint housing authority boards. The governor names the directors of river authorities. County commissioner courts select hospital, noxious weed control, and rural fire prevention district boards. In most cases, district board members are unsalaried. They set basic policy but leave the day-to-day operation of the district to a professional staff. Perhaps the most important task for the board of trustees of a community/junior college district, for example, is to hire a chancellor or president to manage the daily affairs of the college.

Funding

Special districts receive funding from a variety of sources. Many districts levy taxes. Utility districts, port authorities, hospital districts, flood control districts, and community/junior college districts all levy property taxes. Suburban utility districts often assess higher property tax rates than do nearby incorporated municipalities. The funding for sports authorities may come from sales taxes, hotel/motel occupancy taxes, property taxes, or taxes on rental cars. Transit authorities levy sales taxes.

Special districts raise revenues from service charges. Utility districts charge residents for water and sewer usage and for garbage pickup. Students in community/junior college districts pay tuition and fees for the classes they take. Transit authorities raise revenues from ticket charges. Toll road authorities collect tolls from drivers. Funding for coastal subsidence districts comes from fees charged for permits to drill water wells.

Finally, special districts receive funding from other units of government. Federal mass transit aid supports the state's transit authorities. Community/junior college districts benefit from state funding and federal grant money. Hospital districts receive both federal and state funding to support their programs.

Evaluation of Special Districts

Special districts have both defenders and critics. Their supporters argue that they provide services that otherwise would not be available. In contrast, critics identify several problem areas. First, special districts often operate in the shadows, with little state supervision and even less public participation. For example, fewer than a dozen voters may participate in utility district authorization elections. Second, special districts generally operate less efficiently than general-purpose units of local government such as cities and counties.[33] Small districts, particularly utility districts, can be uneconomical. Their operations are often run amateurishly and they are too small to take advantage of economies of scale. The average cost of waste disposal for utility districts is more than twice that incurred by large cities, such as Houston or Dallas.[34] Finally, the multiplicity of special districts in Texas complicates the problems of urban government. For example, many observers believe that utility districts are a major cause of land subsidence in the Houston-Galveston area because of their extensive use of subsurface water resources.

CONCLUSION: LOCAL GOVERNMENT AND PUBLIC POLICY

An influential book on urban policymaking in America is titled *City Limits*.[35] The author's point is that forces beyond local control are primarily responsible for shaping urban-development policy. The same can be said about local policymaking in general. Counties, school districts, special districts, and cities must operate within constraints imposed by the federal and state governments and by the economic environment.

The federal government shapes local policymaking through conditions attached to the provision of federal funds. Every unit of local government receiving federal money—and that includes nearly every city, county, and school district, and many special districts—must conform to federal guidelines on nondiscrimination, equal access for the disabled, environmental protection, historic preservation, union wage rates for construction projects, and buy-American requirements. Schools and other public buildings must be accessible to the disabled. Flood control districts are required to prepare environmental impact statements before beginning projects. Transit authorities are obliged to purchase buses equipped with wheelchair lifts.

Federal court orders place other limits on localities. In 1980, Federal District Judge William Wayne Justice ordered Texas public schools to provide bilingual education in all school grades. A federal appeals court subsequently modified Justice's ruling, instead accepting a program that provided for bilingual education for kindergarten through the elementary grades in school districts with 20 or more students with English-language deficiencies in the same grade. School districts would have to provide bilingual classes or intensive English training in junior high school, and intensive English in high school.[36] Other federal court orders have required county jails to reduce overcrowding and forced school districts to integrate racially.

State government also limits policymaking at the local level. State laws and regulations determine the structures of local government and the scope of local authority. In some areas, state laws are restrictive and specific. Counties, for example, must seek constitutional amendments in order to modify their structures of government. Because counties lack ordinance-making authority, they must receive legislative approval to take such relatively trivial actions as prohibiting the use of fireworks or raising the speed limit on a county road.

Political scientists who study local governments believe that economic factors have considerable influence over local policymaking. Studies have found that the level of municipal expenditures correlates closely with a city's average per capita income. Wealthier cities spend more for public services than do poorer cities.[37] The same can be said for many other units of local government, such as counties and special districts. School district spending is less dependent on local financial resources because of the impact of state school funding reforms.

Nonetheless, it is misleading to suggest that local policymaking is completely determined by outside forces. The relationship between local governments and state and federal authorities is not a one-way street with localities always on the receiving end of instructions from the state and national capitals. Local governments lobby Austin and Washington, D.C., frequently with good effect. After all, representatives elected to the state legislature and to Congress are elected locally from districts that include cities, counties, school districts, and other units of local government. A member of Congress or the Texas legislature chosen from a district located in Dallas, for example, will likely be responsive to the concerns of Dallas County, the city of Dallas, the Dallas ISD, the Dallas Area Rapid Transit Authority (DART), and other school districts and special districts in the area.

In sum, local governments are limited governments. They are at the bottom of the legal structures of American government and, accordingly, must conform to the rules and regulations established by higher levels of government. The policy options of local officials are further constrained by their area's level of economic development. Still, local officials have room to make meaningful policy decisions within the boundaries established by outside forces.

★ REVIEW QUESTIONS

1. Why is basic skills testing controversial?
2. How do counties compare with cities in terms of legal status and governmental powers?
3. What are the most important functions of county government?
4. Who are the elected officials of county government and what do they do?
5. How are county governments funded?
6. What are the strengths and weaknesses of county government?
7. What roles do boards of trustees and superintendents play in managing public education in Texas?
8. How are public schools in Texas funded?
9. What was the impact of *Edgewood v. Kirby* on education funding in Texas?
10. Which of the educational reforms discussed in your textbook do you think is the most effective? Why?
11. What sorts of services do special districts provide?
12. What are the advantages and disadvantages of special district government in Texas?
13. Why are units of local government considered "limited governments?"

★ KEY TERMS

bilingual education
charter school
commissioners court
conflict of interest
federal grant-in-aid programs
Foundation School Program
general-law units of local government
home rule
hospital district
independent school districts (ISDs)

initiative process
long ballot
No Child Left Behind Act
nonpartisan election
ordinance
parental choice
partisan election
Permanent School Fund (PSF)
poll tax
Proposition 227
Robin Hood Plan

School Lunch Program
special district
subpoena
subsidence
tax increment financing
Texas Assessment of Academic Skills (TAAS)
Texas Assessment of Knowledge and Skills (TAKS)
utility district

★ NOTES

1. Greg Mt. Joy, "Taking the TAKS," *Fiscal Notes* (October 2002): 1, 6–7.
2. Greg Winter, "More Schools Rely on Tests, but Study Raises Doubts," *New York Times*, December 28, 2002, available at **www.nytimes.com**.
3. U.S. Bureau of the Census, available at **www.census.gov**.
4. Office of Management Services, Harris County, Texas, available at **www.co.harris.tx.us**.
5. Bob Sablatura, "Contractual Friendships," *Houston Chronicle*, March 24, 1998, p. 1A, 6A.
6. Texas Education Agency, available at **www.tea.state .tx.us**.
7. John M. Bolland and Kent D. Redfield, "The Limits of Citizen Participation in Local Education: A Cognitive Interpretation," *Journal of Politics* 50 (November 1988): 1033–46.
8. Rebecca Winters, "A Job for a Super Hero?" *Time*, February 7, 2000, p. 70.
9. Jim Henderson, "Dallas School Trustees Left Holding Bag Again," *Houston Chronicle*, July 9, 2000, pp. 1A, 21A.
10. Texas Education Agency, *Texas Permanent School Fund, Annual Report, Fiscal Year Ending August 31, 2002*, available at **www.tea.state.tx.us/psf/**.
11. Texas Education Agency, "Snapshot 2002, School District Profiles," available at **www.tea.state.tx.us**.
12. *Financing Public Education in Texas*, 2nd ed., available at **www.lbb.state.tx.us**.
13. "Snapshot 2002, School District Profiles."
14. *Edgewood v. Kirby*, 777 S.W.2d 391 (1989).
15. *Financing Public Education in Texas*, 2nd ed., available at **www.lbb.state.tx.us**.
16. Cindy Horswell, "Schools Struggle with Tax Caps," *Houston Chronicle*, September 22, 2002, pp. 35A.
17. John Kirsch, "New School Finance Plan Unveiled," *Fort Worth Star-Telegram*, May 1, 2002, available at **www.dfw .com.**
18. Charlotte C. Portlewaite, "School Choice Gains Momentum," *State Government News*, (June/July 2003): 29.
19. Janet Elliott and Melanie Markley, "Despite Hopes, Trouble Plagues Charter Schools," *Houston Chronicle*, June 24, 2002, available at **www.houstonchronicle.com**.
20. Melanie Markley, "Many State Charter Schools Rated Low," *Houston Chronicle*, August 3, 2002, p. A35.
21. Kenneth J. Cooper, "For Texas Charter Schools, Shaky Grades," *Washington Post National Weekly Edition*, October 23, 2000, pp. 13–14.
22. "2002 Accountability Manual," Texas Education Agency, available at **www.tea.state.tx.us**.
23. "Snapshot 2002, School District Profiles."
24. Alan Bernstein, "Bilingual Debate Has Texas Twang," *Houston Chronicle*, May 25, 1998, pp. 1A, 16A.
25. Texas Education Agency, "2001–2002 State Performance Report," available at **www.tea.state.tx.us**.
26. Jake Bernstein, "Test Case: Hard Lessons from the TAAS," *Texas Observer*, August 30, 2002, p. 5.
27. Joshua Benton, "TAKS Exposes the Grade Divide," *Dallas Morning News*," June 5, 2003, available at **www.dallasnews .com**.
28. Diana Jean Schemo, "Education Secretary Defends School System He Once Led," *New York Times*, July 26, 2003, available at **www.nytimes.com**.
29. Sharon K. Hughes, "Study Claims 39 percent Drop Out," *San Antonio Express-News*, October 31, 2002, available at **www.mysanantonio.com**.
30. National Center for Public Policy and Higher Education, "Measuring Up 2000: The State by State Report Card for Higher Education," available at **www.highereducation .org/**.
31. Joe Stinebaker, "The Painful Truth," *Houston Chronicle*, July 25, 1999, p. 35A.
32. Paula Lavigne, "Will Sprouting of MUDs Make Mess?" *Dallas Morning News*, October 26, 2003, available at **www.dallasnews.com.**
33. Kathryn A. Foster, *The Political Economy of Special-Purpose Government* (Washington, DC: Georgetown University Press, 1997), pp. 174–83.
34. David W. Tees, "A Fresh Look at Special Districts in Texas." In *Governmental Organization and Authority in Metropolitan Areas* (Arlington: Texas Urban Development Commission, 1971), p. 50; and Virginia Marion Perrenod, *Special Districts, Special Purposes* (College Station: Texas A&M University Press, 1984), p. 76.
35. Paul E. Peterson, *City Limits* (Chicago: University of Chicago Press, 1981).
36. *Houston Post*, July 13, 1982, pp. 1A, 9A.
37. Peterson, pp. 50–64.

ONLINE PRACTICE TEST

Test your understanding of this chapter
with interactive review quizzes at

www.ablongman.com/tannahilltexas/chapter12

State Budget Policy

LEARNING OBJECTIVES

After studying Chapter 13, students should be able to do the following:

★ Summarize the arguments for and against a personal income tax.

★ Identify the most important revenue sources for the state of Texas, including both tax and nontax sources, and trace changes in the relative importance of those sources over the last 20 years.

★ Compare and contrast the tax structure of Texas with the tax structures in other states.

★ Evaluate the tax system in Texas in terms of burden, fairness, and elasticity.

★ Identify and evaluate the various policy options proposed for reforming the state's tax structure.

★ Identify the most important spending priorities for the state of Texas and trace changes in the

relative importance of those priorities over the last 20 years.

★ Describe the issues involved in the longstanding controversy over school finance.

★ Describe the Medicaid and CHIP programs.

★ Identify the primary funding sources for higher education in Texas.

★ Describe the state's welfare program.

★ Compare and contrast state funding trends for the following programs: health care, higher education, transportation, and corrections.

★ Trace the steps in the state budgetary process.

★ Analyze the budgetary process using the policymaking model.

★ Define the key terms listed on p. 376 and explain their significance.

Should Texas have a personal income tax? Texas is one of only seven states (Alaska, Florida, Nevada, South Dakota, Washington, and Wyoming are the others) without one. Those who support the adoption of a state income tax make a number of points in its favor. First, they argue that the state's tax system, which relies heavily on consumer taxes, is incapable of generating sufficient revenue to meet the growing demand for state services. Although some segments of the state's economy are taxed heavily, other sectors of the economy escape taxation almost entirely. As a result, the legislature periodically faces a budget shortfall because the cost of public education, health care, criminal justice, higher education, highway construction, and other state services has gone up faster than the revenues have grown to pay for them. Income-tax supporters believe that a personal income tax would more accurately mirror growth in the economy, thus producing more revenue for state government. Furthermore, the growth of Internet sales, which are not currently subject to state taxation, undermines the sales tax as a foundation for a healthy state tax system.

Second, the supporters of a personal income tax think that it would be a fairer way to raise revenue than the state's current tax system. They note that most economists believe that sales taxes, property taxes, and taxes on gasoline, tobacco, and alcohol fall more heavily on the poor than on other income groups because poor people spend a relatively greater proportion of their earnings on items subject to those taxes than do wealthier individuals. In contrast, an income tax can be designed to spread the tax burden equally among income groups or, if policymakers wish, to tax persons with higher incomes at a greater rate.

Third, federal tax policy favors state income taxes over sales taxes and other forms of taxation. In computing the amount of income tax owed to the federal government, individuals may deduct money paid in state income taxes from their total taxable income, thus reducing the amount of tax they owe. In contrast, sales and excise taxes are not deductible.

Texans who oppose the adoption of a state income tax respond to the points made by income tax advocates with a number of arguments. They belittle the importance of deducting state income tax payments from the federal income tax because the deduction would benefit only those individuals who use the long form in filing their income tax return. Most low- and middle-income taxpayers use the short form, and thus would be unable to take advantage of the deduction. Furthermore, Congress could repeal the deduction for state income tax payments just as it earlier repealed a deduction for state sales tax payments.

The critics of the income tax question its fairness. Because of loopholes and deductions, they say, wealthy individuals have often avoided paying federal income taxes, leaving the tax burden on the backs of middle- and lower-income people. Who would guarantee that a state income tax would be implemented fairly?

Finally, the opponents of a state income tax believe that the real goal of its supporters is to raise revenue to pay for a bigger, more intrusive state government. Instead of replacing or reducing the state sales tax or local property taxes, they predict that a personal income tax would merely supplement other taxes. In the long run, they warn, the adoption of a state income tax would lead to higher taxes for *all* Texans, not just the wealthy.

REVENUES

During the 2002 **fiscal year** (i.e., budget year), the state of Texas generated $55.2 billion in revenue from all sources, including both taxes and nontax sources of revenue. Table 13.1 identifies the various sources of state revenue and indicates their relative importance. Because the table includes data for fiscal years 1983, 1993, and 2002, it also shows changes in the relative importance of revenue sources across time.

Taxes

The state of Texas raises almost half of its total revenue from taxes. The general sales tax is by far the most important state tax source, generating substantially more money than any other tax source. The other major state taxes include a tax on motor vehicle sales and rental, a motor fuels tax, and a corporation franchise tax.

TABLE 13.1   State Revenues by Source, Fiscal Years 1983, 1993, and 2002

Tax Sources of State Revenue as a Percentage of Total Revenue			
Source	1983	1993	2002
General sales tax	24.3 %	27.0 %	26.3 %
Motor vehicle sales and rental	4.3	4.2	5.3
Motor fuels tax	3.6	6.2	5.1
Corporation franchise tax	4.1	3.5	3.5
Taxes on alcohol and tobacco products	4.6	3.0	2.0
Insurance company tax	1.6	1.4	1.9
Severance taxes on oil and gas production	16.6	3.4	1.7
Inheritance tax	0.7	0.4	0.6
Utility taxes	1.7	0.7	0.6
Other taxes	0.1	0.5	0.6
Total Taxes	**62.6 %**	**50.3 %**	**47.6 %**
Nontax Sources of State Revenue as a Percentage of Total Revenue			
Source	1983	1993	2002
Federal funds	21.0 %	29.2 %	32.9 %
Licenses and fees	4.0	6.1	7.9
Interest and investment income	5.9	6.4	3.1
Net lottery proceeds	—	3.3	2.5
Land income	4.3	0.7	0.6
Other nontax revenue	2.2	4.0	5.4
Total nontax sources of revenue	**37.4 %**	**49.7 %**	**52.4 %**
Total net revenue (tax and nontax sources combined)	**100 %** ($13.6 billion)	**100 %** ($33.8 billion)	**100 %** ($55.2 billion)

Source: Texas Comptroller of Public Accounts, "Revenue by Source," various years, available at **www.cpa.state.tx.us**.

The relative importance of taxes to the state's revenue picture has declined over the last 20 years. As Table 13.1 indicates, the proportion of state revenue generated by taxes has fallen from more than 60 percent in 1983 to less than 48 percent in 2002. The trend does not reflect a decline in tax revenues. The legislature and the governor have increased various tax rates and most tax revenues have also increased because of economic growth. Taxes have declined as a source of state revenue relative to total revenues because of the rapid growth of nontax sources of revenue, especially federal funds. Since 1983, federal funds have increased from 21 percent of state revenues to 32.9 percent. Most of the growth in federal funds has been through the **Medicaid program,** which is a federal program designed to provide health insurance coverage to poor people, the disabled, and elderly Americans who are impoverished.

> "Taxes are the price we pay for civilization."
> —Oliver Wendell Holmes, early twentieth century American jurist

General Sales Tax   A **sales tax** is a levy on the retail sale of taxable items. Texas has a relatively high sales tax rate. In 2000, the average Texan paid $1,275 in sales taxes, the 9th highest sales tax bite in the nation.[1] The state levies a sales tax rate of 6.25 percent on the retail purchase of taxable items. Cities and other units of local government may add as much as 2 percent more to the state tax rate, bringing the total sales tax in many areas of the state to 8.25 percent.

Not all sales are subject to taxation. Although restaurant meals are taxable, food purchased at a grocery store is tax exempt (except for ready-to-eat items). The sale of most agricultural items is tax exempt, including the sale of agricultural machinery and parts, fertilizer, feed for animals, and seed. Drugs and medicine are exempt as well, whether sold over-the-counter or by prescription. Only some services are taxable. The list of taxable services includes charges for laundry, dry cleaning, cable television service, credit reporting, data processing, debt collection, landscaping, security, telecommunications, car repair, and janitorial services. The sales tax does not apply, however, to charges and fees for many other services, including legal retainers, accounting services, builder and contractor fees, real estate commissions, brokerage fees, and health care charges.

The growth of Internet sales is undermining the state sales tax base. State governments cannot legally compel an Internet or mail order retailer to collect its sales tax unless the retailer has a physical presence in the state. Sears, for example, charges sales tax on purchases made by Texas consumers because Sears has stores throughout the state whereas L.L.Bean, an Internet and mail order retailer based in Maine with no outlets in the Lone Star State, does not. By 2011, Texas may lose as much as 10 percent of its total expected sales tax collection to Internet sales.[2]

Excise Taxes   An **excise tax** is a tax levied on the manufacture, transportation, sale, or consumption of a particular item or set of related items. It is a selective sales tax. Texas state government levies excise taxes on motor vehicle sales and rentals, motor fuels, alcohol, and tobacco. In 2002, the state's various excise taxes collectively generated more than 12 percent of state revenue, a figure that has not changed appreciably in the last 20 years.

Many states have recently increased excise tax rates, especially taxes on tobacco products and alcoholic beverages. By raising sin taxes, states hope not just to raise revenue but also to discourage people from smoking and drinking, especially

TEXAS ONLINE ★ Forces of Change

Sales Tax Information Online

The sales tax confuses many Texans because rates vary from city to city and because the rules as to what items are taxable are complex. The sales tax rate varies from 6.25 percent to 8.25 percent, depending on the area because local governments have the option of piggybacking sales taxes of their own on top of the state rate. Furthermore, anyone who has ever worked as a clerk knows how difficult it can be to remember which items are taxable and which are not.

The Texas Comptroller of Public Accounts has a website with information on the sales tax:

www.cpa.state.tx.us/taxinfo/salestax.html

Review the information and answer the following questions.

QUESTIONS TO CONSIDER

1. What is the sales tax rate where you live?
2. Do charitable organizations have to pay sales taxes on their purchases?
3. Are children required to collect a tax on the sale of candy or cookies when they are attempting to raise money for a school activity?

> "Either people quit smoking, which is good for everyone, or their habits help us balance the budget."
> —California Assembly Speaker Herb Wesson, defending a proposal to increase cigarette taxes

teenagers. A **sin tax** is a levy on an activity that some people consider morally objectionable, such as smoking or drinking. Fourteen states now have a per pack tax on cigarettes of $1 or more. The cigarette tax in Massachusetts is $1.51 per pack.[3]

In contrast to other states, Texas has not recently increased its excise tax rates, which are now relatively low, especially the state's sin taxes. The cigarette tax in Texas is 41 cents a pack, well below the rate in most other states. Excise taxes on wine, beer, and liquor in Texas are all well below the national average.[4] In the meantime, the Texas motor fuel tax rate of 20 cents a gallon is near the national average.[5]

? WHAT IS YOUR OPINION?

Should the government increase taxes on tobacco products and alcohol to discourage smoking and drinking?

Corporation Franchise Tax   The **corporation franchise tax,** which is a state levy on corporations, is the primary tax assessed by state government on business. (It is not the *only* business tax in the state, however, because local governments also levy property taxes on business property, such as land, warehouses, manufacturing plants, stores, inventory, and office buildings.) Corporations must pay annually the greater of two amounts: 0.25 percent of their net taxable capital or 4.5 percent of corporate profits reported to the federal government for tax purposes. Because of the latter provision, the franchise tax is essentially a corporate income tax by another name. In 2002, the corporation franchise tax generated 3.5 percent of state revenue.

The franchise tax rate is relatively low and the tax has limited coverage. The tax rate of 4.5 percent of corporate profits is lower than the top tax rate in all but 3 other states that have corporate income taxes.[6] Furthermore, a corporation can escape the tax by reorganizing as a limited liability partnership, which is not subject to the tax. In 2001, only 149,040 companies of the state's 500,000 corporations paid the tax.[7] Dell Computer, SBC Communications, Inc. (the parent company of

Texans pay one of the highest sales taxes in the nation.

Southwestern Bell), Luby's Cafeterias, Bluebell Creameries, and many other companies have become partnerships to avoid paying the corporation franchise tax.[8]

Severance Taxes on Oil and Natural Gas Production   A tax levied on natural resources at the time they are taken from the land or water is known as a **severance tax.** The most important severance taxes in Texas are levied on the production of oil and natural gas. The state collects a 4.6 percent tax on the value of oil produced and 7.5 percent on natural gas, rates that are comparable to those charged by other energy-producing states. Texas also levies severance taxes on the production of cement and the extraction of sulfur.

The importance of severance taxes has diminished considerably over the last 20 years. In 1983, severance taxes on oil and gas generated 16.6 percent of state tax revenues. In the late 1970s in particular, rising oil and gas prices provided a bonanza for the state treasury, as the price of oil jumped from less than $10 a barrel in 1978 to more than $35 a barrel in 1981. Beginning in 1982, however, oil prices dropped, falling below $10 a barrel in 1984. Although prices have since recovered to the $20–$30 range, oil production has been declining in the state for years. As a result, severance taxes on oil and gas have fallen dramatically, generating only 1.7 percent of state revenues in 2002.

Other Taxes In addition to the general sales tax, excise taxes, corporation franchise tax, and severance taxes on oil and gas production, the state of Texas collects a number of other levies. These other taxes include an insurance company tax, utility taxes, and an inheritance tax. No one of these taxes accounts for as much as 2 percent of the state's total revenue, but collectively they are an important part of the state's revenue picture.

The state's tax revenue sources also include taxes on **pari-mutuel wagering,** which is a system for gambling on horse and dog racing. The total amount of money wagered on a horse or dog race is pooled and then divided among those who bet on one of the top three finishers, minus percentages that go to the owners of the winning animals, track management, and the government. In 1987, the legislature authorized pari-mutuel gambling on horse and dog racing pending voter approval in a statewide referendum, which passed by a good margin. The legislature permitted the construction of major horse tracks in the Dallas, Houston, San Antonio, and Fort Worth areas, with smaller tracks allowed in other counties pending local voter approval. The legislature permitted the construction of greyhound racetracks in only three counties—Galveston, Nueces (Corpus Christi), and Cameron (Brownsville). Although some observers predicted that taxes on pari-mutuel wagering would eventually produce as much as $100 million a year, the payoff for the state has been insignificant. In 2002, pari-mutuel wagering generated just under $5 million in state revenue, well less than one-tenth of 1 percent of total state revenues.[9]

? WHAT IS YOUR OPINION?

Should the state of Texas allow gambling on dog and horse racing?

Nontax Sources of Revenue

Nontax sources of revenue now account for a majority of total state revenues.

Federal Funds The federal government is a major funding source for state government in Texas, accounting for nearly a third of state revenues. Medicaid is the largest single source of federal financial aid to state government. Federal money also supports highway construction, a variety of welfare programs, and a broad range of other state activities.

Licenses and Fees Texas state government raises money through the sale of licenses and the collection of fees. Texans who wish to drive motor vehicles, operate businesses, go hunting and fishing, attend a state university, or sell alcoholic beverages must purchase licenses or pay a fee for the privilege. In 2002, licenses and fees accounted for 7.9 percent of state revenue, a figure that has doubled over the last 20 years and will likely continue to rise. Although the legislature did not increase taxes in 2003, it raised fees for lawyers, registered nurses, and tow truck operators. College students will pay more as well because the legislature voted to allow university boards of regents to set their own tuition. Most universities planned to increase tuition to partially make up for state budget cuts.[10]

"We have placed a tax on the college students of this state."
—State Representative Rick Noriega, D., Houston

Taxes on pari-mutuel wagering have so far generated relatively little revenue for the state.

Interest and Investment Income   The state of Texas holds billions of dollars in cash and securities that generate dividend and interest income from investment. The largest pool of money is the **Texas Teacher Retirement System (TRS) Trust Fund,** which is a pension fund for the state's public school teachers. The TRS Trust Fund held $70.9 billion in assets at the end of 2002. Similarly, the **Employees Retirement System (ERS) Trust Fund** is a pension fund for state employees. It was worth $20.6 billion in 2002.[11] The TRS and ERS trust funds provide retirement, disability, and death or survivor benefits to their members.

The Permanent School Fund (PSF) and the Permanent University Fund (PUF) support education. The **Permanent School Fund (PSF)** is a fund established in the Texas Constitution as an endowment to finance public elementary and secondary education. In 2002, the market value of PSF bonds and securities stood at $19 billion. The **Permanent University Fund (PUF)** is a fund established in the Texas Constitution as an endowment to finance construction, maintenance, and some other activities at the University of Texas and Texas A&M University. The value of the PUF in 2002 was $7.8 billion.[12]

The state's interest and investment income varies, depending on the investment climate. In the late 1990s and 2000, the value of the state's various trust funds

NATIONAL PERSPECTIVE

The HOPE Scholarship in Georgia

In Georgia, good students go to college for free. When Georgia instituted a state lottery in 1993, it earmarked the revenue to fund college scholarships called HOPE Scholarships. Any student who maintains a B average in high school is eligible for a full scholarship at any public college or university in the state. The program also provides $3,000 a year to eligible students who attend private schools in the state. As long as students maintain a B average, they can keep their scholarships.

The HOPE Scholarship is a popular program. It rewards students who work hard and gives young people an incentive to concentrate on their schoolwork. Because the program is not based on financial need, it helps middle-class students who would not qualify for financial aid but would nonetheless struggle to afford to attend college. Good students have an incentive to stay in the state to attend college because of the scholarship.

Nonetheless, not everyone believes that the HOPE Scholarship is a good idea. Critics charge that the program has widened the educational gap between low-income African American students in Georgia and middle-class White students. Because middle-class students do better academically than low-income students, they benefit disproportionately from the scholarship. Middle-class students would go to college anyway, even without the scholarship. Critics believe that the scholarship program would be more effective if it targeted economically disadvantaged students rather than everyone regardless of financial need.*

QUESTIONS TO CONSIDER

1. Should Texas dedicate lottery revenues to student scholarships even if it means raising taxes to cover the loss of revenue?

2. Do you believe that scholarships should be awarded on the basis of need or the basis of merit (good grades)?

3. Is the HOPE Scholarship a good idea?

*Michael A. Fletcher, "College Aid for the Middle Class?" *Washington Post National Weekly Edition,* June 17–23, 2002, p. 31.

grew as the stock market soared. In 2000, interest and investment income accounted for 3.8 percent of total state revenues. When the stock market slumped in 2001 and 2002, the value of the assets held in the various investment funds fell and the amount of income they generated declined.[13] Interest and investment income represented only 3.1 percent of state revenues in 2002.[14]

Land Income The state of Texas owns more than 20 million acres of land that produce revenue for the state from leases for agricultural use and for oil and gas production. The PSF and PUF hold the largest blocks of land—13 million acres and 2.1 million acres respectively.[15] Income from land held by the PSF and PUF is invested in stocks, bonds, and other securities, which, in turn, generate interest and investment income. In 2002, land income accounted for 0.6 percent of state revenue.

> "Lotteries are a false promise for education."
> —Donald E. Miller and Patrick A. Pierce, political scientists

Lottery Revenue Texas is one of 38 states with a lottery. Since it began operation in 1992, the Texas Lottery has generated more than $10 billion for the state.[16] As Table 13.1 indicates, the lottery accounted for 2.5 percent of state revenues in 2002.

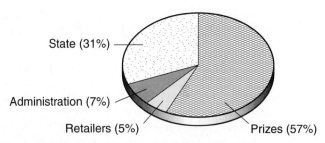

FIGURE 13.1 **Distribution of Lottery Proceeds**
Source: Texas Lottery Commission

Figure 13.1 shows the distribution of money spent on the lottery. A bit more than half of the money that Texans pay for lottery tickets goes for prizes. After sub-tracting money for administration and to compensate retailers for selling lottery tickets, the state realizes 31 percent in revenue of every dollar spent on the lottery.

Lottery proceeds go into the Foundation School Program. When the lottery was created, the legislature funneled lottery earnings into the **General Fund,** which is the state treasury account that supports state programs and services without restric-tion. In 1997, the legislature amended the law to dedicate lottery proceeds to public education. Because the legislature reduced education spending by a sum equal to the amount of anticipated lottery proceeds, the dedication had no impact on the total amount of money spent for education in Texas. Furthermore, research indicates that states that adopt lotteries to fund education tend to decrease funding for education compared to states without lotteries.[17]

The history of lotteries nationwide is that they start strong, but then decline and level off as the novelty wears off. States attempt to slow or reverse the decline by introducing new or different games and by manipulating how jackpots pile up.[18] In 1998, Texas Lottery sales dropped after the legislature reduced prizes in order to increase the amount of money going to the state. The Lottery Commission reacted to the situation by making it more difficult to win. Instead of having to correctly pick 6 numbers from 1 to 50, players had to pick 6 numbers from 1 to 54. The odds of winning increased from 15.8 million to 1 to 25.8 million to 1. By making it more difficult to win, the state hoped to increase the size of jackpots, which would entice more people to spend money on lottery tickets. The strategy worked for a while be-cause lottery sales increased temporarily. When ticket sales slumped again, the state made it even more difficult to win by adding a Bonus Ball, reducing the odds of winning to 47.7 million to 1.[19]

? WHAT IS YOUR OPINION?

Is it morally wrong for the government to use gambling to raise money?

In 2003, the legislature passed and the governor signed legislation authorizing the state's participation in a multistate lottery in hopes of generating additional

The Texas Lottery generates 2.5 percent of total state revenues.

gambling revenue. The Lottery Commission decided to participate in Mega Millions, a game that is offered in ten states. Mega Millions has been attractive to bettors in other states because the long odds of winning, 135 million to 1, have produced some giant jackpots, including a payout of more than $360 million.[20]

> "A person is literally more likely to be struck by lightning than to win a lottery prize. It's the greatest consumer fraud that I can possibly imagine."
>
> —Former State Representative David Hudson

Other Nontax Revenue The "other nontax revenue" category in Table 13.1 groups together a number of miscellaneous revenue sources, which in 2002 collectively generated 5.4 percent of total state revenue. For example, the category includes employee benefit contributions and money withheld from the paychecks of state workers to cover health insurance coverage for their families and other benefits. Although the money is technically revenue to the state, the funds are earmarked for employee benefits.

The category also contains revenue from the tobacco lawsuit settlement. In 1996, Texas brought suit against eight large tobacco companies, their public relations companies, and their research firms, accusing them of violating state and federal law by marketing tobacco products to children and adjusting the nicotine levels in tobacco to cause mass addiction. The suit asked for money to cover the state's share of the health care costs of Medicaid recipients suffering from smoking-related illnesses. Rather than go to trial, the tobacco industry agreed to a $17.3 billion settlement to be paid out over 25 years.[21]

Issues in State Finance

The debate over whether Texas should adopt a personal income tax is only one of a number of issues in state finance.

The Tax Burden How heavy is the tax burden in Texas compared with other states? Table 13.2 compares the state and local tax burden in the Lone Star State with state

TABLE 13.2   Tax Burden in Texas and the United States, FY 2002

Measure	Texas	National Average	Texas's National Rank
State and local taxes per capita	$2,505	$3,100	40
State and local taxes as a percentage of personal income	9.7 %	11.2 %	46
Personal income taxes per capita	0	$1,883	—
State and local sales taxes per capita	$1,275	$1,099	9
State and local property taxes per capita	$950	$885	15
State and local fees and other charges per capita	$1,186	$1,340	37

Source: *Governing*, State and Local Source Book 2003, pp. 31–37.

and local tax rates nationwide. In 2002, the **per capita** (per person) tax burden in Texas was $2,505 compared to a national average of $3,100. Texas was 40th among the 50 states. Measured as a percentage of personal income, the state and local tax rate in Texas was 46th. On average, Texans paid 9.7 percent of personal income in state and local taxes in 2002 compared to the national average of 11.2 percent.

In comparing tax burdens among states, it is important to consider both state and local taxes because states differ in their mix of taxes. Among the 50 states, Texas state government ranks 48th in the proportion of total state and local taxes collected by the state government, with the state raising only 53 percent of all state and local taxes raised. Local governments collect the other 47 percent. On average nationwide, state governments collect 62 percent of state and local taxes.[22]

The legislature and the governor have been able to hold state taxes down somewhat by passing on many of the costs of services to local governments, which must raise the tax monies to pay for them. Although state levies in Texas are relatively low, local taxes are comparatively high. The legislature and governor, for example, have paid for education reform in large part by forcing local school districts to raise property taxes. Property taxes in Texas, the mainstay of local government finance in the state, are relatively high and climbing. Property taxes assessed to support the public schools are especially high.[23]

Furthermore, Texas's status as a state with a below-average tax burden is primarily a reflection of the absence of a personal income tax. Most other state and local taxes are relatively high. As Table 13.2 indicates, Texas has the 9th highest sales tax burden in the nation and the 15th heaviest property tax burden.

Tax Incidence   The term **tax incidence** refers to the point at which the actual cost of a tax falls. When social scientists and policymakers consider the incidence of a tax, they are focusing on who actually pays the tax. Sometimes the people who write the check to the government are not the only people who bear the burden of a tax. Consider the corporation franchise tax. Although corporations pay the tax, the actual expense of the tax is borne by people—stockholders who earn smaller dividends, customers who pay higher prices for the corporation's products, or employees who receive lower wages. Taxes on alcohol and tobacco fall not only on those people who drink and smoke, but also on tobacco and liquor companies because higher prices caused by the tax will reduce consumer demand for their products.

Social scientists use the terms progressive, proportional, and regressive to discuss the impact of taxation on different income groups. A **progressive tax** is a levy whose burden weighs more heavily on persons earning higher incomes than it does on individuals making less money. A luxury tax on expensive yachts and jewelry would be an example of a progressive tax. If we assume that members of the upper-income groups are the only people to purchase luxury items, then the tax would obviously represent a greater proportion of the incomes of wealthier individuals than it would the incomes of low-income people. A **proportional tax** is a levy that weighs equally on all persons, regardless of their income. An income tax that charged everyone the same percentage amount without deductions or exemptions would be a proportional tax because each income group would pay the same percentage of its income in tax. A **regressive tax** is a levy whose burden weighs more heavily on low-income groups than wealthy taxpayers. Economists generally classify sales and excise taxes as regressive because lower-income persons spend a greater proportion of their earnings on items subject to taxation than do upper-income persons. People in upper-income groups pay more in sales and excise taxes because they purchase more taxable items and the items they purchase tend to be more expensive. Sales and excise taxes are regressive because lower-income individuals spend a greater proportion of their incomes on taxable items than do members of middle- and upper-income groups.[24]

? WHAT IS YOUR OPINION?

Do you favor reforming the tax system in Texas to make it more progressive?

> "By letting the rich off easy, Texas has put too much of the tax burden on those who can least afford it."
> —Robert McIntyre, Citizens for Tax Justice

The Texas tax structure is regressive because of its heavy reliance on property, sales, and excise taxes. A study by the comptroller's office estimates that a Texas family with an annual income of $10,250 or less in 2002 paid 10.7 percent of its total earnings in state and local taxes. In contrast, a family making $114,407 a year or more paid only 1.6 percent of its annual income in state and local taxes.[25] Furthermore, comparisons of state tax systems show that the Texas tax structure is among the most regressive tax systems in the nation, ranking 43rd of 50 states.[26]

Tax Fairness   Although everyone agrees that taxes should be fair, observers define fairness in different ways. Some people favor a tax system based on the **ability-to-pay theory of taxation,** which is the approach to government finance that holds that taxes should be based on an individual's financial resources. They argue that people who earn relatively high incomes should pay more in taxes because well-to-do persons can better afford to pay taxes than can people who make less money. The advocates of the ability-to-pay theory of taxation are critical of the tax system in the state of Texas because it is regressive. They favor the adoption of progressive taxes such as the personal income tax.

In contrast, some experts on public finance favor a tax system that encourages economic growth. They think that government should keep taxes low, especially on business, in order to encourage investment and business expansion. The advocates of growth-oriented tax systems believe that progressive taxes such as the personal income tax are harmful because they reduce the amount of money that middle- and upper-income individuals have to invest in economic development. They also oppose high property taxes because of their impact on business. Instead, they prefer the use of consumer taxes, such as sales and excise taxes. The supporters of growth-oriented tax structures give the Texas tax system mixed reviews. Although they applaud the absence of an individual income tax, they worry that local property taxes are so high that they discourage business expansion.

? WHAT IS YOUR OPINION?

What sort of tax system is the best? Why?

Tax Elasticity   The term **tax elasticity** refers to the extent to which tax revenues increase as personal income rises. It is a measure of the ability of tax revenues to keep up with economic growth. If tax revenues grow along with economic growth, then the government has the funds to address the increased demands for services generated by growth, such as new schools and additional roads. If tax revenues fail to keep up with growth, then state government will lack the resources necessary to keep up with the demand for services unless the government raises tax rates. The Texas tax system is relatively inelastic:

- The general sales tax is somewhat elastic because retail sales generally increase as personal income rises. Nonetheless, the sales tax is not perfectly elastic because not all goods and services are taxable. As peoples' incomes rise, they may purchase goods and services that are not taxable, such as stocks, bonds, real estate, accounting services, and legal services. Furthermore, the growth of sales over the Internet is lessening the elasticity of the sales tax.

- Excise taxes on gasoline, alcohol, and tobacco products are inelastic because sales of those products do not necessarily rise as incomes increase. In fact, gasoline tax revenues may fall as income rises because people may trade in their old vehicles for newer model cars that get better gasoline mileage.

- Severance taxes are inelastic as well. Rising personal income is unrelated to oil and gas production.

- The corporation franchise tax may be elastic if the growth in corporate income keeps up with the growth in personal income.

- Property taxes are only mildly elastic because property values do not necessarily rise as rapidly as personal income.

Many economists believe that Texas's relatively inelastic tax system will be increasingly unable to meet the needs of state government. The state can no longer count on raising substantial tax revenues from severance taxes on oil and gas production. Barring a substantial increase in the world price of oil, tax revenues generated by oil and gas production will continue to shrink as a component of state tax revenues. Furthermore, the healthiest, most rapidly growing sectors of the state's economy are largely exempt from the general sales tax. The sales tax does not cover many service industries, including accounting, legal, and brokerage services. Consequently, the service sector escapes paying its share of state taxes and sales tax collections lag behind economic growth.

Policy Options

Critics of the Texas tax system offer a number of policy options designed to make the state's tax structure more equitable, efficient, or productive.

A Personal Income Tax   Most discussions of tax reform in Texas include an examination of the wisdom of a personal income tax. As we discussed in the introduction to this chapter, the proponents of a state income tax make several points. They argue that an income tax could raise a significant amount of revenue that could be used to fund state services and/or reduce sales and property tax rates. The adoption of an income tax would make the state's tax system less regressive. In contrast, the opponents of a state income tax argue that it would simply be an additional tax that would increase every Texan's tax burden. A state income tax would reduce economic growth and retard population growth because people would choose to live and do business elsewhere.[27]

The Texas Constitution prohibits the legislative adoption of a personal income tax without voter approval. The constitution declares that no personal income tax can take effect unless enacted through the legislative process and then approved by the voters in a referendum election. Furthermore, revenues generated by the tax could be used only for education and limiting local school-district property taxes.

Broadening the Sales Tax Base   Another proposal for reforming the state tax system is to enlarge the sales tax base to include more services than are currently taxed. Although the legislature broadened the tax base somewhat in the 1980s, many services, including most of the services provided by architects, lawyers, interior designers, advertising agents, insurance companies, investment counselors, accountants, brokers, and physicians, remain untaxed. The advocates of a widened tax base believe that it would spread the sales tax burden more fairly than it is now. A broader-based tax would also raise more money than the present sales tax system and be more elastic because the service sector is one of the most rapidly growing elements of the state economy. In contrast, critics charge that broadening the sales tax base is just another means of increasing taxes on consumers. Regardless of the rhetoric, they say, taxes on services are taxes on people that use the services. Businesses will inevitably pass the tax along to consumers who purchase their services. Furthermore, extending the sales tax to cover services that are not taxed in other states might make Texas firms less competitive nationwide.

"High taxes discourage business entrepreneurs from locating in a given area; reduce the inflow of new residents into a region and increase the outflow of residents out of a region; and reduce job opportunities and sometimes lead to higher unemployment."
—Texas Public Policy Foundation

"While some claim that being a low-tax state makes us more competitive in attracting business, in fact, it is more important to business that a state have strong public and higher education systems that produce a good workforce."
—Center for Public Policy Analysis

Expanding the Corporation Franchise Tax   Because the corporation franchise tax only applies to businesses organized as corporations, many of the state's business enterprises escape taxation. Some state leaders propose reforming the tax to include most forms of business organization and not just corporations. A broader business tax, they argue, would not only raise more money for the state, but it would also be fairer than the current levy, which taxes a minority of the state's business enterprises.

Tax Relief to Low-Income Families   In recent years, a number of states have enacted special tax exemptions and credits for low-income individuals so that their state tax systems will be less regressive. Thirty-one states allow property owners a partial rebate on their property taxes if the taxes exceed a certain percentage of income (as certified on IRS tax forms).[28] Iowa, for example, grants property tax relief to those people who are eligible (mostly senior citizens and disabled persons) on a sliding scale based on income. New Mexico and Kansas give a sales tax rebate to low-income people.[29]

"Sales tax holidays are nothing more than political gimmicks that accomplish little and leave an unfair system in place."
—David Brunori, tax analyst

In Texas, the legislature and the governor have created a Sales Tax Holiday for the first weekend in August. For 3 days, consumers can purchase clothing and shoes costing less than $100 without paying the state sales tax. Most local governments drop their sales tax as well, although they are not required to participate in the tax holiday.

Analyzing State Tax Systems

Political scientists who study state tax systems have found that states tend to adopt those taxes that are the easiest to impose. States that industrialized early, such as Michigan, were more likely to rely on a corporate income tax than states that were slow to industrialize, such as Texas. States with high personal incomes, such as New York, turned to the personal income tax. States with mineral wealth adopted severance taxes. States also tend to stick with taxes that have been around a long time. A state with a history of reliance on an income tax, for example, is more likely to raise income-tax rates to generate additional revenue than to create a new tax.[30]

State tax policy also reflects politics. The typical tax strategy is to tax the politically weak. When business groups dominate state politics, they shift taxes from business to consumers. When labor unions and consumer groups are more powerful, they reduce taxes on wage earners and consumers while increasing taxes on business and the wealthy.[31]

Scholarship on tax policy helps explain the Texas tax system. The Lone Star State's historic reliance on severance and sales taxes is the result of the state's mineral wealth and the relative strength of its retail sales base in the 1960s when the sales tax was first imposed. Texas's late-developing manufacturing sector and relatively low average levels of personal income help account for the absence of corporate and personal income taxes.[32] All other factors being equal, we would expect the state to stick with its basic tax structure in the future. Powerful political forces oppose major change and precedent favors the current system.

Nonetheless, change is possible in Texas if the present tax structure fails to provide sufficient revenue to cover the cost of government. As oil and gas production continues to fall and as the service sector of the economy continues to expand while the retail sector grows more slowly, the current tax system will have difficulty producing sufficient revenue to fund basic state services. The growth of Internet sales poses a significant threat to the state's revenue stream because many Internet sales are not currently subject to the sales tax. Because of population growth and inflation, particularly for health care, the cost of public services will increase faster than tax revenues will grow. Consequently, the legislature and the governor may be forced to increase taxes, reduce services, or adopt some combination of tax increases and service cuts.

> "Our present tax structure was not designed for our current economy."
> —Wayne Peveto, former state legislator

EXPENDITURES

The state budget for the 2004–2005 biennium was $117.4 billion. Because the Texas legislature meets in regular session only once every two years, the legislature and the governor appropriate money for a two-year budget period, which is known as the **biennium.** The 78th Legislature, which met in regular session in 2003, approved spending $59.6 billion in 2004 and $57.8 billion in 2005.[33]

Table 13.3 identifies the most important items in the state budget and compares spending priorities in 1983, 1993, and 2002. The largest expenditure categories for state government are education, health and human services, transportation, and public safety and corrections. In 2002, those 4 categories accounted for more than 85 percent of total state spending. Since 1983, expenditures for health and human services have more than doubled while spending for public safety and corrections has increased substantially as well. In contrast, the relative importance to the budget of education and transportation has declined.

Table 13.4 compares and contrasts Texas with other states in terms of state and local government spending. Government expenditures in Texas are below the national average but not at the very bottom. Texas is 43rd among the 50 states in total government spending per capita. It ranks 38th in terms of spending as a percentage of personal income.

TABLE 13.3 State Expenditures for Selected Government Functions, 1983, 1993, and 2002

Expenditure	1983	1993	2002
Education	49.4 %	38.3 %	36.3 %
Health and Human Services	15.9	33.7	36.1
Transportation	11.2	8.4	9.0
Public Safety and Corrections	3.8	4.8	6.0
General Government	3.7	4.6	3.3
Other	16.0	10.2	9.3
Total expenditures	**100 %** ($13.5 billion)	**100 %** ($33.4 billion)	**100 %** ($55.7 billion)

Source: "Texas Revenue History by Function, 1978–2002," Comptroller of Public Accounts, available at **www.cpa.state.tx.us**.

TABLE 13.4   State and Local Government Spending, Texas and the United States, FY 2002

Criterion	Texas	National Average	Texas Rank Among the States
Total state and local government spending per capita	$5,258	$6,208	43
State and local government spending as a percentage of personal income	20.4 %	22.4 %	38
Total education expenditures per capita	$1,881	$1,853	21
Elementary and secondary education expenditures per capita	$1,362	$1,298	11
Higher education expenditures per capita	$470	$477	31
Welfare expenditures per capita	$550	$829	47
Highway expenditures per capita	$345	$360	34
Parks and recreation expenditures per capita	$58	$89	41
Environmental expenditures per capita	$187	$265	46
Fire protection expenditures per capita	$66	$82	27
Police protection expenditures per capita	$154	$202	35
Corrections expenditures per capita	$180	$173	15

Source: *Governing,* State and Local Source Book 2003, pp. 11, 12, 21, 38, 69–71, 81, 84, and 90.

"We told the citizens of Texas that, despite tough economic times, we would not raise the price of government to balance the budget. We delivered on that promise."

—Governor Rick Perry

"With this budget, we mark the passage in Texas from compassionate conservatism to just plain old mean-spiritedness."

—State Sen. Eliot Shapleigh, D., El Paso

Few public services in Texas are well funded, at least in comparison with their funding levels in other states. State and local government expenditures per capita for higher education, welfare, highways, parks and recreation, the environment, fire protection, and police protection are all below the national average. The only expenditure categories in which Texas is above the national average are per capita expenditures for education in general, elementary and secondary education in particular, and corrections (prisons). Moreover, the high rank for education expenditures is misleading because it reflects the size of the state's population of school age children rather than a generous commitment to funding education. Per capita expenditures for education are relatively high in Texas because the state has a comparatively large population of school age children. School age children represent 19.1 percent of the population of Texas compared to only 16.8 percent of the population nationwide. Only Alaska and Utah have larger percentages of school age youngsters than Texas. In fact, on a per student basis, funding for elementary and secondary education in the Lone Star State lags behind the national average, $6,850 per student compared to a national average of $7,702 per student.[34]

Texas furthered its reputation as a low-tax, low-spend state during the 2003 regular session of the legislature. Faced with a $9.9 billion budget shortfall, the legislature and the governor chose primarily to cut spending rather than raise taxes. Other states dealt with similar budget crises by taking a balanced approach that combined tax increases and spending reductions. The Texas legislature cut funding for Medicaid, low-income children's health insurance, public school textbooks, higher education, and health insurance for teachers and state employees.

Elementary and Secondary Education

The controversy over local property tax funding of public education has dominated the debate over education finance in Texas for decades. Critics charged that the use of property taxes to support public schools was unfair because it enabled a district with a wealthy property tax base to raise considerably more money than a poor district, even if the two districts levied the same tax rate. In the case of *Edgewood* v. *Kirby* in 1989, the Texas Supreme Court ruled unanimously that Texas's system of financing public education was not just unfair but also unconstitutional.[35] The court ordered the Texas legislature and the governor to remedy the situation, which they did by adopting the so-called **Robin Hood Plan.** It was a reform of the state's school finance system designed to increase funding for poor school districts by redistributing money from wealthy districts. The result of Robin Hood was to increase state funding for property-poor school districts while decreasing funding for wealthy districts.

Education finance remains controversial. Many parents and school officials in poor districts believe that funding equality is not enough because the needs of their students are greater. Although Texas spends a good deal of money to support education, spending on a per student basis lags behind the national average. The average teacher salary in Texas is $39,232 compared to a national average of $44,499. The state ranks 31st in pupil-teacher ratios.[36] Consequently, many Texans believe that the state needs to substantially increase education funding and target students most at risk for failure.

Parents and school administrators in property rich school districts argue that the Robin Hood Plan prevents them from providing a quality education for the youngsters living in their districts. If wealthy districts raise local taxes to improve their schools, most of the money goes to the state. Furthermore, more than 250 districts have increased their property tax rates to the state maximum of $1.50. They lack the ability to raise additional money to support their schools regardless of the need and the wishes of local taxpayers.[37]

Many Texas property owners favor school finance reform because of soaring property taxes. Between 1993 and 2001, the average school tax rate went from $1.33 per $100 of property value to $1.49. Because of rising property values, the actual tax increase for property owners was substantially higher. Between 1993 and 2001, the amount of school property taxes levied increased from $8.7 billion to $15.2 billion.[38]

School finance reform is once again part of the agenda of Texas government. In 2003, the Texas senate passed a measure overhauling the state's school finance system. Although the proposal died in the house, it could serve as a model for future legislative action. The senate plan would replace most local property taxes with a state property tax of $0.75 per $100. The state would raise additional money for education by increasing and expanding the state sales tax. School district voters would have the option of adopting a $0.10 per $100 local property tax to provide additional money for local schools.[39]

Health Care

Medicaid and the Children's Health Insurance Program (CHIP) are the state's major health programs.

Medicaid   The Texas Medicaid program provides medical services to nearly 2.5 million poor or disabled residents of the state.[40] It covers such services as inpatient and

---

"Without a substantial injection of cash, the very near future of the Texas education system will be characterized by plummeting test scores, an increasing number of dropouts, severe cuts in essential curricula and massive teacher layoffs."

—Texas Association of School Boards

"Many districts are looking at deficit budgets. We will have to severely cut programs or go into deficit spending and eventually use up our fund reserve. Those at the [tax] cap are on a crisis cruise."

—John Wilson, Clear Creek ISD

"The only way you can truly restructure public school finance is to have some significant injection of new money."

—State Senator Bill Ratliff, R., Mt. Pleasant

People who do not have health insurance coverage often turn to hospital emergency rooms for health care.

outpatient hospital care, health screening, dental care, hearing evaluations, physicians' services, family-planning services, laboratory fees, x-ray work, and prescription drugs. Although the poor—particularly pregnant women, mothers, and their young children—are the largest group of recipients, most of the spending goes to provide services for the blind, disabled, and impoverished elderly because their medical needs are greater and therefore more expensive to meet.

Medicaid is a **federal grant-in-aid program,** which is a program through which the national government gives money to state and local governments for expenditure in accordance with set standards and conditions. Congress creates the programs and sets guidelines for their implementation while the states administer them. The states and the federal government share the cost of Medicaid, with the size of the state share depending on the state's personal income. The federal government covers 60 percent of the cost of the Texas Medicaid program with the state paying the other 40 percent.[41]

Medicaid is a large and rapidly growing component of state spending. In 2003, Medicaid expenditures in Texas totaled $13.5 billion, nearly 24 percent of state spending. Medicaid spending in Texas rose by 11 percent in 2003[42] and experts predict that it will continue rising at an annual rate of 8–9 percent over the next several years.[43] The rising price of prescription drugs and long-term care for the elderly and disabled are the primary cost drivers for the program.

In 2003, the Texas legislature and the governor cut Medicaid spending to help balance the budget without increasing taxes. They discontinued Medicaid services for pregnant women whose incomes exceed 158 percent of the poverty level, compared with 185 percent of the poverty level before 2003. The Texas Medicaid program no longer covered adult eyeglasses or hearing aids. The legislature and the governor also eliminated Medicaid coverage for podiatric, chiropractic, and psychological services.[44] The proponents of the program reductions argued that the budget cuts were necessary to rein in the expense of a program whose costs are rising more rapidly than the state can afford. Poor families can set priorities to pay for those health care services they really need. In contrast, critics charged that the legislature and the governor were balancing the budget on the backs of the poor. Many poor people would end up in hospital emergency rooms and local health clinics, shifting the cost of indigent health care to local government. Meanwhile, impoverished elderly people in nursing homes would have no money to buy eyeglasses or a hearing aid or to pay for podiatry or mental health care.

Children's Health Insurance Program (CHIP)

The **Children's Health Insurance Program (CHIP)** is federal program designed to provide health insurance to children from low-income families whose parents are not poor enough to qualify for Medicaid. In 2003, more than 500,000 Texas children benefited from CHIP coverage at an estimated cost of $703 million. The state of Texas was responsible for only about 25 percent of the funds, with the federal government providing the other 75 percent.[45]

Because of relatively strict eligibility standards, Texas has failed to take advantage of all the CHIP money available. Between 1998 and 2003, Texas passed up more than $600 million in federal funds because it failed to meet the federal **matching funds requirement,** which is a legislative provision that the national government will provide grant money for a particular activity only on condition that the state or local government involved supply a certain percentage of the total money required for the project or program. The state will pass up even more money during the 2004–2005 biennium because the legislature and the governor cut CHIP funding so they could balance the budget without raising taxes. The legislature and the governor tightened eligibility in ways that were expected to deny coverage to about 167,000 youngsters. Because of the program reduction, Texas will lose $550 million in federal matching funds which will go to other states with more generous funding levels.[46] Furthermore, children remaining on the program will lose access to dental care, vision coverage, and physical and speech therapy.[47]

The reductions in Medicaid and CHIP funding came at an inopportune time for many Texans. According to the U.S. Census Bureau, Texas has the highest percentage of residents without health insurance in the nation. In 2002, nearly one in four Texans was uninsured. African Americans and Latinos were significantly more likely to be without insurance than non-Hispanic Whites.[48] Texas also led the nation in the percentage of children without health insurance coverage.[49] The legislature's

---

"If God was [sic] here and this was [sic] Judgment Day, and the state of Texas was [sic] being judged by the way we treat our mentally retarded, mentally ill, mentally disabled and elderly, we would go to hell."
—State Representative Craig Eilend, D., Galveston

"Where did this idea come from that everybody deserves free education, free medical care, free whatever? . . . It comes straight from the pit of hell. And it's cleverly disguised as having a tender heart. It's ripping the heart out of this country."
—State Rep. Debbie Riddle, R., Houston

"Instead of creating more programs, lawmakers should search for ways to make it easier for us all to plan and pay for our individual health care needs."
—Chris Patterson, Texas Public Policy Foundation

"These folks [in the legislature] have chosen to cut children rather than cut other things, and it's not a priority for them. The reason it's not a priority is because poor children don't make campaign contributions and poor children don't vote. This is not rocket science. You either want to cover kids or you don't."

—State Rep. Garnet Coleman, D., Houston

cuts in state health programs will inevitably increase the number of Texas adults and children without health insurance.

Higher Education

Only California has more publicly supported colleges and universities than Texas, and only California has more students enrolled. In the fall semester of 2002, 1.1 million students attended one of the state's 104 public and independent institutions of higher education. The University of Texas at Austin was the largest center of higher education in the state, registering more than 52,000 students. Enrollment at Texas A&M University exceeded 45,000 students.[50]

More students attend community colleges in Texas than attend universities. Community college enrollment has been growing steadily for years while until recently the number of students attending universities has been falling. Furthermore, Latino and African American students are more likely to attend community colleges than universities. In 2002, 29 percent of community college students were Latino and 11 percent were African American. In contrast, only 20 percent of university students were Latino and only 10 percent were African American.[51]

Higher education funding in Texas lags a bit below the national average and is declining relative to total state spending. In 2002, Texas spent $470 per capita on higher education compared to a national average of $477.[52] Furthermore, as Figure 13.2 demonstrates, the share of state spending allocated for higher education in Texas has fallen by nearly half since the early 1980s. Because the legislature cut

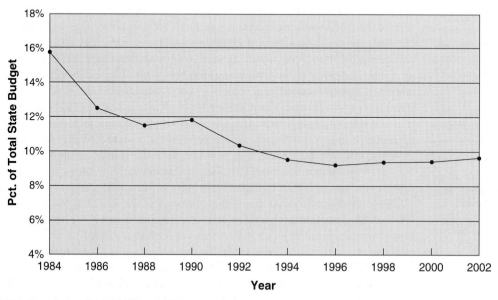

FIGURE 13.2 Higher Education Funding in Texas
Source: Legislative Budget Board

spending for higher education in its 2003 regular session, the share of state spending for higher education will continue to fall.

Colleges and universities in Texas receive funding from a number of sources in addition to the state. Money for community/junior colleges is divided primarily among state funding, student tuition and fees, and local tax support. The state provides 44 percent of the average community college's budget with local property taxes (30 percent) and student tuition and fees (26 percent) supplying most of the rest. Meanwhile, financial support for the state's universities comes from state appropriations, student tuition and fees, research grants, and private donations.[53] Ironically, the government supplies less than half the operating budgets of large state universities in Texas and the nation as a whole. State tax dollars provide only 22 percent of the University of Texas system budget and 32 percent of the budget at Texas A&M University.[54] As the relative importance of state funding for higher education has declined, tuition has risen. Between 1993 and 2002, tuition and fees at Texas universities increased by 104 percent, from $604 for an in-state student taking 14 semester hours to $1,576.[55]

> "Sometimes it is easy to forget that behind every government program, there is a real taxpayer funding it."
>
> —Governor Rick Perry

The University of Texas (UT) at Austin and Texas A&M University at College Station benefit from the Permanent University Fund (PUF). The PUF is a fund constitutionally established as an endowment to finance construction, maintenance, and certain other activities at the University of Texas, Texas A&M University, and other institutions in the UT and Texas A&M University systems. In 1876, the framers of the Texas Constitution set aside a million acres of grassland in west Texas to finance "a university of the first class," including "an agricultural and mechanical branch." A few years later the legislature added another 1.1 million acres. Income from mineral development on the land and agricultural leasing goes into a Permanent University Fund similar to the Permanent School Fund. The PUF may not be spent but is invested to earn dividends and interest. These earnings comprise the Available University Fund (AUF) which is distributed two-thirds to the University of Texas and one-third to Texas A&M University. The PUF money is used to guarantee bonds for capital improvements at schools in the UT and A&M University Systems. Funds from the AUF cover debt service, including payments on principal and interest. Surplus AUF funds can be used at the University of Texas in Austin, Texas A&M in College Station, and Prairie View A&M, for "excellence programs," including scholarships, library improvements, and lab equipment.

In 1984, Texas voters approved an amendment to the Texas Constitution establishing a dedicated fund for construction and other purposes at state-supported colleges and universities outside the University of Texas and Texas A&M systems. This fund, which is called the Higher Education Assistance Fund (HEAF), is financed by an annual legislative appropriation of $175 million. Institutions that are not covered by the PUF can use HEAF money to acquire land; construct, repair, and rehabilitate buildings; and purchase capital equipment and library materials. The 1984 amendment also established an endowed fund similar to the PUF that is financed by a $50 million a year appropriation. Once the new fund, which is called the Higher Education Fund (HEF), reaches $2 billion, its annual income will go to non-PUF schools.

Welfare

The philosophy underlying the nation's welfare system has changed. Before 1996, the unofficial goal of the welfare policy was to provide low-income recipients with a minimal standard of living.[56] Low-income families and individuals who met the eligibility requirements could qualify for various federal programs providing health care, food vouchers, and cash. In 1996, Congress passed and President Bill Clinton signed sweeping welfare reform legislation that explicitly changed the underlying philosophy of government policy from welfare to work. Instead of attempting to supply low-income individuals and families with cash and in-kind benefits sufficient to meet basic human needs, the goal of welfare reform was to move recipients from the welfare rolls to the workforce. Able-bodied welfare recipients would have to find work and/or participate in job training programs in order to receive welfare assistance. Furthermore, the government placed lifetime limits on the amount of time welfare recipients could collect benefits before having to leave the welfare rolls forever.

 WHAT IS YOUR OPINION?

Do you agree with placing lifetime limits on the amount of time an individual can collect welfare benefits?

The welfare reform legislation created **Temporary Assistance for Needy Families (TANF),** which is a federal program that provides temporary financial assistance and work opportunities to needy families. Low-income families and individuals who meet eligibility requirements receive cash and qualify for Medicaid benefits and Food Stamps. The **Food Stamp Program** was a federal program that provided vouchers to low-income families and individuals that could be used to purchase food from grocery stores. To maintain their eligibility, recipients must comply with a Personal

Responsibility Agreement (PRA). The PRA requires recipients to agree not to voluntarily quit a job, stay free of alcohol or drug abuse, participate in parenting skills if referred, obtain medical screenings for their children, and ensure their children are immunized and attending school. People who fail to comply with their PRA may suffer loss of benefits. In Texas, for example, parents who fail to keep their children's immunizations current lose their Medicaid benefits.[57]

Welfare benefits in Texas are among the least generous in the nation. In 2002, Texas ranked 47th in welfare spending per capita, $550 compared to a national average of $829.[58] The average TANF recipient in Texas is a 30-year-old African American or Latino woman caring for 1 or 2 children under the age of 11. She has neither a high school education nor job training and does not have reliable transportation. Her only income is a TANF grant of $208 a month or less.[59]

Welfare reform has helped reduce the welfare rolls, but it has not eliminated poverty. Between 1997 and 2002, the number of TANF recipients in Texas fell by 48 percent and the number of Food Stamp recipients declined by 37 percent. In the meanwhile, the number of Medicaid beneficiaries was little changed, increasing by a mere 2 percent. Critics charge that the decline in the number of welfare recipients reflects the impact of tighter eligibility standards, lifetime limits on benefits, and sanctions forcing people out of programs rather than an improvement in the quality of the lives of low-income Texans. While the number of people receiving welfare benefits was falling, the number of applications for benefits was increasing. Between 1997 and 2002, the number of applications for Medicaid services grew by 49 percent. TANF applications increased by 26 percent and Food Stamp applications rose by 9 percent.[60]

> "Texas is a miserly state when it comes to social services. Everybody is of the attitude that people should take care of themselves."
> —Former state Senator Chet Brooks

Transportation

The Texas Good Roads Amendment has been the foundation of Texas transportation funding for more than 50 years. In 1946, the legislature proposed and the voters ratified an amendment to the Texas Constitution creating the **Dedicated Highway Fund,** which is a constitutionally earmarked account containing money set aside for building, maintaining, and policing state highways. The amendment specified that three-fourths of the motor fuels and lubricants tax be set aside for the construction, policing, and maintenance of state highways.[61] In 2002, money from the Dedicated Highway Fund accounted for 60 percent of the state's $5.8 billion transportation spending, with most of the rest coming from federal matching funds.[62]

The Dedicated Highway Fund is no longer sufficient to fund all of the state's transportation needs. Texas ranks 34th among the states in highway spending per capita, $345 per person compared to a national average of $360.[63] The figure is notably low, especially considering that Texas has more highway mileage than any other state. According to the Texas Department of Transportation (TxDOT), gas tax money and federal funds combined are sufficient to fund only 35 to 40 percent of the transportation projects requested by local officials. This backlog of uncompleted projects contributes to pollution and congestion in metropolitan areas and undermines economic growth.[64] Because the legislature and the governor have been reluctant to increase the gasoline tax to raise additional money, TxDOT has been considering alternative funding approaches, including the use of toll roads and public-private partnerships.[65]

Corrections

The Texas prison system houses 158,131 inmates, making it the second largest prison system in the United States, just 2,000 inmates fewer than California, a state whose population is 60 percent larger than that of the Lone Star State. The Texas prison system is more than twice as big as the prison system in New York even though New York's population is only 12 percent smaller than the Texas population. The incarceration rate in Texas is 685 prison inmates per 100,000 people compared to a national rate of 425. Texas has the third highest incarceration rate in the country, after Louisiana and Mississippi.[66]

During the 1970s and 1980s, the governor and legislature responded to public concerns about crime by getting tough. The legislature passed dozens of anticrime bills, upgrading the seriousness of certain offenses and increasing prison time for offenders. Texas judges and juries began sentencing more people to prison to serve longer terms. The legislature also required that persons convicted of **aggravated offenses** (violent crimes) or crimes using a deadly weapon must serve at least a third of a sentence before becoming eligible for **parole,** which is the conditional release of convicted offenders from prison to serve the remainder of their sentences in the community under supervision. As a result, the prison system stacked up with inmates who could not be paroled.

In the late 1980s, the legislature, the governor, and the voters authorized a massive prison construction program to hold the state's rapidly growing prison population. The legislature proposed and the voters approved constitutional amendments to borrow money to build new prison units. Meanwhile, the legislature and the governor appropriated funds to operate the new prison units and begin the long-term process of paying for their construction. Between 1985 and 2002, the share of state spending devoted to public safety and corrections increased from 3.8 percent of total spending to 6.0 percent.[67]

Although spending for corrections is one of the few budget categories in which Texas exceeds the national average, the Texas prison system is not especially well funded. Despite having the second largest prison system in the country, Texas is 15th in per capita spending on corrections. California, with a prison population only slightly larger than the Texas inmate population, has a corrections budget almost twice as large.[68] Furthermore, the legislature and governor cut the budget for the Texas prison system in 2003, forcing prison officials to reduce funding for food and rehabilitation programs. The cuts will likely force the state to increase its parole rate to control the size of the prison population.

★ THE BUDGET PROCESS

The State of Texas uses **performance-based budgeting,** which is a system of budget preparation and evaluation in which policymakers identify specific policy goals, set performance targets for agencies, and measure results. The governor begins the budget process in the spring of the year before the legislature meets by defining the mission of state government, setting goals, and identifying priorities. Each state

Between 1972 and 2002, the state's inmate population increased from 16,171 to 158,131.

agency develops a strategic plan for accomplishing one or more of the goals. A strategic plan defines the mission of the agency, states its philosophy, and presents a strategy for achieving the goal. The agency also creates a budget to support its strategic plan. Agencies submit their strategic plans and budgets to the governor and the Legislative Budget Board in June, July, and August. The **Legislative Budget Board (LBB)** is an agency created by the legislature to study state revenue and budgetary needs between legislative sessions and prepare budget and appropriation bills to submit to the legislature. Agencies must submit budget requests by the beginning of August.

The philosophy behind performance-based budgeting is that agency budgets are tied to measurable goals. Agencies establish goals, identify quantitative measures to assess progress, and prepare a budget designed to support their efforts. For example, a performance measure used by the Texas Higher Education Coordinating Board is the percentage of university students who graduate within six years of initial enrollment. A performance measure used by the Texas Department of Human Services is the percentage of long-term care clients served in community settings (as opposed to in-stitutional settings). The state rewards managers who achieve their goals by giving them more discretion in the use of funds or allowing them to carry over part of a budget surplus from one budget period to the next.[69]

Professor Thomas Anton identifies three "rules of the budget game" that government agencies follow in making budget requests.

1. Agencies ask for more money than they received the year before and more money than they expect to get so they would have room to cut their budget requests later.
2. Agencies insert some items in their budgets that are obvious targets for spending cuts in hopes that the items that they really want included in the budget will survive the cuts.
3. When agencies want large amounts of additional money, they present the requests as extensions of existing programs because is easier to justify expanding a current program than it is to begin a new initiative.[70]

We could add a fourth rule: When asked to recommend spending reductions, agencies propose cutting programs that are politically popular. Once when the LBB asked the state bureaucracy to prepare budget requests that could be funded without a tax increase, agencies proposed cutting 23,000 poor children from welfare rolls, kicking 12,000 elderly Texans out of nursing homes, and leaving newly built prisons stand unopened.[71] Agency heads want to convince state budget makers that it is wiser politically to look elsewhere for budget cuts than it is to trim their particular piece of the budget pie.

After agencies submit their budgets, the LBB and the governor's staff hold hearings at which agency administrators explain and defend their requests. During the last few months of the year, the LBB drafts an **appropriations bill,** which is a legislative authorization to spend money for particular purposes. Legislators introduce the LBB draft in the house and senate as the basis for legislative deliberations on the budget for the upcoming biennium. The governor usually submits budget recommendations as well, but because the legislative leadership—the speaker and lieutenant governor—control the LBB, its budget serves as the starting point for the legislature rather than the proposals offered by the governor.

The Texas Constitution, similar to most other state constitutions, prohibits the adoption of a budget that is in deficit. A **budget deficit** is the amount by which budget expenditures exceed budget receipts. The state comptroller estimates state revenues for the upcoming biennium at the beginning of each legislative session. The comptroller may issue periodic updates during the session to reflect changing economic conditions or revisions in tax laws. Any spending bill the legislature approves must fall within the comptroller's revenue projections unless the legislature votes by a four-fifths majority to run a deficit, which, of course, is unlikely.

The Texas Constitution also caps state spending to the rate of economic growth. At the beginning of a legislative session, the comptroller projects the rate of economic growth in the state for the next two-year period. The rate of growth in state spending may be no greater than the projected rate of economic growth unless a majority of legislators agree that an emergency exists that warrants additional spending. The limit does not affect the expenditure of federal funds or money generated through dedicated funds.

Most spending decisions are predetermined by federal requirements, court orders, or dedicated funds. The majority of federal dollars are designated for particular activities, such as highway construction, health care for low-income families and children, and vocational education. In order to participate in federal programs, the state must satisfy a matching funds requirement. The national government will provide grant money for a particular activity only on the condition that the state or local government involved supplies a certain percentage of the total money required for the project or program.

The state must also spend money to respond to court orders issued by both federal and state courts. In recent sessions, the legislature has appropriated billions of dollars in response to court rulings concerning state hospitals for the mentally ill and mentally retarded, prisons, public education, and higher education in south Texas. The legislature spent hundreds of millions of dollars to expand educational opportunities in south Texas, for example, because of a lawsuit charging that state higher education funding unconstitutionally discriminated against Latinos living along the border with Mexico. The Texas Supreme Court eventually ruled in favor of the state, at least in part because of the efforts of the legislature to upgrade and expand higher education in south Texas.

The legislature's budgetary discretion is also limited by dedicated funds, such as the Dedicated Highway Fund or the Permanent University Fund. The state has more than a hundred dedicated funds setting aside money for highways, parks, university construction, public schools, retirement funds, and other purposes. Constitutional or statutory dedications accounted for 46 percent of general revenue appropriations in the 2002–2003 budget.[72] The advocates of dedicated funds contend that they enable the state to make long-term commitments to goals. Earmarking revenue is also a means of generating public support for a tax increase because it makes budgeting comprehensible to ordinary people and gives the public confidence that tax moneys will be used as promised. In contrast, critics believe that earmarking contributes to state budget crises by limiting legislative discretion. Dedicated funds deny legislators the option of cutting certain programs, such as the highway construction budget, in order to avoid a tax increase or to find money for other priorities, such as public education or prison construction. Furthermore, dedicated funds, especially those contained in the state constitution, restrict the ability of the legislature to modify budget priorities to reflect the changing needs of the state.

The budget must pass the legislature in a fashion similar to other bills. In the senate, the Finance Committee deals with both appropriations and tax bills, making recommendations to the senate floor. In the house, the Appropriations Committee drafts the budget while the Ways and Means Committee deals with tax measures. In most instances, the final details of the state appropriations bill and most tax packages have to be ironed out by a house-senate **conference committee,** which is a special committee created to negotiate differences on similar pieces of legislation passed by the house and senate. Once legislation receives final legislative approval, it goes to the governor.

On appropriations bills, the governor of Texas (and the governors of most states) has the **line-item veto,** which is the power of the governor to veto sections or items of an appropriation bill while signing the remainder of the bill into law. Although the line-item veto (and the threat of its use) is a potentially potent weapon for influencing the state budget, research shows that it has a relatively small impact on total state spending.[73] In 2003, Governor Perry used the line-item veto to cut $81 million from the state budget of $117 billion, less than one-tenth of 1 percent of total spending.[74] In practice, the legislature has limited the governor's ability to knock out objectionable items by lumping millions of dollars of expenditures together in a single line item. In 1941, for example, the appropriation for the University of Texas at Austin included 1,528 line items. Today, the legislature groups the UT-Austin appropriation into only 23 items. To eliminate a couple of items, the governor would be forced to take the politically risky step of vetoing a major chunk of the university's total budget.[75]

Political scientists who study budgeting have developed models to explain the process. The most common approach is the **incremental model of budgeting,** which is a theoretical effort to explain the budget process on the basis of small (incremental) changes in budget categories from one budget period to the next. Scholars who favor this approach to understanding the budget process believe that agency heads, legislators, and governors all regard an agency's current budget share as its base. Increases or decreases in that base must be justified, while maintaining current levels need not be. Consequently, changes in individual budget items tend to be small. Another explanation for incremental budgeting is that an agency's current budget reflects its political strength relative to the strength of other agencies competing for money. Because the relative political influence of various claimants on the state budget is unlikely to change dramatically from one budget period to the next, budget figures are unlikely to change dramatically either.[76]

Although incremental budgeting may be the norm, not all budget changes are incremental. Between 1983 and 2002, for example, expenditures for public safety and corrections increased by more than 50 percent, rising from 3.8 percent to 6.0 percent of state spending. Exceptions to incrementalism frequently result from a coalescing of political forces sufficient to force a change in longstanding budget priorities. The dramatic rise in spending on public safety and corrections reflected the legislature's response to public pressure to do something about rising crime rates.

The governor and the Legislative Budget Board (LBB) share **budget execution authority,** which is the power to cut agency spending or transfer money between agencies during the period when the legislature is not in session. Between legislative sessions, either the LBB or the governor may propose reductions or shifts in state spending. If the LBB proposes a change, the governor must approve the transfer before it can take effect, and vice versa.

"The item veto itself does nothing to the level of spending."
—Douglas Holtz-Eakin, political scientist

LEARNING EXERCISE

Trends in State Finance

The Legislative Budget Board (LBB) prepares reports analyzing state finance. These reports provide legislators with information as they evaluate the state's budget policies and prepare the budget for the upcoming biennium. Many of these reports are also useful to students of Texas government. "Trends in Texas Government Finance: 1984–2009" is particularly helpful. You can find the report in the "Other Publications and Reports—Miscellaneous" at the LBB website: **www.lbb.state.tx.us**

Use the data in the report and the information in this chapter to answer the following questions.

QUESTIONS TO CONSIDER

1. What is the annual percentage growth in tax revenues that the LBB projects for each year from 2004 through the remainder of the decade?
2. Why would tax revenues increase if tax rates do not go up? Explain.
3. In which expenditure areas does the LBB expect the greatest growth in the last half of the decade of the 2000s?
4. Explain why each of these budget areas is expected to be an area of growth.
5. Of the 15 most populous states, which state has the highest combined per capita expenditures?
6. Where does Texas rank on the list?

CONCLUSION: BUDGETARY POLICYMAKING

The public policy approach offers a useful mechanism for analyzing budgetary policymaking in Texas.

The Environment for Budgetary Policymaking

Environmental and political factors provide the context for budgetary policymaking. Economic development is the single most important factor for explaining state budgetary policies. States with greater levels of personal income have higher tax rates and higher levels of spending for transportation, education, health care, criminal justice, and welfare than do states with lower levels of personal income. In short, wealthy states tax their residents more heavily and provide more generous public services than do poor states.[77] Budgetary policies in Texas are consistent with the state's status as a relatively poor state. Compared to other states, tax rates in the Lone Star State are low and spending programs are poorly funded.

Short-term economic factors affect budgetary policymaking as well. Economic expansion helps the state's budget picture by fueling the growth of sales tax and excise tax revenues. In the late 1990s, the economy boomed and state officials were able to cut taxes and increase spending at the same time. In contrast, state tax revenues decline during a **recession,** which is an economic slowdown characterized by declining economic output and rising unemployment. The recession of 2002 helped produce a budget shortfall of nearly $10 billion in 2003.

? WHAT IS YOUR OPINION?

Do you favor a small state government that provides relatively modest services but holds down taxes or a larger state government that provides more services but costs more?

Texas's budgetary policies of relatively low tax rates coupled with poorly funded public services reflect the state's political culture, interest group environment, and political party balance. **Political culture** is the widely held, deeply rooted political values of a society. Texas's low-tax/low-spend budgetary philosophy is consistent with the state's **individualistic political culture,** which is an approach to government and politics that emphasizes private initiative with a minimum of government interference. Many Texans believe in minimal government. When given a choice between higher taxes with more government services and lower taxes with fewer services, they prefer the latter.

The interest group configuration in Texas is consistent with a low-tax/low-spend government. Interest groups that would favor higher taxes to support better-funded public services, such as labor unions, consumer groups, and racial and ethnic minority organizations, are relatively weak in the Lone Star State. In contrast, business organizations, which typical prefer lower tax rates and less generously funded services, are especially strong in Texas.

The current party balance also supports the state's low-tax/low-spend budgetary policies. The Republican Party, which now controls all three branches of state government, advocates limited government. When faced with a substantial budget shortfall in 2003, Republican leaders in the legislature and the executive branch favored cutting services rather than raising taxes to balance the budget. The Democratic Party, which tends to favor a more active government, has limited influence in the state's policymaking process.

Demographic change may eventually affect the environment for budgetary policymaking in Texas. The Latino population is young and increasing rapidly whereas the non-Hispanic White population is aging. Population growth will invariably lead to political influence. Because the Latinos as a group are more likely to be poor, they are more dependent on public services for health care, education, transportation, job training, and welfare than the non-Hispanic White population. As the political influence of Latino voters grow, the state will likely adopt budgetary policies that shift the tax burden away from consumers and low-income families while increasing spending for government services.

> "The [state] leadership has a long-term philosophical bent to get smaller, meaner government, with the emphasis on meaner."
> —Scott McCown, Center for Public Policy Priorities

> "[R]esponsible leadership doesn't mean raising taxes but controlling spending."
> —Brooke Rollins, Texas Public Policy Foundation

Agenda Building

Budgetary issues are always near the forefront of the state's official policy agenda because of the biennial budget cycle. Adopting a balanced budget that will meet the needs of the state is typically the overriding issue of each legislative session. Whether legislators will have sufficient funds to enact new initiatives or consider a tax cut or whether they will have to cut programs and raise taxes depends on economic conditions. Boom times produce budget surpluses that can be spent while a recession causes a shortfall that must be addressed.

Public officials and interest groups raise budgetary issues because they hope to see their concerns included in the state's official policy agenda. Public school administrators and local property taxpayers want the legislature to reform school finance to increase state funding and to reform the Robin Hood system. Business interests favor the use of tax breaks and government subsidies to promote business expansion. Medical professionals advocate an increase in the state cigarette tax in hopes of discouraging young people from taking up the smoking habit.

Budgetary issues sometimes arise because of external pressures, especially from the courts. *Edgewood v. Kirby* was the lawsuit filed by a number of poor school districts against the state's system of education finance. It forced the legislature and the governor to address school funding issues. A new set of lawsuits may force the governor and the legislature to revisit the issue. In recent sessions, the legislature has considered how to reform the franchise tax in light of successful lawsuits brought by corporations that have diminished tax revenues.

Policy Formulation and Adoption

A broad range of political actors participates in budgetary policy formulation. State agencies make budget proposals and lobby for their adoption. For example, the Texas Higher Education Coordinating Board (THECB) lobbies for increased funding for higher education. The agency's strategy is to focus on the gap in educational attainment between non-Hispanic Whites and the state's two largest minority populations, African Americans and Latinos. THECB officials, joined by allies in higher education and minority rights organizations, argue that closing the educational gap is essential to the future of the state. To achieve that goal, they declare, the state must fund higher education more generously.

The members of the legislative leadership are the key players in drafting a budget and formulating tax policy. The speaker and lieutenant governor control the LBB, which prepares the initial budget document. Their closest political allies chair the house and senate committees that formulate the details of budget policy. In the end, the speaker and the lieutenant governor control the conference committee that prepares the final budget document.

The role of the governor in formulating budgetary policy depends on the interest and the skills of the state's chief executive. In 2003, Governor Perry made clear his opposition to raising taxes, calling instead for the legislature to cut spending to eliminate the budget shortfall. Nonetheless, the governor did not want to become deeply involved in the budget process. When given the opportunity to submit a balanced budget without new taxes at the beginning of the 2003 legislative session, Perry offered a document filled with zeros. Perry explained that his budget symbolized the importance of carefully examining every budgetary item to set priorities and make cuts; his critics accused him of zero leadership.

The federal government has a significant impact on policy formulation in Texas because of federal programs. Some of the most important items in the budget rely heavily on federal funds, including welfare, health care, transportation, and public education. Federal money, however, comes with strings attached. To ensure the continued flow of federal dollars, state budgetary policies must conform to federal guidelines. They must also appropriate billions of dollars in state money as matching funds.

The legislature and the governor adopt budgetary policies through the legislative process. The appropriations bill and tax bills must be passed by majority vote of both the Texas house and Texas senate. The governor must sign them or allow them to become law without signature. If the governor issues a veto, it can be overridden by a two-thirds vote of both chambers of the legislature.

The Texas Constitution establishes special rules for budgetary policymaking that create an atmosphere of budgetary caution. The constitution stipulates that the legislature must adopt a balanced budget unless lawmakers agree by a four-fifths majority to run a deficit. The constitution also demands that state spending may grow no more rapidly than economic growth unless both chambers vote in favor of greater spending. These two provisions create a bias in favor of spending restraint. The clear message of the Texas Constitution is that public officials should focus on limiting the growth of government rather than providing enough spending to meet the needs of the state and its people.

The governor plays a special role in budgetary policymaking because of the line-item veto. On most legislative measures, including tax bills, the governor faces a take-it-or-leave-it choice. The governor can sign the bill, allow it to become law without signature, or veto it. On appropriations measures, however, the governor can pick out individual provisions to veto while allowing the rest to become law. As a result, the governor can play a more active role in budgetary policymaking than in other sorts of policy issues.

Policy Implementation and Evaluation

Private citizens, local governments, and state agencies implement budgetary policies. Retail business establishments collect sales taxes and many excise taxes on behalf of the state. State law requires that retailers obtain a sales tax permit from the comptroller, collect taxes on the retail purchase of taxable items, keep records, and remit tax receipts to the state. In return for acting as the state's tax collector, retail establishments can keep a small portion of the money they collect as compensation for their work.

Local governments play a role in administering the state's programs. Most of the state's spending for education goes to independent school districts, which provide educational services for kindergarten through high school. Community/junior colleges implement higher education policies while hospital districts participate in the implementation of the state's health care policies. County governments collect a number of taxes and fees on behalf of the state, including charges for license plates and certificates-of-title for motor vehicles.

State agencies implement budgetary policies as well. The comptroller is the state's chief tax collector, sometimes collecting taxes directly and sometimes working through intermediaries, such as retail merchants. The Texas Department of Corrections (TDC) administers the state's correctional programs. The Department of

Human Services implements welfare policies. The Department of Mental Health and Mental Retardation operates mental health facilities. The state's public universities provide higher education services to the state's residents.

Performance-based budgeting ensures that state agencies evaluate at least some aspects of their programs. Agencies set goals, plan strategies, and identify measures to determine whether they are achieving their goals. Each year they produce a report showing their progress at achieving their goals.

The comptroller, Legislative Budget Board (LBB), and legislative committees evaluate state programs as well. The websites of the comptroller (**www.cpa.state.tx.us**) and the LBB (**www.lbb.state.tx.us**) include a number of reports evaluating the state tax system and various programs, such as the state's health programs and the Foundation School Program. Legislative committees evaluate state agencies and programs under their jurisdiction. The legislature also evaluates agencies and programs through **sunset review,** which is the periodic evaluation of state agencies by the legislature to determine whether they should be reauthorized.

★ REVIEW QUESTIONS

1. Do you think the state of Texas will adopt a personal income tax within the next decade? Why or why not?

2. How does the growth of Internet commerce undermine the state's tax base?

3. What are the most important tax and nontax sources of revenue for the state?

4. How important is the lottery to the state revenue picture?

5. How heavy is the tax burden in Texas compared with other states?

6. Does Texas have a fair tax system? What is the basis for your answer?

7. If you were giving the state's tax system a grade from A to F, what grade would you give it? Why?

8. What are the most frequently proposed reforms for the state tax system?

9. How have the spending priorities for the state of Texas changed over the last 20 years?

10. Why is the Robin Hood school funding system controversial?

11. What steps did the legislature and governor take to balance the budget in 2003?

12. Why is it that Texas fails to draw down all of the federal money available to finance the Children's Health Insurance Program (CHIP)?

13. How is higher education funded in the Lone Star State?

14. What is the underlying philosophy of the state's welfare system?

15. How does the state fund highway construction?

16. Why has spending for corrections increased over the last two decades?

17. How does performance-based budgeting work?

18. What are the steps in the budget process?

19. In what ways is the legislature's discretion limited in writing a budget?

20. What models do political scientists use to study the budget process?

★ KEY TERMS

ability-to-pay theory of
  taxation
aggravated offenses
appropriations bill
biennium
budget deficit
budget execution authority
Children's Health Insurance
  Program (CHIP)
conference committee
corporation franchise tax
Dedicated Highway Fund
Edgewood v. *Kirby*
Employees Retirement System
  (ERS) Trust Fund
excise tax
federal grant-in-aid program

fiscal year
Food Stamp Program
General Fund
incremental model of
  budgeting
individualistic political culture
Legislative Budget Board (LBB)
line-item veto
matching funds requirement
Medicaid program
pari-mutuel wagering
parole
per capita
performance-based budgeting
Permanent School Fund (PSF)
Permanent University Fund
  (PUF)

political culture
progressive tax
proportional tax
recession
regressive tax
Robin Hood Plan
sales tax
severance tax
sin tax
sunset review
tax elasticity
tax incidence
Temporary Assistance for
  Needy Families (TANF)
Texas Teacher Retirement System (TRS) Trust Fund

★ NOTES

1. "Sales Tax Revenue," *Governing*, State and Local Source Book 2003, p. 34.
2. Penelope Lemov, "The Untaxables," *Governing* (July 2002): 36.
3. "Money for Anti-Tobacco Programs Going Up in Smoke," *Houston Chronicle*, January 8, 2003, p. 21A.
4. Federation of Tax Administrators and the Center for Science in the Public Interest, available at **www.cspinet.org/booze/taxguide/StateRankHL.pdf**.
5. American Petroleum Institute, "State Gasoline Taxes," available at **www.lmoga.com/taxrates.htm**.
6. "Inside the Franchise Tax," *Fiscal Notes* (January 1995): 6–7.
7. Monica Wolfson, "Firms Restructure to Side-Step Tax," *Abilene Reporter News*, June 21, 2003, available at **www.reporternews.com**.
8. *Capitol Update*, May 23, 2003, p. 1.
9. *Year 2002 Annual Report*, Texas Racing Commission, available at **www.txrc.state.tx.us**.
10. George Kuempel and Robert T. Garrett, "Higher Fees to Cost Texans Millions," *Dallas Morning News*, June 3, 2002, available at **www.dallasnews.com**.
11. Texas Comptroller of Public Accounts, "2002 Annual Cash Report," available at **www.cpa.state.tx.us**.

12. Texas Comptroller of Public Accounts, "2002 Annual Cash Report."
13. W. Gardner Selby, "State-Run Funds Suffer a Setback," *San Antonio Express-News*, June 8, 2002, available at **www.mysanantonio.com**.
14. Texas Comptroller of Public Accounts, "Texas Revenue History by Source, 1978–2002," available at **www.window.state.tx.us**.
15. "Solid Ground for Education," *Fiscal Notes* (May 1996): 12–13.
16. Texas Lottery Commission, available at **www.txlottery.org**.
17. Donald E. Miller and Patrick A. Pierce, "Lotteries for Education: Windfall or Hoax?" *State and Local Government Review* 29 (Winter 1997): 34–42.
18. Ellen Perlman, "Losing Numbers," *Governing* (September 2001): 46–47.
19. "Lotto Texas Jackpot Gets Longer Odds," *Houston Chronicle*, March 27, 2003, available at **www.houstonchronicle.com**.
20. Mega Millions, available at **www.megamillions.com**.
21. David W. Winder and James T. LaPlant, "State Lawsuits Against 'Big Tobacco:' A Test of Diffusion Theory,"

State and Local Government Review 32 (Spring 2000): 132–41.

22. Governing, Sourcebook 2001, p. 38.

23. "School Bills Keep Climbing," Fiscal Notes (June 1996): 8.

24. "The Nature of Tax Incidence," Comptroller of Public Accounts, available at www.cpa.state.tx.us.

25. "Texas Tax Incidence," Comptroller of Public Accounts, available at www.cpa.state.tx.us.

26. "State of the Lone Star State: How Life in Texas Measures Up," Texans for Public Justice, available at www.tpj.org/.

27. Richard Vedder, Taxing Texans, Texas Public Policy Foundation, available at www.texaspolicy.com.

28. Texas Weekly, December 23, 1996, p. 3.

29. Steven D. Gold, "Taxing the Poor," State Legislatures (April 1987): 24–27.

30. Richard D. Bingham, Brett W. Hawkins, and F. Ted Hebert, The Politics of Raising State and Local Revenue (New York: Praeger, 1978), p. 21.

31. Irene S. Rubin, The Politics of Public Budgeting: Getting and Spending, Borrowing and Balancing (Chatham, NJ: Chatham House, 1990), p. 39.

32. Michael J. Wolkoff, "Exploring the State Choice of Financing Options," State and Local Government Review 19 (Spring 1987): 73–77.

33. "General Appropriations Act for the 2002–2003 Biennium," available at www.lbb.tx.us.

34. Governing, State and Local Source Book 2003, pp. 14–15.

35. Edgewood v. Kirby, 777 S.W.2d 391 (1989).

36. State and Local Source Book, p. 16.

37. Cindy Horswell, "Schools Struggle with Tax Caps," Houston Chronicle, September 22, 2002, pp. 35A.

38. Jay Root, "Property Tax Levies Continue Steep Rise," Fort Worth Star-Telegram, May 19, 2002, available at www.dfw.com.

39. John Kirsch, "New School Finance Plan Unveiled," Fort Worth Star-Telegram, May 1, 2002, available at www.dfw.com.

40. Texas Department of Health and Human Services, available at www.hhsc.state.tx.us.

41. Texas Health and Human Services Commission, Texas Medicaid in Perspective, April 2002, available at www.hhsc.state.tx.us.

42. Texas Health and Human Services Commission, Texas Medicaid in Perspective.

43. Trinity D. Tomsic, "Managing Medicaid in Tough Times," State Legislatures (June 2002): 13–17.

44. W. Gardner Selby, "State Health Cuts Go into Effect Today," San Antonio Express-News, September 1, 2003, available at www.mysanantonio.com.

45. Mitch Mitchell, "Texas Forgoes Millions for Kids," Fort Worth Star-Telegram, August 25, 2003, available at www.dfw.com.

46. "Mental Health," Houston Chronicle, October 22, 2003, available at www.houstonchronicle.com.

47. Selby, "State Health Cuts Go into Effect Today."

48. U.S. Census Bureau, "Health Insurance Coverage in the United States: 2002," available at www.census.gov.

49. U.S. Census Bureau, "Children with Health Insurance: 2001," available at www.census.gov.

50. Texas Higher Education Coordinating Board, "Statistical Report 2002," available at www.thecb.state.tx.us.

51. Texas Higher Education Coordinating Board, "Statistical Report 2002."

52. Governing, State and Local Source Book 2003, p. 13.

53. Texas Higher Education Coordinating Board, "Facts on Higher Education," available at www.thecb.state.tx.us.

54. Ben Gose, "The Fall of the Flagship," Chronicle of Higher Education, July 5, 2002, p. A 20.

55. Todd Ackerman, "College Costs Walloping Wallets," Houston Chronicle, October 22, 2003, p. 1A.

56. William A. Kelso, Poverty and the Underclass: Challenging Perceptions of the Poor in America (New York, NY: New York University Press, 1994), p. 4.

57. David Harmon, "New Rule Redefines 'work' for Some Welfare Recipients," Austin American-Statesman, October 29, 2003, available at www.statesman.com.

58. Governing, State and Local Source Book 2003, p. 90.

59. Texas Department of Human Services, "Temporary Assistance for Needy Families," available at www.dhs.state.tx.us.

60. Texas Department of Human Services, 2002 Annual Report, available at www.dhs.state.tx.us.

61. Article 8, Section 7a, Texas Constitution.

62. Texas Department of Transportation, at www.dot.state.tx.us.

63. Governing, State and Local Source Book 2003, p. 81.

64. Robert Jones, "On the Road Again," Fiscal Notes (June 2002): 5.

65. Ben Wear, "Road Plan Puts Local Chiefs in Driver's Seat," Austin American-Statesman, August 23, 2003, available at www.statesman.com.

66. Governing, State and Local Source Book 2003, pp. 71–72.

67. Texas Comptroller of Public Accounts, "Texas Expenditure History by Function, 1978–2002," available at www.window.state.tx.us.

68. Governing, State and Local Source Book 2003, p. 71.

69. Karen Carter, "Performance Budgets: Here by Popular Demand," State Legislatures (December 1994): 22–25.

70. Thomas J. Anton, The Politics of State Expenditures in Illinois (Urbana, IL: University of Illinois Press, 1966).

71. Mary Lenz, "$52 billion State Budget Clears Board," Houston Post, December 15, 1990, p. A-1.

72. House Research Organization, "Writing the State Budget, 78th Legislature," available at www.capitol.state.tx.us/hrofr/.

73. James W. Enderaby and Michael J. Towle, "Effects of Constitutional and Political Controls on State Expenditures," *Publius: The Journal of Federalism* 27 (Winter 1997): 83–98.

74. Jim Vertuno, "Gov. Perry Signs $117 Billion, 2-Year Spending Plan," *Houston Chronicle*, June 25, 2003, available at **www.houstonchronicle.com**.

75. Pat Thompson and Steven P. Boyd, "Use of the Item Veto in Texas, 1940–1990," *State and Local Government Review* 26 (Winter 1994): 38–45.

76. Aaron Wildavsky, *The Politics of the Budgetary Process* (Boston: Little, Brown, 1964); David Lowery, Thomas Konda, and James Garand, "Spending in the States: A Test of Six Models," *Western Political Quarterly* 37 (March 1984): 48–66.

77. Thomas R. Dye, *Politics, Economics, and the Public* (Chicago: Rand McNally, 1966).

ONLINE PRACTICE TEST

Test your understanding of this chapter
with interactive review quizzes at

www.ablongman.com/tannahilltexas/chapter13

Glossary

Ability-to-pay theory of taxation: The approach to government finance that holds that taxes should be based on an individual's financial resources.

Abolition movement: The political reform effort in early nineteenth century America whose goal was the elimination of slavery.

Address from office: A procedure for removing judicial officials that is initiated by the governor and requires a two-thirds vote by the legislature.

Ad valorem property tax: See property tax.

Adversary proceeding: A legal procedure in which each side presents evidence and arguments to bolster its position, while rebutting evidence that might support the other side.

Advocacy groups: Organizations created to seek benefits on behalf of persons who are unable to represent their own interests.

Affirm: To uphold a lower court ruling.

Agenda building: The process through which issues become matters of public concern and government action.

Allocational urban policies: Local programs that are more or less neutral in their impact on the local economy.

Allowable: The maximum permissible rate of production for oil and gas wells in Texas as set by the Railroad Commission.

American Association of Retired Persons (AARP): An interest group representing the concerns of older Americans.

American Federation of Labor-Congress of Industrial Organization (AFL-CIO): A national association of unions.

Americans with Disabilities Act (ADA): A federal law intended to end discrimination against disabled persons and eliminate barriers preventing their full participation in American society.

Annexation: The authority of a city to increase its geographic size by extending its boundaries to take in adjacent unincorporated areas.

Appeal: The taking of a case from a lower court to a higher court by the losing party in a lower court decision.

Appropriation bill: A legislative authorization to spend money for particular purposes.

Appropriation process: The procedure through which Congress legislatively provides money for a particular purpose.

At-large election: A method for choosing public officials in which every citizen of a political subdivision, such as a state or county, votes to select a public official.

Authorization process: The procedure through which Congress legislatively establishes a program, defines its general purpose, devises procedures for its operation, specifies an agency to implement the program, and indicates an approximate level of funding for the program but does not actually provide money.

Bicameral legislature: A legislative body with two chambers.

Biennium: Two-year budget period.

Bilingual education: The teaching of academic subjects in both English and a student's native language, usually Spanish.

Bill: A proposed law.

Bill of rights: A constitutional document guaranteeing individual rights and liberties.

Blame avoidance: The effort on the part of government officials to assign responsibility for policy failures to someone else.

Block grant program: A federal grant-in-aid program that provides money for a program in a broad, general policy area, such as elementary and secondary education, or transportation.

Bond: A certificate of indebtedness issued to investors who loan money for interest income; in lay terms, a bond is an IOU.

Bond election: An election for the purpose of obtaining voter approval for a local government going into debt.

Boosters: People who promote local economic development.

Branch banking: A business practice whereby a single, large bank conducts business from several locations.

Budget deficit: The amount of money by which annual budget expenditures exceed annual budget receipts.

Budget execution authority: The power to cut agency spending or transfer money between agencies during the period when the legislature is not in session.

Building codes: Municipal ordinances that set minimum standards for the types of materials used in construction, building design, and construction methods employed in all building within the city.

Burden of proof: The legal obligation of one party in a lawsuit to prove its position to a court.

Cabinet system: An administrative structure in which subordinate executive officials report to a single chief executive.

Capital expenditure: The purchase by government of a permanent, fixed asset, such as a new city hall or freeway interchange.

Capital punishment: The death penalty.

Catching the late train: Giving money to candidate after an election is over.

Categorical grant program: A federal grant-in-aid program that provides funds to state and local governments for a fairly narrow, specific purpose, such as removing asbestos from school buildings or acquiring land for outdoor recreation.

Caucus method of delegate selection: A procedure for choosing national party convention delegates that involves party voters participating in a series of precinct and district or county political meetings.

Cause groups: Organizations whose members care intensely about a single issue or a group of related issues.

Charter schools: Independent, publicly funded schools that operate under the terms of a formal contract or "charter" with the state.

Checks and balances: The overlapping of the powers of the branches of government so that public officials limit the authority of one another.

Children's Health Insurance Program (CHIP): A federal program designed to provide health insurance to children from low-income families whose parents are not poor enough to qualify for Medicaid.

Christian Coalition: A conservative Christian organization.

Citizen groups: Organizations created to support government policies that they believe will benefit the public at large.

City charter: The basic law of a city that defines its powers, responsibilities, and organization.

City manager: A professional administrator hired by the city council in the council-manager form of city government to manage the day-to-day affairs of city government.

City ordinances: Laws enacted by the governing body of a municipality.

Civic culture: A political culture that is conducive to the development of an efficient, effective government which meets the needs of its citizens in a timely and professional manner.

Civil case: A legal dispute concerning a private conflict between two or more parties—individuals, corporations, or government agencies.

Civil defendant: The party who responds to a lawsuit.

Civil liberties: The protection of the individual from the unrestricted power of the government.

Civil union: A legal partnership between two men or two women that gives the couple all the benefits, protections, and responsibilities under law as are granted to spouses in a marriage.

Class action lawsuits: Suits brought on behalf of a group of people wronged in the same way, even though some potential clients may not know that a suit has been filed.

Closed primary: An election system that limits primary election participation to registered party members.

Coattail effect: The political phenomenon in which a strong candidate for one office gives a boost to fellow party members on the same ballot seeking other offices.

Commissioners court: The board of directors for county government composed of four county commissioners and the county judge.

Common Cause: A group organized to work for campaign finance reform and other good-government causes.

Communities Organized for Public Service (COPS): A predominantly Latino neighborhood reform organization in San Antonio.

Commutation: The reduction of punishment for a criminal offense.

Concurring opinion: A written judicial statement that agrees with the majority opinion's ruling but disagrees with its reasoning.

Conference committee: A special committee created to negotiate differences on similar pieces of legislation passed by the house and senate.

Conflict of interest: A circumstance in which the personal interests of a public official may clash with that official's professional responsibilities.

Conservatism: The political view that seeks to preserve the political, economic, and social institutions of society against abrupt change. Conservatives generally oppose most government economic regulation and heavy government spending while favoring low taxes and traditional values.

Constitution: The fundamental law by which a state or nation is organized and governed.

Constitutional amendment: A formal, written change or addition to the state's governing document.

Constitutional law: Law that involves the interpretation and application of the constitution.

Constitutional revision: The process of drafting a new constitution.

Contract case: A civil suit dealing with disputes over written or implied legal agreements, such as a suit over a faulty roof repair job.

Coordinated expenditures: Funds spent by a national party organization to support the party's candidates, including expenditures for polls, advertising, issue research, and fundraising.

Corporation franchise tax: A state tax levy assessed on corporations.

Council-manager form of city government: A structure of municipal government in which the city council/mayor appoints a professional administrator called a city manager to act as chief executive of the municipality.

Creation science: An approach to the origin of the universe that is consistent with the biblical story of creation.

Criminal case: A legal dispute dealing with an alleged violation of a penal law.

Criminal defendant: The party charged with a criminal offense.

Cumulative voting system: An election system that allows individual voters to cast more than one ballot in the simultaneous election of several officials.

Dedicated funds: Constitutional or statutory provisions that set aside revenue for particular purposes.

Dedicated Highway Fund: A constitutionally earmarked account containing money set aside for building, maintaining, and policing state highways.

Deed restrictions: Private contractual agreements that limit what residential property owners can do with their houses and land.

Delegate approach to representation: An approach to representation in which legislators attempt to reflect the views of their constituents in a mirror-like fashion.

Democracy: A system of government in which the people hold ultimate political power.

Developmental urban policies: Local programs that enhance the economic position of a community in its competition with other communities.

Dillon's rule: The legal principle that a city can exercise only those powers expressly allowed by state law.

Direct democracy: A political system in which the citizens vote directly on matters of public concern.

Disfranchisement: The denial of voting rights.

Dissenting opinion: A written judicial statement that disagrees with the decision of the court's majority.

District election: A method for choosing public officials in which a political subdivision, such as a state or city, is divided into districts and each district elects one official.

Domestic-relations case: A civil suit based on the law involving the relationships between husband and wife, and between parents and children, such as divorce and child custody cases.

Double jeopardy: The constitutional principle that an individual may not be tried a second time by the same unit of government for a single offense if acquitted in the first trial.

Dual school system: Separate sets of schools for White and African American youngsters.

Edgewood v. Kirby: A lawsuit filed by a number of poor school districts, including the Edgewood Independent School District in San Antonio, against the state's system of education finance.

Election precinct: Voting district.

Electoral College: The system established in the U.S. Constitution for the selection of the president and vice president of the United States.

Electoral mandate: The expression of popular support for a particular policy demonstrated through the electoral process.

Elite theory (elitism): The view that political power is held by a small group of people who dominate politics by controlling economic resources.

Employees Retirement System (ERS) Trust Fund: A pension fund for state employees.

Enfranchise: To grant the right to vote.

Enterprise zones: A state program that allows local governments to designate certain areas called enterprise zones in which private investors can receive property tax abatements, local sales tax rebates (refunds), and government-backed low-interest loans.

Entitlement programs: Government programs providing benefits to all persons qualified to receive them under law.

Environmental Protection Agency (EPA): The federal agency responsible for enforcing the nation's environmental laws.

Equal Protection Clause: The constitutional provision found in the Fourteenth Amendment of the U.S. Constitution that declares: "No State shall . . . deny to any person within its jurisdiction the equal protection of the laws."

Equal protection of the law: The legal principle that state laws may not arbitrarily discriminate against persons.

Excise tax: A tax levied on the manufacture, transportation, sale, or consumption of a particular item or set of related items.

Exit polls: Surveys based on random samples of voters leaving the polling place.

Extraterritorial jurisdiction (ETJ): The authority of a city to require conformity with city ordinances and regulations affecting streets, parks, alleys, utility easements, sanitary sewers, and the like in a ring of land extending from one-half to five miles beyond the city-limits line.

Federal grant-in-aid programs: Programs through which the national government gives money to state and local governments for expenditure in accordance with set standards and conditions.

Federal mandate: The legal requirement placed on a state or local government by the national government requiring certain policy actions.

Federal preemption of state authority: An act of Congress adopting regulatory policies that overrule state policies in a particular regulatory area.

Federal system *or* federation: A political system that divides power between a central government, with authority over the whole nation, and a series of state governments.

Feedback: The impact of policy evaluation on the policy process.

Felony: A serious criminal offense, such as murder, sexual assault, or burglary.

Filibuster: An attempt to defeat a bill through prolonged debate.

Fiscal note: An analysis of a legislative measure indicating its cost to state government if any.

Fiscal year: Budget year.

Food Stamp Program: A federal program that provides vouchers to low-income families and individuals that can be used to purchase food.

Forcible entry and detainer suit: An effort by a landlord to evict a tenant.

Formula grant program: A grant program that awards funding on the basis of a formula established by Congress.

Foundation School Program: The basic funding program for public education in the state of Texas.

Franchise: The right to vote.

Frostbelt: The Northeast and Midwest.

General election: A statewide election to fill national, state, and some local offices, held on the first Tuesday after the first Monday in November of even-numbered years.

General Fund: A state treasury account that supports state programs and services without restriction.

General law city: A municipality that is limited to those governmental structures and powers specifically granted by state law.

General-law units of local government: Units of local government that are limited to those structures and powers specifically granted by state law.

General obligation bonds: Certificates of indebtedness that must be repaid from general revenues.

Gerrymandering: The drawing of legislative district lines for political advantage.

Global economy: The integration of national economies into a world economic system in which companies compete worldwide for suppliers and markets.

Good business climate: A political environment in which business would prosper.

Grand Old Party (GOP): Nickname for the Republican Party.

Grange: An organization of farmers that influenced the content of the Texas Constitution of 1875.

Gross State Product (GSP): The total value of goods and services produced in a state in a year.

Habeas corpus, writ of: A court order requiring a government official to show cause why a person is being held in custody.

Harmless error: A mistake committed by a trial court that is not serious enough to warrant a new trial because it could not have affected the outcome of the original trial.

Hate-crimes legislation: A legislative measure that increases penalties for persons convicted of criminal offenses motivated by prejudice based on race, religion, national origin, gender, or sexual orientation.

Height limitation: A city regulation restricting the height of buildings within the city.

High technology industries: Industries that are based on the latest in modern technology, such as telecommunications and robotics.

Home rule: The authority of a unit of local government to take actions not prohibited by the laws or constitutions of the United States or the state.

Home rule city: A municipality that can take any actions not prohibited by state or federal law or the constitutions of the United States or the state of Texas.

Homestead: Legal residence.

Homestead exemption: A property tax reduction granted to homeowners on their principal residence.

Hopwood v. Texas: A lawsuit filed by several unsuccessful non-Hispanic White applicants to the University of Texas Law School who believed that the university's admissions process violated the Equal Protection Clause of the U.S. Constitution because it granted applicants a preference based on their race or ethnicity.

Hospital district: A special district that provides emergency medical services, indigent health care, and community health services.

Housing codes: Local ordinances requiring all dwelling places in a city to meet certain standards of upkeep and structural integrity.

Impeachment: A formal accusation against an executive or judicial officeholder.

Incorporated municipality: A city under the laws of the state.

Incremental model of budgeting: A theoretical effort to explain the budget process on the basis of small (incremental) changes in budget categories from one budget period to the next.

Incremental model of policy formulation: An approach to policy formulation that assumes that policymakers, working with imperfect information, continually adjust policies in pursuit of policy goals that themselves are subject to periodic readjustment.

Incumbent: Current officeholder.

Independent expenditures: Funds spent on behalf of a candidate that are not coordinated with the candidate's campaign.

Independent School Districts (ISDs): Units of local government that provide public education services to district residents from kindergarten through the twelfth grade.

Individualistic political culture: An approach to government and politics that emphasizes private initiative with a minimum of government interference.

Initiative process: A procedure available in some states and cities whereby citizens can propose the adoption of a policy measure by gathering a prerequisite number of signatures. Voters must then approve the measure before it can take effect.

Interest groups: Organizations of people who join together voluntarily on the basis of some interest they share for the purpose of influencing policy.

Interim committee: Committee established to study a particular policy issue between legislative sessions.

Interstate Commerce Clause: The constitutional provision giving Congress authority to "regulate commerce . . . among the several states."

Issue network: A group of political actors that is concerned with some aspect of public policy.

Jacksonian democracy: The view (associated with President Andrew Jackson) that the right to vote should be extended to all adult male citizens and that all government offices of any importance should be filled by election.

Joint and several liability: The legal requirement that a defendant with "deep pockets" held partially liable for a plaintiff's injury must pay the full damage award for those defendants unable to pay.

Joint resolution: A resolution that must be passed by a two-thirds vote of each chamber.

Judicial review: The authority of courts to declare unconstitutional the actions of the other branches and units of government.

League of United Latin American Citizens (LULAC): A Latino interest group.

Legal briefs: Written legal arguments.

Legal writs: Written orders issued by a court directing the performance of an act or prohibiting some act.

Legislative access: An open door through which the interest group hopes to influence the details of policy.

Legislative Budget Board (LBB): An agency created by the legislature to study state revenue and budgetary needs between legislative sessions and prepare budget and appropriations bills to submit to the legislature.

Legislative oversight: The process through which the legislature evaluates the implementation of public policy by executive branch agencies.

Legislative Redistricting Board (LRB): An agency composed of the Speaker, lieutenant governor, comptroller, land commissioner, and attorney general that is responsible for redrawing the boundaries of Texas house and senate seats when the legislature is unable to agree on a redistricting plan.

Legislative turnover: The replacement of individual members of a legislature from one session to the next.

Liberalism: The political view that seeks to change the political, economic, or social institutions of society to advance the development and well-being of the individual. Liberals believe that government should foster social progress by promoting social justice, political equality, and economic prosperity. Liberals usually favor government regulation and high levels of spending for social programs. On social issues, such as abortion and pornography regulation, liberals tend to support the right of adult free choice against government interference.

Line-item veto: The power of the governor to veto sections or items of an appropriation bill while signing the remainder of the bill into law.

Litigants: The parties in a lawsuit.

Lobbying: The communication of information by a representative of an interest group to a government official for the purpose of influencing a policy decision.

Local bills: Proposed laws that affect only a single unit of local government.

Local governments: Subunits of states.

Local-option elections: Elections held to determine whether an area will legalize the sale of alcoholic beverages.

Lone Star State: A nickname for the state of Texas.

Long ballot: An election system that provides for the election of nearly every public official of any significance.

Low-information rationality: The concept that because most voters have a limited understanding of the political world, they decide how to vote by using informational shortcuts about parties, candidate behavior, personal characteristics, and the relationship candidates have with familiar groups and people.

Magistrates: Judicial officers.

Majority-minority districts: Legislative districts with populations that are more than 50 percent minority.

Majority *or* deciding opinion: The official written statement of a court that explains and justifies its ruling and serves as a guideline for lower courts when similar legal issues arise in the future.

***Mandamus,* writ of:** A court order directing a public official to perform a specific act or duty.

Mark up: The process in which legislators go over a piece of legislation line-by-line, revising, amending, or rewriting it.

Matching funds requirement: A legislative provision that the national government will provide grant money for a particular activity only on condition that the state or local government involved supply a certain percentage of the total money required for the project or program.

Mayor-council form of city government: A structure of municipal government in which the voters elect a mayor as the chief executive officer of the city and a council that serves as a legislative body.

Medicaid program: A federal program designed to provide health insurance coverage to poor people, the disabled, and elderly Americans who are impoverished.

Merit selection (Missouri Plan): A method for selecting judges that combines gubernatorial appointment with voter approval in a retention election.

Minimum wage: The lowest hourly wage that an employer can pay covered workers.

Misdemeanor: A relatively minor criminal offense, such as a traffic violation.

Mothers Against Drunk Driving (MADD): An interest group that supports the reform of laws dealing with drunk driving.

Moralistic political culture: An approach to government and politics in which people expect government to intervene in the social and economic affairs of the state, promoting the public welfare and advancing the public good.

National Association for the Advancement of Colored People (NAACP): An interest group organized to represent the interests of African Americans.

National Organization for Women (NOW): A group that promotes women's rights.

National Rifle Association (NRA): An interest group organized to defend the rights of gun owners and defeat efforts at gun control.

National Supremacy Clause: The constitutional provision that declares that the Constitution, the laws made under it, and the treaties of the United States are the supreme law of the land.

New Deal program: The name given Franklin Roosevelt's legislative program for countering the Great Depression.

No Child Left Behind Act: A federal law that requires state governments and local school districts to institute basic skills testing as a condition for receiving federal aid.

Nonpartisan elections: Election contests in which the names of the candidates appear on the ballot but not their party affiliations.

Normative analysis: A method of study that is based on certain values.

North American Free Trade Agreement (NAFTA): An international accord among the United States, Mexico, and Canada to lower trade barriers among the three nations.

Off-street parking requirement: A city regulation that business owners provide off-street parking for clients and customers.

Official policy agenda: Those problems that government officials actively consider how to resolve.

One person, one vote: The judicial ruling that the Equal Protection Clause of the Fourteenth Amendment to the U.S. Constitution requires that legislative districts be apportioned on the basis of population.

Open primary: An election system that allows voters to pick the party primary of their choice without disclosing their party affiliation.

Opinion leaders: Individuals whose views shape the political attitudes of the general public.

Pardon: The exemption from punishment for a criminal offense.

Parental choice: An educational reform that allows parents to choose which school their children will attend in hopes that schools will be forced to improve because they must compete for students.

Pari-mutuel wagering: A system for gambling on horse and dog racing.

Parole: The conditional release of convicted offenders from prison to serve the remainder of their sentences in the community under supervision.

Partisan election: An election contest in which both the candidates' names and their party affiliation appear on the ballot.

Party faction: A subgroup within a political party.

Party platform: A statement of party principles and issue positions.

Per capita: Per person.

Performance-based budgeting: A system of budget preparation and evaluation in which policymakers identify specific policy goals, set performance targets for agencies, and measure results.

Permanent School Fund (PSF): A fund established in the Texas Constitution as an endowment to finance public elementary and secondary education.

Permanent University Fund (PUF): Money constitutionally set aside as an endowment to finance construction, maintenance, and some other activities at the University of Texas, Texas A&M University, and other institutions in those two university systems.

Plaintiff: The party who initiates a lawsuit.

Plea bargain: A procedure in which a defendant agrees to plead guilty in order to receive punishment less than the maximum for an offense.

Plural executive: The division of executive power among several elected officials.

Pluralist theory (pluralism): The view that diverse groups of elites with differing interests compete with one another to control policy in various issue areas.

Policy adoption: The official decision of a government body to accept a particular policy and put it into effect.

Policy cycle: The passage of an issue through the policy process from agenda building through policy evaluation.

Policy evaluation: The assessment of policy.

Policy formulation: The development of strategies for dealing with the problems on the official policy agenda.

Policy implementation: The stage of the policy process in which policies are carried out.

Policy outcomes: Actual government policies.

Policy outputs: The situations that arise as a result of the impact of policy in operation.

Policymaking environment: The set of factors outside of government that impacts the policymaking process either directly or indirectly.

Political Action Committee (PAC): An organization created to raise and distribute money in political campaigns.

Political campaign: An attempt to get information to voters that will persuade them to elect a candidate or not elect an opponent.

Political culture: The widely held, deeply rooted political values of a society.

Political machines: Entrenched political organizations headed by a boss or small group of leaders who held power through such techniques as patronage, control over nominations, and bribery.

Political party: A group of individuals who join together to seek public office in order to influence public policy.

Political patronage: The power of an officeholder to award favors, such as government jobs, to political allies.

Politico approach to representation: An approach to representation in which legislators behave as delegates on issues that are highly visible to their constituents, while acting as trustees on other questions.

Politics: The process that determines who shall occupy the roles of leadership in government and how the power of government shall be exercised.

Poll tax: A tax that prospective voters had to pay in order to register to vote.

Population bracket laws: State laws designed to target particular cities based on their population.

Poverty line: The amount of money an individual or family needs to purchase basic necessities, such as food, clothing, health care, shelter, and transportation.

Preclearance provision of the VRA: The requirement that state and local governments in areas with a history of voting discrimination to submit redistricting plans to the federal Department of Justice for approval *before* they can go into effect.

Presidential preference primary election: An election in which party voters cast ballots for the presidential candidate they favor and in so doing help determine the number of convention delegates that candidate will receive.

Primary election: An intraparty election during which a party's candidates for the general election are chosen.

Probate case: A civil suit dealing with the disposition of the property of a deceased individual.

Probation: The suspension of a sentence, permitting the defendant to remain free under court supervision.

Problem-solving court: A judicial body that attempts to change the future behavior of litigants and promote the welfare of the community.

Progressive tax: A levy whose burden weighs more heavily on persons earning higher incomes than it does on individuals making less money.

Project grant program: A grant program that requires state and local governments to compete for available federal money.

Property case: A civil suit over the ownership of real estate or personal possessions, such as land, jewelry, or an automobile.

Property lien: A financial claim against property for payment of debt.

Property taxes: Taxes levied on the value of real property, such as land and buildings.

Proportional tax: A levy that weighs equally on all persons, regardless of their income.

Proposition 227: A California state ballot measure passed in 1998 which was designed to outlaw bilingual education in the state.

Prosecutor: The attorney who tries a criminal case on behalf of the government.

Prospective voting: The concept that voters evaluate the incumbent officeholder and the incumbent's party based on their expectations of future developments.

Public policy: The response, or lack of response, of government decision makers to an issue.

Public policy approach: A comprehensive method for studying the process through which issues come to the attention of government decision makers, and through which policies are formulated, adopted, implemented, and evaluated.

Punitive damages: Monetary awards given in a lawsuit to punish a defendant for a particularly evil, malicious, or fraudulent act.

Puritanism: A religious reform movement.

Racial profiling: The practice of a police officer targeting individuals as suspected criminals on the basis of their race or ethnicity.

Radical Republicans: Members of the Republican Party that wanted sweeping social change to take place in the South after the Civil War.

Rational comprehensive model of policy formulation: An approach to policy formulation that assumes that policymakers establish goals, identify policy alternatives, estimate the costs and benefits of the alternatives, and then select the policy alternative that produces the greatest net benefit.

Recall election: A procedure allowing voters to remove elected officials from office before the expiration of their terms.

Recession: An economic slowdown characterized by declining economic output and rising unemployment.

Redistributive urban policies: Local programs that benefit low-income residents of an area.

Redistricting: The process of redrawing the boundaries of legislative districts.

Reform Party: The political party founded by Dallas billionaire Ross Perot.

Regressive tax: A levy whose burden weighs more heavily on low-income groups than wealthy taxpayers.

Religious right: Individuals who hold conservative social views because of their religious beliefs.

Remand: To return a case to the trial court for reconsideration in light of the appeals court decision.

Representative democracy *or* **republic:** A political system in which citizens elect representatives to make policy decisions on their behalf.

Reprieve: The postponement of the implementation of punishment for a criminal offense.

Resolution: A legislative statement of opinion on a certain matter.

Responsible party: A political party that clearly spells out issue positions in its platform and, when in office, faithfully carries them out.

Retrospective voting: The concept that voters choose candidates based on their perception of an incumbent candidate's past performance in office or the performance of the incumbent party.

Reversible error: A mistake committed by a trial court that is serious enough to warrant a new trial because the mistake could have affected the outcome of the original trial.

Right to work law: A statute prohibiting the union shop.

Robin Hood Plan: A reform of the state's school finance system designed to increase funding for poor school districts by redistributing money from wealthy districts.

Rulemaking: A regulatory process used by government agencies to enact legally binding regulations.

Rules: Legally binding regulations adopted by a regulatory agency.

Runoff primary election: An election between the two top finishers in a primary election when no candidate received a majority of the vote in the initial primary.

Sales tax: A levy on the retail sale of taxable items.

School Lunch Program: A federal program that provides free or inexpensive lunches to children from poor families.

Select *or* **special committee:** A committee that is established for a limited period of time to address a specific problem.

Senatorial courtesy: A custom of the Texas senate that allows individual senators a veto over nominees who live in their districts. By tradition, senators will vote against a nominee if the senator from the district in which the nominee lives declares opposition to the nomination.

Seniority: The length of continuous service a member has with a legislative body.

Separation of powers: The division of political authority among legislative, executive, and judicial branches of government.

Setback ordinance: A city requirement that construction take place a specified minimum distance from the street right-of-way.

Severance tax: A tax levied on natural resources at the time they are taken from the land or water.

Sierra Club: An environmental organization.

Sin tax: A levy on an activity that some people consider morally objectionable, such as smoking or drinking.

Social lobbying: The attempt of lobbyists to influence public policy by cultivating personal, social relationships with policymakers.

Solid South: A phrase used to refer to the usual Democratic sweep of southern state electoral votes in presidential election years.

Sovereignty: The authority of a state to exercise legitimate powers within its boundaries, free from external interference.

Special district: A unit of local government created to perform specific functions.

Special election: An election called at a time outside the normal election calendar.

Split-ticket voting: Citizens casting their ballots for candidates of two or more parties for different offices during the same election.

Standing committee: A permanent committee established to handle legislation in a certain field.

Statutory law: Law made by a legislature.

Straight-ticket voting: Citizens casting their ballots only for the candidates of one party.

Subpoena: A legal order compelling the attendance of a person at an official proceeding, such as a trial.

Subsidence: The sinking of the surface of the land caused by the too rapid extraction of subsurface water.

Suffrage: The right to vote.

Sunbelt: The South and Southwest.

Sunset review: The periodic evaluation of state agencies by the legislature to determine whether they should be reauthorized.

Super delegates: Democratic officeholders and party officials who attend the national party convention as delegates who are not officially pledged to support any candidate.

Tax abatement: A program that exempts property owners from local property taxes on new construction and improvements in a designated tax abatement district for a set period of time.

Tax elasticity: The extent to which tax revenues rise as personal income rises.

Tax incidence: The point at which the actual cost of a tax falls.

Tax increment financing: A program in which a local government promises to earmark increased property tax revenues generated by development in a designated area called a tax increment financing district to fund improvements in the area, such as roads, parks, sidewalks, and street lighting.

Term limitation: The movement to restrict the number of terms public officials may serve.

Texas Abortion and Reproductive Rights Action League (TARAL): An organization that supports abortion rights.

Texas Assessment of Knowledge and Skills (TAKS): A state mandated basic-skills test designed to measure student progress and assess school performance.

Texas Association of Business (TAB): A trade association for business firms ranging from giant corporations to small neighborhood business establishments.

Texas Civil Liberties Union (TCLA): The Texas affiliate of the American Civil Liberties Union (ACLU), which is a group organized to protect the rights of individuals as outlined in the United States Constitution.

Texas Commission on Environmental Quality (TCEQ): The state agency responsible for enforcing pollution control regulations in Texas.

Texas Equal Rights Amendment (ERA): A provision in the Texas Constitution that states the following: "Equality under the law shall not be denied or abridged because of sex, race, color, creed, or national origin."

Texas Medical Association (TMA): A professional organization of physicians.

Texas Right to Life Committee: An interest group opposed to abortion.

Texas Teacher Retirement System (TRS) Trust Fund: A pension fund for the state's public school teachers.

Texas Trail Lawyers Association (TTLA): An organization of attorneys who represent plaintiffs in personal injury lawsuits.

Top 10 percent rule: A policy that guarantees the admission to state colleges and universities of students who graduate in the top 10 percent of their public high school classes without regard for their SAT or ACT scores.

Tort case: A legal dispute concerning personal injury or damage to property, such as a lawsuit stemming from an automobile accident.

Tort reform: The revision of state laws to limit the ability of plaintiffs in personal injury lawsuits to recover damages in court.

Trade associations: Organizations representing the interests of firms and professionals in the same general field.

Traditionalistic political culture: An approach to government and politics that sees the role of government as the preservation of tradition and the existing social order.

Trial: A formal examination of a civil or criminal action in accordance with law before a single judge who has jurisdiction to hear the dispute.

Trustee approach to representation: An approach to representation in which legislators do what they believe is in the best interests of their constituents.

Truth in taxation laws: Laws that block local governments from raising the total amount of property taxes they collect from one year to the next when assessed values go up.

Two-party system: The division of voter loyalties between two major political parties, resulting in the near exclusion of minor parties from seriously competing for a share of political power.

Unicameral legislature: A legislative body with one chamber.

Unincorporated area: Territory that is not part of a legal city.

Union or closed shop: A workplace in which every employee must be a member of a union.

Urban planning: The formulation, adoption, and implementation of public policies designed to promote the orderly development of metropolitan areas.

Urban sprawl: The excessive geographic expansion of cities.

Utility district: A unit of local government that provides utilities such as water and sewer service to residents living in unincorporated urban areas.

Veto: An action by the chief executive of a state or nation refusing to approve a bill passed by the legislature.

Voting Rights Act (VRA): A federal law designed to protect the voting rights of racial and ethnic minorities.

White primary: An election system that prohibited African Americans from voting in Democratic primary elections, to ensure their continued control of the Democratic Party.

Yellow Dog Democrat: A loyal Democratic voter.

Zoning: The governmental designation of tracts of land for industrial, commercial, or residential use.

PHOTO CREDITS

Index